Miners on Strike

D0222925

Miners on Strike

Class Solidarity and Division in Britain

Andrew J. Richards

BERG

Oxford • New York

First published in 1996 by
Berg
Editorial offices:
150 Cowley Road, Oxford, OX4 1JJ, UK
70 Washington Square South, New York, NY 10012, USA

Berg is an imprint of Oxford International Publishers Ltd.

Library of Congress Cataloging-in-Publication Data

A catalogue record for this book is available from the Library of Congress.

British Library Cataloguing-in-Publication Data

A catalogue record for this book is available from the British Library.

ISBN 1 85973 172 4 (Cloth)
1 85973 177 5 (Paper)

Typeset by JS Typesetting, Wellingborough, Northants.
Printed in the United Kingdom by WBC Book Manufacturers, Bridgend,
Mid Glamorgan

Contents

Contents

Acknowledgements

This book is derived from a doctoral dissertation defended at the Department of Politics, Princeton University, in 1992, and from research conducted in the British coalfields in 1989 and 1990. It could not have been completed without the invaluable assistance of many individuals and several organizations.

At Princeton University, I am especially grateful to my dissertation supervisors, Professors Nancy Bermeo and Ezra Suleiman, and to the other members of my examining committee, Professors Atul Kohli and Kathleen Thelen. In addition, the University's Council on Regional Studies, under the Directorship of Professor Ezra Suleiman, and the Center of International Studies, under the Directorship of Professor Henry Bienen, provided me with generous grants with which to undertake my field research.

Many other individuals have helped me along the way by commenting on various parts of the text: Kristin Mattson, Judith Barish, Michael Hanchard, Michael Jones-Correa, Miriam Golden, Michael Goldfield, Vincent Wright, Pratap Mehta, Marta Fraile and Javier Polavieja. I thank especially Manuel Jiménez, and also Paloma Aguilar, César Colino and Jacqueline de la Fuente, for invaluable help in preparing the final version of the manuscript.

In Britain, my sincere thanks go to the 217 miners in the South Wales, Nottinghamshire, Yorkshire and Derbyshire coalfields who, between November 1989 and July 1990, were gracious and patient enough to allow me to interview them about their experiences of a troubled time in the coal industry. For their help and cooperation in facilitating contacts and my research in general, I am especially grateful to the following: Ron Stoate, NUM Lodge Secretary, Penallta colliery, South Wales; Tyrone O'Sullivan, NUM Lodge Secretary, Tower colliery, South Wales; Philip Turner, NUM Branch Treasurer, High Moor colliery, Derbyshire; Henry Richardson, General Secretary, Nottinghamshire Area NUM; David Amos, UDM Branch Secretary, Annesley colliery, Nottinghamshire.

For allowing me access to invaluable archive and research material, I am grateful to Dr Hywel Francis, Director of the South Wales Miners' Library at University College, Swansea; Mick Clapham, Industrial

Acknowledgments

Relations Section, NUM National Headquarters, Sheffield; Ruth Winterton, Northern College, Barnsley; staff members at the library of British Coal National Headquarters, London; officials of the Coalfield Communities Campaign, Barnsley, and Tony Benn MP. I thank also the NUM Lodge, and British Coal management, at Taff Merthyr colliery, South Wales, for arranging a memorable five-hour underground tour of the colliery in November 1989 – now, at least, I have an inkling of what my grandfather and great-grandfather endured on a daily basis.

I express my eternal gratitude to the late Bernard Savage, former NUM Branch Delegate at Blidworth colliery Nottinghamshire, and to members of his family – Irene Stone, David Huzij, Carol Huzij, Peter Savage and the late Betty Savage – for their friendship, encouragement and hospitality during six wonderful months spent in the Nottinghamshire coalfield between February and July 1990.

At Berg, I am extremely grateful to the anonymous reviewer of the manuscript for a host of trenchant comments and criticisms, and to Kathryn Earle, Editorial Director, for her advice and immense encouragement.

In addition, I express my gratitude to my many new friends at the Center for Advanced Study in the Social Sciences, Juan March Institute, Madrid, and in particular to José María Maravall, José Ramón Montero, Leopoldo Calvo-Sotelo and Martha Peach. In terms of the often arduous task of producing a manuscript, they could not have provided me with a warmer, more encouraging and more stimulating environment.

Finally, I thank, as ever, my family. To my sisters, Gail and Carol, and to my brothers-in-law, Keith and Wayne, I am grateful for all manner of assistance whilst I was in Britain in 1989 and 1990. Most of all, I thank my mother and father, who have been a constant source of encouragement and who have unselfishly and unstintingly helped me throughout my education. This manuscript is dedicated to them.

Glossary of Abbreviations

AEU	Amalgamated Engineering Union
AIS	Area Incentive Scheme
ASLEF	Associated Society of Locomotive Engineers and Firemen
BACM	British Association of Colliery Management
BC	British Coal
BR	British Rail
BS	British Steel
CEGB	Central Electricity Generating Board
CINCC	Coal Industry National Consultative Committee
CGT	Confederation General du Travail
CLP	Constituency Labour Party
COHSE	Confederation of Health Service Employees
COSA	Colliery Officials and Staffs Association
CPGB	Communist Party of Great Britain
EETPU	Electrical Electronic Telecommunications and Plumbing Union
EPEA	Electrical Power Engineers' Association
GMB	General, Municipal and Boilermakers Trades Union
ILO	International Labour Organization
ISTC	Iron and Steel Trades Confederation
LRD	Labour Research Department
MFGB	Miners' Federation of Great Britain
NACODS	National Association of Colliery Overmen, Deputies and Shotfirers
NALGO	National and Local Government Officers' Association
NCB	National Coal Board
NEC	National Executive Committee
NMA	Nottinghamshire Miners Association
NPLA	National Power Loading Agreement
NUM	National Union of Mineworkers
NUR	National Union of Railwaymen
NUS	National Union of Seamen
NUT	National Union of Teachers
PLP	Parliamentary Labour Party

SOGAT'82   Society of Graphical and Allied Trades
SWMF   South Wales Miners Federation
SWMIU   South Wales Miners Industrial Union
TGWU   Transport and General Workers Union
TUC   Trades Union Congress
UCATT   Union of Construction, Allied Trades and Technicians
UDM   Union of Democratic Mineworkers
UFCW   United Food and Commercial Workers (USA)

Introduction: Consciousness and Action amongst British Miners

Britain's Miners in Victory and Defeat

In the national coal strikes of 1972 and 1974, the National Union of Mineworkers (NUM), after a decade of industrial contraction and declining wage levels, inflicted two memorable defeats on the Conservative government of Edward Heath. On both occasions, miners voted overwhelmingly to heed the union's recommendation to strike for higher pay, and on both occasions the government eventually capitulated. Indeed, the 1974 strike contributed, at the very least, to the downfall of the government in the February 1974 General Election. In the wake of these dramatic confrontations, the miners 'won considerable gains and came to be seen as the strongest working community in Britain, the vanguard of the labor movement' (Kahn 1987: 57).

History appeared to be repeating itself when, in March 1984, in a deteriorating political and economic climate, the miners embarked on strike action against the Conservative government of Margaret Thatcher. This time, however, the stakes were even higher than in the early 1970s, and the issues more fundamental. Indeed, the strike – destined to last an entire year – was a momentous and unprecedented event in recent British political history which saw an astonishing mobilization of the union membership and the mining communities, and a steadfast determination on the part of the government to break the strike. The strike was called in order to oppose the pit closure programme of the National Coal Board (NCB) and to defend existing mining communities against further job losses. It was unprecedented in that it was fought not on the issues of pay or working conditions but explicitly on the question of employment levels in the coal industry. As such, the strike challenged the very core of Thatcherism's strategy towards the nationalized industries in particular and the trade union movement in general.

During this struggle, the miners suffered a catastrophic defeat. In March 1985, in the face of a continuing drift back to work by a demoralized workforce, a Special Delegate Conference of the NUM voted 96 to 91 to end the strike. The strike had failed to force the NCB to withdraw its pit closure programme; the miners returned to work without any agreement whatsoever on this issue. The consequences of defeat were disastrous. The union had been split from the start of the strike because of the refusal of the majority of miners in the profitable Notting-hamshire coalfield (the nation's second largest) to join the strike. Soon after the strike, they voted to break away from the NUM (of which they had been founder members) and form the Union of Democratic Mine-workers (UDM). Furthermore, the miners were unable to prevent the phenomenal contraction of the coal industry which took place after the strike. Between March 1984 and March 1992 the number of operating mines in Britain fell from 170 to 50, while the workforce was reduced from 181,000 to 46,000.[1] By early 1994, only 17 deep mines remained in Britain, employing fewer than 11,000 miners.[2] As the British Coal Chairman commented: 'All this. . .represents a restructuring unmatched in depth and speed in any major UK industry in recent history.'[3] From the point of view of the miners, however, Griffin's characterization of the strike's outcome as 'a shattering and divisive defeat . . . without parallel in recent labour history' is no exaggeration (1985: 10). Cer-tainly, by March 1985, the triumphs of 1972 and 1974 were but a distant memory – the idea of the NUM as 'the vanguard of the working-class was buried. . . it is now but one of many beleaguered and declining unions' (Francis 1985a: 56).

The history of the miners and their Union in the 1970s and 1980s obviously shows that the unity achieved in the national strikes of 1972 and 1974 proved difficult to preserve. The national wage parity which had underpinned strike action in the early 1970s was effectively destroyed in 1978 by the reintroduction of incentive payments into the industry. Meanwhile, the uneven impact of the pit closure programme adopted by the NCB after the election of the Thatcher government in 1979 made it an inherently divisive issue on which to build a united front. Undoubtedly, by the early 1980s, the NUM leadership was exper-iencing growing difficulty in maintaining the unity of an increasingly fragmented workforce. As such, the fate of the miners during this period conforms to a pattern identified in 1978 by Hobsbawm in an influential analysis of the changing fortunes of organized labour,[4] and the state of class consciousness, in advanced industrial societies: 'We now see a growing division of workers into sections and groups, each pursuing its own economic interest irrespective of the rest . . .there's not much doubt that sectionalism is on the increase'(1978: 284). Many commentators viewed the outcome of the 1984–5 miners' strike in these terms. Igna-tieff, for example, claimed that 'the miners' strike is not the vindication of class politics, but its death throes' (cited in Meiksins Wood 1986: 181). Hall argued that 'the miners' strike certainly contained a powerful "class" dimension. But politically it was not. . .a "class-versus-class" showdown because, far from "the class" being united, it was deeply divided. . .the internal divisions within the miners' union had real, material and ideological conditions of existence. . .' (1988: 204).

But are such judgements valid? Did the defeat of the miners reflect, and was it synonymous with, the demise of the working class in particular and class-based politics in general? After the strike, did notions of working-class consciousness, identity and solidarity (with which the miners were strongly associated) now belong to a bygone era rapidly receding into history? In this book, I reject such perspectives on two principal grounds. First, despite a post-strike legacy of division and defeat, the bonds of solidarity among miners remained resilient. Second, the experience of struggle laid the basis for a changed and raised consciousness among miners themselves (and indeed, among those who sought to support them). These contentions rest upon the construction of a refined notion of class consciousness, a recognition of the concrete constraints under which workers labour, and a sober assessment of the extent to which workers in struggle are able and willing to escape the confines of their own traditions. Ultimately, therefore, the study seeks to demonstrate, through the eyes of a group of industrial workers undoubtedly running against the tide of history, the continuing complexity and resilience (rather than the disappearance) of class consciousness in advanced capitalist society.

The Problem of Class Consciousness

The Problem of Revolutionary Consciousness

Both Marx and Lenin have exerted considerable influence on the study of class consciousness. For Marx, 'it makes no sense. . .to speak of a class-conscious proletariat which is not engaged in the activity of overthrowing capitalism' (Ollman 1972: 3). This image, remote though it may seem in the late twentieth century, none the less continues to form the benchmark against which the attitudes and actions of workers in industrial societies are measured. Whether working within, or in opposition to, the Marxist tradition, the principal concern of students of working-class politics has been to explain the continuing failure of workers to attain such an 'ideal-type' consciousness: 'why, in advanced capitalist societies, have working-classes not become revolutionary classes?' (Marshall 1988: 98).

Several reasons have been advanced to explain the failure of the industrial proletariat to achieve its revolutionary potential. Many authors argue that the objective structural factors which Marx held to be necessary (though not sufficient) for the creation of conditions in which revolutionary consciousness could emerge, have not developed in the way he envisaged. Instead of the expansion and immiseration of the industrial proletariat, the latter has diminished in size and a blurring of class lines has taken place. The rise, instead, of routine non-manual work and of the service sector has led to the emergence of 'contradictory class locations' (Wright 1985: 42–57) and to the fragmentation of the industrial working class (Hobsbawm 1978). The consequences, however, of such structural change continue to be examined in terms of the agenda bequeathed by Marx: 'what are the consequences of this diversity for class consciousness and action? In short, who now will make the revolution?' (Marshall 1988: 99).

Lenin's adaptation of Marx's model of the class-conscious worker was equally important in shaping explanations for the attitudes and actions of workers: without the help of a revolutionary élite, workers' actions would be hopelessly circumscribed by their spontaneous (and largely material) motivations: 'the history of all countries. . .shows that the working class exclusively by its own effort is able to develop only trade union consciousness' (1973: 37, cited by Gallie 1983: 19).

Without question, the material factors that so concerned Lenin have been emphasized by those seeking to explain workers' actions, attitudes and consciousness in a variety of geographical, historical and institutional settings. Indeed, the notion that workers are motivated by little more than their immediate material concerns has underpinned explanations for both action and inaction on the part of workers – materialist explanations exist for both the 'deradicalization' and 'militancy' of workers. With respect to the former, the failure of the industrial proletariat to achieve its revolutionary potential is accounted for by the material gains it has achieved under capitalism. Increasing affluence has been accompanied by a process of deradicalization (Przeworski 1980a: 126). Militancy, to the extent that it emerges, is of a strongly instrumental type. Thus Hyman, in his critique of the 'affluent worker' studies (Goldthorpe *et al.* 1968, 1969) remarks: 'The prototypical semi-skilled production worker, they argue, experiences no significant intrinsic attachment to his work, regards employment merely as a necessary evil sustaining the standard of living to which he aspires in his domestic life, and is conscious of few ties of solidarity outside the immediate workplace' (1978: 53).

Similarly, Parkin argues that 'workers will either confine their aspirations to economic gains within the social order or be overwhelmed by "fatalistic pessimism"' (1971: 95, cited by Gallie 1983: 19). And in his survey of the post-war British labour movement, Hobsbawm underscores the impact of growing material differentiation within the working class. Strike action often amounts to nothing more than a narrow wages militancy more likely to hinder rather than promote the solidarity of workers as a whole (1978: 286). The emergence, meanwhile, of materially-based sectionalism, demarcation and stratification forms the core of current problems of socialist strategy (1978: 283–4; see also 1982). In short, the primacy assigned to materialist explanations ensures that the great majority of workers' attitudes and actions are banished to the realms of 'trade union consciousness'.

The assumption that workers act in line with their material interests is most explicitly stated by Przeworski who uses a rational choice model to explain why workers in capitalist societies have not opted for socialism: '. . .I will assume that workers under capitalism have an interest in improving their material welfare, and I will base the entire analysis of their political preferences and strategies on this narrow assumption. . .' (1980a: 126). He concludes that workers have not opted for socialism because the process of transition, for a variety of reasons, is costly in material terms (1980a: 144; see also Przeworkski 1980b; Przeworkski & Wallerstein 1982).

Within the capitalist system, the instability of corporatist wage regulation structures is testimony to the vigour with which workers defend their material well-being.[5] Thus Panitch, in a radical critique of the corporatist state, points to the conflict that inevitably emerges between the trade unions – as essentially agents of wage restraint – and their own rank and file: '. . .in so far as wage restraint is practised continually or intensified to the point of producing falling real wages, there is an increasing likelihood that, through the mobilization of opposition within union organizations. . .or through the expression of unofficial strikes on a large scale, trade unions will withdraw from. . . corporatist political structures' (1981: 54–5; see also Layne n.d.: 28).

Indeed, Panitch argues that much of the rank-and-file militancy throughout Europe in the late 1960s was due to resentment against corporatist policies of wage-restraint. Certainly, Britain's 'winter of discontent' in 1978–9 was a glaring example of workers throwing off the shackles of wage restraint and ignoring the pleas of their union leaderships to adhere to corporatist agreements.

Overall, Lange's observations serve as a reasonable summary of the perspectives on workers' attitudes and actions outlined here:

> Whether the starting point is Marxist/neo-Marxist or individualist/rationalist the underlying assumptions are that workers' interests are objective, that their demands and behaviours will come to reflect these interests and that. . .they want to maximize their individual income and/or class power. As a result, workers will resist union policies that are unresponsive to these interests and which instead claim to promote collective and/or systemic values. (n.d.: 6)

The Problem Reassessed

The two principal perspectives outlined above – first, that changes in the class structure have critical implications for the formation of working-class consciousness, and second, that this consciousness has limited itself to the defence or pursuit of material well-being – are both flawed as means of understanding how, and from where, working-class consciousness is generated.

It is certainly true that economic and industrial change has profoundly affected the class structure of capitalist societies. None the less, problems arise with 'the analytical priority accorded thus far to the dichotomous couplet of structure-consciousness' (Marshall 1988: 119). Historically, the nature of this relationship is anything but clear. Certainly, 'the image of a strong and united working class movement marching behind the socialist banners of the party has stuck in the popular and historical memory, and constitutes the "base line" from which subsequent changes are measured' (Cronin 1983: 128). Yet such a 'memory' is empirically suspect: 'the connections were never so close and automatic as the happy coincidence of outcomes might seem to suggest, and it was never obvious to contemporaries that class membership was easily translated into political ideologies or allegiances, or that social structural change had inevitable political consequences' (Cronin 1983: 131).

For example, 'by a truly perverse logic, the greatest and longest lull in overt industrial conflict lasted from 1927 to 1955, more or less the precise period noted for its class-based politics' (Cronin 1983: 133).[6] While 'networks of working people have been extremely resilient. . .the picture of the traditional defensive working-class community being eroded by the anomie of privatised dwellings and the lure of consumerist mass media, is more than a little overdrawn' (Cronin 1983: 135).

An historically grounded assessment of working-class politics therefore suggests that the relationship between structure and consciousness is not a deterministic one. Divisions, fragmentation and intra-class conflict are historic and long-standing hallmarks of working-class politics, not developments new to the present era which may then be contrasted with an alleged 'golden age' of cohesion and solidarity. Current divisions within the working class do not therefore support the thesis that changes in the class structure are leading to a withering away of class consciousness (Milibaud 1964). Nor do they mean that the possibilities for the generation of a radical consciousness are any more remote now than they were in the nineteenth century: '. . .when we did have a classic class structure of a kind that would have made every Marxist go to sleep happily at night, we always had a Tory government. We never had socialism in the 19th century when there was great oppression. . .or in the [19]30s when millions of people were organised in unions in their overalls, we never had socialism' (Benn 1985: 14).

If, however, the link between structure and consciousness is weak, the problem none the less arises of how, and from where, class consciousness *is* generated. A critique of materialist explanations and of the ideal-type model of class consciousness suggests that the actions of workers themselves are of prime importance. This, in turn, highlights the need for a more refined conception of class consciousness. With respect to materialist explanations, even if it were accepted that workers' actions are, in the first instance, instrumental and shaped by a 'trade union consciousness', do they not contain a transformative potential? Can actions and consciousness rooted in narrow material concerns flower into something broader? In this context, several authors have critically examined the tenuous link between material concerns and ensuing action. Blackwell and Seabrook, for example, argue that attempts by workers to redirect the impersonal forces of capitalism 'according to a more human design' may entail a much more ambitious endeavour: 'daring to dream of an altogether different way of ordering the energies and passions of social life' (1985: 33). Both Hyman and Westergaard argue that the consequences of action motivated by material concerns are anything but predictable. Hyman argues that in economically unstable situations characterized by closures and redundancies: 'The notion of "instrumentalism" fails to indicate the type of conflict which can derive from even wage-oriented trade unionism. . .[e]conomic instability puts employment itself at risk: wages can be protected only through demands and actions which transcend mere wage-bargaining' (1978: 53).[7] Westergaard, underlining the brittle and potentially explosive quality of the 'cash nexus' argues that 'the single-stranded character of the "cash orientation" implies a latent instability of workers' commitments and orientations. . .' (1970: 130; see also Westergaard & Resler 1975: 379)

Similarly, Gaventa describes how action can transform both the issues involved and the consciousness of the participants:

> . . .the development of consciousness of an issue re-enforces the likelihood of attempted action upon it, in turn re-enforcing consciousness. A single victory helps to alter inaction owing to the anticipation of defeat, leading to more action and so on. Once patterns of quiescence are broken on one set of grievances, the accumulating resources of challenge – e.g. organization, momentum, consciousness – may become transferable to other issues and other targets. (1980: 24–5)[8]

The idea that action – however humble its origins and motivations – can *raise* consciousness challenges the wisdom of adhering to a conception of a 'true' consciousness as necessarily 'socialist' or 'revolutionary'. Certainly, taking class consciousness as in Marx's schema as a theoretical reference point has lent coherence to the study of working-class attitudes, culture and action. It is, however, a one-dimensional perspective. With such a demanding definition, workers either have to fuse a set of 'components' of consciousness in order to become 'revolutionary' (Mann 1973: 12–13), or negotiate a nine-stage obstacle course (Ollman 1972: 8). Mann, for example, argues that it is necessary to distinguish between four main elements in the conception of class consciousness – class *identity*, class *opposition*, class *totality* and the conception of an *alternative* society. He concludes that a true revolutionary consciousness is a combination of all four, and is 'obviously a rare occurrence' (1973: 13). By these criteria, it is rare indeed. And the effect of adopting such a model is to consign virtually all working-class attitudes and actions to the realm of Lenin's trade union consciousness. Ollman, for example, argues:

> A similar misconception. . .has 'class consciousness' referring to the workers' general resentment and feeling of being systematically cheated by the boss, where any aggressive action from complaining to industrial sabotage is viewed as evidence. . .Though obviously components of class consciousness, resenting the boss and the insight that he is taking unfair advantage are not by themselves sufficiently important to justify the use of this theme. (1972: 4)

But why not? To dismiss such evidence on the grounds of its alleged remoteness from an ideal-type revolutionary consciousness is effectively to overlook a wealth of activity whereby we may be able to identify how consciousness is generated and to better understand the 'process by which class and other political actions actually come about' (Rees 1985: 390). Thus 'to study class consciousness as if it were a simple continuum from right to left, or from trades union to political-revolutionary awareness, is to exclude an enormous variety of other dimensions of class consciousness' (Marshall G. 1988: 121). In this respect, the dangers of using a static or extreme model of class consciousness have been emphasized by some students of working-class history in the United States – where, of course, the absence of working-class consciousness is taken almost as a given. Wilentz, for example, argues that the USA only appears 'exceptional' because a 'powerful working-class socialist movement' is assumed to be the '*sine qua non* of true class consciousness. . .once class consciousness is equated with working-class socialism, American history seems to acquire a certain distinctive narrowness' (1984: 2–3). He goes on to argue that 'the failure of the American working class to live up to some preconceived (usually, unexamined) platonic standard has led us to read history backwards, rather than to come to grips with complex historical developments on their own terms' (1984: 5). Thus a more richly historical approach to the problem leads Wilentz to conclude that the limits of labour radicalism in Europe indicate that the 'social, political, and ideological history of the United States and its labor movements may not have been so exceptional after all'. In addition, 'US workers' use of natural rights theory and their belief in private property in no way negated the class-conscious character of their remarks', that is, 'if we equate working-class consciousness with Marxism or socialism, this no doubt sounds like a tame, even primitive, critique of capitalist class relations. . .but taken on its own terms and placed in a broader historical context, the powerful class character of the argument emerges' (1984: 11).

Similarly, Zolberg argues that the dominance in the United States of a 'narrowly construed business unionism' should not hide the fact that the language of the American working class was 'hardly a benevolent one. . .American workers were obviously not revolutionary-minded; but if the criterion of a high degree of class awareness is a revolutionary disposition, then one is led to the absurd conclusion that hardly anywhere in the capitalist world of the early twentieth century was a genuinely aware working class to be found' (1986: 426).

In the European context, Tilly and Tilly argue that '. . .such demand-ing standards for class conflict nearly banishes class conflict from history; however engaging the vision of workers speaking articulately in class terms and acting decisively on the basis of an accurate assessment of their interests and enemies, the event itself has been rare indeed. We settle for a less demanding and wider ranging conception of class conflict' (cited in Fantasia 1988: 18).

The point here is not to arrive at a situation where the study of class consciousness becomes an exercise in a subjective, indeterminate empiricism or where, to put it crudely, 'anything goes'. Instead, there is a need to formulate a conception of class consciousness with two key features. First, its *dynamic quality* should be highlighted (Fantasia 1988: 8). There must be a 'realization that class consciousness, like class itself, is a relational phenomenon. It does not exist as a separate entity with a reality *sui generis* but only as consciousness *of* something: of the structures that impinge on workers' lives and the opportunities for action within these. . .' (Marshall 1988: 122–3).

Consciousness is therefore 'generated in and changed by social action'; it is not 'a discrete component of social reality carried around inside people's heads and dipped into at pertinent moments' (Marshall 1988: 119–20). This dynamic dimension to class consciousness has been captured well by Allen: 'It is not the case that consciousness is contained in compartments. That there is "trade union consciousness" in its own box, useful for immediate needs but useless for altering the system, and that there is "class consciousness" of a different order, in its own box, labelled "for revolutionary purposes only" [*sic*]. Consciousness is a complex, contradictory phenomenon' (1977: 75).

Second, the actions of workers themselves must be *taken seriously*.

Marshall has noted drily that the tendency to underestimate working-class action 'can perhaps be attributed to the widely held belief among academic observers that it is somehow necessary for men and women to encompass society intellectually before they can attempt to change it. This premise is not confirmed by the history of class action on either a revolutionary or on a more modest scale' (1988: 106).

Thus workers' actions should be judged *on their own terms*, and not with reference to an abstract and demanding model of class consciousness which constantly derides their efforts as rudderless, spontaneous and doomed to failure.[9] And in allowing workers at the grass-roots level the capacity to act with initiative and foresight, the need arises to examine their actions in the most concrete way possible if a more refined conception of class consciousness is to be developed. Or, as Marshall has argued,

> consciousness is. . .an integral component of social action rather than a distinct something that somehow causes or is caused by it. The two cannot be studied in isolation. Experience has shown that it is the relationships and actions that are important and that these *can only be studied context-ually*. . .*Working-class consciousness*. . .*must be investigated as a component or dimension of everyday class practices.* (1988: 120; emphasis added)

The Miners and the Problem of Class Consciousness

The history of Britain's miners embody the problems of class consciousness, and of class politics in general, that have been discussed so far. The fate of the coal industry, the miners and their communities is a particular example of general changes in the economic, industrial and class structure of Britain during the twentieth century. In 1921, there were 1.132 million miners, accounting for 6.3 per cent of the working population. By 1983, the deep coal-mine workforce was 231,600, or less than 1.0 per cent of the working population. In 1922, 15 per cent of all trade unionists were miners. By 1984, however, only 2.3 per cent were miners (Callinicos & Simons 1985: 223).[10] Michael McGahey, Scottish miners' leader and National Vice-President of the NUM during the 1984–5 strike, reflected:

> We've seen this *change*. . .shall we say, in the *pattern* of the working class – the big battalions are no longer there like we used to have. An example, in my lifetime – I started in the industry in 1939 – there were 850,000 miners in Britain, there were 80,000 miners here in Scotland. Now, there's 3,000 in Scotland, and there's hardly 60 to 70,000 nationally. . .The steel industry, when I started work. . .had over 600,000 workers, and now they've declined to less than 100,000. The railway industry has declined. . . these big battalions of the working class are no longer there.[11]

Table 1. The Rise and Fall of the British Coal Industry

Year	No. of mines	Output (m. tons)	Workforce (000s)	Rate of Unionization (%)
1891		185.6	621.6	
1892		181.9		59.5
1895	2 935	189.8		
1901		219.1	778.7	68.7
1911		272.0		74.1
1913	2 705	287.5	1 095.2	
1921*		163.3	1 144.3	76.7
1926*		126.3	955.1	61.9
1929		257.9	939.4	55.1
1936		228.4	751.7	73.2
1941		206.3	697.6	
1948	940	211.5	716.5	86.4
1960	698	196.7	602.1	95.9
1964	576	251.5	517.0	93.5
1968	376	173.6	391.9	89.9
1972*	289	122.3	281.5	92.4
1974*	259	108.8	252.0	96.1
1979	223	119.9	234.9	
1983	191	120.9	207.6	
1984*	170		181.0	
1994	17		<11.0	

* major strike years

Sources: Ashworth 1986: 672–5; Bain and Price 1980: 45; Church 1986: 86,189,388; *FT*, 5/3/94; *I*, 26/3/92; NCB, *Report and Accounts 1984/5*, pp. 28–9; Supple 1987: 8–9.

The figures for 1994 refer to the remnants of the state-owned deep mine industry; by this time, nearly 2,000 other miners were working in 140 private pits (*G*, 10/2/94).

As Table 1 illustrates, a contrast may therefore be drawn between the miners as the backbone of the labour movement in the first quarter of the twentieth century and as a besieged and beleaguered section of organized labour in the 1980s. Yet this history of decline also under-scores the tenuous nature of the relationship between structure and consciousness. For the class experience of the miners was always beset by difficulties. The miners, like the British working class in general, *never* enjoyed a golden age of solidarity with which the immense problems engulfing the NUM in the early 1980s could somehow be ruefully contrasted. Instead, structural and material factors ensured that obstacles to unity amongst miners were, historically, severe. The miners, like any other section of the working population, struggled to overcome the divisive effects of industrial expansion and contraction, and material differences within their own ranks. Solidarity, to the extent that it was achieved, was never a 'given', but a *highly contingent*, and painstakingly constructed, phenomenon.

Yet despite these historic difficulties, and throughout a century-long process of economic and industrial change, it *is* possible to identify a collective class-based identity[12] amongst Britain's miners. For one thing, loyalty to the Union played a critical role in underpinning a wider sense of belonging to the extent of overcoming, on occasions, deep material differences. No doubt the miners' collective identity – which encompassed division as well as unity, local rivalries as well as national solidarity, strikebreakers as well as strikers – appears highly problematic when compared to an abstract model of revolutionary consciousness. Measured on its *own* terms, however, it is decidedly more impressive. Thus miners during the twentieth century may not have actively engaged in 'overthrowing capitalism'. Nor did they always succeed in overcoming divisions within their own ranks. However, in their constant battles with the employer, in their bruising encounters, at times of acute crisis, with the State, and in times of high unemployment and severe deprivation, they showed initiative and resilience, against heavy odds, in endeavouring to create for themselves an element of security in conditions otherwise characterized by uncertainty and hardship. *This* is the benchmark to use when examining the class consciousness of miners, and it is in this context that an assessment of the national coal strike of 1984/5 is undertaken. The motivations, perceptions and actions that shaped (and were shaped by) this monumental dispute, and any elements of continuity and change in the consciousness of miners, are best understood in terms of the miners' own history and experience. My empirical analysis of consciousness and action amongst British miners in 1984–5 is therefore undertaken with Thompson's critical claim firmly in mind that

> If we stop history at a given point, then there are no classes but simply a multitude of individuals with a multitude of experiences. But if we watch these men over an adequate period of social change, we observe patterns in their relationships, their ideas, and their institutions. Class is defined by men as they live their own history, and, in the end, this is its only definition. . .we cannot understand class unless we see it as a social and cultural formation, arising from processes which can only be studied as they work themselves out over a considerable historical period. (1966: 11)

Furthermore, by examining the actions of miners in terms of their own history and experiences, I favour Wilentz's definition of class consciousness 'not as any particular set of ideas, doctrines, or political strategies but far more broadly as the *articulated resistance* of wage workers. . .to capitalist wage-labor relations'. (1984: 6; emphasis added)

Notes

1. Source: NCB, *Report and Accounts 1984/5*, pp. 28–9; *I*, 26/3/92.
2. *FT*, 5/3/94.
3. BC, *Report and Accounts 1988/9*, p. 3.
4. As such, the fate of the NUM in the 1970s and 1980s was in keeping with the declining fortunes of trade unions throughout the advanced capitalist world. In an increasingly hostile economic, political and industrial environment, which generated generally higher rates of unemployment and fostered the growth of part-time and temporary work, the bargaining strength of unions was sapped, especially at the national level. Heavily unionized sectors of the economy tended to give way to those which, historically, had been difficult to organize. As a result, the 1980s saw generally reduced rates of unionization (or union 'density'), while the long-term process by which the ranks of organized labour were being recomposed was greatly accelerated: the rise of white-collar unionism, the growing presence (relatively) of women trade unionists and, above all, the demise of the male, blue-collar, industrial worker as the traditional mainstay of trade unionism.

    For comparative overviews of these developments, see Richards 1995; Western 1995; Regini (ed.) 1992; Coggins *et al.* 1989; Visser 1989, 1992; Hall 1987; Pérez-Díaz 1987; Crouch 1986, 1992, 1995; Walsh 1985; Bain and Price 1980. For an overview of the decentralization of industrial relations in the 1980s and 1990s, see Katz 1993. For studies of the multiple difficulties faced by British trade unions since 1979, see Beaumont and Harris 1995; Disney, Gosling and Machin 1995; Morris 1995; Smith and Morton 1994; Edwards 1992; Green F 1992; Dorey 1991; Maksymiw, Eaton and Gill 1990; Coates 1989; Hobsbawm 1989; Marsh 1989; Towers 1989; Winchester 1989; Longstreth 1988; Beaumont 1987; MacInnes 1987; Jacobi *et al.* 1986.

    On the acute contemporary crisis of trade unionism in the USA, see Davis and Sprinker (eds) 1988; Brody 1994; Cobble 1994; Craver 1993; Salvatore 1992; Trumka 1992; Geoghagan 1991; Gifford 1990; Green H 1990; LaBotz 1990; Feldman and Betzold 1988; Goldfield 1987; Davis 1986; Lipset (ed) 1986; Aronowitz 1983; Edwards R 1979.

    On white-collar unionism, see Smith, Knights and Willmott 1991; Lockwood 1989; Hyman and Price (eds) 1983; Bain and Price 1972. On women and trade unionism, see Kingsolver 1989; Boston 1987; Coote and Campbell 1987; Phillips 1983. For empirical analyses of the decline of traditional industrial unionism, see Rhodes and Wright

1988; Strath 1987; Mény and Wright (eds) 1986; Hartley, Kelly and Nicholson 1983.

5. Radical resistance to encroachments on material security has not, of course, been confined to the industrial worker. Both Popkin (1979) and Scott (1976) provide essentially materialist explanations for peasant rebellion in Southeast Asia. While the latter emphasizes a moral and normative dimension to the basis of rebellion (1976: vii), the behaviour of the peasant is none the less labelled 'risk-averse' (1976: 4). As such, the capitalist transformation of the countryside damages the peasantry's ability to maintain a minimum income (1976: 7,9) and provokes the need to rebel (1976: 40).

   In similar fashion, Zeitlin links economic insecurity with radical action by explaining the post-revolutionary attitudes of Cuban workers as a function of their pre-revolutionary levels of economic security (1966: 35). Meanwhile, Lipset argues that with respect to nineteenth-century agrarian upheavals in Canada, the main site of protest was the economically (and climatically) vulnerable wheat belt (1950: 10, cited by Zeitlin 1966: 35, n.4).

6. Miliband also argues that the 1930s in Britain 'save for very active pockets of intellectual, political and industrial dissent and militancy, were years of middle-class complacency and working-class apathy and resignation, with more "deferential" support for the Conservatives among the working classes than they have ever enjoyed in later years' (1964: 99; see also Miliband 1985).

7. Similarly, Fosh observes a strong tendency in the British industrial relations literature to separate 'instrumental' from 'ideological' forms of union orientation, whereby union 'members are statically seen as having one or the other'. Yet, in fact, 'most rank-and-file members' conception of unionism can contain elements of both instrumentality and ideology' (1993: 580).

8. Green makes a similar case in his riveting account of the 1985–6 strike waged by members of Local P-9 of the UFCW against the Hormel meatpacking company in Austin, Minnesota (Green H. 1990).

9. Many authors persist in conceiving of class consciousness as something that can be taught to or implanted in the working class. Nairn, for example, argues that '(t)he English working class, immunized against theory like no other class, by its entire historical experience, *needed* theory like no other. It still does' (1964: 57; original emphasis).

10. The fate of the British coal industry is not unique in the advanced industrial world. International Labour Organization statistics highlight the declining fortunes of this traditional sector in the

economies of most advanced industrial countries. The ILO estimates that employment in mining and quarrying in France fell from
136,000 in 1981 to 81,000 in 1991. During the same period, and in
the same economic sectors, levels of employment in Spain fell from
94,000 to 76,000; in Canada, from 208,000 to 174,000, and in the
USA from 1,118,000 to 733,000. In Germany, levels of employment
in mining and quarrying fell from 232,000 in 1984 to 182,000 in
1991, and in Australia from 102,000 in 1986 to 93,000 in 1991
(ILO, *Bulletin of Labour Statistics 1992–4*, pp. lxi–lxv).

11. Interview, Edinburgh, 15/12/89.
12. Quite obviously, the miners do not constitute a 'class' per se. I
present the miners, therefore, as a particular occupational group of
workers whose attitudes, values and actions are none the less shaped
and constrained by their position in the wider class structure. In
doing so, I am indebted in particular to Atul Kohli for helping me
to think through this issue, and also to Rick Fantasia who, in his
study of consciousness and action amongst American workers,
writes: 'My subject is not class conflict, if one's conceptual requirement is class "writ large", but class action as it is expressed in
specific industrial conflicts and framed by institutionalized trade
unionism and the industrial relations system in which it operates'
(1988: 19).

The Basis of Solidarity

Introduction

> What with the dejected countenances of the men, occasioned by their poverty and hard labour, and what with the colour or discolour which comes from the coal, both to their clothes and complexions . . . they are, indeed, frightful fellows at first sight.
>
> Daniel Defoe, *A Tour through the Whole Island of Great Britain, 1726* quoted in M. Pollard, *The Hardest Work under Heaven*

> Here, encamped on a vast raft of coal . . . was a tribe of Englishmen so distinctive in their way of life that, had they been situated on a remote island in the South Seas, they would have been the subject of a dozen ethnographic monographs. . . .
>
> M. Benney, 'The Legacy of Mining', in M. Bulmer (ed.), *Mining and Social Change*

These two comments underscore an historical irony: while coal production was central to Britain's industrial development, those producing the coal were long regarded as a breed apart. The brutality of their work, the isolation of mining settlements and their consequent emergence as 'occupational communities' did much to reinforce such perceptions on the part of both miners and non-miners alike. Furthermore, several studies argue that such characteristics made mining communities more militant than other segments of the working population (Gaventa 1980: 37, n.14).

The nature and history of coal mining, and the development of mining communities and institutions certainly underpinned a tradition of resilience, solidarity and militancy. But why? This chapter examines hose factors which promoted such solidarity amongst miners.

The 'Ideal-Type' Mining Community

Isolation, homogeneity of occupation and cultural insularity were long regarded as the defining characteristics of mining communities. In his influential typography of 'working-class images of society', Lockwood presented coal mining as one of the bastions of 'proletarian traditional-ism' – that is, an industry which tended '. . . to concentrate workers together in solidary communities and to isolate them from the influences of the wider society' (1975: 17). Geographical isolation and dependence on a single employer produced a 'distinctive occupational culture' (1975: 17). Moreover, its predominantly one-class population and low rates of geographical and social mobility made the mining community an 'inward-looking society', and served '. . . to accentuate the sense of cohesion that springs from shared work experiences' (1975: 18). In class terms, therefore, social consciousness in the mining community was 'centred on an awareness of "us" in contradistinction to "them" who are not a part of "us". "Them" are bosses, managers . . . and ultimately, the public authorities of the larger society' (1975: 18).

The *consequences* of isolation and insularity, however, were never clear. Kerr and Siegel, for example, formulated an isolated mass hypo-thesis to explain the position of mining as a highly strike-prone industry. The location of a worker in society determined his propensity to strike; this location was heavily influenced by an industrial environment in which the '. . . [e]mployees form a largely homogenous undifferentiated mass' (1954: 191, 192). Steady contact between workers generated co-hesion which in turn created the basis for permanent organization (such as a trade union) (1954: 193, n.9). In sum, industries would be highly strike-prone when workers formed a relatively homogenous and cohesive group unusually isolated from the general community (1954: 195).

However, Kerr and Siegel never made clear why militancy was a *nec-essary* consequence of the cohesion of mining communities.[1] Thus Rimlinger argued that 'the inherent environmental tendency toward strike proneness may be counteracted or reinforced by sociocultural factors' (1959: 405). For example, the 'paternalistic discipline' of employers in the Ruhr basin explained the deference of German miners, while the failure of either the state or employers in Britain to accept responsibility for workers' welfare during industrialization explained the general militancy of British miners (1959: 403).

Bulmer, meanwhile, criticized the hypotheses outlined above for failing to explain the 'dynamics' of mining communities (1975: 66). Thus the limitations of (Lockwood's) class conflict model '. . . lies in its neglect of endogenous change. What role does human motivation and collective action at the local level play in the course of events in mining settlements? Is human social behaviour entirely the product of exo-genous forces external to the community?' (1957: 67). Similarly, the '. . . isolated mass hypothesis is an oversimplified view of the social structure of mining communities. In a sense it replaces the over-emphasis on class factors in the "archetypal proletarian" view, with an overemphasis upon the *industrial* characteristics of mining settlements' (1975: 71, original emphasis). And while Rimlinger's hypothesis improved on that of the isolated mass, in that it '. . . emphasises the importance of *different* reactions to the industrial setting . . .' (1975: 73, original emphasis), it does not '. . . specify *how* the socio-cultural influences in fact operate' (1975: 76, original emphasis). Bulmer concluded by presenting a traditional model of the ideal-type mining community as a means of assessing the nature of social change in the coal industry. That is, the traditional mining community possessed the following characteristics: physical isolation, economic predominance of mining, dangerous work, social insularity arising from occupational homogeneity and isolation, communal leisure activities, rigid division of labour between the sexes, economic and political conflict between mine-owner and miner, and the communal character of social relationships (Bulmer 1975: 85–8). In addition, however, he emphasized 'the relatively neglected problem of industry-community linkages' (1975: 76). Understanding how such linkages promoted solidarity amongst miners and their communities is the focus of the remainder of this chapter. The *meaning* of such terms as 'solidarity', 'cohesion' and 'militancy' has to be understood in order to assess the problems of collective action at the national level. What follows is not a comprehensive account of the rich culture of mining communities, but an attempt to highlight those aspects of such a culture which generated the possibilities for collective action amongst miners.

The Working Environment

> You see, what other folk don't understand . . . is the bond of the miner. I work in a place . . . where . . . we're working against the atmosphere that's highly explosive, I trust you not to take a match, a cigarette, to ignite and blow us all to smithereens. I trust you to set that pit prop, to hold the roofs up, when you've been on shift before me, *secure*. I trust *you* . . . and it gets a *bond* between you, because you're both in same conditions – it's a great leveller down in pit – it doesn't matter if you've got a mansion [or] . . . a shanty-hut – because you're *all* the same – you're all black, sweaty, mucky, and wear rags, and you're on your hands and knees – it doesn't matter what you've got up there – it's a great *leveller*. (D51)

Solidarity in the mining community was rooted in the working environment. In their classic study, Dennis *et al.* noted that 'the team of colliers, with this system of mutual dependence, is the hub of the social structure of coalmining . . .' (1969: 45), while Benney argues that '. . . it is the work at and around the coal face that determines the attitude of the whole mining community to mining as an occupation' (1978: 55). Certainly, the point of production in mining heavily shaped the attitudes and actions of the work-force. The 'continual presence of physical danger in mining'

(Bulmer 1978a: 25) underpinned any mutual dependence amongst miners. The history of the industry was scarred by the deaths of thousands of miners, and the serious injury of many thousands more. Even among those who survived their working lives physically intact, many were condemned to retirements plagued by emphysema, bronchitis and, most notoriously, pneumoconiosis ('black lung').[2] Between 1951 and 1971 more than 17,000 British miners and ex-miners died from pneumoconiosis alone (Allen 1981: 94). While technology had possibly eliminated the threat of appalling underground disasters characteristic of the past, mining in Britain remained in modern times the most dangerous of occupations: 'the rate of fatal and major injuries . . . in 1985 for coal extraction etc., is over three times the average for manufacturing and 1.3 times that for construction' (LRD 1989: 4). By 1987/88 non-fatal major industries in coal mining were 2.7 times those for construction (LRD 1989: 4).

Several authors have considered the effects of an environment in which the '. . . face worker is engaged, in the last analysis, in a daily wager with death' (Samuel 1986: 8). The ever-present threats of fires, floods, poisonous gases and collapsing roofs encouraged 'dependence on and responsibility for fellow-workers' and explained why importance is attached to working among tried and known companions' (Bulmer 1978b: 246; see also Reid 1981: 98–9). In addition, the underground environment created a 'collective or group orientation to work among miners' (Bulmer 1978a: 25) in which work was experienced not simply as a means towards an economic end but as a group activity. This, in turn, led to a high level of work involvement on the part of the miner (Bulmer 1978a: 25).[3]

The unpredictability of mining work is well captured by Douglass who asks: 'The earth is pried open for our industrial convenience. How long will it accept the indignity?' (Douglass & Krieger 1983: 4). However, levels of unpredictability varied from job to job underground; this, it is argued, led certain groups of miners to show greater solidarity (*vis-à-vis* management) than others. This was seen most clearly in the predominant role assumed in mining trade unionism by that minority of men underground working at or near the coalface. In any mine, this was the most arduous, dangerous and generally the best-paid work. Yet it was also the most unpredictable, prone to constant interruption (roof falls, faults in the coal seam, mechanical breakdowns, etc.). This ensured that faceworkers, especially at times when payment was by results (that is, before and after the era of the National Power Loading Agreement (NPLA), 1966–77) were 'constantly being thrown into a bargaining position with management' (Dennis *et al.* 1969: 87). This tended to place them in the forefront of trade unionism[4] – indeed, 'though trade union militancy has never been isolated to any one section of the men, the heart of NUM organisation and activity is located on the coal at the point of production' (Pitt 1979: 84; see also Dennis *et al*. 1969: 48, 49, 56, 87). In contrast, other underground work, and surface work, was characterized by greater levels of predictability and safety. As such, 'one proof that unionism in . . . coal-mining . . . derives much of its strength from the unexpected circumstances which constantly arise in the course of work is that among that group which does not experience these vagaries, the surface-workers, trade unionism has never had such a strong appeal' (Dennis *et al*. 1969: 87).

Differentiations such as these, however, did not undermine the *general* impact that the working environment had on miners collectively – there was a '. . . universal recognition by the men of their common condition in "the same hole"' (Pitt 1979: 29). Even if miners working at or near the coalface took a leading role in industrial action and union affairs, they did not do so as a sectionalised, self-serving élite. For example, the wave of unofficial strikes which swept the coalfields in 1969 and 1970 were instigated by faceworkers on behalf of surface-workers whose conditions of work had not altered since the defeat of the General Strike of 1926.

Overall, therefore, the working environment underground was the cornerstone of the solidarity demonstrated so often above the ground. In this respect, '. . . the comradeship of the picket line and the readiness to stand up to police charges might . . . usefully be related to a working environment which privileges physical courage and endurance and makes reciprocity and trust a very condition of survival' (Samuel 1986, 8).

Coal and Community

> . . . when a pit is sunk . . . the village . . . come[s] second. The village is built around the colliery and . . . all the social life . . . everything . . . is directly connected to the colliery . . . and when the pit . . . dies, you lose the community of the villager and the surrounding area and if you look at the South Wales valley[s] as an whole – where every pit *is*, there's a village attached to it . . . you've your miners' welfare halls, where you had your snooker and your chess clubs, your libraries . . . it was all built around the colliery. (W1)

Historically, while the presence of coal determined the location of mines and the working environment of miners, the location of the mine, in turn, became the centre of the community that subsequently emerged in its vicinity. For example, Throckley in Northumberland 'was built up as a community of miners quite deliberately by the coal company which sank the pit there in the late 1860s' (Williamson 1982: 6). Indeed, the fact that communities were created *because* of the presence of coal ensured that 'the pit loomed large over every activity' (Bulmer 1978a: 28). Thus the mining village was very much a 'constructed community' (Williamson 1982: 6, 230)[5] whose occupational homogeneity ensured, amongst other things, that 'the income of a whole village population [was] dependent on the fortunes of a single pit' (Benney 1978: 57). The issue of pit closures was therefore fundamental: 'The pit is the village, paying its wages, supporting its shops, keeping the community together. There is little other industry . . . The pit is the reason for the village and if the pit dies the village dies also' (Marshall P. 1984: 39).

The Pit Disaster

Yet even if the livelihoods of miners and their families were generally hostage to the economic fortunes of the local mine, nothing demonstrated more graphically the degree to which communities were at the mercy of the industry than the pit disaster. The bloody history of the industry has already been noted; indeed, 'no other industry has such a catalogue of mass killings which have continued despite statutory controls and management and union regulations to prevent them' (Allen 1981: 94). And while the death toll consisted largely of isolated fatalities scattered over time and through the various coalfields (Allen 1981: 92), it was the large-scale underground disasters – in which tens or hundreds were killed – that characterized the industry for the outsider and which were long remembered in the mining communities themselves:[6] 'While coal picked off most of its victims in ones and twos . . . it could sometimes jump on a community and kick it to pieces' (Pollard 1984: 21).

Mining communities throughout Britain suffered in this way. For example, communities in the four NUM areas in which research was undertaken suffered *at least* one major disaster in the course of the twentieth century. In Yorkshire, two underground explosions at Cadeby Main colliery in July 1912 killed 88 men. In Derbyshire, 79 men died in October 1938 at Markham No. 1 mine. In Nottinghamshire, 80 miners died in an underground fire at Creswell colliery in September 1950 (33 bodies were sealed in the workings). And in October 1913, in the worst disaster in British mining history, a massive explosion at the Universal colliery, Senghenydd, killed 439 miners, thereby confirming the grim reputation of the South Wales coalfield as the most dangerous in the country.[7] That in the latter case, the dependents numbered more than a thousand underscored the monstrous impact of such an event on a single community: 'Such statistics could hardly be grasped by the mind when related to one obscure valley. It seemed out of all proportion to nature that one small area of the country should meet with such a savage blight' (Duckham & Duckham 1973: 171).

A final example, however, epitomizes the chronic agony of the mining community. If the above cases ensured that wives were left without husbands, and children without fathers, the 1966 tragedy in Aberfan, South Wales, demonstrated in the most brutal manner imaginable how the industry could rip the very heart out of a community. The disaster occurred when a large section of one of several waste tips towering above the village on the surrounding hillsides collapsed. Some two

million tons of coal dust, rubble and soaking industrial waste material
careered down the hillside, engulfing a farmhouse, several homes, and
burying Pantglas Infants' and Junior School to a depth of forty-five feet.
Twenty-eight adults and 116 infants and young children were killed. One
in two families in Aberfan were bereaved; one in five at the nearby
village of Merthyr Vale.[8]

The impact of such shocking disasters could not, however, be
measured in concrete terms alone. In becoming 'part of the bloody
backcloth against which the miner carries on his working life . . . ' (Pitt
1979: 35), they assumed immense symbolic importance, and helped to
underpin the powerful and bitter sense of history pervading most mining
communities. The fact that there was 'blood on the coal'[9] did not just
reflect the often destructive way in which the fate of communities was
at the mercy of the industry. In addition, it generated a *moral* claim on
the local mine – '[t]his is *our* pit' (Beynon 1984: 113; original emphasis;
see also Samuel 1986: 22). This helped explain the continuing fierce
attachment by a community to a mine which may, in fact, have caused
immense suffering. This was certainly the case with respect to Aberfan.
After the disaster, the NCB pledged that the local mine would not shut
until its reserves were exhausted. However, the announcement by BC in
July 1989 of the impending closure of the mine outraged the local community. While some objections were formulated on commercial grounds,
most argued that a moral responsibility arising from the 1966 disaster
was being abrogated. One retired miner commented, 'I suppose the Coal
Board think that if they can shut down a community with a history like
Aberfan's, they can shut down most of the South Wales coalfield with
no trouble.' Another ex-miner commented, 'I've worked hard for this
mine all my life . . . I challenge Mrs. Thatcher or anyone to come here
to the colliery to meet me and hear what this village has been through.
They would not go ahead if they had any feelings at all.' No comment,
though, captured better the paradoxical relationship between coal
industry and community than that of the local NUM Lodge Secretary:
'The decision is despicable on moral grounds, because the mine is what
keeps this village alive.'[10]

Collective Identity and the Mining Community

Pit disasters demonstrated how mining communities suffered *as* communities. They also showed how, on occasions, the hazardous nature of
an occupation *central* to the livelihood of a community ensured that
suffering was on a collective rather than an individual level. None the
less, they alone cannot explain how, in mining communities, the identity
of the individual was so often subsumed by that of the collective. Thus
any tendency towards a 'collective culture' sustained by the brutality of
the working environment and occupational homogeneity was 'reinforced

by the social and geographic isolation which turns the community in upon its own resources' (Bulmer 1978a: 26). Isolation was the most concrete manifestation of the miners' 'apartness'; this, in turn, had implications for the dominance of collective identity in mining communities. The history of the Kent coalfield is instructive. Kent, alongside Nottinghamshire, was one of the last coalfields in Britain to be developed. Work on Betteshanger colliery, the last of the area's four pits, did not commence until 1924 (Pitt 1979: 22). There were no indigenous miners in Kent; all the required skilled labour had to be imported from the established coalfields (Pitt 1979: 22).[11] The Kent coalfield therefore epitomized the peculiar way in which the mining industry 'constructed' communities. Unlike other branches of industrial capitalism, which tended to concentrate labour into cities, the sheer 'immovability of the coal measures' ensured that '[c]apital had to go to the coal, and men, women and children were compelled by necessity to follow' (Pitt 1979: 22).

Moreover, the miners entering the Kent coalfield encountered not only the 'worst physical conditions in British mining', but also an 'alien, hostile social environment' (Pitt 1979: 23). Certainly, the arrival, in the 1920s and 1930s, of thousands of men from Scotland, Durham, Staffordshire, Yorkshire and Wales in search of regular work was a rude awakening for an area in which 'the industrial worker was almost unknown' (Pitt 1979: 68, 22). Some Kent miners ascribed the initial hostility of local people to their first contact with the 'sinkers' – that particularly tough and cohesive group of itinerant workers, mainly Scots, Welsh and Irish, who sank the shafts of the new collieries and then moved on elsewhere (Pitt 1979: 69). Indeed, the isolation endured by these early arrivals in the coalfield was the foundation for the later distinctiveness of 'pit villages'. Similarly, the local hostility which greeted them laid the basis for the astonishing system of 'social apartheid'[12] suffered by subsequent generations of miners in Kent (Pitt 1979: 70).

Such social isolation lent the mining community a certain insular quality: '[t]he reaction of the miners has been to turn in on the community, and back towards their own people . . . It wasn't so much that the miners consciously looked inwards, they couldn't very well look outwards' (Pitt 1979: 70, 72) And even in environments less hostile than the 'near-feudal milieu' (Pitt 1979: 94) of Kent, *geographical* isolation had similar consequences. For example, even though the massive economic, political and social role played by the South Wales miners guaranteed them a venerated position in Welsh society,[13] the geographical isolation of pit villages in remote, steep-sided valleys perpetuated the perception of the mining community as a 'world apart'. Such perceptions in South Wales in 1984–5 were, it seems, common to miners, employers and outsiders. Thus a miner from Mardy colliery commented: 'We're a different breed here. Thatcher . . . will never understand that.'[14] The NCB's South Wales Area Director noted acerbically: 'Show me a valley where you can't get out at the top without ropes, and I'll show you a place with union troubles.'[15] Meanwhile, the perspectives of the ubiquitous outsider did not appear to have progressed much beyond that of Daniel Defoe. An English journalist, about to enter the South Wales coalfield, described himself as being 'on the threshold of hell'. For good measure, he referred to Trethomas, a pit village on the edge of the coal-field, as being '. . . so far removed from middle Britain. . . that it could be Africa. It looks scruffy, clapped-out, and awful' (Marshall P. 1984: 39).

Isolation, therefore, compounded the tendency towards a sense of collective identity in mining communities engendered initially by the underground working environment and occupational homogeneity. Furthermore, the 'immense pressure for conformity' in most mining communities did not just *reflect* the recognition by miners of the need to maintain unity in the face of a hostile working environment and a dominant employer (Pitt 1979: 59, 86). It was also a *result* of how iso-lation obstructed social mobility out of the mining community − 'for many the village was a prison' (Chaplin 1978 cited in Bulmer 1978a: 43). This had both positive and negative connotations for the 'idea of the community as a prison implies both constraint and lack of opportunity' (Bulmer 1978a: 43–4). Nowhere is this seen more powerfully than in the subordinate position of women in the mining communities.

Gender Relations and the Mining Community

Social control in mining communities rested on, and was expressed through, the male domination of women and an intensely *masculine* culture.[16] Indeed, the 'lives, consciousness and action of women', in and of themselves, have tended to be overlooked in studies of mining com-munities (Warwick & Littlejohn 1992: 72).[17] Instead, studies such as Bulmer's 'ideal-type' community tend to perpetuate the view that there were distinct 'men's' and 'women's' worlds, with the former, of course, being far more important as a means of understanding the solidarity of the mining community − the men's world was one of 'economic and political activity, where working-class consciousness is made and remade', while women were merely 'domestic managers' (Warwick & Littlejohn 1992: 73). Given this, '[h]ow far this ever was entirely the truth is a good question, and how far this has been a product of men's own definition of the situation is another' (Warwick & Littlejohn 1992: 73). While an analysis of the role of women themselves in shaping the culture and identity of mining communities is beyond the scope of this study, it is none the less critical to emphasize how the solidarity of miners, and the development of mining itself, entailed the subordination of women. Only then can the role of women in the 1984–5 strike be placed in proper context.

Thus in an historical overview of the development of the coal industry, Allen underscores how mining exemplified the way in which capitalism's structural requirements created and enforced a rigid sexual division of labour. While men derived their power and status from involvement in market-determined production (which was almost exclusively in their own hands[18]) the task of social reproduction became the responsibility of women. Through a range of activities (child-rearing, washing, cleaning, cooking), women ensured that 'the coalowners would have an adequate supply of male workers tramping to the pits each day' (1981: 75). Moreover, such activities were 'performed at no cost to the employers for the domestic labour of women had no price on it and was not paid for. It was not even designated as work' (1981: 75, 79). Furthermore, the status of women as 'unpaid domestic labour to provide back-up services' for the coal industry was legitimized by the circulation of ideas − internalized by the miners − about 'man's work', the responsibilities of women in the home, and the virtues of subordination to a man's needs (1981: 79). If, therefore, the isolated community was a prison for the miners, the family − as a site for the reproduction of gender inequality − became a prison for women within the same communities.

Historically, therefore, the women of the coalfields led separate and subordinate lives. Moreover, Williamson, who offers a lucid account of the daily routines of miners' wives (1982: 118–32), notes that even in times of acute crisis, the role of women was a decidedly domesticated one. Thus his own grandmother's role in the 1926 lock-out was to 'bear the burden of the budget and never to question my grandfather's reasons for sticking. . . to his union's decisions. . . to make do with nothing and scratch resources together as best she could' (1982: 176). As such, 'her experience of class conflict, as it were, in the kitchen was just as sharp as my grandfather's in the pit' (1982: 176).

In their study, in the mid-1950s, of a Yorkshire pit village, Dennis *et al.* describe (though in curiously benign fashion) a near-brutal sexual division of labour involving a strict separation of duties and routines (in ways nearly identical to those described by Williamson in the 1920s) in which the miner's economic *in*dependence (and conversely, his wife's economic *de*pendence) led to separate working *and* social lives (1969: 180–6; 201–7).[19]

Gender relations within mining communities were never, of course, static. Indeed, the post-war decline of the industry (ironically) ameliorated women's conditions of oppression as they themselves entered the labour market to combat insecurity and declining living standards (Allen 1981: 79). Indeed, Warwick and Littlejohn note how 'where mining was not quite so dominant in the labour market, there could be more equal status for both genders, brought about by a more open competition for jobs' (1992: 84). Yet these same authors emphasize the force of tradition in mining communities – how the legacy of sexist practices and attitudes remained intact (Allen 1981: 79), and how contemporary residents of the village originally studied by Dennis *et al.* in the 1950s felt that the community *remained* male-dominated, with men and women tending to lead separate lives as a consequence of pit work (1992: 31).[20]

The Strikebreaker and the Mining Community

If, however, the historic position of women in mining communities reminds us that the foundations for solidarity *within* such communities were uneven, the legendary treatment meted out to the strikebreaker demonstrated how, in the face of the 'enemy' *without*, they were also 'close-knit highly integrated collectivities' able to 'exercise powerful social control over their members' (Bulmer 1978a: 43–4). Such treatment validates Benney's assertion that 'the mining community. . . makes its demands on life *as* a community, and not as a collection of individuals' (1978: 58; original emphasis).

Lloyd describes how the 'depth of feeling expressed against a "scab" in a mining community is not easily understood by an outsider, and is shocking in its intensity. . .' (1985: 33). The undying hatred earned by the strikebreaker was explained by a Derbyshire miner:

> . . . if someone . . . goes back to work, when we have a dispute, he's broke a trust. Because I've been pals . . . a comrade-at-arms with him . . . not in a struggle, but at my actual *work* – it's a life and death situation . . . He's broke that bond . . . but if he comes back to work in my team again, I'm going to be thinking . . . when we got us backs to wall, when going got tough – he gibbed out . . . got some money . . . all the time, at the back of my mind, I'll be thinking: can I trust him? . . . because he's looking after himself, he's not with us, a team . . . he's on his own and . . . *that's* the bond that he's broke. (D51)

Furthermore, in conditions of occupational homogeneity, any breaking of trust underground became a betrayal of the mining community as a whole. Thus while the breaking of the code of loyalty to one's 'mates' could have serious consequences in any industry, for the miner '. . . his whole life, not only his work, can be affected by the actions and words of his fellows. The "blackleg" miner must be made a social outcast in every way, and not only at work' (Dennis *et al.* 1969: 79–80). Moreover, the recognition by the mining community of 'facing a common enemy and a common fate' (Dennis *et al.* 1969: 80) made strikebreaking a par- ticularly emotive issue. For example, in Throckley, Northumberland, an enduring bitterness was generated by police baton charges into miners demonstrating against strikebreakers in 1926 (Williamson 1982: 190–1). And in the Durham pit village of Easington in 1984–5, Beynon describes the demoralization of a community caused by a single strikebreaker, and the violence accompanying the intrusion of state power as a means of ferrying him into work – 'All this, all this for one bloody man' (1984: 113).

In such circumstances, strikebreaking created ill-feeling long after the specific troubles in which it arose were over (Williamson 1982: 191). Strikebreakers themselves were vilified for the rest of their lives.[21] Furthermore, a powerful emphasis was placed on *total* loyalty. When four miners at Cortonwood colliery in Yorkshire returned to work one day before the end of the 1984–5 strike, pickets at the pit gate ' . . . could not understand why the four should have guaranteed themselves a working life of isolation and vilification instead of waiting just another 24 hours to join the official return to work'.[22] Similarly, a miner at Allerton-Bywater colliery, Yorkshire, acknowledged that by returning to work three days before the official Monday resumption of work, he would be known thenceforth as a 'Friday man'(Y48). And a Derbyshire striker whose family was in particularly dire circumstances towards the end of the 1984–5 strike related how he had returned to work in order to spare his son (also on strike) the ignominy of being labelled a 'scab' for the rest of his life (D9).

However, underscoring how mining communities tended to have 'their own moral and socio-political values' (Francis 1985e: 269), it is noteworthy that overt violence directed against strikebreakers was the exception rather than the rule: 'In times of intense struggle, those who break strikes place themselves outside such communities. But the methods used to extract discipline and solidarity invariably, but not always, have been forms of non-violent direct action such as the social boycott, social ostracism and stay-in strikes' (Francis 1985e: 269).

Indeed, strikebreakers, in return for their collaboration with the state and employers, were doomed to suffer a degree of ostracism not dissimilar to that inflicted by outsiders on the miners of the Kent coalfield. Thus at Taff Merthyr colliery where in the 1930s the South Wales Miners Federation (SWMF) struggled with the company-backed South Wales Miners Industrial Union (SWMIU), the community enforced just such a system: 'To isolate those who supported the "scab union", cinemas and shops were boycotted, there were expulsions from football teams, bands and choirs and "scabs" were compelled to sing on their own in chapel services. "Scabs" witnessed their own "death" in communities which no longer accepted them' (Francis 1985e: 269).

Therefore, while 'the use of police as an arm of the State during mining strikes is as old as mining itself . . . [v]iolence is not endemic in the British coalfields . . . '[23] (Francis 1985e: 270). Instead, violence for the most part only occurred during the escorting of strikebreakers to work by police or troops. What was said of the South Wales coalfield in 1984–5 was applicable to many other coalfields during the twentieth century: 'violent intimidation is not practised if only because it is not needed. Ostracism happens spontaneously, and is more effective.'[24] This demonstrated not only the 'apartness' of mining communities, but also their impressive ability to act, in the face of challenges from within, *as* communities.

The Roots of Community Action

Mining communities were never static entities jarred occasionally by pit disasters or the tensions and hardships accompanying strike action. Instead, the great swings of fortune experienced by the coal industry, and the ensuing social and economic hardships, meant that mining communities endured adversity on a continuous basis. Thus while much of a mining village's life had to be understood 'on its own terms', it was also 'massively shaped by society as a whole' (Williamson 1982: 5–6). The expansion and contraction of the industry ensured that Throckley 'was never a static community, its structures frozen in time' (Williamson 1982: 231).

What was true of a Northumberland pit village was applicable to other coalfield areas. This was demonstrated, for example, by the maelstrom of economic and industrial change endured by the mining communities of the Rhondda valley in South Wales. Between 1860 and 1920, the population of the Rhondda increased from 950 to more than 160,000. Coal was central to such growth; by the turn of the century, the Rhondda had become the largest coal-producing area in the world. In 1911, of the approximately 150,000 people in the valley, all but about 7,500 were either working in or dependent upon the coal industry (Pollard 1984: 15). In 1920, 67 per cent of the people were directly involved in work at the mines. However, for the communities shaped by this phenomenal expansion, the effects of the 1926 strike defeat, and the onset of economic depression and mass unemployment in the 1930s, were devastating. The number of collieries in the Rhondda fell from 53 in 1913 to only 12 in 1947.[25] By the mid-1930s '*mining* communities were becoming or had become *unemployed* communities' (Francis 1985d: 13; original emphasis; see also Ginzberg 1991 (1942)).

The adversity arising from industrial change brought not just the insecurity associated with unemployment but also extreme social hardship. Social conditions in mining areas before 1914, and during the inter-war period, were shocking (Bulmer 1978a: 29). A combination of poor housing, insanitary conditions and high incidence of ill-health marked out mining districts from other areas.[26] Indeed, much of Orwell's masterful portrayal of the horrors of industrial Britain in the 1930s centred on mining areas (1986: 18–68). Furthermore, in the pre-nationalization era, the coal owners tended to separate industrial and social responsibilities (Benney 1978: 58). Up to the late nineteenth century, whenever a new pit was opened ' . . . the owner built a few rows of houses around it to house the workers he required, and so called a village into being without any further thought of obligation' (Benney 1978: 58). Typically, both employers and central government were reluctant to alleviate harsh social conditions; the mining community, therefore, 'had, in the main, to meet its needs from within' (Bulmer 1978a: 26, 29). Hence it was the efforts of miners themselves, through the construction of various institutions, that effected the transformation of a crude pit settlement into something akin to a 'community' with a way of life valued by its inhabit-ants, and which enjoyed at least *some* degree of autonomy from an otherwise dominant employer. This long-term effort to counteract an hostile economic and social environment had both a 'defensive' and 'offensive' dimension. Miners and their families were tenacious in defending a way of life when the survival of their communities was severely threatened. My intention here is not to present a comprehensive review of the array of institutions that emerged in mining communities in the nineteenth and twentieth centuries – for example, the Miners' Welfares, the Miners' Institutes, local Labour and Communist Party branches and, of course, the union itself. Instead, I assess the *motivations* involved in their construction.

Mining communities were remarkably successful in undertaking an essentially *defensive* endeavour – alleviating severe physical and social conditions, and attaining a degree of security in circumstances of insecurity. Thus in the early twentieth century, when issues of public health and housing were of particular concern to local trade unions and political movements, ' . . . it is important to emphasize the extent to which political power was used in mining areas simply as a means of improving the social conditions of the working class . . . ' (Bulmer 1978a: 29). Yet such motivations, while essentially defensive in scope, also contained an important offensive dimension. Given employers, and a state, which generally abrogated any social responsibilities, any improvement in social conditions largely rested upon a degree of initiative on the part of miners and their families.[27] As such, not only was there 'a sense in which some of the more positive aspects of mining communities derive from the negative features of local social life' (Bulmer 1978a: 44), but also ' . . . there is no question that villages owe all their horror to the colliery owners who built them, and all their redeeming features to the organisational energies of the people who live in them' (Benney 1978: 51).

Underpinning such initiative was a desire for autonomy from the coal owners deemed responsible for the very social ills which miners were attempting to alleviate. Thus in an environment where colliery owners controlled both jobs and housing, the building of council housing by Labour-controlled councils was to be both a way of improving housing standards, and of wresting control from the coal owners (Bulmer 1978a: 30). Similarly, the Co-operative movement attempted, as an economic organization, 'to maintain the autonomy of the working-class community from outside control' (Bulmer 1978a: 31; see also Williamson 1982: 6). The construction, therefore, of such institutions as the Miners' Welfare, the Workingmen's Club and the co-operative store reflected, in a profound sense, the recognition by miners and their families that their own welfare, and any improvements in their social conditions, rested ultimately on their own efforts.[28] Such institutions were rooted firmly in a powerful sense of mutuality and the need for self-help. Indeed, 'each village was, in fact, a sort of self-constructed, do-it-yourself counter-environment. The people had built it themselves. There was everything there, in the pit village . . . you had a sort of complete welfare system' (Chaplin 1978: 80–1). Patton notes how miners always had to create their own entertainment, through the Workingmen's Clubs and Miners' Welfares, and how they always looked after 'their own' in a host of ways – for example the Aged Miners' Homes (1978: 221). Williamson describes how the ' . . . [m]en who came to Throckley built a life for themselves, as far as they could, free of the constraints of the company and its rules and the vicissitudes of winning coal. The community which developed had "that necessary habit of mutuality" which many writers have detected as central to working-class communities' (1982: 230; see also 1982: 6).

The emergence of village institutions underpinned the 'significant regularities' within and between mining communities over time (Bulmer 1978a: 33). Yet within the construction of such institutions lay the potential for the most 'offensive' dimension of all: 'a positive commitment to a very different kind of social order' (Williamson 1982: 202). Thus the Workingmen's Clubs provided a setting and means for the development of collective consciousness (Thorpe 1978: 112),[29] while the structures within mining communities were not 'simply defensive': 'the union lodge, the Labour Party, the co-operative store had an offensive rationale, too, displaying at different points in time changing images of a better society' (Williamson 1982: 230). This should not be exaggerated; community institutions served largely to make a generally harsh environment more tolerable. None the less, the ability, at certain times, of mining communities to foster, from within, a genuine 'counter-culture' should not be underestimated either. The role of the Miners' Institutes in the South Wales coalfield is a good example.

Miners' Institutes served as facilities for both learning and leisure. Many were notable for their fine lending libraries. Francis traces the development of the institutes, noting that miners' contributions towards their construction dated from the 1880s (1976: 185). A surge in their construction was caused by the great influx of people into the central valleys in the period immediately before and after World War One. By the 1920s, the rest of the South Wales coalfield had begun to catch up with the 'vanguard' position of the central valleys (1976: 187). Institutes enabled miners coming into the valleys to ' . . . escape from the cramped atmosphere of their lodgings' while '[i]n the absence of universal state secondary education . . . the institutes more than filled the yawning gap'. They also served as a meeting place, away from the influence of pubs and clubs, for the SWMF (1976: 185).

While each institute had its own individuality and personality according to cultural, linguistic and geographical variations within the valley communities, '[e]ach institute and its library was very much at the service of its community' (Francis 1976: 188). Some were less politically oriented than others;[30] certainly, though, at its most 'offensive', the institute became the backbone of highly politicized communities such as Mardy and Tredegar. For example:

> [j]ust to stand outside the Mardy Institute in the 1920s and 1930s was tantamount to declaring yourself a 'red'. Politics in such a community, which came to be known as 'Little Moscow' at this time, spilled over into every human activity – and all were centred on the Institute . . . in such an intense atmosphere the Library quite naturally came to be seen as a revolutionary weapon for the coming crisis of capitalism. (Francis 1976: 188)[31]

Meanwhile, '[t]he Workmen's Institute at Tredegar became a most effective proletarian weapon in moulding the cultural and political taste of the town for more than a generation' (1976: 189). The Tredegar Institute, in addition to funding a lending library of over 20,000 books, supported a cinema, operatic society, choral society, town band and music festivals, and brought eminent British intellectuals and politicians to the town (1976: 190). Hence '[w]ith [Aneurin] Bevan as the M.P., a miners' medical aid scheme and a labour controlled town council, it was as if a socialist republic existed at Tredegar with its natural focal point being the Workmen's Institute – a veritable workers' assembly' (1976: 190).

The phenomenon of such institutes and libraries, on a *universal* scale, was peculiar to the South Wales coalfield (Francis 1976: 190). However, in terms of the motivation that informed their construction, and the role that they fulfilled, they represented a phenomenon applicable to the coalfields in general. Indeed, the fact that 'the towns and villages of the coalfields stand, historically, as places of immense political and cultural stability' (Beynon 1985: 403) reflects the success with which mining communities throughout Britain negotiated their way through continual economic and social adversity. In this respect, Chaplin's reflections on the Durham coalfield serve both as a poignant reminder of the struggles involved in achieving success, and as a hint of the tenacity with which miners could be expected to defend their gains. The achievements of the pit villages

> . . . cry out for celebration. Against all the odds, they and the folk who inhabited them built up communities prepared for every contingency, little societies of great strength and resilience and full of vigour and humour . . .

and while one recognises that all things have to go . . . one also has to recognise that there was a very great achievement and that the greatest of these achievements was that with the poorest of materials, in the poorest of circumstances, fighting a battle underground and fighting a battle against bad housing and bad sanitation on the surface and poor wages, people banded together and built in their villages little communities which were quite something to live for. (1978: 71, 81)

Conclusions: History and the Mining Community

Given their harsh working environment, occupational homogeneity, social and geographical isolation, and the various adversities encountered and overcome, 'of all the industrial workers in Britain, the miners appear to have the greatest sense of their own history . . .' (Francis 1985e: 267).[32] Such a powerful sense of history underpinned the fierce resistance put up by miners when their livelihoods and communities were threatened. The impetus for collective action amongst miners, and the form that such action assumed, was *historically* driven. What, though, was the basis of this sense of history?

First, 'it is necessary to insist from the beginning on the great age, both of the workings and of the traditions in these parts' (Benney 1978: 50–1). This is an obvious but important consideration. Many of the collieries in existence prior to the 1984–5 strike were over one hundred years old. Thus the individual miner's own life, and that of preceding generations, were entwined with the fortunes of the local colliery. This undoubtedly generated a profound sense of history – few miners, for example, underestimated what was at stake with the closure of the local colliery. A South Wales miner, one of six men sealing the main shaft of the now defunct Celynen North colliery, reflected: 'my grandfather sank this shaft, now I'm filling it in . . . it took them two years to dig this shaft – by hand; it will take two weeks to fill it up'(W51). And a Derbyshire miner, surveying the site of his former colliery, commented: 'When I first saw the colliery site after the pit had closed, they'd pulled the headstocks down. I wept, it was very upsetting . . . I never thought I'd live to see the day when this had happened, when the pit had closed. I thought there'd be jobs here for other lads . . . I worked at this colliery for forty years, you just can't divorce yourself from that, it's a part of your life'(D45).

However, if communities acted, and suffered, *as* communities, they also *remembered* as communities. Francis points to 'the strength and vitality of what has been called the received collective memory in maintaining solidarity' (1985e: 268). Bulmer notes how a community's solidarity was strengthened by a shared history of living and working in one place (1978a: 26; see also 1978a: 33; 1978b: 247). Such a 'received collective memory' was, of course, rooted in the harsh environment and adversity traditionally endured by mining communities. Thus common memories of past struggle helped to bind together the mining community – that is, a 'fund of shared experiences' (for example the 1926 strike defeat, poverty and unemployment in the inter-war period) worked towards the conditioning of each miner along the lines of the general values and characteristics of the rest of his community (Dennis *et al.* 1969: 14, 80, 81). Indeed, a knowledge of the collective experience of massive unemployment in the 1920s and 1930s was as important to an understanding of the mining community as a knowledge of the activity of mining itself (Patton 1978: 220; see also Bulmer 1978a: 26).

Certainly, memories of the miners' worst ever defeat – that of 1926 – loomed large in the collective consciousness of miners: '[t]he bitterness is still recalled and is still a potent force . . . among older people. For miners as a whole it helped confirm their self-definition as a maligned, exploited group' (Williamson 1982: 1687). Indeed, the uneasiness with which miners embarked on the 1972 national strike was rooted in the defeat suffered in 1926: '[t]hey were particularly afraid of a long strike of mutual attrition. The memories of 1926 and the starvation of families were indelibly printed on their minds' (Pitt 1979: 180). *During* the 1972 strike, it was the old men of the village – the retired miners – who 'were glad to see the young men struggling for a decent wage, and "getting up off their knees". Their attitude was that the miners had lost in 1926, and it was up to this generation to make sure that they did not lose this time' (Pitt 1979: 181). Not surprisingly, the ensuing victory in the strike was viewed in similarly historic terms: '[f]or miners with long memories or with a sense of history, 1972 was the effective answer, not just to the years of contraction, but to the disaster of 1926' (Howell 1989: 39).

Mining communities therefore greatly valued their 'continuity with the past' (Douglass & Krieger 1983: 13). This, however, did *not* mean a romantic hankering for the past, for such a past had a double image: 'on the one hand a nostalgic picture of family and community, on the other a picture of poverty and squalor which they would be glad to forget' (Williamson 1982: 231).[33] *Instead*, their sense of history was a product of the various adversities which communities had to endure and which they attempted to overcome. In short, '[h]istory preserves [the miner's] dignity' (Douglass & Krieger 1983: 14). Moreover, it also preserved the motivations which had informed the construction of community institutions – motivations which challenged the concerns and priorities of employers and the state and which were informed by a very different set of values.[34] And by helping to perpetuate the counter-environment constructed by preceding generations, such a sense of history had important implications for the ability, and willingness, of miners to defend themselves against current threats to their livelihoods and communities.[35]

For all its adversity, therefore, the mining environment gave the miners an extraordinary capacity to draw on the most positive aspects of an otherwise grim past. This capacity, manifesting itself in a powerful sense of history, promoted *defiance* in the face of successive material threats to livelihoods and communities. Of these, the pit closure programme of the early 1980s – which threatened the existence of large swathes of the British coalfield – was the most severe yet.

Notes

1. There are dangers in substituting 'militancy' for 'cohesion.' Coal mining may represent an industrial environment in which 'the habit of solidarity suggests itself naturally' (Hobsbawm 1952, cited in Kerr and Siegel 1954: 191, n.6). But while it may encourage a general uniformity of action, this may not be of a 'militant' nature, as events in the pit villages of Nottinghamshire in 1984–5 demonstrated. For a re-evaluation of the Kerr-Siegel hypothesis, see Church *et al.* 1991.
2. Between 1951 and 1971 more than 17,000 British miners and ex-miners died from pneumoconiosis along (Allen 1981: 94).
3. Benney argues that the difficulties and frustrations encountered by miners underground helps explain the 'peculiarly obsessive hold their work has on them'. This was manifested, for example, in constant talk, during leisure hours, about work (1978: 56).
4. (i). The overwhelming majority of Branch officials and committee-members (both NUM and UDM) interviewed in the course of research were, or had been, workers at or near the coalface.
   (ii). With respect to the militancy of miners in this group, it was suggested to me that of those in Nottinghamshire who *did* support the 1984–5 strike, a disproportionate number were faceworkers.
5. This contrasted with the recently developed Selby complex of mines on the northern edge of the Yorkshire coalfield. While BC had to induce miners, through financial incentives, to move into the area, it conspicuously did *not* construct a community for the incoming workforce. Thus miners who moved there, only to find themselves dispersed throughout the existing villages, complained about the lack of

community life. A Stillingfleet miner reckoned that the absence of close-knit mining communities explained the relatively high return-to-work rate in the area before the end of the 1984–5 strike (Y39). Additionally, the NUM Branch President at Barnsley Main colliery, in the central Yorkshire coalfield, described how several miners had 'emigrated' to Selby only to return south soon afterwards, regardless of financial loss (Y14). (See also *G*, 20/5/88.)

6. In 1977, hundreds in the Scottish mining village of Blantyre commemorated the centenary of a disaster at the local pit which had killed more than 200 miners (Allen 1981: 95).

7. For a catalogue of major disasters in the South Wales coalfield, see 'South Wales Coalfield – Disasters' (BC, Public Relations Office, Cardiff, August 1986).

8. For a full account, see Miller 1974; for recent reassessments (upon which this brief description is based), see: Robert Kee, *The Listener*, 7/6/90; Tony Geraghty, *The Weekend Guardian*, 12–13/8/89; Kate Muir, *I*, 25/7/89.

   Moreover, the world-wide attention gained by the Aberfan disaster did not prevent a similar tragedy occurring only six years later when, in West Virginia in February 1972, a massive coal-refuse pile owned by the Buffalo Mining Company collapsed without warning, and unleashed more than 130 million gallons of water and waste materials on to Buffalo Creek Valley below, and its sixteen small mining communities. Over 125 lives and 1,000 homes were lost (Stern 1977).

9. *The Weekend Guardian*, 12–13/8/89.

10. *I*, 25/7/89. Similar sentiments were recorded elsewhere in the 1980s. Indeed, the imminent closure of Creswell colliery was announced in 1990 as villagers prepared for the fortieth anniversary of the underground disaster referred to above. The UDM Branch Delegate commented: 'It's still a family pit, which gives you more pride because deep down there is that feeling that it's yours . . . It also means that closure would be that much harder to take' (*DT*, 6/8/90).

   In late 1988, miners at Marine colliery in South Wales put up spirited opposition to the closure of the pit. The Lodge Secretary said: 'We don't intend to hand the pit over on a plate – it's not the coal board's, it's the community's' (*G*, 6/12/88).

   And when, in 1989, Barnburgh became the eighth of twelve pits in Dearne Valley, Yorkshire, to close within a decade, an ex-miner commented: 'What happened to the men and these communities was immoral . . . ' (*I*, 7/2/90).

11. After the 1926 strike, 'the stream of trade union militants and political activists into the Kent pits became a flood as the coal-owners

purged the coalfields of "red agitators" and "union troublemakers"' (Pitt 1979: 83). This helps explain the fiercely militant tradition of the area and, indeed, its links with the older militant coalfields. A young Kent miner addressed South Wales miners at the start of the 1984–5 strike thus: 'I was born in . . . [Wales] . . . thirty years ago. My parents moved to Kent in search of work . . . There has always been a close bond between our coalfields . . . ' (Francis and Rees 1989: 43).

12. Shop windows advertised 'miners' bacon' or 'miners' cups'; notices at vacant lodgings stated 'Rooms to let – miners need not apply' or 'No miners or dogs allowed'. Most memorable of all was a local newspaper headline proclaiming 'Man in fight with Miner' (Pitt 1979: 69–70).

13. Historian Deian Hopkin commented: 'Wales owes the miners everything: every national institution today has been built on their sweat and sacrifice' (Francis and Rees 1989: 60–1).

14. *G*, 26/3/84.

15. *FT*, 17/12/84. Again, though, the weakness of the hypothesized link between isolation and *militancy* is illustrated by the fact that Mardy's legendary militancy was not matched by collieries in similarly isolated locations. (For example, the growth of company unionism in the 1920s and 1930s in South Wales occurred at semi-isolated pits like Raglan, Taff Merthyr and Bedwas.)

16. For general discussions of this theme in the British context, see Allen, S. 1989; Allen, Littlejohn and Warwick 1989 and Campbell, B. 1986. For discussions of masculinity and mining culture in Appalachia, USA, see Trent and Stout-Wiegand 1987 and Yarrow 1992. For a discussion of the theme in the construction industry, see Maynard 1989.

17. As in the case of labour history in general. See Scott, J. 1988.

18. Indeed, women in Britain were prohibited from working in mines by the 1842 Mines Regulation Act (Humphries 1981).

19. For the life of a miner's wife in pre-Depression USA, see Ellis 1980 (1929); for contemporary Bolivia, see Barrioz de Chiungara and Viezzer 1978.

20. It is in this overall historical context, therefore, that the very great achievements of women in the 1984–5 strike – and the miners' own assessments of those achievements – must be placed.

21. Dennis *et al.* refer to the fate of a 'blackleg' in 1926 who was subsequently ostracized by his workmates, friends and sons, none of whom attended his funeral in 1946 (1969: 88, n.2).

   Numerous examples of intra-family ostracism, as a result of strikebreaking, were encountered in the course of research, especially in Nottinghamshire.

22. *T*, 5/3/85.
23. Unlike some of the US coalfields where '"the right to bear arms" on picket lines bears witness to a completely different kind of tradition' (Francis 1985e: 270; 271, n.15).
24. *FT*, 17/12/84. The reporter described the fate of a lone strikebreaker at the Phurnacite coking plant at Aberdare: 'At a meeting this week . . . the lodge chairman called on all members to "make the man's life hell". The women of the village are doing the same for his wife . . . When she visits Tesco's supermarket most of the shoppers and even the check-out ladies walk out and she is served more or less under protest by the manager. When she gets onto a bus, the driver refuses to move, and so on. Or so I was told, gleefully, by union officials.'
   Similar non-violent tactics were used in 1985 by the villagers of Ystradgynlais in South Wales who gathered outside a strike-breaker's house and sang hymns. Unfortunately, their target was still working his shift at the local colliery (*WM*, 10/1/85).
25. *The Times Saturday Review*, 29/9/90.
26. As, indeed, they continued to do so. In 1990, the five central valleys of the South Wales coalfield had the highest level of youth unemployment in Britain, the highest proportion of permanently sick and the highest proportion of householders with no bath or lavatory. They also had the highest premature death rate in Europe – the main illnesses were cancer, heart attacks, hypertension and respiratory diseases. Some 10,000 people a year died of heart attacks. In the Rhondda valley, male unemployment exceeded 25 per cent (*The Times Saturday Review*, 29/9/90).
27. Though see Thorpe who argues that 'oppositional' institutions developed initially out of a space provided for them by an enlightened local ruling class that believed in 'rights and duties' (1978: 112).
28. A miner at Taff Merthyr colliery, South Wales, reflected: ' . . . we've only ever got what we've been strong enough to take' (W3).
29. Samuel notes how, in 1984–5, the Miners' Welfare was at 'the heart of . . . communal bonding' (1986: 10).
   In the divided pit villages of Nottinghamshire, in 1984–5, the Miners' Welfare emerged as a place of symbolic, as well as practical, importance. In Ollerton, striking miners, though in a small minority, were determined that the Miners' Welfare should be their strike headquarters. A striker in the village recalled with pride that they had succeeded in doing just this (N1). In contrast, in the northern Nottinghamshire village of Meden Vale (adjacent to Welbeck colliery), a non-striker explained how only members of *his* union (the UDM) now used the Miners' Welfare – NUM members had to do their drinking down the road at The Three Lions (N15).

30. Thus '[i]n spite of its fine library, Bargoed Institute was noted more for its boxing and snooker tables than its books' (Francis 1976: 188).

31. The reputation of Mardy as 'Little Moscow' came to the fore once again in the 1984–5 strike. There was a complete absence of strike-breakers in the village. Not once was a picket ever mounted at the pit gates. As such, the village attracted considerable press attention. See, for example, *FT*, 6/3/85; *T*, 25/2/85; *G*, 2/1/85; *G*, 26/3/84; *T*, 12/3/84.

32. The most visual aspect of this were the NUM branch/lodge banners displayed by the miners at rallies, demonstrations, strike marches and annual regional miners' galas. Kellingley colliery's banner, for example, 'celebrates the nobility of the mineworker. A bare-chested collier stands on a plinth, throttling the snake of capitalism with his left hand. Steps proclaiming "Socialism leads to prosperity" lead up to pithead winding gear. The slogan underneath [reads] "Only the strong survive"' (*IS*, 3/6/90).

33. Chaplin warns against 'waxing poetic' on the traditional mining community as 'a sort of pitman's *Paradiso*, safely set in the remote past. The corrective is to remember the harshness, the disease, the filth, above all the smells' (1978: 70–1).

34. In a tribute to such alternative values, Thompson remarks: 'The miners have always had difficulty in comprehending the simplest of propositions as to the market-regulation of wages, and have clung tenaciously to unscientific notions such as "justice" and "fair play"' (1980: 66).

    For an account of the alternative values which informed the fierce defence of mining communities in 1984–5, see Williams R. 1985.

35. I draw here on Scott's discussion of 'The Remembered Village' (1985: 178–83). The ability of mining communities to see threats in historic terms has parallels with the villagers of Sedaka, who 'collectively created a *remembered village* and a *remembered economy* that serve as an effective ideological backdrop against which to deplore the present' (1985: 178).

—2—

The Limits of Solidarity

Introduction

A diversity of traditions within and between the coalfields made the construction of solidarity at area and national levels highly contingent. Solidarity amongst miners was strongly local and insular in character; in reality, coalfield areas were precarious coalitions of a diverse range of local traditions. Moreover, the post-war rationalization of the coal industry, whereby the number of miners fell from 700,000 in 1956 to 296,000 in 1970 (Allen 1982: 17), further fragmented the miners as a collectivity. Both industrial contraction and measures to boost productivity levels accentuated the diversity of traditions within the coalfields. As such, the problems of mobilizing collective action amongst miners reflect a more general problem applicable to the working population as a whole: 'Village life . . . is transcended, though never with any certainty, by a collective recognition extending hesitantly to a feeling of common cause with other working men, perhaps, even, to the abstraction of a working class as a whole . . . Such a shift is not a natural one; nor is it ever-present . . . it has always been contingent and precarious' (Williamson 1982: 7).

Diversity in the Coalfields

> . . . class is . . . something which is experienced; it is a mode of social recognition bringing, under certain conditions, a consciousness of belonging . . . The boundaries of that recognition, that sense of belonging, are intensely local . . . The family, the street, the village and . . . the pit, define most of them.
>
> B. Williamson, *Class, Culture and Community. A Biographical Study of Social Change in Mining*

With respect to national and area collective action, the implications of powerful local-level solidarity were ambiguous. On the one hand, many factors lent mining communities a remarkable capacity to act with initiative and resilience. On the other hand, the strong links that developed between mine and community underpinned a certain *insularity* which

ensured that individual communities acquired their own particular traditions and culture.

Localism and Insularity

That the culture of individual mining communities was somewhat insular
is not surprising. The local dominance of coal, the age of the local mine
and the relative isolation of the pit village made the mining community
very much a 'world of its own'. Despite the existence of hundreds of pit
villages in the Durham coalfield in the early twentieth century '. . . one
lived in one's own village and it was sufficient. One was hardly aware
of the villages next door. There was a tremendous sense of insularity . . .
and isolation and one became terribly attached to one's village . . .'
(Chaplin 1978: 62–3). Moreover, such impulses were prominent in times
of particular hardship. For example, when mass unemployment hit the
Northumberland coalfield in the 1930s, the Throckley union lodges
attempted to regulate how the available work should be shared: 'A
strong sense of locality and community emerges from these efforts, the
lodges seeking to protect the employment of Throckley men against
those defined as "strangers"' (Williamson 1982: 199).

Nothing, however, underscored the strong attachment to the locality
than the miners' general fear of moving elsewhere: 'Consciousness of
having lived in a place for a long time, in relative isolation, reinforces
the sense of participating in a close-knit network of social relations. To
leave this community is to cut oneself off from one's roots' (Bulmer
1978a: 36). Even moves that did not require leaving the local community (that is, transfers to pits within travelling distance) were
generally detested. The working environment was an important
consideration. To achieve *some* security in an otherwise dangerous
environment, value was placed on working with tried and trusted
companions, and becoming familiar, over time, with the particular
hazards of the local mine. Thus a transfer entailed moving not to just
'another hole in the ground' but to an entirely new environment. This
created a fear of moving to even a nearby mine. A Derbyshire miner
forced to move, after 22 years, from Langwith colliery to nearby Warsop
Main commented:

> It's like waiting for the electric chair. I really worried about it – you knew
> everyone at Langwith, you wondered about being able to fit in at a new
> colliery. Luckily we joined a good bunch of men at Warsop. But when you
> knew you were going to have to move, it was like waiting to be hanged . . .
> We three times refused the manager's request to leave Langwith. (D33)

In describing the closure in 1969 of Tudhoe Park colliery in the south-
west Durham coalfield, Bulmer notes the difficulty encountered by the

NCB in attempting to transfer men to South Hetton on the eastern edge of the coalfield. The Tudhoe management, wishing to transfer fifty miners to South Hetton, failed to entice a single miner to do so. This was despite their '. . . stated intention to try to create a "little Tudhoe" at this colliery. A whole face was set aside, it was said, where conditions were very similar to those at Tudhoe' (1978b: 242). In explaining the management's failure, a '. . . very significant internalised constraint upon freedom of action was the importance attached to locality. Four-fifths of the miners lived within three miles of the pit. One-third could walk to work; two-thirds could get there in less than 15 minutes by various means . . .' (Bulmer 1978b: 245).

Furthermore, the local union secretary described Tudhoe as a 'family pit', the features of which '. . . included not only the fact that people had kinship ties, but that everybody knew everybody else, and that miners lived in the locality, which produced a happy atmosphere with easy relations between man and man' (1978b: 246).[1] What miners feared most, therefore, was that a 'shared consciousness of common work experience' was threatened by closure of the mine: '[a] network of social ties had been built up which could only partially be re-created by [workmates] going to work together elsewhere' (1978b: 247).[2] In sum, '. . . the picture of strong diffuse and particularistic local ties showing long attachment to and familiarity with particular pits, is striking. The [NCB] operates at area, regional and national level, but for many of its employees, the particular enterprise is the focus for loyalties and involvement' (Bulmer 1978b: 255).

Localism and Diversity

> Tower always has been a militant pit. It's difficult to explain why some pits are more militant and others not. It is not a question of leadership, though. Tower has had moderate trade union leadership – decent people, though – but has always voted for strike action. (W24)

The roots of diversity within and between the coalfield areas are complex. Williamson argues that the comparative study of mining is not so well developed that explanations for such diversity can be stated sys-tematically (1982: 229). Important factors, however, would include the age and geological character of the coalfield, the structure of ownership of the industry, the degree of isolation of the community, the structure of working relationships underground and the character and commitment of local union leaders and politicians (1982: 229; see also Laslett 1974: 6). An examination of another related factor – the impact of labour migration – underlines the complexity of the problem.

At an *inter*-area level, Kent and Nottinghamshire may be compared. Kent, as a 'cosmopolitan' coalfield, was developed relatively late and drew its entire workforce from established coalfields. The particular characteristics of the incoming workforce, and the physical and social conditions they encountered, combined to produce a very militant political tradition (Pitt 1979: 67–99). The Nottinghamshire coalfield was also developed relatively late, and also drew thousands of miners from other coalfields (including militant Scotland and South Wales) during the inter-war depression and post-war contraction of the industry. Yet unlike Kent, the absence of both severe physical conditions and social isolation hindered the development of a militant political tradition. Thus the 'cosmopolitan' nature of the Nottinghamshire miners is often presented as a factor explaining the area's relatively moderate political tradition: 'while it may still be true that "most Notts miners are related by blood to those who work in the pits of Scotland, Durham and Wales"[3] a historical sense of mining *community* is virtually absent from most of Nottinghamshire' (Winterton & Winterton 1989: 75; original emphasis).

On an *intra*-area level, Campbell analyses two districts in the Lanarkshire area of the Scottish coalfield in the nineteenth century: '. . . Coatbridge, renowned for its lack of union strength, and Larkhall, a union stronghold' (1974: 9). He differentiates between '. . . the district union in Coatbridge, whose "degraded slaves" were content with working fourteen hours a day in the pit . . .' and '. . . the "honourable men" of Larkhall, whose maintenance of output restriction ensured them a higher rate [of pay]' (1974: 9). A principal factor explaining the contrast was the degree of Irish immigration into the Scottish coalfield. Irish immigrants posed a threat both as skilled labourers and as potential strikebreakers; as such, they incurred the wrath of local Scots miners. Campbell concludes:

'As more Irish became absorbed into the mining labour force, Orange and Green disputes further fragmented the miners' occupational group. Coatbridge had one of the worst records of sectarian strife, and miners were prominent on both sides in religious riots. Such divisions inevitably retarded the development of trade unionism . . . In contrast, Larkhall, with its consistently lower Irish population, was notable for its lack of communal strife' (1974: 10).

The arrival, however, in the early twentieth century, of a small community of Spanish miners in the central valleys of the South Wales coalfield had a markedly different effect. Noting that '[t]heir attitudes towards the colliery owners was [*sic*] nothing short of contemptuous' (1980: 173), Francis describes how their arrival 'had a leavening effect on industrial militancy in the area . . . Oral tradition has it that they were the best trade unionists' (1980: 172).[4] A local union secretary commented: 'I've never found any Spaniard in arrears with his union contribution . . . And whenever there was a ballot held, they used to go . . . to the secretary and ask him – "Which of these is the Communist?" "Communista", they said. Their vote was invariably for the Communist candidate' (Francis 1980: 172). In this manner, an influx of immigrants helped foster an emerging militant tradition in South Wales.

The multiple effects of labour migration illustrate not only the complex roots of diversity within the coalfields but also the plain fact that '. . . given the same task, digging coal from the ground, men act differently' (Williamson 1982: 230). Moreover, such localism ensured that solidarity amongst miners was precarious enough at *area* level, let alone *national* level. Thus it is important to note the diversity of trad-itions within areas (Allen 1981: 310). For example, the branch secretary at Barnsley Main colliery surveyed the Yorkshire coalfield thus:

> Be aware of the differing political traditions within the Yorkshire coalfield. Barnsley is very loyal to Scargill . . . traditionally militant . . . we sent out more pickets than any other panel area in 1984–5 . . . Doncaster is still quite militant, though becoming more moderate . . . North Yorkshire – the Selby complex – was traditionally moderate, middle of the road, but now is becoming quite militant . . . South Yorkshire – very moderate – lots of Nottinghamshire and Derbyshire influence . . .[5]

Indeed, 'the very notion of a culture characteristic of [a coalfield] *as a whole* should be treated with caution' (Rees 1986: 472; original emph-asis).[6] In this context, a brief comparison of the South Wales and Nottinghamshire coalfields shows that neither the overall 'militancy' of the former, nor the overall 'moderation' of the latter should be exag-gerated.

With respect to the historic militancy of the South Wales coalfield, its characterization as 'a semi-mythical Red Belt of the British working class' is astute (Williams G. 1982: 185, cited by Rees 1986: 173). Until the 1890s, South Wales was the least densely unionized region in Britain. And while, by the inter-war years, Communists controlled the union leadership (Rees 1986: 473), the same period witnessed constant battles between the SWMF and the company-backed SWMIU (Rees 1985: 398). Indeed, the latter gained between 2,000 and 6,000 members locally; as such, it 'was more strongly represented in South Wales than in any other coalfield area outside of Nottinghamshire and Derbyshire . . . a fact which is difficult to reconcile with the supposed "popular socialism" of the region' (Rees 1986: 473).

Internally, too, the South Wales coalfield was riven by 'contrasting tendencies' between its militant and moderate areas (Allen 1981: 310). Historically, a cultural and political divide existed between the anthra-cite coalfield in the rural west, and the steam and coking coalfield in the central valleys. Francis describes how '[i]n stark contrast to the dynamic cosmopolitan qualities of the central and eastern valleys, the rural anthracite coalfield to the west experienced a much slower rate of proletarianisation . . .' (1980: 175). There developed within these 'tightly-knit anthracite villages' a strongly Welsh, anti-English insularity whereby miners joining the local workforce from as near as fifteen miles away were regarded as 'strangers', and where '[e]ven into the 1930s non-Welsh speaking Welshmen from [the central valleys] were considered English, and would have great difficulty in obtaining work . . .' (Francis 1980: 175–7). Yet out of the central valleys, in the same decade, and in contrast to the insularity of the rural west, '. . . came the largest groups of Welsh volunteers for the International Brigades: arguably the highest form of proletarian consciousness' (Francis 1980: 175). Dozens of miners left in 1936 to fight in the Spanish Civil War.[7]

Echoes of this historic divide were evident at the end of the 1984–5 strike. As late as February 1985, mines in the central valleys remained solidly on strike.[8] Yet at Cynheidre, an anthracite mine, and the coal-field's most westerly pit, solidarity was breached as early as November 1984. By February 1985, 127 miners, out of a total workforce of some 1,000, had returned to work.[9] Thus levels of solidarity varied, from east to west, even within this traditionally militant coalfield.[10]

Similarly, it is dangerous to label Nottinghamshire, blanket fashion, as a 'moderate' coalfield. Certainly, Nottinghamshire's *reputation* as a politically quiescent coalfield was well-entrenched. Miners elsewhere invariably viewed Nottinghamshire's refusal to strike in 1984–5 as being rooted in the area's role as a bastion of 'scab' unionism after the 1926 General Strike and during the 1930s. Thus a miner at Taff Merthyr colliery, South Wales, commented: 'I think it's going on . . . tradition, more or less, . . . of the old Spencer union[11] . . . many years ago, and . . . I think it's embedded in them . . . that they were rather moderate . . . I don't think they were so – how can you put it? – adamant to get their way as what we were down here'(W3).

Yet such a reputation merits certain qualifications. For example, despite Spencerism, the Nottinghamshire Miners Association (NMA) remained loyal to the MFGB and

> . . . always retained a substantial representation in the coalfield. Indeed, in 1928, a ballot organised by the TUC revealed that 32,277 Nottinghamshire miners wished to be represented by the NMA out of a total workforce of some 40,000. Even as late as 1937, after a decade of pressure from the colliery owners to join the Spencer union, nearly 10,000 miners retained their membership of the NMA . . . (Rees 1986: 473)

This presence of a substantial militant strand within an otherwise moderate coalfield indicates, therefore, that 'coalfield cultures' are not 'internally consistent entities' (Rees 1986: 474). This was demonstrated in the Nottinghamshire Area ballot on industrial action at the start of the 1984–5 strike. That 73.5 per cent of miners, including all the Area's thirty-one branches, voted against striking, certainly confirmed Nottinghamshire's status as a weak link in the chain of militancy. Yet there was considerable variation in levels of branch support for joining the strike. While eleven branches recorded 'yes' votes of below 20 per cent, four branches recorded 'yes' votes of 40 per cent or more. At Bestwood, 4.1 per cent of miners voted to strike, compared to 46.4 per cent at Blidworth.[12] The case of Blidworth illustrates, in fact, the resilience of local militancy within a generally more moderate area tradition.[13] The pit was one of only six NUM branches in Nottinghamshire (out of a total of thirty-three) to reject the National Incentive Scheme in October 1977.[14] The Branch Secretary at the pit reported that during the 1984–5 strike the police besieged the village only when it became apparent that the strike was gaining popular support amongst local miners.[15] Certainly, the stance of the Blidworth union leadership during the strike was noted by NUM members elsewhere. The Branch President at Goldthorpe/ Hickleton colliery in Yorkshire recalled a warm welcome from NUM officials at the pit, before a substantial police presence made picketing ineffective (Y9). Thus when BC embarked in 1989 on its campaign to close the colliery, it was considered that '. . . of all the Nottinghamshire villages Blidworth is probably the toughest nut to crack' (Gray 1989: 30).

In sum, the range of locally based traditions had important implications for the mobilization of national collective action amongst miners – the problems of solidarity were rooted not just in differences *between* areas but in the 'internal complexities and inconsistencies' within (Rees 1986: 474).

Industrial Decline and the Undermining of Community

The diverse traditions within the coalfields must be assessed in the context of the rationalization that the coal industry underwent in the post-war period. This process involved two principal components: contraction (mine closures, job losses and reductions in output), and increasing productivity levels. Between 1947 and 1983–4, deep-mined output fell from 187.5 to 90.1 million tonnes, the number of collieries from 958 to 170, and industrial manpower from 718,400 to 191,700. Meanwhile, overall levels of productivity increased from 1.09 to 2.43 tonnes of output per manshift.[16]

However, 'the sharp differentiation between the areas of the British coalfield in their experience of patterns of development in the coal industry' is critical (Rees 1985: 391). Above all, a clear distinction emerged between the hardest-hit older peripheral coalfields such as Durham, Lancashire, Scotland and South Wales, and the central area stretching from North Yorkshire to South Nottinghamshire (Rees 1985: 391). This became particularly pronounced during the severe programme of pit closures in the 1960s and early 1970s, '. . . the impact of which was felt most acutely in the older coalfields. In South Wales, for example, even as late as 1960, 85 000 miners were raising 20 million tonnes of coal. By 1973, almost 100 pits had been closed, employment had fallen by over 50 000 and output . . . cut to a little over 7 million tonnes . . .' (Rees 1985: 391).[17]

Contraction in the declining coalfields also had consequences at an intra-area level: '. . . even *within* the peripheral coalfields, closures were distributed unevenly; in South Wales, for instance, it was the central area – incidentally, traditionally the most militant – which was most affected, with the Rhondda valleys especially hard-hit' (Rees 1985: 391; original emphasis).

Similarly, steady increases in productivity accentuated the differences both between and within areas of the coalfield. Such increases were

> . . . achieved by the adoption of new mechanised methods, and in particular, the integrated power-loading system. The ease with which such methods could be introduced in existing geological conditions was a major determinant of the spatial distribution of closures. Hence, from the late 1950s onwards, the NCB's overall strategy was to shift the focus of production from the peripheral older coalfields to the low-cost central fields and especially to the East Midlands . . .' (Rees 1985: 391)[18]

Geological conditions (and hence output levels), however, could also vary within a single area. In this respect, the Area Incentive Scheme (AIS) (introduced in 1977), which tied earnings to output levels, ensured that drives to increase productivity exacerbated differences within, as well as between, areas of the coalfield.

Industrial Contraction and the Undermining of Community

> [I've] lived in Bentley since 1938. [There've been] vast changes. Now, the village is no longer a mining community. About 600 men work at [the] pit, about 500 of them . . . from outside the village. Previously, most men [came] from the village. [It was] close-knit. (Y26a)

> A pit village is not a pit village like it used to be. It isn't here in Shirebrook – you have men coming into work at the pit from a 20-mile radius. They come in to work and then they go. (D39)

These comments reflect the changes wrought by the contraction of the coal industry. Such changes were well under way before the 1984–5 strike, though they became especially pronounced afterwards. The impact of wider socioeconomic change shows how mining communities were never static entities (Williamson 1982: 231). For example, pit closures in Kent saw mining employment fall from 5,000 in 1956 to 3,500 in 1972. Such a closure programme had '. . . a dramatic effect on the occupational structure of the villages. Whereas in the past, a miner's son would look to the pit for work, poor wages and the threat of redundancy made him take his father's advice not to go down the pit, and find work on the outside' (Pitt 1979: 106).

Thus the character of traditional mining communities changed. The *uneven* impact of pit closures within areas, however, sharpened the distinctions between mining and ex-mining communities. In those communities whose pits closed, miners either retired, transferred to other pits, moved into alternative employment, or became unemployed. The economies of such communities were severely damaged (Glyn 1984), as the NUM Branch Secretary at Blidworth colliery in Nottinghamshire noted: 'We're very afraid of losing our community here. It's a very easy thing to do, to lose a community. To see how easy, just go across into Yorkshire and look at the towns there, whole streets empty, boarded up' (Gray 1989: 30). The cohesion and solidarity of mining communities were also affected by the closure of their local pits: 'In what are still, to a remarkable extent, hereditary occupational communities, a change in job location, when younger people move away, destroys . . . intergenerational solidarity . . .' (Samuel 1986: 37). Bulmer observes, with respect to the displaced miner, that '. . . where place of work and place of residence no longer coincide, the extent of an individual's social contacts and involvement in the place where he lives may be reduced' (1978a: 35).[19]

Yet if the character of communities changed where the local pit closed, the same was true of communities where the local pit survived. Here, the composition of their work-forces was transformed as miners displaced by pit closures elsewhere joined the local work-force. The general contraction of the industry was accompanied by the emergence of what miners invariably labelled 'receiver' or 'cosmopolitan' pits. For example, the NUM Branch President at Denby Grange in Yorkshire reflected that as recently as the late 1970s, the colliery had been a 'village pit . . . men walked to work'. Most miners travelled to work from within a radius of only five to six miles. Twenty-five per cent of the men at the pit came from the local village of Netherton, and another 25 per cent from nearby Middlestown. By 1990, however, only 10 per cent of the men came from Middlestown and a mere 5 per cent from Netherton – 'the rest are just everywhere'. Indeed, the local work-force had become so fragmented that some miners from Denby Grange were now working in the far north of the Yorkshire coalfield: '. . . now we have men travelling from *here* to Selby, which is an 80-mile round trip.'[20]

What, though, did this mean for the collective solidarity of miners within an area? In one sense, the displacement of miners from one workplace to another weakened the insular characteristics of the traditional, isolated, mining community where the links between local pit

and village were immensely strong.[21] However, attachment to the locality remained strong both on the part of miners forced to work elsewhere,
and of miners at pits acquiring 'cosmopolitan' status. With respect to the
former, it is noteworthy that most men displaced from Denby Grange
colliery to the northern Yorkshire coalfield were reluctant to actually
reside there: 'Most men don't want to uproot themselves and go and live
there. The locals won't mix with them, so those that *are* there are trying
to set up their own clubs.'[22] In the Durham coalfield, the thousands of
men bussed daily from their own villages into the eastern 'receiver' pits
such as Easington were regarded by the local communities as 'travellers'
or 'strangers' (Beynon 1984: 112).

    However, whether *insularity* per se was eroded or not, the increasing
fragmentation of the mining work-force underpinned a growing differentiation between those mining communities which remained, in the
traditional sense, relatively close-knit, and those whose work-forces
became considerably dispersed (Francis 1985e: 268). This had grave implications for collective action amongst miners, both at a local and area
level – especially in times of crisis. The plain fact that, increasingly, '. . . not
all miners lived within the narrow corral of a mining community close
to the pit' (Adeney & Lloyd 1988: 219) posed problems for local-level
NUM leaderships in coordinating action amongst their members. Strike
action in 1989 at Tower colliery in South Wales underscores the point.

    Tower became, during the 1980s, a 'receiver' pit. The Lodge Sec-
retary reported to the NUM's 1990 Annual Conference that up until the
early 1980s, 90 per cent of the pit's work-force had come from the local
towns of Hirwaun and Aberdare. Currently, however, 'Men were coming
in from all over.' Fifty buses arrived at the pit every day.[23] The problems
posed by this transformation were illustrated in late 1989 during a strike
at the pit precipitated by the dismissal of a miner for 'disciplinary'
offences. In order to gauge the opinion of the entire work-force on the
matter, the NUM Lodge officials had to organise three separate meetings
to cover the morning, afternoon and night shifts at the mine. By this
time, much of the spontaneous outrage at the dismissal of the worker had
been sapped. Lodge officials explained that in earlier times, with a much
more locally based work-force, a general meeting could have been
quickly arranged and the situation rapidly assessed. With a greatly dispersed work-force, however, this was no longer possible.[24]

    In addition, an increasingly dispersed work-force further fragmented
the solidarity of miners at an *area* level. For example, towards the end
of the 1984–5 strike, patterns of strikebreaking suggested that distinctions between striker and 'scab', and between pits where the strike was
solid and those where it was crumbling, had assumed a 'core–periphery'
quality. That is, loyal strikers tended to be members of more traditional
close-knit mining communities while strikebreakers tended to live

outside such communities. Similarly, the most solid pits tended to be situated in the heartland of a given coalfield, with the less solid pits situated on the periphery of the area[25] (Winterton & Winterton 1989: 178–208). Winterton and Winterton discovered just such a pattern in their analysis of the strike in Yorkshire (1989: 182). This pattern became more pronounced as the strike continued – by January 1985, while only 9 per cent of the Yorkshire work-force as a whole had returned to work, 20 per cent of miners had done so at pits on the southern edge of the coalfield compared to only 3 per cent in the central areas of Doncaster and Barnsley (1989: 199). By its final week, the '. . . strike was still relatively solid in the heart of the coalfield, with under five per cent at work in eighteen collieries and under ten per cent at a further seven' (1989: 201). However, over *50 per cent* had returned at nine peripheral pits in the south, west and far north (1989: 210).[26] Strikebreaking in South Wales, though on a smaller scale, displayed a similar trend – pits where solidarity *was* significantly breached (by February 1985) were situated in the far west and extreme south-east of the coalfield. However, the NCB had to recognize that the pits in the central coalfield remained solidly on strike.[27]

The pattern identified by Winterton and Winterton is a compelling one and would appear to support the notion that the 'undermining of community' through industrial contraction fragmented the solidarity of miners. However, the *local* conditions for such an erosion of solidarity were diverse. That is, the ways in which the nine peripheral Yorkshire pits suffered a collapse of solidarity may have differed depending on the peculiarities of their particular locality. The workforce at Denby Grange in the west was considerably dispersed. The recently developed Selby group of mines in the north, as noted, lacked the infrastructure of the traditional mining community. And the southern peripheral pits – perhaps reflecting the erosion of insularity – were very close to the strongly anti-strike pits of Nottinghamshire.[28]

Industrial contraction therefore exacerbated divisions at an intra-area level, between those communities whose local pits closed and those whose pits survived. In the latter category, a growing differentiation may be observed between mining communities whose work-force remained relatively close-knit and locally based, and mining communities which became increasingly 'cosmopolitan' in character. It is important to note, however, that both 'close-knit' and 'cosmopolitan' communities represent formidable obstacles to solidarity at the area level. The former retained the insular quality described earlier which underpinned a strongly local type of solidarity. With the latter, any benefit derived from the erosion of insularity was circumscribed by the problems of solidarity and coordination associated with an increasingly fragmented work-force.

Miners on Strike

The Area Incentive Scheme and the Undermining of Community

... for a long, long period of time, the collier in the local Welsh pits was paid a lesser rate ... than his counterpart in England ... it's always been there, the split. (W3)

Table 2. Average Weekly Earnings by Area in Relation to National Average (Percentage variation above or below national average wage)

Area	70/1	71/2	72/3	73/4	74/5	75/6	76/7	77/8	78/9	Ave. 70–9
YORKS	0.0	-0.9	−0.4	+0.3	+1.2	+0.2	+0.6	+0.5	+0.5	+0.2
DERBS	+4.5	+3.6	−0.1	+1.5	+3.4	−0.3	−0.2	+4.1	+5.0	+2.4
NOTTS	+6.8	+4.5	+3.6	+1.5	+2.1	+0.7	+0.1	+3.1	+4.3	+3.0
S.WALES	−5.8	−3.6	−2.6	−4.2	−6.6	−9.4	+3.1	−5.7	−8.2	−4.8
SPREAD	12.6	8.1	6.2	5.7	10.0	10.1	3.3	9.8	13.2	8.8

Sources: NCB, Report and Accounts: 1971–72, Vol.II, Accounts and Statistical Tables, p.101, Table 23; *NCB Statistical Tables 1973/74,* p.12, Table 12; *NCB Statistical Tables 1975/6,* p.12, Table 14; *NCB Statistical Tables 1976–7,* p.12, Table 14; *NCB Statistical Tables 1978/9,* p.12, Table 14.

A South Wales miner's comments summarize succinctly the 'view from the periphery' regarding the long-standing differences in earnings within the British coalfield. Indeed, national wage parity amongst miners was attained, as Table 2 shows, for only a brief period in the early 1970s.

Table 2 illustrates the national trend in the 1970s initially towards, then away from, wage parity across the British coalfield. In 1976–7, only 3.3 percentage points separated the highest paid from the lowest paid area. However, by 1978–9, after the introduction of the AIS, the gap had widened to a degree exceeding that recorded for the start of the decade. Thus the NUM Left's long-cherished goal of common wages for all miners was achieved for a short time only. Wage differences within and between areas were therefore the historical norm. This section highlights how the drive to boost productivity levels exacerbated such differences.

The introduction in 1978 of the AIS was a crucial part of the NCB's attempts to increase productivity levels in the industry. By operating on a 'performance index' (NUM 1983) – that is, tying earnings to *output* rather than *effort* – the AIS threatened to not only undermine the general wage parity achieved by the National Power Loading Agreement (NPLA) but also to divide the older, peripheral coalfields beset by geological difficulties from the newer, central coalfields where more accessible coal seams generated higher productivity levels. A Derbyshire miner commented:

The NPLA came into place just prior to my starting on the coalface. *Before* the NPLA, the men working in good conditions earned more than men working in bad, difficult conditions. Therefore, in the late 1970s, I saw the incentive scheme as a return to the old contract system . . . where men working in good conditions earned more money than men in difficult and wet conditions who earned only the basic norm. It was unfair. (D20)

Miners were balloted twice on the issue of the introduction of an incentive scheme into the coal industry. In November 1974, miners, nationally, rejected the scheme by a vote of 63 per cent to 37 per cent. In October 1977, to the amazement and delight of the NUM Left, miners again rejected the scheme – this time by a vote of 55 per cent to 45 per cent. However, *within* the British coalfield, there was considerable variation, in both ballots, in levels of support for the AIS. Such variation tended to be closely tied to variations in levels of productivity. Miners at high-productivity pits in the central coalfields viewed the AIS as an opportunity for '. . . more money for no extra work'(N3). For others, though, it was unfair and divisive: 'We needed any increase to go on the basic wage. The AIS set men against men'(Y15).

Despite the ballot results of 1974 and 1977, however, the AIS was none the less subsequently introduced into the industry.[29] Consequently, the national wage parity that prevailed in the mid-1970s was undermined. As Table 3 shows, productivity figures for the period between 1978 and 1984 showed a huge gulf in earnings opening up between areas like South Wales (at the bottom) and Nottinghamshire (at the top).

Table 3. Area Productivity Levels in relation to National Average Level

Area	1978/9	1979/80	1980/1	1981/2	1982/3	1983/4
YORKS	+6.3%	+3.9%	+3.9%	+4.2%	+5.7%	+5.8%
DERBS	+29.5%	+29.4%	+38.4%	+38.8%	+35.2%	+19.3%
NOTTS	+23.7%	+23.8%	+23.3%	+22.1%	+21.7%	+21.4%
S.WALES	−37.1%	−39.4%	−37.1%	−38.8%	−39.8%	−35.4%

Source: NCB, *Report and Accounts*, for *1978–79* (p.5); *1980–81* (pp.34–5); *1982–83* (pp.22–3); *1984–85* (pp.28–9).

The AIS therefore succeeded in rekindling the historic differences between areas over wage levels which had only been temporarily smothered by a brief period of wage parity. A Welsh miner reflected:

> . . . it was only in the '74 strike that the Scottish area and the South Wales area came up to *parity* with the rest of the British coalfield. Because then Yorkshire, the Midlands, Nottinghamshire – they were *all* on big money, then. *Far* better than we were. And it's only . . . in '74 that we came up to

parity . . . And of course . . . when we had . . . the Incentive Scheme . . . the
big gap came again . . . in wages. (W8)

Furthermore, such fragmentation ensured that potential national solidarity on the wages issue (which had underpinned the 1972 and 1974
national strikes) was badly damaged: 'Incentive earnings constituted an
increasingly important component of pay and were susceptible to local
pressure. As collective bargaining was fragmented, national wage unity
was destroyed, so a strike in support of a national pay claim became
improbable' (Winterton & Winterton 1989: 17).

Meanwhile, the widening gulf in productivity levels between 'core'
and 'periphery' threatened the continued viability of pits in the older
coalfields: '[d]ifferences in bonus earnings between the central and peripheral coalfields . . . added to the inherent divisiveness of pit closures
. . .' (Winterton & Winterton 1989: 17–18). On an inter-area level, therefore, the drive to increase productivity exacerbated long-standing
differences within the British coalfield, both in terms of wage levels and
vulnerability to pit closures. As such, the NUM Lodge Secretary at
Penallta colliery, South Wales, lamented:

> . . . in '72 and '74, the incentive bonus scheme wasn't in being whereas in
> '84 [it] *was* in being. And there were pits around the country..and *areas*
> around the country, earning *good wages* – so why should they lose them
> wages over some – as it was put – 'Victorian hole in the ground' in South
> Wales, or Kent, or Scotland, or some other peripheral areas. Because that's
> where the main axe was going to fall. (W7)

However, varying geological conditions (and hence output levels) within
individual areas (and, indeed, within individual pits) ensured that the
fragmentation of solidarity extended well below the inter-area level. A
Derbyshire miner commented: '[t]he trouble with incentive schemes is
that they make men greedy. There's more falling out between men over
incentive and bonus agreements than anything else. They're a union
man's nightmare'(D30). Local variations in working conditions ensured
that earnings from the AIS differed significantly *within* areas of the
coalfield. This applied even to central 'core' coalfields such as Nottinghamshire[30] and Yorkshire. Thus while average bonus earnings *between*
areas varied by plus or minus 18 per cent,[31] 'bonus earnings *within*
Yorkshire ranged from +36 per cent to -15 per cent of national average
earnings in 1983' (Winterton & Winterton 1989: 76; original emphasis).
A local miner claimed that while 'decent bonus payments' were
available in the North and South panel (NUM-organized) Areas of the
Yorkshire coalfield, they were 'non-existent' in the central Doncaster
area (Y9).

In a bitterly critical assessment of the effects of the AIS undertaken in 1983, the NUM demonstrated how the scheme had caused considerable differences in wage levels within the Yorkshire coalfield. It found that average earnings per week in 1983 varied between the coalfield's four panel areas as follows: North Yorkshire – £188.00; Barnsley – £185.70; South Yorkshire – £183.56; Doncaster – £155.24 (NUM 1983: 11). The variation within individual panel areas was even more pronounced. For example, in South Yorkshire, faceworkers at the top pit earned 43 per cent more than those at the bottom. A similar pattern was observed within the three other panel areas (1983: 5–8). The study therefore labelled the AIS a 'shambles', with 'as much as 85 [pounds] per week difference in the incentive pay of face workers in the same coalfield' (1983: 15).

However, the impact of the AIS cannot be measured solely in terms of how it fragmented national wage parity. In addition, varying incentive pay compounded the 'undermining of community' caused by industrial contraction. The NUM in its study noted that when the AIS was first introduced in 1978, the NCB – perhaps mindful of miners' fears of a return to the old pre-NPLA piece-work system – had given

> the impression that [the scheme] would not be allowed to be varied at local level . . . In other words the Board were suggesting that the scheme would have built into it an element of positive discrimination, to assist those collieries in Areas where the geological conditions are adverse and to hold their own against high technology pits. *In addition of course, greater equality of earnings between collieries assist community stability by reducing labour mobility between pits.*(NUM 1983: 4; emphasis added)

It was the NCB's belated recognition of this latter fact, the NUM argued, that explained its subsequent decision to allow incentive payments to vary widely: 'It is evident that the Board are aware of the wide variations in pay between pits. This in turn suggests they are using the scheme to facilitate mobility of labour in the hope that it will speed up colliery closures' (1983: 15).

Therefore, the AIS not only destroyed wage unity but contributed to the 'undermining of community' noted earlier. As such, many strikers in 1984–5, including those from the central coalfields, ruefully pinpointed the introduction of the AIS as a particularly important source of division within and between areas of the coalfield. A miner from Thurcroft colliery in Yorkshire reflected: '[the] incentive scheme broke [the] union – it was set up to do this'(Y23).[32] A miner at Goldthorpe colliery was even more blunt: 'It was a "divide and rule" tactic, the most important single factor in undermining the NUM'(Y9).

Summary and Conclusions

> There's always been this buffer between Yorkshire and Nottinghamshire –
> they've never forgiven us for 1926 and Spencerism. (N28)

> Both my father and grandfather were on strike in 1926, and I'd often
> wondered, until 1984, how they'd managed without anything for six
> months. My father always used to say that the Nottinghamshire men would
> let us down again. (Y22)

The reflections of two miners, the first a Nottinghamshire non-striker,
the second a Yorkshire striker, capture the essence of the arguments
made in this chapter. They underscore the historic, and obstinately local,
basis of diversity within the British coalfield. Thus just as the many
factors which laid the basis for solidarity were historically driven, so too
were those factors which limited solidarity. The oft-repeated proclamation of the NUM activist that 'there is more that unites us than divides
us' was, in fact, an implicit recognition that the powerful basis for
solidarity amongst miners was tempered by long-standing and well-
entrenched differences within the coalfield.

Such historic diversity was exacerbated as the coalfield, through
rationalization from the late 1950s onwards, acquired a distinct 'core'
and 'periphery'. Meanwhile, within individual areas, the 'undermining
of community' ensured that while many local mining traditions died,
others remained intact, and others still changed considerably. The 'shift-
ing sands' of the British coalfield therefore constituted a precarious
foundation for the mobilization of collective action amongst miners at
area and national levels:

> It is . . . apparent, from divisions and differences between various coalfields
> . . . that the material inequalities which are literally inscribed in the earth
> have profound effects on the possibility of any wide and agreed social order
> . . . The most profitable coalfields, and the pits with the easiest seams, can
> see quite different futures for their own immediate communities. The
> theoretical ability of a national union . . . to compose these differences into
> a single policy, a single alternative order, is sharply limited by these very
> practical differences of circumstances. (Williams R. 1985: 9)

Notes

1. Several interviewees referred to mines from which they had been transferred as 'family pits', underscoring the importance attached to knowing one's workmates.
2. Other factors reinforced their reluctance to move elsewhere, not the least of which was the increased travelling involved. A Derbyshire miner reflected: 'It used to be just a five-minute walk across the field to Shirland. Now it's over half an hour on the pit bus to Shirebrook'(D36).

   In the difficult terrain of South Wales, increased travelling distances could worsen an already grim working day. A delegate from Tower colliery told the 1990 NUM Conference that even a fifteen-mile journey to the pit could entail getting up at 4.10 a.m. for the 7.00 a.m. shift, and leaving the pit at 2.15 p.m. to arrive home at about 5.00 p.m. (Tyrone O'Sullivan, Motion 22, NUM Annual Conference, Durham, 10/7/90).
3. Richards F. 1984: 25.
4. Though the presence of non-unionized Spaniards in Merthyr Tydfil in the early twentieth century and in the anthracite coalfield during and immediately after the First World War is noteworthy. My only claim here is that immigrant labour did not necessarily hinder union militancy.
5. Interview, 19/4/90. See also Winterton & Winterton 1989: 5–8.
6. Rees 1986: 472; original emphasis. Rees responds to Sunley's argument that '. . . a key role in the determination of the distinct patterns of mobilisation in the different coalfields during the 1984–5 strike was played by the "cultures of the coalfields": for example, "popular socialism" and "political radicalism" in South Wales, "independence and individualism" and "political quiescence" in the Midlands coalfields' (Rees 1986: 471, in reference to Sunley 1986: 466–77).
7. *FT*, 1/8/84. See Francis 1984.
8. *FT*, 6/2/85.
9. *FT*, 6/2/85; *FT*, 26/2/85.
10. Such geographical contrasts should not be overstated. A 'league' of militancy existed among the pits of the central and eastern coalfield (Allen 1981: 310), while, historically, strikebreaking in the militant areas was not unknown. Indeed, in 1985, the only other pit in the South Wales coalfield to experience a significant return to work before the end of the strike was South Celynen in the extreme east of the coalfield (*FT*, 17/12/84).
11. 'The Spencer Union was established in Nottingham under the

leadership of George Spencer MP, following the negotiation of an
independent Nottingham settlement to the miners' lockout of 1926.
It was purportedly a "nonpolitical" union and was widely regarded
as closely aligned with the coal-owners. It eventually amalgamated
with the [NMA] (and hence the [MFGB]) in 1937' (Rees 1985:
398, n.6).

12. Source: *NUM, Nottingham Area, Minutes, 1984*; p.114.

13. The former NUM Branch Delegate at the colliery, Bernard Savage,
    described it as historically 'a good militant pit' (*G*, 3/3/89).

14. Source: *NUM, Nottingham Area.*

15. Conversations with Peter Savage between February and July 1990,
    Blidworth, Nottinghamshire. Only two men went to work at Blid-
    worth at the start of the 1984–5 strike (though only sixty-four men
    stayed out for the entire strike) (*G*, 3/3/89).

16. *British Coal Corporation, Report and Accounts 1988/9*, pp. 28–9.

17. This is when miners earned their reputations as 'industrial gypsies',
    as thousands moved from the peripheral areas to central England
    (*G*, 6/12/88; Rees 1985: 391).

18. Thus it is argued that a 'fundamental cause' of the South Wales
    coalfield's demise was the way in which difficult geological
    conditions consistently held down productivity levels (*FT*, 5/4/91).

19. This is not, however, to underestimate the way in which aspects of
    mining community culture persisted after the industrial base which
    initially spawned them disappeared. For example, in Spennymoor,
    north-east England, 'the social patterns and attitudes of a single-
    occupation community have outlasted the extinction of coal-mining
    (in the town) since the war . . . [t]he strong attachment and identity
    with Spennymoor seems to be connected with behaviour patterns
    associated with a long established traditional, socially homogenous
    "community"' (Taylor and Townsend 1976: 141, 144, cited by Bul-
    mer 1978a: 41).

20. Interview, 18/5/90. A similar fragmentation of the workforce occur-
    red at Renishaw Park colliery in North Derbyshire. By 1985, only
    58.6 per cent of the colliery's 565 miners lived in the immediately
    adjacent villages of Renishaw and Eckington; the remaining 41.4
    per cent were scattered around several other villages, with some 10
    per cent of the workforce living in the suburban areas of the region's
    two largest urban centres, Sheffield and Rotherham. (Source: *The
    Case for Renishaw Park*, Derbyshire County Council and North
    East Derbyshire District Council, December 1987, p. 21.)

21. For example, with respect to the divisions between the western and
    central parts of the South Wales coalfield discussed earlier, 'such
    apparently enduring localised attitudes' were eventually '. . . eroded

by internal mobility between the anthracite and the steam coalfields
. . .' (Francis 1980: 177).

22. Interview with the NUM Branch President, Denby Grange colliery,
18/5/90.

23. Speech by NUM Lodge Secretary, Tower colliery, on Motion 22,
NUM Annual Conference, Durham; 10/7/90.

24. Conversations with the Secretary, Vice-Chairman and other members of the NUM Lodge Committee, Tower colliery; 24/11/89.

25, An NCB tactic during the strike was to target miners living in the
greatest individual isolation, outside mining communities, and bus
them into work under police protection (Beynon 1984: 112–13).

26. For example, in the west, 96 out of approximately 350 miners at
Denby Grange remained on strike for the whole year (Interview with
the NUM Branch President, Denby Grange colliery, 18/5/90).

27. *FT*, 26/2/85.

28. Though despite its undoubtedly 'cosmopolitan' character, only
sixty-one of 2,169 miners at Easington colliery had returned to work
by the eleventh month of the strike (*FT*, 6/2/85).

29. See Chapter 3.

30. Thus while 66 per cent of Nottinghamshire miners supported the
scheme in the October 1977 ballot, there was considerable variation
between the area's thirty-three branches, with four recording 'yes'
votes of 80 per cent or above, and six branches recording 'yes' votes
of below 50 per cent. (Source: *NUM, Nottingham Area.*)

(Notably, of the forty-three miners interviewed who refused to
support the 1984–5 strike, twenty-seven (or 62.8 per cent) had supported the introduction of the AIS. In contrast, all twelve miners
interviewed who supported the strike had opposed the AIS.

31. *FT*, 17/4/84.

32. For the argument that this may well have been the intention of the
NCB all along, see Winterton & Winterton 1989: 10–11.

The Union and the Problems of Solidarity

Introduction

'I make no distinction between the NUM and the men. The men *should* be the Union.' (D20)

The perennial hope of a Derbyshire miner – of the workforce being 'at one' with the Union – was undoubtedly realized in 1974 when 81 per cent of miners supported the NUM leadership in a national strike ballot. With large majorities from militant and moderate areas alike favouring strike action, 'It is difficult to imagine a greater expression of solidarity with a union than the miners expressed on this occasion' (Allen 1981: 239). Yet this occasion was a rarity – miners, *nationally*, were seldom 'at one' with their Union. Instead, history demonstrates that the path from local-level to national-level solidarity was hazardous. Collective action in the mines took place usually at the pit level, occasionally at the area level and only rarely at the national level. The 1972 strike was the first national-level action undertaken by the miners since the 1926 General Strike – 'it was as if a giant asleep for half a century had come awake' (Pitt 1979: 17).

The relationship between miners at the local level, and the Union at area and national levels, was often uneasy. Miners, locally, often 'jumped the gun', sometimes forcing the hand of a tentative area or national leadership.[1] On other occasions, local action disintegrated after the Union's refusal to sanction 'unofficial' action from below.[2] On more occasions, miners locally refused to follow a 'vanguard' position adopted by an area or national leadership.[3] Overall, therefore, '[m]ilitancy in the coalfields, though often heroic, has almost always been unco-ordinated' (Douglass & Krieger 1983: 90). As such, 'It was always clear that the path from individual consciousness to collective action passed through institutions . . . [e]xperience in the (NUM) . . . showed, however, that the path was an institutional maze containing obstacles and diversions . . .' (Allen 1981: 321). Thus the strengths and weaknesses of the Union as an institution capable of forging Britain's miners into a nationally collectivity was rooted in the fact that the British coalfield was 'national' only to the extent of being an uneasy coalition of fiercely independent localities. An analysis of the Union as a national institution, therefore, must be undertaken with the predominance of locally-based solidarity and identity firmly in mind.

The Meaning of the Union

> . . . I think the grass roots of any union, be it miners or anybody else . . . they're not really interested in politics and the union as a whole – it's only . . . the minority . . . of leaders by definition isn't it? The rest of the people just go to work for their wages, they're concerned about their . . . wages, they're concerned about their bonus, they're concerned about their shifts, concerned about whether they'll have a donkey-coat or whether they're having a new pair of boots. They don't really concern themselves with the wider issues. (W5)

The vast majority of the concerns with which miners, on a daily basis, confronted the Union were of a decidedly 'nuts and bolts' nature. Yet within the membership's supposed lack of interest in the 'wider issues' lay a paradox. For the Lodge Chairman quoted above was able to acknowledge the extraordinary loyalty that local miners, for all their alleged political apathy, had shown the Union in the 1984–5 strike, when only *three* men at the colliery broke ranks before the end of the strike. In this section, I show how supposedly mundane concerns could in fact generate the impressive loyalty shown on this occasion.

That the bulk of miners' concerns were of a 'nuts and bolts' nature is unsurprising, given the dangers continually encountered by miners in their working environment (Allen 1981: 301). Visits in 1989 and 1990 to twenty-seven NUM and ten UDM branches[4] confirmed that the Union office, at times of shift changes, rapidly became an arena for an array of complaints such as discrepancies in pay packets, or uncomfortably high water or temperature levels underground (see also Pitt 1979: 85). Union offices also acted as sources of information and assistance for retired miners (for example, regarding compensation claims for industrial deafness), and also for miners' widows (for example, regarding deliveries of concessionary coal). Thus in the everyday industrial setting, Union branch officials – no matter how politically active and motivated – were mostly engaged in resolving the concrete problems arising from the hazards of mining. For example, the NUM Branch Secretary at Brodsworth colliery in Yorkshire estimated that 90 per cent of his duties involved the prosecution of compensation claims for miners injured at the pit.[5] In addition, the traditional isolation of mining communities ensured that the Union, in performing such duties, was viewed in a very localized way: '[t]hrough the physical and social isolation of the pit and the pit village, and the long history of local wage bargaining, the loyalty of a miner to the Union is primarily a loyalty to the pit lodge and its officials. A . . . problem . . . will trigger off the automatic response, "I'll see the Union", and "the Union" is the branch' (Pitt 1979: 84–5). Moreover, as the NUM Branch Secretary at Shire-brook colliery in Derbyshire acknowledged, in order to retain credibility, the Union *had* to be seen as efficient and responsive:

> When you're talking to the men, they don't want some [person] willy-nillying about. If they've got a problem – alright, it might seem to you a [minor] thing – they want some action taken on it . . . and if you say to them 'come back tomorrow', then when they come back tomorrow, you've got to have an answer for them. And it's that sort of service people want . . . and that's what we try to provide, isn't it? If someone's paying three quid to [the] Union, per week, they want to see what they're getting out of it, don't they? And, really, it's like protection – if they're in a situation where . . . they have accidents, or they've got problems with officials or gaffers . . . then of course they come here, if they want that problem resolved. You know, you can't always *do* it, and then you've got to be honest and say 'you've got nowt to . . . come', like, . . . but we usually have a bash at everything . . .[6]

This, however, was not the whole story. Clearly, the Union had to *earn* the respect and loyalty of the workforce. But the fact that most problems presented to the Union were of a concrete nature did not necessarily mean that the Union was viewed solely in instrumental terms.[7] Instead, the problems arising from the struggles of working life could lay the basis for a much deeper sense of attachment.

The very fact that better pay and conditions had to be constantly struggled for is testament to the grossly uneven structure of power within which miners traditionally found themselves. A Welsh miner recalled the words of a deceased colleague thus: 'British Coal have never given us anything that we were entitled to, just because we were entitled to it. They've never given us it just because we *deserve* it. The only thing we've ever got off . . . British Coal is what we were strong enough to take. We've never had it as a right.' The miner himself continued: 'And that goes for wages, conditions . . . everything. They don't want to give you nothing, only what we're strong enough to take' (W5; see also Allen 1981: 300). Implicit in such remarks was a conception of the Union in a much broader sense – as a defender of rights, security and dignity in a harsh working environment. In this way, the local Union could be viewed as something more all-encompassing. Thus a Derby-shire miner, reflecting on twenty-five years working underground, demonstrated how, for him, the Union had become an object of trust: 'I've been a Union man all my life, and I'd sooner believe the Union than the Board'(D34). A retired South Wales miner spoke of the Union thus:

. . . the Union means *everything*, because you've got to have a Union. Because when I . . . started in the pits thirty-five years ago . . . they ruled with a big iron rod in their hands. And you done as you were told . . . you had no *say* in things. And the Union was over there to back you up and you had your say and . . . you were listened to . . . Oh, the Union to me, in my working life, has been *everything*. I've always joined a union . . . and I don't regret it at all – it's been very good to me, in every part of my job. Wages, everything else . . . (W17)

Such loyalty ensured that the Union in many localities acquired much *more* than an industrial role, and exerted a considerable pastoral, and even hegemonic, influence in local society. Historically, this was demonstrated most powerfully in the pit villages of South Wales, where 'the Checkweigher, the Lodge Secretary and the Miners' Agent were as powerful as the RC priests in Irish villages and "this power rested completely upon service"' (Edwards 1936: 225–8, cited by Francis & Smith 1980: 34).[8] The notion of the Union being at the service of the community was important for miners in many localities. As such, striking miners in 1984–5 were outraged at being described by Thatcher as Britain's 'enemy within'. The Lodge Chairman at Penallta colliery commented: '. . . we've been called "the enemy within", we've been vilified by the papers – the miners of South Wales have built hospitals up and down these valleys that are now old age pensioners' homes. There's hospitals all over these valleys built by the miners. And we're entitled to be treated with a little bit of respect' (W5).

This image of a social role for the Union was also articulated in 1990 by the Branch leadership at Shirebrook colliery in Derbyshire. Even in the desolate aftermath of the 1984–5 strike, Union officials remained convinced of the need for the NUM to persevere and to play a wider role in the life of the local village. The Branch was therefore active in fundraising for local schools, and organizing parties for schoolchildren at the local Miners' Welfare Hall.[9]

Occasionally, at certain points in history, the Union assumed a pastoral role on an Area basis. Again, the experience of the South Wales coalfield is illustrative. Because of the sheer dominance of coal in the local economy, the SWMF, by the 1930s, 'was, literally, the fount of control in other spheres as well as that of the industry itself' (Francis & Smith 1980: 34). It was, therefore, 'a lot more than a trade union; it was a social institution' (Paynter 1972: 110–11). This pastoral role played by the Union in the narrowness of the mining valleys also extended into wider Welsh society. For example, not only was the Union instrumental in constructing, in the pit villages, the Miners' Institutes, but it also played an important role in the development of the education system in Wales as a whole (Francis 1976: 192; Lewis 1993).

The case of the Union in South Wales – at least as an area-wide phenomenon – may indeed be unusual.[10] But it does illustrate how the Union could, through tending to the everyday concerns of the workforce, transform purely instrumentalist attachments and become, for the miner, something much deeper and more all-encompassing. This is critical to understanding the way in which intense loyalty was shown to the Union on those occasions when the daily routine of struggle at pit level gave way to a national situation of acute crisis and confrontation demanding a solidarity transcending localized concerns. Only then is it possible to understand, for example, the determination with which miners in 1926 resisted the coal owners' attempts to reduce wages and impose longer working hours. Rallying to MFGB Secretary Arthur Cook's battle cry of 'not a minute on the day, not a penny off the pay' (Williamson 1982: 171), the miners led a general strike and then, isolated, endured a bitter six-month lock-out. The episode remains one of the most powerful examples of the ability of the Union to command astonishing loyalty in the most dire circumstances.

Sixty years on, in 1984–5, in a similar situation of extreme crisis, the Union again displayed this capacity. A Nottinghamshire striker remained loyal to the Union despite losing all he had: '. . . the electric was cut, the gas was cut . . . the house was snatched. But eventually you don't care – you reach rock bottom and you can't go down any further'(N7). A Derbyshire striker commented: 'Arthur [Scargill] told me to come out, and he told me to go back. And that was enough for me'(D34). Nor should the agony of many of those miners forced to 'scab' be forgotten:

> We had a lad here, a face chargeman, about six foot six. I'd been saying to him since Christmas [1984] – 'hold on, hold on, there'll be a settlement to this [strike]'. His wife had left him, and he was . . . going to lose his home, his daughter was getting married in May [1985] – he'd got no money for that, he'd spent all his money. And he was down at my house, crying, and . . . I put him off till February [1985], and then he went back to work. But his *only* worry was that he didn't want to lose face with the Union. And after all that . . . how on earth could you call him a 'scab' or 'owt like that? He'd given his all, hadn't he?[11]

Many Branch officials, in fact, expressed incredulity at the loyalty shown to the Union during the 1984–5 strike. At Sharlston colliery in Yorkshire, the Branch Delegate reflected: 'I don't know how we kept [the men] out for a whole year, I just don't know. Right to the last day . . . there was a blind loyalty to the NUM'(Y40). At Betws colliery, South Wales, the Lodge Secretary commented: 'The loyalty to the NUM in this area is incredible; I reckon only the NUM could have sustained a strike like that for twelve months . . . if the NUM called the men out today on strike, they would come out' (W36).

The Union acted, and was viewed, in a multiplicity of ways – from being the provider of services and protection in the everyday workplace to being an organization capable of inspiring fierce loyalty in situations of acute crisis. As Samuel describes in the case of the 1984–5 strike, the bond that emerged on occasion between workforce and Union was form-idable:

> [t]he function of the Union . . . was seen as protective, as much, perhaps, for what it stood for as for what it did. It was the only safeguard for the miners' welfare, the only security for their conditions of work. In the rhetoric of the strike it appears as a kind of 'philanthropic Hercules' . . . a purveyor of 'friendly benefits' as much as a pillar of strength. It represented a higher principle of unity than those to be found in the localities. It incarnated a wider sense of belonging. In the words of an old trade union song, it was 'The Miners' Lifeguard' . . . As miners put it . . . 'Without the union, we would be lost'. (1986: 28)

None the less, such bonds of loyalty between workforce and Union were never a given (Francis 1985c: 28–9). The national strikes of 1926, 1972, 1974 and 1984–5 were the only examples this century of industrial action which *truly* encompassed the entire British coalfield; they demon-strated the kinds of solidarity that could *potentially* be achieved. For the most part, however, the Union struggled to forge the miners into a national collectivity – achieving a 'higher principle of unity' and 'incarnating a wider sense of belonging' often proved elusive goals. Thus the fierce loyalty described here had a latent, or potential, quality. How well-equipped, though, was the Union, in terms of its institutional development and structure, to tap such potential?

The Structure and Development of the Union

> My own . . . view is that if we . . . decided to get rid of the structure that we've got, we should have problems with our members. They like this link. They [have] got something they can call on and identify with, rather than something remote, centralized. And personally, whether [or not] it affects our ability to galvanize action against our employer at a certain time, I'm not sure that I've been convinced by an argument for a centralized structure or area structures because . . . we tend to roam about in other people's areas at that time [that] we're trying to galvanize support . . . in practice, the area set-up doesn't hold you back . . . from galvanizing national action[12]
> Interview with Financial Secretary, Derbyshire Area NUM, 11/10/89

> I always believed it was [the] NUM member first, and [the] Nottinghamshire member second. My loyalty was *always* to the national union . . . and I always believed, for example, that this federation game were a nonsense anyway – we should be just one national union and to hell with the areas . . .[13]
> Interview with General Secretary, Nottinghamshire Area NUM, 10/10/89

These contrasting views of two neighbouring Area leaders underscore the historic tension within the Union between those pushing for the
construction of a wider unity and those guarding against any infringe-
ments of local autonomy. This tension is a product of the way in which
mining trade unionism developed in Britain – that is, very much from the
grass roots upwards. Certainly, once the Union *was* established at the pit
level, there was much that laid the basis for coherent organization: '[t]he
very nature of pit work, its physical isolation and the mutual dependence
of the men, is conducive to an exceptionally high degree of trade union
organization' (Pitt 1979: 79). This was supplemented by the establishment of the closed shop when the coal industry was nationalized in 1947
and the newly-formed NUM acquired sole bargaining rights for Britain's
miners.[14] Furthermore, 'the NUM had a distinct advantage over other
unions in enforcing the closed shop because "we have all our members
in the same hole"'. Thus for the individual miner, union membership
became 'an unquestionable and unchallengeable fact of life in the pit'
(Pitt 1979: 79).

Such organizational coherence at the pit level, however, did little to
help the national union to *institutionalize* a wider identity amongst
Britain's miners. Instead, the Union's strength at pit level and the
localized identity of the Union acted as brakes on attempts to do so.
Historically, the construction of a national union was delayed by
constant concessions to local autonomy – both in terms of the relationship between Branch and Area leaderships, and between Area and
National leaderships. This was true, moreover, of both the pre- and post-
nationalization eras. The history of British mining unionism therefore
conforms to a general pattern: '[t]he institutional history of coalmining
unions in most Western societies is a complicated web of mergers and
splits between unions attempting to submerge particular ethnic, religious, political, or institutional loyalties to form more encompassing, and
therefore more effective, alliances' (Marks 1989: 161).

Examples from both the pre- and post-war periods, and at both the
intra- and inter-area levels, illustrate the point. Francis and Smith
describe how even in South Wales, the SWMF, which eventually became
a revered Area-wide institution, was none the less a product of a protracted struggle to overcome local loyalties and internal rivalries within
the coalfield (1980: 1–44). Poor inter-valley communication, varying
geological conditions, and localized wage bargaining fostered a loyalty
to the Union extending no further than the local Lodge: '[s]ince the
collier's wages depended heavily on the local customs and price lists
that his local leadership negotiated, his defence, he felt, had to be at this
level. Only half of the monthly contribution . . . went to the new Central
Executive' (1980: 4). Thus despite the 'commonalty induced by similar
labour, similar living conditions and similar work, . . . the demands for
a greater degree of centralisation in the affairs of the federated Union

foundered on the rocks of local pride' (1980: 7). For example, in 1908 the Union's Rhondda Number One District opposed any centralization of funds: '[d]elegates spoke against any loss of "Home Rule of the District" and of their fears that centralisation might put them under "some Czar or other" . . .' (1980: 7–8).

Such tensions also extended to the *inter*-Area level:

> . . . what mattered took place in the individual coalfields, where local con-ditions of production, marketing opportunities and problems, the strength and weaknesses of local management could best be appreciated. Beyond such practical considerations, there lay parochialism and a coalfield chauvinism that could be developed by District Officials keen to establish their credibility both locally and nationally – a battery of unavoidable considerations and emotional sentiments that could threaten any national strategy by the MFGB. (Howell 1989: 5)

The difficulties encountered by the MFGB in prosecuting just such a national strategy were exposed during the 1926 strike. The *Newcastle Journal* described in August 1926 how Arthur Cook recognized the inherent weakness of the MFGB in maintaining the solidarity of a diverse group of coalfields:

> 'Does it look as if we are beaten when our delegates are touring all parts of the world to collect funds to help us? The only way we can be defeated is by the district settlements, and it will require all the power of local com-mittees to prevent them being accepted.'
> Mr. Cook expressed himself 'sick and tired' of different organisations pulling different ways, and said the great need was for one large Federation. (cited in Williamson 1982: 188)

Cook's remarks were, of course, prophetic. The strike collapsed when the Nottinghamshire miners negotiated their own local settlement and seceded from the MFGB. Eleven years were to pass before they were persuaded to rejoin the national federation.

Nor did the need for compromise between areas of the coalfield evaporate with nationalization and the formation of the NUM. On the contrary, even long-time supporters of 'the ideal of One Miners Union' (Howell 1989: 9) such as Arthur Horner[15] recognized that the structure of the NUM would inevitably reflect the realities of a diverse British coalfield. In 1943, as the MFGB began discussing a new rule book for what would eventually become the NUM, he remarked: 'This we are now proposing is an attempt to make a superstructure over what already exists, and we cannot do it independently of what exists' (cited in Francis 1985b: 22; see also Arnot 1961: 411). This realistic approach, borne of the inter-war years of defeat, division, unemployment and company unionism, prevailed when the NUM was formed in 1945.[16] The NUM, structurally, differed little from its predecessor (Howell 1989: 5).

As such, it was as limited by the power of local autonomy as the MFGB had been in the pre-war period: 'The constituent unions of the old Federation became areas of the National union; their officials became Area Officials of the NUM, but retained much of their power. The areas collected money and retained a sizeable proportion. Such a resource facilitated the continuation of the diverse sentiments which went along with divergent procedures and a range of industrial and political policies' (Howell 1989: 9).

In short, as Tony Benn observed, '. . . the NUM never really got past being the MFGB'.[17] In failing to do so, long-standing differences within the British coalfield remained firmly embedded.

Thus within individual coalfields, tensions between Branch and Area leaderships persisted in the post-war period. In Kent, for example, even after the establishment of the NPLA, which transferred wage bargaining from the local to the national arena, 'the pit branches still jealously guarded the principle of local autonomy' (Pitt 1979: 84). As such, the powers of Branch delegates, in relation to the Area Union, were restricted: 'Area delegates represent "the pit", and must always be looking over their shoulder to "the men". A surrender of branch interests on the Area council by an Area delegate will bring down on his head accusations of treachery and betrayal from the branch, and the curt reminder that "we put you there to do a job". A controversial decision at Area [level] can even raise the cry, "Stop the money! Let's go it alone!"' (1979: 89)[18]

In the *national* context, it is important to emphasize the sheer durability of Area-based structures and traditions. In Lancashire, for example, Howell describes how 'So much had changed, yet through the disputes, the inter-war depression, two wars, nationalisation, more closures, the routines of the Union continued . . . Successive full-time officials might leave individual imprints on the Union, but the routine of meetings continued . . . The procedures of the Union seemed to carry on regardless of external crisis . . .' (1989: 4; 1–14).

Such well-entrenched traditions, identities and loyalties[19] ensured that as a *national* institution, 'the Union has had to cope with its own history' (Allen 1981: 265). For any national leadership trying to construct a wider unity, 'the NUM is a difficult union to lead . . . In practice it is a federation with its various areas acting with the mentality of autonomous county unions . . .' (Allen 1982: 21; see also 1981: 265).

An examination of the Union's National Executive Committee (NEC)[20] illustrates the impact that concessions to area autonomy had on the structure and development of the NUM. First, it is important to note how the membership of the NEC viewed itself: 'The composition of the [NEC] reflects these area differences for its members go to [national headquarters] as leaders of the South Wales, Scottish, Yorkshire, Derbyshire miners and not as representatives elected by a given proportion of members divided on geographical basis. They descend . . . as plenipotentiaries. They are not, therefore, easily controlled' (Allen 1982: 21).

In addition, NEC members sat 'on the basis of equality . . . each member . . . has his own vote irrespective of his membership' (Allen 1982: 21). Such an anomalous system was a result of the process in the early 1940s in which the old constituents of the MFGB amalgamated to form the NUM:

> . . . each Area irrespective of its size had at least one [NEC] representative while the maximum number was three . . . this method of representation favoured the small areas from the outset . . . the reason for starting off with such an inequitable system was given . . . in August, 1944, when it was stated that the spheres of interest of the county unions had to continue for some time after the amalgamation otherwise the amalgamation would not even materialize. (Allen 1981: 266)[21]

Despite a subsequent 'patchwork alteration' (Allen 1981: 266), no basic change in this system occurred after 1958 '. . . and at no time did the [NEC] attempt to view the Union as a whole in an endeavour to remove the anomalies and undemocratic tendencies which the amalgamation compromises had left' (Allen 1981: 267). Instead, attempts at successive Annual Conferences to effect a reorganization of the NEC along more representative lines were continually thwarted not only by Area Officials 'who wanted to protect their petty domains' but also by 'the ordinary members who were conscious of their county identities, proud of their local traditions and jealous of their financial autonomy' (Allen 1981: 267).

Furthermore, the general but uneven contraction of the industry from the late 1950s ensured that 'the discrepancies in the sizes of Areas widened as some were reduced to the size of individual branches in others' (1981: 267). By 1979, the anomalies 'were not only marked but ridiculous . . . Cumberland's [914] members had exactly the same voting power on the [NEC] as Scotland's 16,373 members. Voting situations could, and did, occur where a minority on the [NEC] commanded a majority of votes in the coalfields' (Allen 1981: 267–8).

The way in which the durability of Area traditions and the NUM's federal structure hindered the construction of a wider unity amongst miners was underscored in 1978 when the AIS, twice rejected in national ballots in 1974 and 1977, was none the less introduced through the 'back door' at Area level.

Attempts to reintroduce a productivity-related incentive scheme into the industry's wages system threatened to destroy the national wage unity which had underpinned the 1972 and 1974 strikes. As such, furious clashes erupted at the NUM's 1977 Annual Conference between delegates from those Areas (such as South Derbyshire) which stood to gain most from the reintroduction of incentives, and those from Areas (such as South Wales) seeking to preserve wage parity. A Welsh delegate pleaded: 'We do not want to go backwards. We do not want to allow anybody to shatter this unity that we have got now. If we allow ourselves to retrogress back to our divided directions, then it will be a crime against all those old miners who fought over the years to get what we have got now.'[22]

Despite the fact that the South Wales resolution was carried at the Conference,[23] tensions persisted within the Union. The Kent Area's appeal in the Chancery Court against the NEC's decision in October 1977 to conduct a national ballot as a means of overturning the Conference decision failed, and 'the right of the [NEC] at its own initiative to conduct a ballot of its entire membership was categorically confirmed'.[24] However, to the delight of opponents of the incentive scheme, miners rejected the NEC's recommendation by a vote, in October 1977, of 110,634 to 87,901.[25] Even in Nottinghamshire, which was generally favourable to incentives, nearly 40 per cent of miners voted against (Howell 1989: 53). Even this, however, failed to prevent the undermining of national unity on the issue. Instead, at an acrimonious NEC meeting in November 1977, the NUM President, with majority backing, ruled that while 'the Committee must accept the result of the ballot on a National [Incentives] Scheme . . . the Committee did not have the democratic right to stop Areas raising the question of whether they could introduce Area schemes'.[26] This effectively paved the way for the reintroduction of incentives 'through the back door' at the Area level. At an NEC meeting on 8 December 1977, the Union President accepted a motion 'that Areas should now be allowed to introduce incentive schemes'.[27] Opponents argued that the Committee 'was obliged not to act in defiance of decisions of Conference . . . and . . . that the [NEC] had no power to overrule previous decisions and give authority to Areas to have local schemes'.[28] This position was defeated, however, by a majority on the NEC which:

> . . . pointed out that the National Incentive Scheme had been rejected, and that the [NEC] had accepted this decision. However, there was now pressure for local arrangements . . . and the [NEC] was obliged to consider such applications and had the right either to withhold approval, or to endorse any such local arrangements, or to delegate power to Areas to enter into such arrangements. There was no need for those Areas, who did not wish their members to have incentive bonus schemes, to have them.[29]

Legal action was immediately taken by the Kent, South Wales and Yorkshire Areas 'to prevent the operation of the [NEC]'s decision to delegate power to those Areas who wished to enter into a production incentive scheme', but was subsequently dismissed by the courts.[30]

Thus only three months after a majority of miners, nationally, had supported the maintenance of national wage unity, manoeuvrings on the NEC had negated such an expression of solidarity. The earlier successes enjoyed by those opposed to incentives 'had counted for nothing' (Howell 1989: 56). National wage unity was dead. Instead, the 'incentives imbroglio not only heightened factional rivalries and eroded confidence in the Union's procedures, increasingly it was seen by many as fracturing the solidarity of the early seventies' (Howell 1989: 57). The reintroduction of incentives was therefore a watershed in the recent history of the Union. The *manner* of its introduction, however, exposed once again the power of entrenched Area interests within the national Union, and its ability to undermine a wider unity expressed emphatically in two successive national ballots. Nationally, therefore, the debacle highlighted the problems of maintaining 'the solidarity of a federal union whose fissiparous tendencies are notorious' (Thompson 1980: 70). A Welsh miner reflected:

> ... the point about incentives ... [is] ... it created disunity in the mines – that was the beginning of the end, as far as the union in the mines is concerned ... and Joe Gormley *forced* that upon us ... even after national ballots ... And when ... Gormley ... allowed areas to go their own way ... then everybody were getting worried that they were losing out and they all wanted to jump on the bandwagon because maybe, *some* of their pits were more lucrative to earn incentives in rather than the next pit – [Gormley] allowed it, and that's when disunity crept in. (W4)

Overall, as a union capable of institutionalizing and maintaining the national solidarity of miners, the NUM was woefully inadequate. Any national action that *did* emerge did so in spite of, rather than because of, the structure of the NUM: 'an unsentimental demythologised reading of the history shows that the NUM ... is not, and never has been, sufficient as a model for a miners' union' (Howell 1989: 218). The intention here, though, is not to focus exclusively on the problems of generating national solidarity but to emphasize that the *strength* of the Union lay very much at the local level. In times of crisis, however, the obduracy of local power made relations between miners and the national Union uneasy. For an NUM national leadership struggling to maintain solidarity in a national crisis, such local power could be a source of both resilient support for, and stubborn resistance to, the strategy being pursued nationally. As such,

> Local initiatives are no doubt a feature of any national strike, and so are regional differences. What gives them special purchase in the coalfields is the molecular character of mining trade unionism as reflected in the federal make-up of the NUM's national executive, the financial independence of

the regions, and the relative autonomy of the miners' lodge . . . centripetal
influences have survived forty years of amalgamation . . . almost untouched:
whatever the constitutionalities of the matter, miners are accustomed to
acting on their own. (Samuel 1986: 22; see also Hyman 1986: 344)

These, then, were the 'facts of life' with which successive national
leaders of the NUM had to contend and which, with varying degrees of
commitment, they sought to overcome. Any national leadership –
whether militant or moderate – had to contend with the obduracy of Area
traditions and, below these, the jealousy with which local interests and
autonomy were guarded. It is in this context that one must view the political transformation of the NUM's national leadership at the end of the
1970s, when a conciliatory leadership, dedicated in the 1970s to the
preservation of a beleaguered Labour Government, was replaced by a
militant leadership confronting a hostile Conservative Government.

Leadership and the Union

Gormley was one of the finest secretaries the NUM had – the way he went
into business and sorted things out with the (NCB) before he went to the
members with ballots . . . he really went into it and worked hard at his job.
Whereas Scargill when he went to the NCB, if they said 'no', first time, it
was 'we'll have them out on strike' – which to me is a load of rubbish – he's
very poor at negotiations. (N31)

Scargill was a man of principle, with a commitment to the trade union
movement and his membership. Joe Gormley was moderate, he would
compromise – was this right for the 1970s when trade unions had a lot more
muscle? He could have made more of it. (Y24)

These contrasting views of two successive national leaders of the NUM
– Joe Gormley, President of the Union from 1971 to 1981, and Arthur
Scargill, President since 1981 – reflect the political transformation of the
NUM's national leadership that occurred during the 1970s and early
1980s. In the coal industry, as with British politics in general, an era
of consensus was giving way to one of confrontation. Yet given the
constraints imposed on the national leadership by the traditions of the
Union, how important were such changes at the top?

National Leadership and the Post-war Consensus

The nationalization of the mines in 1947 promoted cooperation between
the NCB, NUM and successive post-war British governments. As an
historic goal, 'nationalisation of the pits clearly brought goodwill from
the miners' (Lloyd 1985: 5) who 'were no longer prepared to work for

the private coal owners' (McCormick 1979: 47, cited in Lloyd 1985: 5). Replacing the bitter years of private ownership and inter-war depression, an elaborate system of consultation and conciliation was established, within which the NCB was awarded 'monopoly rights to produce coal in the UK' and the NUM was awarded sole bargaining rights for the manual workforce (Lloyd 1985: 4). The 1946 Coal Industry Act ensured that

> [b]esides being prepared to direct policy so as to secure the welfare of their employees, the NCB had to direct it so as to get the benefit of the knowledge and experience of the employees in the organization and conduct of the operations; and they were also required to establish joint machinery with employees' organizations for the settlement by negotiation of the terms and conditions of employment (with provision for arbitration) and for consultation on various matters, including the organization and conduct of operations. (Ashworth 1986: 594)

Both militant and moderate wings of the NUM's national leadership recognized the values of such provisions; as such, the hallmark of industrial relations in the post-war period became one of consultation (if not always agreement). The discussion of a multitude of issues – from manning agreements to wage levels – was structured through consultative committees established at the pit, area and national levels. Wage questions at the national level, for example, were dealt with by the Joint National Negotiating Committee consisting of sixteen NCB representatives and sixteen NUM representatives (Handy 1981: 23). By the 1970s, the structures for consultation in the industry were extensive: 'To the pit level consultative committees and to the national level consultative council [was] added the national level Joint Policy Advisory Committee; together with national committees on health and safety and recruitment, training and welfare. In any given year, a minimum required number of joint meetings would amount to 17 at national level, 72 at area level and around 4,000 at pit and workshop level' (Lloyd 1985: 7).

Complementing this elaborate machinery[31] was the fact that 'on the employer's side there was a long period when the national board almost always included someone with a long practical experience of the affairs of the NUM' (Ashworth 1986: 604). Thus while the NUM's national leadership always opposed any representation on the board for *current* NUM officials (Ashworth 1986: 594; Lloyd 1985: 6), this did not prevent a limited flow of former miners and NUM officials to the upper echelons of management. For example, Sam Watson, the Durham miners' leader, and a leading figure in the NUM, became a part-time board member after his retirement from union office (Ashworth 1986: 604). Lord Robens, NCB Chairman in the 1960s, was an ex-miner and Union member. As late as 1976, NUM President Joe Gormley was offered the chairmanship of the NCB by Energy Secretary Tony Benn (Gormley 1982: 168). Overall, such a 'cosy consensus' (Lloyd 1985: 14) seemed to epitomize the general position of coal as the 'paradigm case' in industry of the post-war political consensus (Francis & Rees 1989: 41).[32]

How, though, did the miners respond to such a consensus at the top, and what does this say about the capacities and influence of national leadership? After all, cooperation with the NCB by successive NUM leaderships amounted in the post-war period to agreeing to the radical overhaul of a fragmented and well-entrenched wage bargaining system, and accepting, with reduced demand for coal, a *massive* rundown in manpower levels from 658,000 in 1959 to 305,000 in 1970 (Jackson 1974: 120). Not surprisingly, support amongst miners for their leadership's participation in a 'consensus' which had such dire consequences was never wholehearted. The consensus was therefore not without its strains. Nationalization in and of itself did not eradicate industrial action in the coal industry (Ashworth 1986: 595). One consequence of the NUM's support for NCB policy in the late 1940s and early 1950s was a growth of unofficial strikes amongst rank-and-file members 'who felt that their interests had been forgotten or were being ignored' (Jackson 1974: 123). Indeed, in 1957, 78 per cent of all recorded disputes in British industry and services were in the coal industry (Ashworth 1986: 596). Many of these strikes 'do show signs of being caused, at least in part, by disenchantment between national officials of the NUM and rank and file members' (Jackson 1974: 174). Thus while the NUM leadership cooperated with the NCB to improve the efficiency of the industry, the 'attitude of the rank and file members was by no means as clear-cut as that of the NUM leadership' (Jackson 1974: 127).

Nevertheless, successive national leaderships of the Union, at least until the late 1960s, largely succeeded in containing rank-and-file discontent. The basis of the NCB-NUM consensus was never fundamentally challenged. Most unofficial strikes in the 1940s and 1950s 'were very small, very short and very localized (often only one shift in one face in one colliery), and though numerous, they were not nearly as numerous as the disputes which were settled peacefully through the conciliation arrangements . . .' (Ashworth 1986: 595–6). Furthermore, after the late 1950s, when world demand for coal slumped, both the NCB and the NUM leadership acquiesced in the belief that there was little the miners could do but accept the consequences of market changes – that is, a huge programme of pit closures. Yet the number of strikes in the industry between 1959 and 1968 (that is, the period of severe industrial contraction) actually dropped markedly: 'the coal industry ceased to be the outstandingly bad example of proneness to dispute' (Ashworth 1986: 596). In 1959, there were 1,307 stoppages, and 363,000 man-days lost through stoppages, in the industry. By 1968, there were only 227 stoppages in the industry with 57,000 man-days lost (Jackson 1974: 124). While such a fall in strike action did not indicate positive support for the strategy of the NCB and NUM, by the same token, 'there is little evidence that there was any major increase in hostility on the part of the miners, either to the Board's actions or to their union's support for most of these actions' (Jackson 1974: 127).

Thus for a long time an NUM national leadership eager to make nationalization 'work' and ready, as a consequence, to accept painful change, played an important role in shaping the response to such change of miners as a whole. Not surprisingly, the NCB was fulsome in its praise for the cooperation it had received. The NCB Chairman proclaimed in 1963: 'I believe that the working relationship of the Board and the . . . unions has contributed more to the rebirth of the British coal-mining industry than any other single factor' (Jackson 1974: 122). The role of the miners in overhauling the wages system was noted in 1972 by the Wilberforce Committee: 'There has been quite exceptional co-operation shown by the miners in the last few years in moving from piecework schemes to day-working schemes in the interests of greater efficiency. This co-operation has been a model to industry as a whole' (Jackson 1974: 123).

However, as the eruption of massive unofficial strikes in several parts of the British coalfield in 1969 and 1970 demonstrated, there were limits to the ability of a national leadership to contain grass-roots discontent. With rising unemployment, 'the context of industrial relations began to change' (Ashworth 1986: 606), as 'the conventional wisdom about the uncontrollable, all-powerful laws of the market disseminated by the Government, the N.C.B. and Union officials appeared rather sour to miners faced with the prospect of unemployment' (Allen 1981: 137). The election of Scottish miners' leader Lawrence Daly, a Communist, as national General Secretary of the NUM reflected growing discontent in the coalfields (Allen 1981: 141). In October 1969, unofficial strikes in Yorkshire, over wages, grew to encompass 130,000 miners from 140 pits in Scotland, South Wales, Derbyshire, Kent, Nottinghamshire and the Midlands (Allen 1981: 156). In November 1970, the failure to obtain, in a national ballot, the two-thirds majority required for strike action did not stop 103,000 miners from South Wales, Scotland and parts of Yorkshire from staging unofficial strikes (Allen 1981: 163–4; Lloyd 1985: 5). Thus the NUM leadership in this period 'had to run to keep control of a wages militancy which surprised and temporarily disoriented them' (Lloyd 1985: 5).

The 1972 and 1974 strikes, which grew in large part from the unofficial actions of 1969 and 1970, were obviously major disruptions to the post-war consensus in the industry. Moreover, their success not only boosted the morale of a disheartened workforce but resurrected strike action as a credible industrial weapon. Yet even then, the desire for consensus at both local and national levels remained strong. In 1971, in the election for National President, Joe Gormley, the moderate leader of the Lancashire miners, comfortably beat the Scottish miners' leader Michael

McGahey (a Communist) – a result which not only disappointed the
NUM Left, but probably reflected the desire of miners to balance the
Communist General Secretary they had elected in 1968 with a more
moderate President (Allen 1981: 167).

Furthermore, consensus of a kind was restored – somewhat ironically
– after the 1974 national strike. The 1974 Plan for Coal, with its guar-
antees of security for the miners, laid the basis for a tripartite agreement
between a resurgent NUM, a chastened NCB and an incoming Labour
Government anxious to restore tranquility to the coalfields and secure
the cooperation of the miners in the implementation of key components
of its economic policy. Indeed, Gormley's presidency after 1974 and the
adoption of the Plan for Coal 'marked the closest relationship between
the Board and the union in their joint histories' (Lloyd 1985: 7).
Throughout the 1970s, warm relations existed between the NCB
Chairman and the NUM President (Ashworth 1986: 611). As a 'convinced advocate of the consultative approach' (Lloyd 1985: 7), the
NUM President was a powerful influence for wage restraint as a means
of cooperating with the Labour Government. Typically, he viewed the
reintroduction of incentive payments not just as a means of raising
miners' earnings, but also of cooperating with the NCB to boost levels
of production and productivity. Those who opposed such efforts were
labelled 'wreckers' (Gormley 1982: 146–72).

However, the 1970s marked the ending, rather than the reinforce-
ment, of the era of consensus. While Gormley, throughout the 1970s,
was able to win a majority on the Union's NEC for his position, 'it was
a narrow majority, and the demands of the opposition were both more
divergent and more sharply presented than had been customary'
(Ashworth 1986: 611). Increasingly, the 'NUM President had to struggle
. . . to contain his powerful left-wing and deliver national level peace'
(Lloyd 1985: 7). Indeed, the 1969, 1970, 1972 and 1974 strikes trig-
gered a process of political change within the Union which would
culminate, in the NUM's 1981 Presidential election, with the emphatic
victory of Arthur Scargill – a leader whose political and industrial outlook could not have differed more sharply from that of his predecessor.

Political Change and the Breakdown of Consensus

Negotiating has been my life.

J. Gormley, *Battered Cherub. The Autobiography of Joe Gormley*

I'm not prepared to pay for the crisis of capitalism at the expense of the
people that I represent.

A. Scargill, 'The New Unionism', *New Left Review*

Scargill's election victory in 1981 was the outcome of a long period of mobilization within the NUM dating from the upheavals of 1967 when, in a situation of growing concern about the unexpectedly harsh fate of the coal industry under Wilson's Labour Government, representatives from Derbyshire, Kent, Scotland, South Wales and Yorkshire met to select a left-wing candidate to succeed the retiring Communist General Secretary of the NUM, Will Paynter (Adeney & Lloyd 1988: 32). The unofficial 1969 strike, meanwhile, united thousands of miners around 'a common tactic and programme of demands' (Douglass & Krieger 1983: 89), and bolstered the confidence of the Left in the Yorkshire coalfield (Adeney & Lloyd 1988: 32).

In focusing on Scargill's platform and victory, therefore, my intention is not to personalize what was largely a rank-and-file reaction to consensus. None the less, as a co-founder of the radical Barnsley Miners' Forum, Scargill played a leading role in the critical transformation of the Yorkshire coalfield from being a cornerstone of the NUM's post-war accord with the NCB to being, from the late 1960s onwards, a bastion of industrial militancy (Taylor 1984; Scargill 1975). Moreover, following his role in the 1972 strike, and his election in 1973 as President of the Yorkshire miners, Scargill became one of the leading standard-bearers of the Left within the NUM (Taylor 1982: 218). Indeed, by 1980, Scargill was the undisputed candidate of the Left in the battle to succeed Gormley as Union President.[33] His 'meteoric rise in the NUM' should therefore be viewed as a product of the 'reaction to the post-war, post-nationalization history of the coal industry, especially to what is regarded as the betrayal of the industry and the miners by the 1964–1970 Labour government' (Taylor 1982: 218). This reaction contained three key components.

First, in keeping with many militant predecessors, Scargill based his platform on the wages issue – the miners were to be at the top of any wage 'league' (Taylor 1982: 219). To achieve this goal, he supported the vigorous pursuit of free collective bargaining with the employer, and rejected any participation in incomes policies or other forms of wage restraint, regardless of the political complexion of the government attempting to implement them (Scargill 1975: 24). Unlike his predecessors, therefore, Scargill in the 1970s was a vehement critic of the Labour Government's Social Contract with the unions in which the NUM, under Gormley, participated (Scargill 1975: 29). Furthermore, the collapse of the Social Contract, and the ensuing 'winter of discontent' of 1978–9, merely reinforced his conviction that no union should become entangled in an incomes policy: '[t]his union must never again accept wage restraint' (Scargill 1981: 8).

Second, Scargill differed sharply from his predecessors on the question of industrial contraction. Gormley, like many other post-war NUM leaders, had believed that there was little the miners themselves could do to control the size of their industry (Lloyd 1985: 20–1). Scargill disagreed, noting that 'the biggest cutbacks were made by a Labour government. And we accepted them, which was totally wrong. They should have been resisted' (1975: 24). In 1981, he referred to miners (particularly those in South Wales, Scotland and the North east) who were 'still paying a heavy price for the butchery imposed by the pit closure programme of successive Tory and Labour Governments' (1981: 4). And in 1982, in his inaugural Presidential address to the NUM Conference, he declared:

> If we do not save our pits from closure then all our other struggles become meaningless. I do not subscribe to the philosophy of John L. Lewis, who encouraged contraction so that the wages of those who are left could be raised . . . Protection of the industry is my first priority, because without jobs all our other claims lack substance and become mere shadows. Without jobs our members are nothing – they have no power or means of subsistence, because we live in a society which penalises people who have no jobs. I hope, therefore, that this conference will endorse my call to make opposition to pit closures its central task. (Lloyd 1985: 13, 19–20)

The third component of Scargill's platform was what he deemed the need for the democratization of the Union. He criticized the unrepresentative nature of the Union's NEC and its role in continually thwarting the decisions of the NUM's Annual Conferences and campaigned for the need to elect it on more representative lines, and to reassert the supremacy of the Annual Conference: 'The union constitution is democratic. It states clearly that power resides in the annual conference and that the task of the N.E.C. is to interpret and apply policy handed to it. Under no circumstances should the N.E.C. violate or act contrary to the wishes of the annual conference' (1981: 10).

On becoming Union President, Scargill stated to the 1982 NUM Conference: '. . . no matter what judges say or will say, the decisions of this conference are sacrosanct and binding on the NEC and the union as a whole . . . I give an undertaking that whilst I am National President, this conference will never be trivialised – dismissed as being out of touch with reality . . . it must be recognized that I am not giving a personal view, but simply repeating a union rule' (cited in Lloyd 1985: 20).

This, again, distinguished him from his predecessors – whereas previous leaders had attempted 'to balance the various centres and mechanisms of NUM power' (Lloyd 1985: 20), Scargill, by reasserting the supremacy of the national conference, 'cut through all such considerations' (Adeney & Lloyd 1988: 37). In doing so, he 'was not giving an uncontroversial re-statement of the Rules: he was making clear his intention of running the union and its policies through that forum which, because it is composed of the most active, committed and (usually) leftist members would be most likely to support his radical policies' (Lloyd 1985: 20).

Before assessing the scale and effects of Scargill's 1981 election victory, it is worth emphasizing the astonishingly unbending nature of his political and industrial objectives, and his unflinching adherence to militant means of achieving them. Indeed, his reflections on the 1972 strike serve as a testament to his lifelong outlook as a trade unionist: 'We were fighting a class war and you don't fight a war with sticks and bladders. You fight a war with the weapons that are going to win it' (1975: 14). As such, he described the famous incident in Birmingham during the 1972 strike when a combined mass picket of miners and engineering workers succeeded in forcing the police to halt 'scab' deliveries of coal from leaving the Saltley Gate Coke Depot: '. . . it was the greatest victory of the working class, certainly in my lifetime . . . Here had been displayed all that's good in the working-class movement . . . Here was living proof that the working class had only to flex its muscles and it could bring governments, employers, society to a total standstill. I know the fear of Birmingham on the part of the ruling class' (1975: 19).

Such a 'world-view' remained consistent throughout the 1970s, 1980s and into the 1990s. In 1987, he lambasted the current of 'new realism' sweeping the labour movement as 'a rejection of . . . class strug-gle' (Scargill 1987: 7). He continued to call for further strike action to halt pit closures long after the 1984–5 defeat,[34] and in 1990 dismissed allegations of financial misdeeds by himself and the NUM's General Secretary during the 1984–5 strike as a 'political campaign to discredit any trade union leader prepared to resist the Tory juggernaut'.[35] Typically defiant, he declared: 'I . . . have an unshakeable belief in my political outlook, which leads me to believe that they will continue to attack . . . Our struggle in 1984–85 was an inspiration. People today still talk about it . . . and the last thing they want is a symbol of that kind . . . [The courts say] that we're guilty of defying the law. We're guilty and proud of it.'[36]

Overall, therefore, the policies and strategies espoused by Scargill represented a major rupture with those pursued by his predecessors at the national level for most of the post-war period: '[c]lass struggle . . . came into the NUM leadership, undiluted, with the assumption of Scar-gill to the presidency in 1982' (Adeney & Lloyd 1988: 33). Did this, however, effect and reflect a radical transformation of the Union membership as a whole?

The Limits of Political Change

Scargill's election victory in December 1981 was emphatic. In an 80 per cent poll, he received 70.3 per cent of the vote, thereby crushing the challenge of his opponents – the Colliery Officials and Staffs

Association (COSA) leader (with 17.3 per cent of the vote), the Notting-hamshire Area President (9.1 per cent) and the Lancashire Area President (3.3 per cent).[37] Thus in a Union renowned for its closely-contested elections, the scale of victory was 'unprecedented' (Campbell & Warner 1985: 3).[38] Indeed, it suggests strongly that Scargill received considerable backing from moderate as well as more militant coalfield areas (Campbell & Warner 1985: 11). Of miners interviewed, all 52 (100 per cent) in Yorkshire had voted for Scargill, 52 of 54 (or 96.3 per cent) in South Wales, and 48 of 53 (or 90.6 per cent) in Derbyshire. Even in Nottinghamshire, 41 of 56 (or 73.2 per cent) had supported him.[39] What, though, was the meaning of this triumph? With some justification, Scargill interpreted his majority as 'an emphatic vote in favour of the policies I pursued during the election campaign' (Adeney & Lloyd 1988: 37). Yet its impact was mixed.

The least ambiguous consequence of Scargill's victory was the subsequent transformation of the *national* leadership of the Union. Undoubtedly aware of the constraints imposed by a right-wing NEC on previous militant leaders (Allen 1981: 118–24), Scargill none the less declared to the 1982 NUM Annual Conference: 'I have no intention of allowing the job to frustrate my intentions . . . I do not underestimate either the constitution of the union, nor any constraint with which I have to contend, but I do not accept that these should be reasons for not being true to one's word' (cited in Lloyd 1985: 19).

In the two years before the 1984–5 strike, Scargill succeeded to a remarkable degree in this mission. A narrow right-wing majority on the NEC gave way to a 'solid left majority through the replacement of Gormley supporters by his own, or, more importantly, by the incorp-oration of the old right into the left camp for most practical purposes' (Adeney & Lloyd 1988: 39). This transformation of the NEC – critical for understanding how it buttressed the Union's national leaders throughout the 1984–5 strike – was undoubtedly facilitated by a deteriorating political and industrial environment in the early 1980s which undercut moderate members of the committee. The Labour Party's defeat in the 1983 General Election removed any hope, for the time being, of a political solution to the industry's problems. Instead, the appointment later in 1983 of Ian MacGregor as NCB Chairman eclipsed the role of more conciliatory NCB managers to whom moderate NEC members had traditionally appealed as a counterweight to the Left faction on the NEC. The veteran leader of the Durham miners reflected: 'I used to be a moderate: but with Thatcher's hard regime, I have been pushed to the left' (Adeney & Lloyd 1988: 43).

In addition, the leftward drift of the NEC was reinforced in January 1984 when Peter Heathfield, the Derbyshire miners' leader, and a candidate of the NUM Left, was elected the Union's General Secretary. With Scargill as President and McGahey as Vice-President, 'the national leadership became the preserve of a triumvirate of the Left, an unprecedented position in the NUM' (Campbell & Warner 1985: 23). By the time of the 1984–5 strike, therefore, Scargill had 'an executive which was no longer at odds with the will of conference. He had achieved what he laid out in his inaugural presidential speech. The public policy of the union was his policy. At leadership and activist level, the union was his' (Adeney & Lloyd 1988: 43).

However, the success of the NUM President in the early 1980s in pushing the Union at the leadership level into a more confrontational stance was not matched at the grass roots-level. For in three national ballots in 1982 and 1983, miners voted down strike action (see Chapter 4). Such results 'showed that Scargill's election majority did not ensure in itself the miners' commitment' (Campbell & Warner 1985: 11). Indeed, research in Nottinghamshire underscored this point: of the forty-three Nottinghamshire miners interviewed who did *not* support the 1984–5 strike, no fewer than twenty-eight (or *65.1 per cent*) had none the less voted for Scargill in 1981.[40] Electoral support for Scargill in 1981 did not, therefore, necessarily translate into support for strike action three years later.

Furthermore, the aforementioned victory of Heathfield in the election for NUM General Secretary in January 1984 was an extraordinarily narrow one. Heathfield, a nationally-known figure within the NUM, only managed to scrape home, with 51.2 per cent of the vote, against his unknown challenger, the Compensation Agent for North Yorkshire (Campbell & Warner 1985: 3–4). As such, the result represented a warning shot from the rank and file across the bows of the Union's national leadership: 'The closeness of the election . . . was not so much a vote of confidence in any of the traditional right-wing leaders in the NUM, as a challenge to the new aggressive stance taken by Scargill's "vanguardist" strategy' (Campbell & Warner 1985: 8).

These developments demonstrate, once again, that the significance of national leadership in the Union has to be assessed with the mood of miners at the local level firmly in mind. In the late 1960s and early 1970s, a rising militancy at the grass-roots level eventually limited the ability of a moderate national leadership to continue participating in a structure of consensus; indeed, such militancy ultimately forced the Union leadership into the confrontations of 1972 and 1974. Now, in the early 1980s, recalcitrance at the grass-roots level limited the impact of a dramatic political transformation at the national level.[41] National leadership mattered – as ever, though, it had to contend with the mood of miners below.

Summary

What's the point . . . in passing [Conference] resolutions you know you're not going to carry at . . . branch [level]. It's no good, is it?"

Interview with NUM Branch Secretary, Shirebrook colliery, Derbyshire,
27/6/90

Either we are going to adhere to Conference decisions, or we're *not* going to adhere to Conference decisions. If we're *not* going to adhere to Conference decisions, there's no point in holding Conferences. (W15)

The reflections of two Branch officials – so often the men in the firing line between the needs of the workforce and the demands of the Union – capture the difficulties that the NUM faced in forging the mining workforce into a collective entity. On the one hand was the recognition that if the Union was to have any strength at all, it had to accommodate the needs of the local workforce. Yet on the other hand, if the Union was to institutionalize a wider sense of identity, then its authority, at that wider level, needed resonance and meaning. This tension was never satisfactorily resolved – the relationship between workforce and institution was a complex one. The Union acted, and was viewed, in many ways and at many levels. Yet the overriding fact that power in the Union was essentially locally based is *key* to understanding both its strengths and weaknesses as an institution. Thus while locally-based power often proved to be a source of resilience and intense loyalty in times of crisis, it also limited the institutionalization of a wider sense of identity, and constrained the power of national leaders.

Therefore, in attempting in the early 1980s to construct a united response to a particularly divisive threat and a hostile Government, the NUM faced a perennial problem. And the Union's national leaders knew it. Surveying in 1984 the forces ranged against the NUM, the newly-elected General Secretary of the Union declared: 'Whether we defeat this rabble or not depends upon our ability to weld the NUM together nationally . . . We must all be part of the "Central Block". That means that we have to convince the miners of Nottingham, Derby, Yorkshire and the rest of the Midlands that the fight for the South Wales, Scottish and North Eastern miners is also their fight' (Campbell & Warner 1985: 17). The deficiencies of the NUM as an institution capable of doing this ensured that such a task was formidable.

Notes

1. An NUM leader commented before the 1974 strike: 'If the strike is called off, the members might walk all over us' (Wolfe 1985: 433).
2. In June 1959, the Scottish Area NUM demobilized an unofficial strike by 25,000 miners at forty-six pits to oppose the closure of Devon colliery (Allen 1981: 68).
3. In 1980 Welsh miners refused to support their Area leadership's call for industrial action to aid striking steelworkers (*FT*, 1/8/84).
4. See Appendix One.
5. Interview, 26/4/90.
6. Interview, 27/6/90.
7. Arthur Scargill observed astutely that any progress for a politically charged Union leadership lay, initially, in its efficiency in dealing with the concrete needs of the workforce (1975: 27).
8. See also Paynter 1972: 110–11.
9. Interview with NUM Branch Secretary, Shirebrook colliery, 27/6/90.

    Similarly, on 15 October 1992 – one day after BC announced it was to be 'mothballed' – Maltby colliery in Yorkshire won a Business in the Community Award. It was praised for organizing special projects that linked local schools with the mine (*The Irish Times*, 16/10/92).
10. Thus the ability of the Lancashire Area NUM to establish an hegemony over the region's unionism and politics was hindered by the fact that coal was rivalled by glass-making and cotton as the region's largest source of employment (Howell 1989: 6).
11. Interview with NUM Branch Secretary, Shirebrook colliery, Derbyshire, 27/6/90.
12. Interview with Financial Secretary, Derbyshire Area NUM, 11/10/89.
13. Interview with General Secretary, Nottinghamshire Area NUM, 10/10/89.
14. Both these foundations of the NUM's power were effectively broken during the 1984–5 strike and its aftermath.
15. Horner was President of the SWMF from 1936 to 1946 and the NUM's national General Secretary from 1946 to 1958 (Allen 1981: 120).
16. Similarly, at the NUM's 1986 Annual Conference, Mick McGahey urged that such lessons of the past be heeded if the NUM was to cope with the divisive aftermath of the 1984–5 strike (Francis 1986: 60).
17. Interview, London, 24/10/89.

18. (Though see Howell (1989: 10–11) who describes the considerable power which the one-time Lancashire Area Secretary wielded over many local union branches.)

19. Notably, apart from Arnot's four-volume official history of the MFGB (Arnot 1979, 1961, 1953 and 1949), Allen's 1981 study, and the NUM's own pictorial centenary book of the MFGB/NUM (1989), the vast literature on mining unionism in Britain is *regional* in focus. See for example: Howell 1989; Taylor 1984; Waller 1983; Francis and Smith 1980; Pitt 1979; Garside 1971; Griffin 1962; Williams 1962.

20. In between NUM conferences, the NEC administered the business and affairs of the Union. Under the NUM's constitution, the NEC performed 'all the duties laid down for it by resolution of Conference, and it shall not at any time act contrary to, or in defiance of, any resolution of conference' (Allen 1981: 264).

21. Certain occupational categories, as well as geographical areas, entertained misgivings about joining the NUM. For example, skilled specialists like the winding enginemen were, throughout the postwar period, particularly recalcitrant members of the national union (Ashworth 1986: 602; Seifert and Urwin 1987: 7). Indeed, in the North Staffordshire coalfield, before and during the 1984–5 strike, the winders took unofficial strike action against the national overtime ban imposed by the NUM, and eventually joined the UDM (Seifert and Urwin 1987: 7; 7–16).

22. *NUM Annual Report and Proceedings, 1977*, p. 418.

23. Ibid., p. 523.

24. Ibid., p. 769.

25. Ibid., p. 776.

26. Ibid., p. 771.

27. Ibid., p. 813.

28. Ibid., p. 814.

29. Ibid., p. 814.

30. *NUM Annual Report and Proceedings, 1978*, p. 2.

31. For fuller accounts, see McCormick 1979; Handy 1981; Ashworth 1986: 289–316, 593–612.

32. Thus long before the advent of Thatcherism, the NCB's headquarters 'became a favourite Tory symbol of Socialist bureaucracy' (Sampson 1962: 539).

33. During the 1970s, Scottish miners' leader Michael McGahey remained a strong contender to succeed Gormley. However, Gormley's calculated decision to remain as NUM President after 1980, when McGahey was 55 (and thereby ineligible under Union rules to stand for national office), scotched the chances of the man he had beaten

in 1971 to now succeed him (Adeney & Lloyd 1988: 52).

34. See, for example, *NUM: Annual Conference, 1988, Presidential Address*, p. 2.
35. *G*, 31/8/90. For an account of this episode, see Milne 1994.
36. *G*, 31/8/90; see also Scargill 1990.
37. Source: *NUM, Annual Report and Proceedings, 1981*, p. 729.
38. Of the ten elections for the two top posts in the MFGB and NUM since 1918, 'only one resulted in less than 50 votes for the runner-up per 100 for the winner' (Campbell & Warner 1985: 2).
39. The Nottinghamshire Area NUM General Secretary remarked that 'Scargill . . . quite openly canvassed on Left policies . . . [and] . . . amazingly enough, received 80 per cent of the Nottinghamshire miners' vote' (Interview, 10/10/89).
40. Of the thirteen Nottinghamshire miners interviewed who *did* strike in 1984–5, all had voted for Scargill in 1981.
41. In this context, a Derbyshire surfaceworker reflected: 'If Scargill had been in Gormley's era, and Gormley in Scargill's era, I'd have classed them on a par – they each came at the wrong time. In Scargill's period, we needed someone with a bit of guile; when Gormley was in office, we needed someone with a bit of punch'(D20).

—4—

The Problems of Strike Action

Introduction

> It was . . . probably the most noble long strike . . . of the traditional kind that
> I've been involved in in my lifetime. Because it wasn't about materialism,
> it wasn't about two pounds extra – it was about men and women fighting
> . . . giving up everything . . . in order that some young man in another street
> in another colliery village could have a job. Now, you can't get more noble
> than that.
>
> Interview with Dennis Skinner MP, 9/11/89

The 1984–5 coal strike was, in many ways, unprecedented. Sustained
for a year, it became the most important battle in the war between the
Thatcher government and the British labour movement. That the strike
was waged over the question of pit closures was, as a Yorkshire Branch
Delegate commented, all the more notable: 'wage militancy naturally
took a big part in industrial actions in the past – it were *unique* to have a
strike over jobs. But . . . once we got into the strike, our membership was
with us, apart from some isolated areas . . . they were definitely with us'
(Y40). For these reasons, the strike was 'a major social and political
event in postwar European history . . . the first major strike of long
duration to be fought over mounting unemployment in Western Europe,
. . . it seemed to defy the notion that unemployment would create fear,
resignation, and industrial timidity among workers' (Kahn 1987: 57).

Furthermore, the strike was all the more remarkable given the historic
difficulties miners had faced in resisting industrial contraction. The issue
of pit closures had always proved to be inherently divisive – as ever, the
closures announced by the NCB in March 1984 directly affected only a
minority of miners. Yet they were eventually joined on strike by a majority of fellow workers who themselves were in no immediate danger.
This is not to ignore the minority of miners who defied the strike; rather,
it is to emphasize that for the miners to wage a strike over this issue, with
the degree of unity they achieved, was significant. The NUM Lodge
Secretary at Oakdale colliery, South Wales, reflected:

... in 1974, of course, we were all on the same wages level and so there was a great deal of unity on the question of wages. And that did make it much easier. But, in an *historical* sense it's easier as well, because *historically* I mean that's what trade unions were formed *for*, was to fight for wages and better working conditions and safety at work and shorter hours – but *all* to do with conditions of work. But fighting on closures is a much more complicated, and *political* issue which . . . means . . . that it was *far* more difficult to achieve unity. And . . . so in a sense, we had a . . . tremendous amount of unity *despite* all the difficulty, you know, and despite not having Nottingham out – there's still a high level of unity in 1984 when you think about it, on such a complicated question as pit closures. (W11)

The Divisiveness of Pit Closures

An Historic Problem

It's always been the most difficult . . . case to fight on . . . the closure . . . programme. And we seen it in this valley in the early [19]60s, when there was a small pit up [the valley], Rhigos. And at that . . . time, in the Rhondda, Merthyr and Aberdare valleys, there were about 22 pits. And we *couldn't* get a collective action to defend Rhigos. Rhigos men were willing to fight for the pit and the only pit, to our credit, was Penrhiwceiber, we come out for a week with Rhigos . . . it was a *very close* community [but] we still couldn't get unanimity then over the way to fight pit closures. As there was a view by the Area [Union] Officials at the time, that it was a hopeless battle, pits had to go, there was too much coal being produced etc., and of course we had oil being pushed into the country at a very cheap price. But the *main* issue is: it's a minority, at the stage they select a pit [for closure], that pit is virtually on its own, it's a minority of men being affected. (W14)

Miners facing the closure of their local pit were nearly always isolated – pit closures in the post-war period were generally implemented one by one. Without a general threat of closure, therefore, the impending demise of a single pit was a rickety foundation on which to build any kind of collective resistance – with only a minority of miners affected at any given time, the parochialism of unaffected mining communities tended to come to the fore (Pitt 1979: 91–2). As a Nottinghamshire miner commented, the unaffected miner found it far easier to relate to an issue like pay rather than that of another pit's fate: '[the] pay issue [is] something tangible that happens that *will* affect everyone, rather than a pit closure that might affect 900 men in an area where 35,000 men work – it's something that's tangible to everyone rather than something that "might happen to us, but then again it might not". It's the known quantity against the unknown factor'(N55).

Of course, a problem up until 1972 for miners at threatened pits was that 'neither the NUM Left nor the Union as a whole managed to formulate an effective strategy on the closure question' (Howell 1989: 61). During the 1960s, the NUM leadership acquiesced in the massive contraction of the industry. Its loyalty to the Labour Government and its belief that resistance to trends in the energy market was futile served to reinforce parochial tendencies at the local level (Howell 1989: 62). However, even after 1972, when the NUM officially declared its oppo-sition to closures 'resulting from reasons other than exhaustion of seams or safety' (Howell 1989: 62), generating resistance remained as difficult as ever. When in 1975, for example, the NCB announced the closure of Langwith colliery in Derbyshire, miners nationally voted against striking to defend the pit (Howell 1989: 62–5). Similarly, when the NCB announced, in 1979, the closure of Teversal colliery in Nottinghamshire, local miners voted heavily against defending the pit (Allen 1981: 303).

Soon afterwards, the fate of Deep Duffryn pit in South Wales became a focus of concern for local miners. Local coal stocks had begun to accumulate during 1978; when, therefore, the NCB announced the impending closure of Deep Duffryn, it 'served as a focus for the under-lying fear about widespread closures' (Allen 1981: 303). The local NUM Lodge organized opposition to the closure throughout South Wales, while at the NUM's 1979 Annual Conference, the South Wales Area Presi-dent's pleas for help in the fight to save the pit received considerable support. What is notable in this case, however, was the absence of a ballot either in South Wales or beyond. Allen, noting the role of spontaneity in overcoming the divisiveness of the closures issue, draws an important conclusion:

> The South Wales officials took no constitutional steps to test the feelings of their members. They realized that the divisive elements generated by pit closures would predominate . . . if miners were asked to assess the closure in a detached, rational manner and in relation to their own interests. A protest about pit closures . . . had to be an emotional thing, generated by sympathy and anger, during which formal decisions were avoided whenever possible. (1981: 304)

The difficulties that the NUM faced in the early 1980s in resisting pit closures were therefore long-standing. However, with the onset of eco-nomic recession, and the election of a Conservative Government hostile to the public sector, 'the world of the seventies collapsed' (Howell 1989: 65). As such, the problems of generating strike action against closures were exacerbated.

Fighting Pit Closures in the 1980s

> I think the election of Margaret Thatcher in 1979 was the signal for a *dram-atic* change in the political climate and context in which any struggle was going to take place in the future . . . in 1972 and 1974, there was *still* at least a *residue* of what was known as consensus politics in Britain. (W11)

The sharp deterioration in the coal industry's fortunes after the election of the Thatcher Government in 1979 is illustrated in Tables 4 and 5. Under the 1974–9 Labour Government, the industry continued to contract, albeit more slowly than in the 1960s. Between 1974 and 1979, though the number of mines in Britain fell by 13.9 per cent from 259 to 223, manpower levels dropped by only 4.2 per cent from 242,500 to 232,400. As ever, some areas suffered more than others. Mine closures and job losses in South Wales greatly exceeded the national average, while in Nottinghamshire, the number of mines remained unchanged and manpower levels actually increased.

Table 4. Contraction of the Coal Industry, 1974–79, on an Area and National Basis

Area	No. of mines 1974	1979	% change	Manpower 1974	1979	% change
YORKS.	66	64	−3.0%	64400	64800	+0.6%
DERBS.	14	11	−21.4%	12800	12100	−5.5%
NOTTS.	27	27	0.0%	32000	33600	+5.0%
S. WALES	48	37	−22.9%	30900	27400	−11.3%
NATIONAL	259	223	−13.9%	242500	232400	−4.2%

Source: NCB, Report and Accounts, for 1973–74 (Statistical Tables, p. 5, Table 3); for *1978–79 (Statistical Tables,* p. 5, Table 3).

In contrast, Table 5 illustrates the sharp contraction of the industry between 1979 and the start of the 1984–5 strike. The number of mines in Britain fell by 23.8 per cent, while 51,000 miners left the industry – a reduction of *22.1 per cent.* Again, some areas suffered more than others. Contraction in South Wales continued to exceed the national average, while in Nottinghamshire it was well below.

Table 5. Contraction of the Coal Industry, 1979–1984, on an Area and National Basis

Area	No. of mines 1978/9	1983/4	% change	Manpower 1978/9	1983/4	% change
YORKS.	64	53	−17.2%	64800	53900	−16.8%
DERBS.	11	9	−18.2%	12100	10400	−14.0%
NOTTS.	27	25	−7.4%	33600	29200	−13.1%
S. WALES	37	28	−24.3%	27400	20100	−26.6%
NATIONAL	223	170	−23.8%	232400	181100	−22.1%

Source: Statistics for 1978–79: as for Table 4; statistics for 1983–84, *NCB, Report and Accounts, 1984/85,* pp. 28–9.

The 1984–5 strike did not emerge out of the blue: 'March 1984 marked an escalation in the conflict rather than its origin; a strike had been inevitable since the first Thatcher Government took office' (Winterton & Winterton 1989: 53). From 1979 onwards, relations in the industry became polarized between a Government-backed NCB management determined to eliminate excess capacity and an NUM leadership increasingly drawn into adopting militant means of defending what remained of the industry. March 1984 did not, therefore, represent the first attempt by the miners to strike against the pit closure programme. Instead, between 1979 and 1984, several skirmishes between the NUM and the NCB illuminated the way in which strike action eventually came about, nationally, in 1984: 'the failed attempts to launch a major confrontation earlier illustrate the problems of mobilization in general and help explain much of the 1984 strike' (Winterton & Winterton 1989: 53).

Strike action against pit closures erupted in South Wales in January 1980. The Welsh coalfield was particularly vulnerable to government efforts to encourage BS to import more coking coal and simultaneously cut its capacity. By the end of 1979, it was estimated that two-thirds of the area's pits were in jeopardy (Allen 1981: 306). A Welsh steel and coal strike was planned for 21 January 1980. On this occasion, however, the NUM National leadership refused to support the Welsh strike while the TUC 'downscaled' it into a Day of Action on 28 January 1980: 'Gormley's right-dominated NEC was able to isolate the conflict in 1980 because only South Wales appeared to be at risk. The NCB did not immediately embark on a closure programme and denied the existence of a hit list, making it more difficult to raise membership consciousness' (Winterton & Winterton 1989: 53–4).

By mid-1980, however, the NUM as a whole was increasingly suspicious of the NCB's intentions (Howell 1989: 65). The Coal Industry Bill, introduced by the Government in 1980, and designed to make the industry 'self-supporting' by 1983–4, demanded a cut in capacity of 4 million tonnes for 1981–2 – 'well above the rate in previous years' (1989: 66). At a meeting of the Coal Industry National Consultative Committee (CINCC) on 10 February 1981, the NCB called for the closure of '20 to 50' pits over the following five years entailing a loss of 20,000 jobs from the industry's current labour force of over 230,000[1] (Winterton & Winterton 1989: 55). The Lancashire Area NUM Secretary recalled: 'Within ten minutes you could have cut the air with a knife. It was the most rumbustious meeting that I have ever attended. There was shouting and threats being bandied about the room' (Howell 1989: 66).

This meeting provoked the most serious confrontation between the NUM, NCB and the Government prior to the 1984–5 strike; the episode is significant for several reasons. First, while the NCB fragmented the timing of the proposed closures, its decision 'brought an unusual degree of unanimity for action from the [NUM] because all areas could have been at risk' (Winterton & Winterton 1989: 55). The NUM President's declaration that 'he was not going to officiate at a requiem mass for the industry'[2] was supported by militant and moderate area leaders alike. For example, in Kent, where the NCB planned to close one of the area's three remaining pits with the loss of 960 jobs,[3] the Area Secretary argued that the 'whole British coalfield must now be brought to a halt'.[4] Even in Nottinghamshire, the 'heartland of pit moderation', the Area President warned that the NCB's proposals, involving the loss of 1,000 jobs in two years, could lead to industrial action.[5]

Second, hastily introduced plans by the government to substantially increase redundancy payments to miners[6] failed to prevent strike action. The NUM Vice-President declared: 'I want to warn those who believe that any revision upwards in redundancy payments will solve the problem with a "buy-out" that they are living in a fools' paradise'.[7] Such views were endorsed locally. At Coegnant colliery in South Wales, the NUM Lodge Secretary commented: 'The government must change its policies. We are not interested in redundancy payment, what we want are jobs'.[8]

Third, the subsequent decision by the NUM to seek a meeting with the Government and to ballot its membership for a strike, was overtaken by action at the local level – 'spontaneous, uncoordinated strikes swept through the coalfields' (Winterton & Winterton 1989: 55). In South Wales, miners at Coegnant colliery struck immediately, ahead of their Area Leadership's decision to sanction a strike. Having recently been praised for opening a new coalface,[9] miners were infuriated by the NCB's abrupt decision to close the colliery. The NUM Lodge Secretary declared: 'Our closure announcement was a bolt from the blue. Many of the men here regard themselves as middle-of-the-road moderates, but they are absolutely incensed at the way the board has done this'.[10] By 16 February, half of the South Wales coalfield was at a standstill (Winterton & Winterton 1989: 55), with the Area's Vice-President promising an imminent shutdown of the entire Welsh coalfield: 'This action will go ahead regardless of anything nationally unless something drastically changes'.[11] Within forty-eight hours, the Kent and Scottish miners were on strike – the latter in protest at the closure of three local pits (Winterton & Winterton 1989: 55). Derbyshire miners, though under no immediate threat themselves, agreed to strike in support of the Welsh miners from 23 February (Allen 1981: 311). In Durham, where four closures had been announced,[12] Union delegates voted to support the NUM's call for a strike, with some demanding immediate unilateral action.[13] Three closures were also announced in Yorkshire, including Park Hill colliery whose workforce immediately went on strike (Winterton & Winterton 1989: 55). Soon, 10,000 Yorkshire miners were on strike ahead of their Area Council's formal endorsement: 'Responses were moving ahead of the constitutional timetable . . . picketing was beginning to spread; the prospects for a near-complete shutdown before any national ballot became clear' (Howell 1989: 67).

At this stage, the government conceded. The Energy Secretary pledged fidelity to the 1974 Plan for Coal, agreed to relax financial constraints on the NCB and to reduce imports of coking coal. The NCB, meanwhile, withdrew the closure proposals: 'Superficially it could seem like 1972 and 1974 all over again; the Miners had flexed their muscles, even this tough government had climbed down – and at a time when trade union successes were sparse' (Howell 1989: 67).

Yet the outcome of this confrontation merely underscored the continuing problems faced by the NUM in sustaining a coherent response to pit closures. Miners were divided by the government's turnaround, with some returning to work immediately and others remaining on strike. The Union's NEC voted to return to work at a time when the strike was diminishing in some areas and solidifying in others. In particular, Area leaders from South Wales, Kent, Scotland and Yorkshire remained sceptical about what the NUM had actually achieved.[14] The latter, for example, argued that the 'strike must continue until there are firm assurances on the table'.[15] In the event, the authority of the NEC's call for a return to work prevailed and the dissident coalfields agreed to end the strike.[16] Several Area leaders, however, retained serious misgivings. For example, the Kent Area leader declared: 'We are dealing with cunning people and, for the present, the Kent Miners have a guarded mistrust of the new situation'.[17] He warned the next day that 'once the dust has settled, they will pick us off one by one'.[18]

Such doubts proved to be well founded. By October 1981, half of the national closure programme had been implemented, and by June 1982, fifteen of the twenty-three named pits from February 1981 had been closed through the local Review Procedure: '. . . in most cases the NCB was able to obtain branch agreement after softening the workforce with redundancy terms' (Winterton & Winterton 1989: 56). The rationale of the NCB's decision, after the 1981 confrontation, to return to its policy of contraction by stealth was emphasized by its Western Area Director: 'I preferred the "salami" technique when dealing with economic and social problems – as a slice at a time improves the digestion' (Howell 1989: 68). In reality, therefore, 'February 1981 settled nothing for the NUM' (Howell 1989: 68). Contraction of the industry continued, albeit in a more gradual manner. As such, the episode came to be seen as something of a missed opportunity for the NUM in the struggle over pit closures: 'In retrospect it could seem the great lost opportunity for the Union to defend jobs' (Howell 1989: 68; see also Winterton & Winterton 1989: 55). The episode is therefore of great significance.

First, the confrontation demonstrated how the Government, through a timely concession, could demobilize widespread industrial action. This is not to say that the Government's retreat was a phoney one. The settlement damaged its plans for public spending cuts,[19] and was criticized by its supporters throughout British industry[20] and by the press which labelled it a major 'U-turn'.[21] Yet for all the short-term hysteria, the

Government, by ensuring that the NCB reverted to the more traditional manner of closing pits one by one, continued to achieve its objectives in the wake of what had appeared to be a severe setback. The decision of the Government to bide its time meant – as a Welsh miner reflected ruefully – that it remained a difficult opponent:

> We had action in 1981 . . . over pit closures, which was spontaneous . . . we had the coalfield out . . . within a short space of time, Thatcher done a U-turn . . . And I think that was perhaps the one vital mistake we made in '81, that we went back to work then on promises – they were verbal promises, there was nothing written on paper . . . and even if you get it on paper, it's no assurance that they're going to carry out these promises or those agreements . . . but when we just had them verbally, they just ignored them and within a matter of months . . . it was totally ignored. (W14)

Second, the 1981 confrontation said much about relations between local, area and national levels of the NUM in a time of crisis. The response of the NUM to the NCB's announcement was shaped, in the first instance, by local-level action. The decision of the Coegnant miners in South Wales to strike created the possibilities for widespread industrial action: 'Perhaps the men of Coegnant did not realize it when they voted to strike over the Coal Board's plan to shut their pit, but they have stirred uneasy memories of the early Seventies'.[22] Their action quickly engulfed the entire South Wales coalfield; this, in turn, propelled other Area leaderships into a position of defiance including those not directly affected by the closures. The Northumberland miners' leader, for example, declared: 'If it's them today it's us tomorrow'.[23] Grass-roots action in 1981 therefore overcame, to a large degree, the parochialism which had traditionally hampered the miners' efforts to resist closures. A miner from Oakdale colliery, South Wales, reflected: '*Prior* to [1984], the strike weapon was hardly used *at all* . . . on closures . . . with the exception of . . . 1981, when they did really start to build up a momentum . . . a growing, sort of, understanding that we were heading for a *massive* round of pit closures'(W11). However, as the crisis developed, the impact of leadership at the national level came to the fore. Initially, this took the form of attempting to restrain 'unofficial' action underway in several areas ahead of the national leadership's plans for a ballot of the entire workforce. Thus as South Wales pickets began to lobby miners throughout the British coalfield, the NUM President urged them to 'hold their fire'.[24] With a 55 per cent ballot majority required under union rules to sanction a national strike, he argued 'There are many people in the country today, even members of this union, who have the ability to go to law to make sure the union does not take action if it is against the rules'.[25] Once the Government had made its concessions, moreover, the NUM's national leadership was successful in demobilizing the efforts of dissident coalfields to prolong the strike. The NUM President expressed his hope that 'no area would take the decision to carry on with industrial action. I hope that they will accept the authority of the national executive'.[26]

The pattern of events in 1981 therefore epitomized the class politics of the miners – namely, the robust nature of action and initiative at the local level, combined with an uneasiness and lack of co-ordination between local, area and national levels of the Union. Additionally, however, the role of *grass-roots action* in a situation of growing crisis anticipated the manner in which the 1984–5 strike emerged. As such, the NUM's wry reflections on the 1981 confrontation are noteworthy: 'The miners' response was swift. Within days, over half the British coalfield was on strike, including areas such as Nottingham and the Midlands, traditionally known as "moderate". It is interesting to note that this strike action took place without a ballot or even a conference decision' (NUM 1989: 102).

The end of 1981 saw Arthur Scargill elected NUM President and, consequently, the adoption by the Union of a far more aggressive stance on pit closures. Yet this in and of itself could not overcome the threat posed by the Government and NCB as they reverted to more traditionally divisive methods of implementing closures. Instead, the problems faced by miners at threatened pits were exacerbated: 'the package of closures which had been collectively rejected was being processed at local levels in a fragmented way through the Review Procedure without the focus of publicity on it' (Allen 1981: 315). Soon after the confrontation of February 1981, Lancashire miners, for example, accepted the first pit closure in their Area for a decade (Howell 1989: 78–9). Undoubtedly, in the absence of a general threat, improved redundancy terms and/ or transfer payments proved attractive to many miners thereby facilitating the NCB's efforts to reduce manpower levels while simultaneously sapping the NUM's ability to build a unified response to continuing industrial contraction: 'The construction of any collective solidarity ran against a mass of individuals each pursuing their private benefits' (Howell 1989: 79).

The transformation of the NUM's national leadership from 1981 onwards must therefore be placed in a context of continuing divisions on the issue of pit closures within the coalfield as a whole. Many miners 'believed they had been outwitted and they could do little about it because the mood for unified action which had characterized the [1981] strike had been dissipated. Such moods are not easily recreated' (Allen 1981: 315). Indeed, this was demonstrated by the subsequent repeated failure of the NUM leadership, in three successive national ballots, to win majority support for strike action. In January 1982, only 45 per cent of miners opposed the NCB's 1981 pay offer: 'Wage militancy was clearly no substitute for raising consciousness over pit closures' (Winterton & Winterton 1989: 56). Instead, this episode demonstrated, once again, the power of a national leader to demobilize possible industrial action – the day before the ballot, outgoing NUM President Joe Gormley urged miners, in the pages of the *Daily Express*, to accept the pay award and avoid a strike (Winterton & Winterton).

During 1982, two pit closures – Snowdown in Kent and Kinneil in Scotland – were contested but resistance remained local. When the NUM subsequently met with the NCB in August 1982 to discuss the closure of Snowdown, the NBC's Deputy Chairman referred to 'technological unemployment' and the need to abandon inefficient pits (Winterton & Winterton 1989: 56). At this stage, 'hoping to combine the support for action over closures in the militant areas with the wage militancy assumed to exist in the moderate areas', the NEC imposed an overtime ban from 11 October 1982 and agreed to link the issues of pay and pit closures in a ballot for strike action to be held at the end of October 1982 (Winterton & Winterton 1989: 56–7). However, only 39 per cent of miners, nationally, voted to strike, causing the NUM Vice-President to declare: 'The lesson of the miners' campaign is to recognize that the Union must be a campaigning, crusading union, not only in periods of wage negotiations or fighting in the conditions decided by the Coal Board. The Union must campaign every day in educating our members about the situation at the base level, namely at the pits' (Winterton & Winterton 1989: 57).

After the October 1982 ballot result, the overtime ban was terminated by the NUM and the NCB formally announced the closure of the troubled Kinneil colliery. Miners at the pit immediately struck and deployed pickets throughout the Scottish coalfield. However, there were angry scenes at some pits, and the NUM's Area Executive, anxious to avoid local divisions and isolation from the rest of the NUM, recommended acceptance of the closure. This provoked an unofficial, and ultimately unsuccessful, strike by the Kinneil miners during Christmas of 1982.

In February 1983, strike action erupted again in South Wales when the NCB announced the closure of Blaengwrach and Ty Mawr/Lewis Merthyr collieries. Twenty-eight miners at the latter pit staged an immediate stay-down strike – much to the annoyance, initially, of the Union's Area leadership (Adeney & Lloyd 1988: 82). Seven neighbouring pits joined the strike and on 23 February 1983, a delegate conference of the South Wales Area NUM decided to call a strike ballot. By the end of the month, the entire South Wales coalfield was at a standstill as Welsh miners began to lobby other coalfields. On 28 February the Yorkshire Area Council instructed local miners to strike from 6 March (Winterton & Winterton 1989: 58–9). On 1 March, the Lancashire Area Executive met with Welsh miners and agreed to ballot its membership with a recommendation to strike. By early March, three pits in North Derbyshire and one pit in Kent had stopped work, while Scottish miners had agreed to strike from 6 March. Area ballots with recommendations to strike were planned in Northumberland, Durham and Nottinghamshire (Howell 1989: 86). Once again, grass-roots action at a single pit had generated the possibility for widespread industrial action.

Against this background, the NEC met on 3 March and, at the President's urging, considered officially sanctioning the strike already in progress in South Wales, but instead decided to hold a national ballot – 'a decision for which the right-wing caucus claimed responsibility' (Winterton & Winterton 1989: 58–9). This ballot was viewed by many within the NUM as a 'make-or-break' opportunity for the union in its campaign against pit closures. The Lancashire miners' leader, for example, returned to his coalfield and declared: 'We are at the brink . . . this is the last chance . . . it could be Lancashire's turn next' (Howell 1989: 86). However, widespread pessimism concerning the likely outcome of a ballot for strike action over the closure of a single Welsh pit involving no compulsory redundancies proved well-founded as miners, nationally, subsequently voted by 61 per cent to 39 per cent against defending the stricken collieries in South Wales. As such, the result represented a watershed in the Union's efforts to resist the closure programme. In particular, it reinforced assumptions, on the part of miners in threatened areas, and the NUM's beleaguered national leadership, that miners in secure positions would not strike over an issue which did not affect them directly. In these circumstances, the very credibility of the Union was threatened (Howell 1989: 87).

The period of the first Thatcher Government (1979–83) was therefore a demoralizing and sobering one for those in the NUM committed to resisting the contraction of the coal industry. Miners in various coalfields had, on occasion, been willing to fight; such 'false starts' (Winterton & Winterton 1989: 53), however, merely underscored the chronic difficulty faced by the NUM in building a united front on the issue. In this context, the fiasco of March 1983 was 'the sombre clarification of a longstanding problem. The NUM had never succeeded in developing an effective national resistance to pit closures . . . in 1983, with economic insecurity all pervasive and a mounting toll of trade union failures against the Thatcher Government, effective resistance seemed even more problematic" (Howell 1989: 87). It is therefore against this background that the solidarity achieved in the 1984–5 strike should be judged.

Divisions Overcome: The Mobilization of Strike Action in 1984

The Collapse of Consensus 1983–4

'Sooner or later our members will have to stand and fight.'
Comment by NUM National President Arthur Scargill *(The Times*, 6/6/83)

Within months of the March 1983 ballot failure, the NUM's predicament deteriorated still further. The re-election of the Thatcher Government in June 1983 destroyed the possibility of an alternative strategy of expansion for the coal industry to which the Labour Party had committed itself during the election campaign (Winterton & Winterton 1989: 59). Instead, the period between June 1983 and March 1984 saw relations between the NCB and the NUM enter a deepening crisis.

Within days of the election, the NCB announced its intention to shed approximately 65,000 jobs over the next five years.[27] In response, delegates at the NUM's 1983 Annual Conference supported unanimously the NEC's emergency motion proposing an intensive campaign in the coalfields to be followed by a ballot on strike action 'at a time deemed most appropriate'.[28] However, there was considerable unease regarding the Union's ability to unify the workforce in the face of this latest threat. The North Derbyshire miners' leader urged delegates to 'stop basking in the glory of 1972 and 1974. It's a completely different ball game.' The NUM Vice-President, meanwhile, acknowledged that the Union had failed 'to win the hearts and minds of its members . . . There is a credibility gap, but we can close that gap by embarking on a campaign which springs from the rank and file'.[29]

However, time was fast running out for the NUM's national leadership. Shortly after the Union's conference, three more pits were closed resulting in the loss of 4,000 jobs. A month later, the NCB threatened to close Coedely coke works and Wyndham Western colliery (both in South Wales) and then announced the closure of Cardowan colliery in Scotland and Brynlliw in South Wales (Winterton & Winterton 1989: 60). The latter two closures provoked particular anger amongst local miners. At Brynlliw, miners accused the NCB of reneging on agreed investment at the pit and of ignoring the findings of a joint union-management study which had suggested ways of extending the life of the pit by fifteen years. The Area Vice-President declared that the 'credibility of the system, under which the difficulties of pits were reviewed jointly, was at risk by the NCB's attitude'.[30] Meanwhile, the NCB's decision to transfer 1,080 miners from the doomed Cardowan pit provoked strikes at neighbouring Scottish collieries destined to take on the displaced miners. Production was suspended at Polmaise colliery when local miners formed picket lines and urged Cardowan miners to return to their own pit.[31] All 1,350 miners at Polkemmet colliery struck after learning that up to 300 men would be offered voluntary early retirement pay-offs to make way for miners transferred from Cardowan. NUM Branch officials claimed that management had not consulted them on the retirement deals and possible transfers.[32] As such, the Scottish miners' leader accused the NCB's Area director of 'riding roughshod over consultative procedures with the miners . . . Never in my 40 years as an activist have I come across such tactics. He is not only breaking every rule in the book, but running over people as well. He has locked out miners from their pits. . . he is attempting to break the miners' unity. But he is not an independent agent. He is acting under orders from the NCB bosses in London and they are under orders from No. 10 [Downing Street]'.[33]

As such, incidents at the local level were beginning to reflect the wider breakdown of the largely consensual relationship between the NCB and the NUM that had prevailed for most of the post-war period. In July 1983, the NUM decided for the first time not to invite the NCB Chairman to its Annual Conference.[34] In September 1983, the Government appointed as the new NCB Chairman Ian MacGregor – 'an outsider not just to the coal industry but to post-war British culture' (Adeney & Lloyd 1988: 42). He had long since gained notoriety amongst American miners as a union-buster (1988: 55). More recently, he had been dubbed 'Mac the Knife' by British steelworkers for his role, as Chairman of British Steel (BS), in cutting the workforce from 150,000 to 85,000 (1988: 61). His appointment as NCB Chairman therefore completed the process by which coal's position as the 'paradigm case' of the post-war consensus was being eroded in the early 1980s. His detestation of the NCB's management was exceeded only by that which he reserved for the NUM itself. As such, a Welsh miner reflected: 'When MacGregor was appointed, it was only a matter of time before a strike was going to happen. We all knew that'(W38).

Undoubtedly, the appointment of MacGregor heralded a new management offensive on the issues of discipline, productivity, excess capacity and manpower levels. On 20 September 1983, MacGregor warned miners at Bilston Glen colliery in Scotland: 'Perform and you have a future; don't and you have no future, it's as simple as that' (Winterton & Winterton 1989: 60). Ten days later, he rebuffed the NUM's demand for a substantial pay increase by making a 'first and final' offer of 5.2 per cent and announcing that not only would there be no slowing down of the NCB's closure programme but that a further five pits (including two in Nottinghamshire) would be added to it. On 21 October 1983, a Special Delegate Conference of the NUM voted unanimously to impose an overtime ban in the industry, effective from the end of the month, as a means of prosecuting the pay claim and resisting further pit closures (People of Thurcroft 1986: 43). These events highlighted 'the changing temper of the industry' (Adeney & Lloyd 1988: 68) as the NCB, attempting to reduce capacity and inefficiency, clashed with miners determined to guard local custom and practice. MacGregor himself was often greeted by miners with fear and hostility. In November 1983, he was pelted with flour-bombs while visiting Brodsworth colliery in Yorkshire; in February 1984, at Ellington colliery in Northumberland, he was knocked to the ground by local miners protesting job cuts at a neighbouring colliery (Adeney & Lloyd 1988:

68). One demonstrator yelled: 'We will hear what he has to say, then we will tear his head off' (Bone *et al.* (eds) 1991: 53).

Prior to the imposition of the national overtime ban, conflict over pit closures and the increasingly imperious management style of the NCB tended to remain localized. Fourteen thousand miners from the Barnsley area of the Yorkshire coalfield went on strike in late September 1983 in protest at the dismissal of a local miner for an alleged disciplinary offence. A week-long strike took place at Westoe colliery in Durham to oppose altered shift times, while 560 miners at Cronton colliery in Lancashire struck for the day when the closure of their pit was announced on 10 October 1983. Miners at Monktonhall colliery in Scotland, on strike for a month against the closure of their pit, were supported by a one-day strike throughout the coalfield (Winterton & Winterton 1989: 60–1).

It was, however, the overtime ban imposed by the NUM's national leadership from the end of October 1983 that was to lay the basis for more widespread resistance to pit closures. An overtime ban had been an important prelude to the national strike of 1974, not least for the way it 'committed the membership to further action in order to recoup the necessary investment of lost earnings, and prepared miners for the forthcoming deprivation' (Winterton & Winterton 1989: 62–3). Similarly, in 1983, the NUM expected the overtime ban to reduce coal stocks sufficiently to make a strike effective, though in the light of recent reversals, it was reluctant to conduct another national ballot (Winterton & Winterton 1989: 62–3). Though by no means universally popular, the overtime ban was adhered to by the NUM membership as a form of 'cut-price' industrial action, while 'the *de facto* 3- or 4-day working week stimulated demands for reduced hours and demonstrated the inadequacy of the basic wage' (Winterton & Winterton 1989: 63). As such, 'the ban held. Miners wanted to take *some* action . . . even if a majority weren't prepared to strike yet. The traditions of absenteeism and local disputes meant that miners were used to, and prepared to tolerate, the loss of wages involved' (Callinicos & Simons 1985: 45).

In response, NCB managers resorted to provocation to break the ban. At Westoe colliery, 200 overmen struck when managers took over safety checks. Miners at Kellingley colliery in Yorkshire were locked out for a week after refusing to allow rope-capping at the weekend. At Wearmouth colliery, miners threatened to strike when managers argued that rope-capping would mean a three-day week (Winterton & Winterton 1989: 63–4). Meanwhile, in January 1984, miners at Polmaise colliery went on strike upon hearing that their pit – labelled in 1982 the 'success story of the Scottish coalfield' – was to close (Callinicos & Simons 1985: 46).

By early 1984, therefore, the industry was in ferment. The NCB appeared determined to break the overtime ban while the NUM received demands from some miners to end it and from others to transform it into a full-scale strike (Winterton & Winterton 1989: 63). It is in this situation of mounting crisis that grass-roots action was to form the foundations for widespread resistance to further closures.

Grass-roots Action and the Mobilization of the 1984–5 Strike

Alongside the localized disputes taking place throughout the British coalfield, the Yorkshire Area became the site in February 1984 of several clashes between Union and management arising from the national overtime ban. On 20 February, managers at Manvers Main colliery attempted to introduce uniform 'snap times' (meal times) as a means of extending working hours. In doing so, they circumvented the usual conciliation procedures and in addition, changed the time of shaft inspections unilaterally and tried to introduce a four-shift system without an agreement (People of Thurcroft 1986: 43; Winterton & Winterton 1989: 65). The miners at Manvers took immediate strike action and asked the NUM Yorkshire Area Council to sanction an Area-wide strike. Though this was rejected, 10,000 of South Yorkshire's 14,000 miners were none the less on strike by 5 March over the dispute at Manvers colliery.[35]

However, it was the announcement on 1 March that another South Yorkshire pit – Cortonwood – was to close that 'provided a focus for the separate strands which constituted the roots of the [1984–5] strike' (Winterton & Winterton 1989: 66). Two aspects of the closure ensured that it became the basis for more widespread strike action throughout the British coalfield. First, as Area leaders observed, Cortonwood represented the first purely 'economic' closure which the NCB had announced in Yorkshire (People of Thurcroft 1986: 44). The NCB's Area Director argued that the pit was to be closed because its output matched the cuts in capacity which he was under instructions to implement in South Yorkshire for the 1984–5 financial year, and because there was 'no market' for its high-quality coking coal.[36] Cortonwood's miners, owever, were astonished. The NCB had recently invested over one million pounds in the pit and had guaranteed the pit a further five years' working life. Moreover, when nearby Elsecar colliery had closed only a few weeks earlier, displaced miners had been transferred to Cortonwood (Winterton & Winterton 1989: 67). Thus the NUM Branch Delegate at the pit declared: 'The reaction is one of total, stunned shock for the branch and the men concerned. This has come out of the blue. We shall be recommending total strike action'.[37] Moreover, his argument that, effectively, *no* pit in Yorkshire was safe undoubtedly resonated with miners at other collieries. A Thurcroft miner reflected: 'The Cortonwood closure – with massive reserves – came out of the blue. If they could do it with them they could do it with any pit – this is the crux of the matter. People in their late 50s and early 60s had been given assurances, a guarantee of five to seven years at Cortonwood. If they could get away with Cortonwood, they could get away with any closure'(Y23).

Second, the *manner* in which the closure was announced was in breach of the procedure agreed by the NCB and the NUM. The decision was conveyed to the Union by the NCB at a regularly scheduled review meeting. According to procedure, however, it should have made Cortonwood the subject of a reconvened review meeting thereby enabling the NUM to investigate the pit and to organize the attendance of Cortonwood's Branch officials. Instead, it abruptly announced its decision to close the pit. The Yorkshire Area NUM President declared: 'We have been given four weeks' notice of closure of the pit. It is diabolical'.[38] The way in which this closure was announced was therefore very much in keeping with the manner in which closures had recently been implemented in the more threatened peripheral coalfields. As such, miners in these areas viewed the NCB's decision to close Cortonwood not simply as economically dubious but as an ominous breach of trust. At Penallta colliery, South Wales, the NUM Lodge Secretary commented:

> There was . . . always an agreement, see, before . . . the 1984 strike, that pits would be closed in consultation with the *Union*. Now Cortonwood, which was . . . the straw that broke the camel's back . . . now just a month or six weeks prior to . . . the closure . . . being announced, they had been told that they had at least five years' work there. So . . . it was clear that they were just going to unilaterally close pits as and when they saw fit. And they didn't give a damn about the workforce, or what was going to happen to the workforce, or any consultation *with* the workforce, at all. (W7)

Overall, therefore, the Cortonwood closure, which had taken place 'before exhaustion, without agreement and in breach of procedure, contained the essential ingredients to overcome colliery parochialism and trigger a general stoppage' (Winterton & Winterton 1989: 67). To a very remarkable degree, the closure had precisely these effects, especially as it was complemented by the disputes, arising from the overtime ban, that were underway at other collieries. The Cortonwood miners themselves reacted swiftly to the closure decision. At a rowdy Branch meeting on 4 March, over 500 miners voted unanimously to fight the closure, picket other collieries in South Yorkshire and lobby the NUM's Area leadership to sanction an Area-wide strike. By the time the Yorkshire Area Council of the NUM met on 5 March, fourteen of the fifteen pits in South Yorkshire were at a standstill, while elsewhere in Yorkshire, strikes either continued, or commenced, at Goldthorpe (over bonus earnings), Yorkshire Main (over unsafe face conditions) and Askern (over management proposals to reduce the number of chock fitters at the pit). The Cortonwood closure, however, dominated the proceedings of the Area Council, and resulted in a vote to instruct all Branches in the Area to strike from the last shift on 9 March. In addition, national approval for the Yorkshire strike would be sought, under Rule 41, on 8 March. Between 5 and 9 March, four more collieries joined the strike (Winterton & Winterton 1989: 67). Once the strike became official in Yorkshire on 9 March 1984, support for it was generally very high (though levels of compliance varied between the four panel areas of the coalfield[39]). Indeed, Yorkshire soon emerged as one of the most solid coalfields in the 1984–5 strike.

Events in Yorkshire, however, were soon overtaken by a national confrontation between the NCB and the NUM. Having lost 600 million pounds, and made 20,000 miners redundant during the 1983–4 financial year, the NCB now sought to cut the production budget for 1984–5 by 8.2 million tonnes, involving the loss of a further 20,000 jobs.[40] In response, the Union's NEC voted (21 to 3) to endorse, under Rule 41, the strikes already underway in Yorkshire and Scotland, and to extend approval to any other coalfield area joining the strike. This decision – to spread the strike on a 'rolling' basis rather than through the mechanism of a national ballot – was underscored by the Union's National Vice-President: 'We are not dealing with niceties here. We shall not be constitutionalized out of a defence of our jobs. Area by Area will decide, and in my opinion it will have a domino effect' (Howell 1989: 101). Levels of compliance with this 'domino' strategy were, at best, uneven. The majority of Nottinghamshire's 32,000 miners quickly emerged as the most determined opponents of strike action, though they were not alone. The much smaller coalfields of South Derbyshire (with a membership of 3,000) and Leicestershire (2,500) also became bastions of opposition to the strike. Indeed, not one of the eight coalfield areas that held Area Ballots in early March 1984 recorded sufficiently high majorities to sanction the strike, though Derbyshire and Northumberland came close. Even more damaging, potentially, to the prospects of a successful national strike was the result of individual pithead ballots in South Wales where, to the dismay of local NUM leaders, only ten of the Area's twenty-eight Lodges voted to strike. Yet despite these shaky beginnings, the initial recalcitrance seen across the British coalfield in early March 1984 was, in the course of a few weeks, largely overcome. By April 1984, 80 per cent of miners, nationally, were on strike. An assessment of how this was achieved is essential to understanding how the strike was eventually sustained for an entire year.

First, the role of rank-and-file miners in seizing the initiative and attempting to spread the strike by picketing should be underscored. This was particularly true of the Yorkshire coalfield where, despite the pleas of Area leaders, pickets streamed into Lancashire and Nottinghamshire. A miner at Hatfield Main colliery reflected:

Phone calls were made and we decided to go out [picketing] on the Monday before the [Yorkshire Area] executive meeting on the Tuesday to make them think – to make them *know* – how the lads felt. And we honestly believed – well I do – that we swung the [Yorkshire Area Executive] to our way of thinking. Before we were picketing our [Branch] secretary said, 'You can't do this, you can't do that' – you know – and I mean, [the Area leadership] said, 'You can't do it.' But we did. We went out and we closed two pits in one night. (Samuel *et al.* (eds) 1986: 70)

A faceworker from Armthorpe colliery spoke similarly:

This branch first started going into Nottingham picketing and we got a roasting there. We went to [Harworth colliery] first and [the Yorkshire Area NUM President] got on phone and told us to come out because Nottingham were having a vote. He said leave it up to vote and see what happens. And we said no chance – if we're out, they're out. It's their jobs and all, sort of thing. So we went picketing . . . And we all got together and had a mass picket at [Harworth] and it shut pit down. (Samuel *et al.* (eds) 1986: 71)

The role of rank-and-file miners was acknowledged by an Area leader:

To be honest, we thought there'd be a revolt in Yorkshire. So we held the pickets back in case of wanting to get Yorkshire out. Because the position always was to get your own coalfield out before you go and see anybody else. But Armthorpe being like it was, and everybody was on hooks, Armthorpe just said 'Come on, we're going', so half the bleeding pickets went with them. Didn't wait for us. So when we did have the meeting, it was already an accomplished fact – either you deploy the pickets or the pickets will deploy themselves. (cited in Samuel *et al.* (eds) 1986: 70)

Such a pattern was repeated later in South Wales, where rank-and-file miners travelled to Nottinghamshire despite the misgivings of some local NUM leaders. The Lodge Secretary at Oakdale colliery recalled:

I mean South Wales [miners] went up there within about four weeks . . . six weeks . . . with a leaflet which was absolutely *appalling*. They called [the Nottinghamshire miners] and quoted from Jack London about blacklegs being lower than snakes . . . and I 'phoned up [the South Wales Area President] on the night the buses went up and said for Christ sake . . . stop those buses going up, or at least stop the miners giving out those leaflets – you imagine what the effect was going to have on the Nottingham families and . . . the miners' children reading what they were calling their fathers, husbands, and brothers. I said: is that the way to win them . . . over? Because lumping them all as 'scabs', and 'traitors', and all that – but of course, [the Area President] said, they're on the buses now, I can't stop them, and they went up. (W11)

The success enjoyed by miners in picketing Areas of the coalfield other than their own was mixed. Yorkshire and South Wales pickets undoubtedly enjoyed some early successes in the Nottinghamshire coalfield. A faceworker from Maltby colliery claimed that during the first week of the strike, Yorkshire pickets received '95 per cent support' from miners at Pye Hill colliery, while at Annesley, 'we had them out'(Y29). Such successes proved short-lived, however, in the face of a rapidly growing police presence in the Nottinghamshire coalfield.[41] In Lancashire, miners at Bold colliery respected a picket line formed by Yorkshiremen, while at Cronton colliery, four Yorkshire pickets turned back 90 per cent of the Branch membership (Howell 1989: 107). Elsewhere, Lancashire miners were less enthusiastic. At Parkside, the Branch Secretary declared that the Yorkshiremen should leave the Area, though he none the less acknowledged the respect shown by his membership for their picket line (Howell 1989: 109). At Agecroft colliery, however, the local workforce was bitterly critical of the allegedly violent behaviour of Yorkshire pickets (Howell 1989: 109).

Perhaps reflecting the miners' localized world, however, picketing by miners *within* their own coalfields proved far more effective. In Scotland, for example, three of the Area's ten pits worked on the first day of the strike, yet within 48 hours all had been picketed out. In Durham, local picketing ensured that 'the strike soon secured firm and widespread backing' (Howell 1989: 105). The strike in Yorkshire was also solidified by the impact of local pickets in the northern and southern edges of the coalfield (Howell 1989: 105; Winterton & Winterton 1989: 69). Nowhere, though, did the picket line play a more decisive role in overcoming initial opposition to the strike than in South Wales.

Given the vulnerability and traditional militancy of the South Wales coalfield, the opposition to strike action recorded at eighteen of the Area's twenty-eight NUM Lodges was at first glance perplexing, as well as being potentially lethal to the success of a national strike. Undoubtedly, considerable resentment remained in South Wales at the lack of support given by miners, nationally, to the Area's previous efforts to resist pit closures – particularly the March 1983 episode when miners nationally had failed to defend the threatened Ty Mawr/Lewis Merthyr pit:

> I voted 'No' at the start of the strike . . . because 12 month previous, we were on strike, over Ty Mawr/Lewis Merthyr, and . . . we sent the delegates all over the coalfield, and the response we had was virtually nil. So . . . come '84, when it was happening in the Yorkshire coalfield, that was still in the back of my mind, and then I thought – well, they didn't want to know us, so, why should we support them? (W8)[42]

After the pithead ballot, however, miners from the ten pits that had voted to strike travelled around the area and, within twenty-four hours, set up picket lines at those that had voted against. Such actions were not always welcomed. Sharp criticism came from miners at Cynheidre colliery where a faceworker described how the men were 'seething with anger'.[43] Even at the militant Penrhiwceiber colliery, a miner described how 'I have been appalled and disgusted with the behaviour of a minority of men who call themselves miners . . . the minority want to rule the majority'.[44] Certainly, such picketing violated the area's rules, yet within a week the entire South Wales coalfield was on strike. The NUM Lodge Secretary at Penallta colliery recalled:

> . . . more pits voted *against* strike action, according to Area rule, than voted for. Now, Penallta, we didn't have our general meeting till the Sunday. And a lot of men in the meeting were saying a majority of the pits had voted against strike action. I said, well, I'm not concerned about the majority of pits, I'm concerned about Penallta, and I got the vote for strike action. Now, I said we'd have a follow-up meeting on the Monday night, to decide what's happening, but I didn't expect *anybody* to work on the Monday . . . nobody worked. Now [when] I called the general meeting for the Monday night, I had a letter off the Area Executive calling on *all* members to support those that were on strike. So they're asking us to support ourselves! So we *couldn't* vote to go back to work . . . although [eighteen pits] had voted for going back to work . . . so therefore they broke the rule . . . or *twisted* the rules. And . . . we picketed then and the majority of our pits came out, and we stayed solid . . . There's a *bigger* rule – trade union solidarity. (W9)

The sanctity of the picket line therefore proved critical in overcoming initial recalcitrance within the Area. Thus a miner at Taff Merthyr colliery reflected:

> I would have preferred a ballot and that's why Taff Merthyr . . . continued working for three days because . . . the feeling was . . . in my own pit, that we wanted a national ballot . . . but . . . because of the loyalty that we have always shown to one another in Wales . . . we recognised that if there was one picket outside a gate . . . that our loyalty to that person . . . whether right or wrong . . . we would never cross a picket line. Which we didn't, you know. (W1)

It is important to note, moreover, that from such initial misgivings emerged an intense loyalty to the national strike that was to remain unsurpassed by any other Area in the British coalfield. This, as local NUM leaders noted, said much about the history and culture of the mining communities in South Wales. The Lodge Secretary at Tower colliery commented that 'the tradition of South Wales [has] always been: "never, ever cross a picket line". I knew, once picket lines were out . . . that

Welsh miners would ever cross a picket line . . . and that's how [the strike] rapidly grew'.[45] The Area President concurred:

> I had no doubts, even from the first reaction of . . . reluctance – understandable reluctance, really . . . that the element of loyalty within South Wales to the Union . . . was still very great and . . . that, despite this *initial* reluctance, that in a very short time, everybody would certainly be there behind us. *That* you must put down to our heritage, to tradition, to custom – you can't explain it – other than to say it goes back throughout our history.[46]

The successful picketing of otherwise unenthusiastic pits therefore laid one of the foundations for the 1984–5 strike. An NUM Branch Committeeman at Markham colliery in Derbyshire observed bluntly: 'The thing was, we fetched a lot of pits out through picketing – pits that would have carried on working if we hadn't picketed them out'(D22). Yet the impact of picketing cannot entirely explain how adverse ballot results were overturned, and support for a national course of action generated. Instead, in a situation of uncertainty – but also of growing adversity – a latent gut loyalty to the NUM emerged to reinforce the mixed results achieved by picketing. Thus at Hatfield Main colliery in Yorkshire, the NUM Branch Delegate presented to the local workforce a near-apocalyptic vision of what was now at stake. He declared: 'Everyone knew this day would come. It's here. There is no place to hide; we have it to face . . . Cortonwood is the acid test of loyalty to this Union, fail this test of loyalty, abandon Cortonwood and this Union might just as well close down lock, stock, and barrel' (Douglass 1986b).

While dwelling largely on the economic aspects of the Cortonwood closure, and the economic vulnerability of Hatfield Main itself, the Delegate stressed that the miners, their communities and their Union had 'no place left to run . . . [our] backs are to the wall'. In short, larger issues were at stake than the fate of a neighbouring colliery: 'This isn't just a fight for Cortonwood, nor even for Hatfield, but for the right to have an effective Union to represent you! (Sustained applause).' Moreover, in the light of a Conservative MP's advice to the miners to 'go and eat grass', the Delegate retorted: 'I'd rather eat grass and fight to maintain our dignity and self respect . . . than to surrender to Thatcher and the Board and learn to eat shit! (Cheers, stamping).' Finally, he declared: 'This brothers, is the last ditch battle of the Miners' Union. If you make the wrong decision now, you'll have the rest of your life on the dole queue to regret it.' In the ensuing ballot, only five miners voted against striking (Douglas 1986b).

While the solidarity expressed here was impressive, it should none the less be remembered that the position of the NUM in Yorkshire was fortified by the 85.6 per cent majority it had obtained in a January 1981 Area Ballot to strike against 'the closure of any pit unless on the grounds of exhaustion' (Winterton & Winterton 1989: 54). Elsewhere, however, the Union's position was more precarious. More typical was the dilemma faced by NUM leaders in Derbyshire, where local miners had voted very narrowly (50.1 per cent to 49.9 per cent) against striking. Such a result, however, created the possibility of chaos in the Derbyshire coalfield. Seven NUM Branches in the Area had voted in favour of joining the strike, and seven against. At Markham colliery, where the NUM had two Branches, one had voted in favour and the other against. This raised the spectre of men from the same pit being on opposite sides of the picket line. As such, the Derbyshire miners' leaders effectively sought to overturn the adverse ballot result by appealing to all local miners to strike 'for the sake of unity'. The Area General Secretary remarked: '. . . the Derbyshire Area . . . leadership . . . was in a dilemma . . . We saw a situation developing where we would have miner against miner in the Area . . . where we as Area leaders would not be in control of our membership . . . and we would virtually hand the running of the organisation – either strike or no strike – to the police. And of course in that situation . . . we . . . decided to go on strike'.[47] This decision was not, however, warmly received. Branch leaders at those mines which had rejected strike action faced the daunting prospect of persuading hundreds of disgruntled miners to set aside their votes and commit themselves to the strike. Particularly unenviable was the task of the Branch leadership at Shirebrook, the area's largest pit, where 64 per cent of the men had voted against striking. The Branch Secretary recalled:

> I got the [Branch] committee together . . . and to their credit . . . the committee unanimously agreed to support the strike call, and we would take that to [a] mass meeting . . . Well, I went to mass meeting at Welfare [Hall] . . . there must have been 800 people there, and of course they weren't very happy – the majority. And I explained to them . . . the reasons the Area had took the decision . . . there were a lot of shouts . . . for a vote . . . and I said 'There's no more votes, that was it, now we're on strike.' And I [asked for] those that are interested . . . in picketing duties and we want everybody on picket line at 4.30 in morning. And they duly obliged . . . when I come here . . . at 5 o'clock the following morning, and there were . . . probably 300 . . . Shirebrook lads picketing.[48]

Eventually, miners at Shirebrook and elsewhere in the Derbyshire coalfield rallied to the cause of national strike action. But what kind of appeal had won them over? As at Hatfield Main colliery, the Branch Secretary reflected on how, in a situation of considerable uncertainty, an appeal for loyalty to the Union had been one of the most important factors:

> Well, really it was two or three things. One, in that position, you've got to make a stand, it had been sort of looming for some time . . . and we'd had an overtime ban and that sort of thing . . . and people were . . . concerned

about jobs and the future. Another one – bar . . . not taking any action at all
and saying that we were going to work wouldn't have got us nowhere
anyway, because we'd have had . . . other pickets here picketing us out . . .
[And] of course, the Union had said it were strike action, and I've been
brought up to believe whatever Union says, that that does one – for them
reasons, we supported [strike action]. But . . . in that meeting . . . it got a
little bit . . . 'hot', really, and . . . one or two people were looking for back
door . . . .[49]

Levels of Solidarity in the 1984–5 Strike

The 1984–5 strike therefore emerged from a situation of general crisis
in the coal industry, and was mobilized on the basis of several ongoing
disputes in different parts of the coalfield not all of which were immediately concerned with the question of pit closures. Yet from these
decidedly ragged beginnings an intense loyalty to the Union was
generated which sustained the strike for a year despite the traditional
divisiveness of the issue upon which it was fought, and despite the
repeated attempts by the Government and the NCB to weaken the
miners' resolve. Nowhere was such fortitude seen more clearly than
in the early days of the strike, when Government efforts to demobilize
strike action through the introduction of massively increased redundancy
payments failed to deter miners from their chosen course of action.[50] Yet
the NUM's fears that this would deter its membership from fighting the
closures proved unjustified. A Cortonwood striker dismissed the measures as a 'cheap ploy . . . just another attempt to buy us off and weaken
our resolve'.[51] Instead, miners displayed a grim determination to fight
on regardless of the cost. At Manvers Main colliery, miners saw the
Government's decision to freeze tax rebates and reduce social security
benefits as attempts 'to starve us out'. One miner declared: 'We will not
give up. We have been provoked by the coal board.' Another added: 'I
just don't know how we'll manage but we will keep on. If I have to steal
for my family then I will – we're fighting for our jobs. It's as simple as
that'.[52] And at Penallta colliery, South Wales, the Lodge Secretary noted
the limited impact of increased redundancy payments:

I think the redundancy agreements . . . were so good for a lot of older
people, like myself, and . . . in the start of the '84 strike, I made that clear to
our General Meeting that, you know, fighting for jobs . . . was not for me,
or for the Chairman [of the Branch] – because the both of us was over 50.
But I said, if the younger people are prepared to fight for their jobs, the same
as I've done nearly *all* my working life – fight for the right to work in the
pit – then I'd be prepared to vote with them. And the majority of our older
men *voted for strike action* in the '84–'85 strike. Although they had *nothing*
really to *gain*, see . . . and they did commit themselves. (W9)

Similarly, the worries of Union activists that increasing financial commitments had sapped the willingness of miners to support strike action proved, ultimately, to be unfounded. In an era of (potentially) high bonus earnings and of the sale of council and NCB houses to erstwhile tenants, many miners claimed that low levels of support for strike action over wages and jobs in the early 1980s were a function of increasingly heavy financial commitments. An NUM Lodge official commented:

> I think probably one of the factors was the fact that . . . we were now on an incentive bonus scheme throughout the pits . . . there were wages being earned now, and I think it deterred men from . . . the very thought of losing this sort of money . . . I think people's lifestyles were beginning to change anyway with the onset of the Tory government, the attitudes were beginning to be subtly changed – you know, the affluent society . . . we were starting to have cars, starting to have holidays that hitherto . . . we didn't enjoy so much – we were becoming more affluent . . . there was an element of influence in that direction. (W12)

Yet the link between increased material well-being, increased financial commitments and reluctance to strike is anything but clear (Przeworski 1980a; 1980c). The link between mortgage commitments, for example, and propensity to strike was tenuous. Research in Nottinghamshire revealed that 67.5 per cent of non-strikers (n=43) had mortgages compared to only 46.2 per cent of strikers (n=13). But the proportion of miners with mortgage commitments in Nottinghamshire as a whole (62.5 per cent) was not markedly different from Yorkshire (58.5 per cent) and Derbyshire (59.3 per cent), and, indeed, was lower than in South Wales (67.9 per cent). Yet in these three other areas, support for the 1984–5 strike was much more solid. The resolve demonstrated by the majority of miners in foregoing short-term material interest for the sake of more threatened colleagues, and in recognizing that larger issues were at stake, are therefore key to understanding how the 1984–5 strike lasted for so long.[53]

Inevitably, assessments of just *how* solid was the 1984–5 strike are coloured by the complete unity achieved by the NUM in the much shorter strikes of 1972 (seven weeks) and 1974 (five weeks). Yet a year-long strike, fought over a divisive issue in extremely difficult circumstances, represented an entirely different enterprise involving appalling losses not seen in British industry since the 1926 miners' strike. For these reasons alone, the solidarity that *was* achieved in 1984–5 remains impressive. Because there never was total unity in 1984–5, the actual extent of solidarity in the coalfields became the source of a fierce propaganda battle between the NUM and the NCB. As such, it is difficult to determine precisely how many miners were on strike and how many were not. Nationally, the greatest number on strike was probably reached on 16 March 1984, when the Nottinghamshire coalfield staged a brief strike to conduct its Area Ballot, and the NCB conceded that only eleven of Britain's 174 pits were working.[54] The strike was most solid from March to August 1984 when approximately 80 per cent of miners, nationally, were on strike.[55] Indeed, between April and mid-August 1984, only 8,000 miners returned to work to rejoin those who had never come out on strike – 48,000 miners were now working, with 133,000 (73 per cent) still on strike.[56] Solidarity was breached in early November 1984 when 5,000 miners responded to the NCB's offer of a £1,400 pre-Christmas bonus payment in return for abandoning the strike.[57] Even so, the rate at which miners subsequently returned to work disappointed the NCB, and by late November 1984, it conceded that the strike would continue into 1985.[58] At this stage, the NUM reported that 144,428 of its total membership (196,000) were still on strike.[59] However, 24,000 miners returned to work between 17 January and 28 February,[60] though in mid-February, the NUM claimed that 64 per cent of miners remained on strike.[61] The NCB's claim on 27 February 1985 that 50 per cent of miners had now returned to work was hotly contested by the NUM, whose own figures on 1 March 1985 – that is, only two days before the strike ended – showed that 60 per cent of miners (116,810 of 196,000) remained on strike.[62]

In terms of Area solidarity, significant variations emerged. Of the major Areas, Nottinghamshire became the most important bastion of working miners, while South Wales, Yorkshire, Scotland and the North East remained (in descending order) the most solid. In Nottinghamshire, the strike, at its height, may have attracted the support of about one-third of the local membership,[63] though an account sympathetic to non-strikers argues that no more than 3,500 of the Area's 29,200 miners were ever on strike (Griffin 1985: 8). The NUM, halfway through the strike, could only point to one pit in the Area (Bolsover) where more than half the workforce was on strike,[64] though on 1 March 1985, it claimed that 22 per cent of the Area's miners were on strike.[65]

In comparison, solidarity in South Wales remained astonishingly robust for the entire year. On 20 August 1984, only *one* miner had returned to work in the Area,[66] while in mid-December 1984, of the twenty-six pits in Britain that had *no* miners working, twenty-one were located in South Wales.[67] The solidarity shown in the Scottish, Yorkshire and North East coalfields was only slightly less impressive. In August 1984, only 125 of Scotland's 12,500 miners had returned to work, while strikebreakers totalled only nine (out of 53,000) in Yorkshire and twenty-three (out of 22,400) in the North East.[68] By mid-February 1985, the NUM claimed that 98 per cent of miners were still on strike in South

Wales, 90 per cent in Yorkshire, 75 per cent in Scotland and 73 per cent in the North East.[69] Overall, Table 6 demonstrates the variation in solidarity, by Area, at three stages of the strike.

Table 6. Levels of Solidarity in the 1984–85 Strike, by Area

Area	Manpower	% on strike on 11/19/84	% on strike on 02/14/85	% on strike on 03/01/85
South Wales	21500	99.6	98	93
Kent	3000	95.9	95	93
Yorkshire	56000	97.3	90	83
Scotland	13100	93.9	75	69
Cokeworks	4500	95.6	73	65
North East	23000	95.5	70	60
Workshops	9000	55.6	–	50
Derbyshire	10500	66.7	44	40
Lancashire	6500	61.5	49	38
Midlands	13000	32.3	15	23
Nottinghamshire	30000	20.0	14	22
South Derbyshire	3000	11.0	11	11
Leicestershire	1900	10.5	10	10
North Wales	1000	35.0	10	10
NATIONAL	196000	73.7	64	60

Sources: Industrial Relations Section, NUM National Office, Sheffield. Bulletins of 19/11/84, 14/2/85 and 1/3/85.

By the time the strike ended on 3 March 1985, the coalfields were seriously divided. However, some Areas remained relatively solid, while very high levels of strikebreaking tended to be confined to the smaller Areas of the coalfield. Moreover, more than 70 per cent of those who had originally joined the strike in March 1984 were *still* on strike a year later. As both friends and foes of the NUM acknowledged, 'no other industry could do it' (Adeney & Lloyd 1988: 218).

The Problem of Strike Action

> . . . until you cause disruption, no one will listen to you, once other roads are exhausted. (D20)

> [The strike] is our only weapon, I suppose, if you've got a government . . . or Coal Board . . . who are intransigent – they don't want to bother with you . . . I would term it as not just *mine* workers', but *every* worker's atomic bomb, really – that's all we've got left . . . that's our main and biggest weapon, to withdraw our labour. (W5)

The constant clashes between the NCB, the Government and the NUM between 1980 and 1984 underscored two difficulties faced by the miners at a time of political and industrial change. First, miners highlighted the *uncertainty* that had enveloped their daily working lives. A miner at Goldthorpe colliery in Yorkshire described how 'everybody felt under threat, we didn't know what was going on from one day to the next'(Y8), while the NUM Lodge Secretary at Penallta colliery, South Wales, reflected:

Well, we seemed to be in a constant . . . mood of 'Are we going . . . on strike this year, and if we are, when?' You couldn't plan for anything . . . And then once that passed, 'are we going on strike this year over this *next* issue?' And that went on for a number of years, from about '81 right up until the [1984–5] strike. Every year, there was strike action looming on the horizon. Everybody knew it was coming. But it was just . . . hanging over us like a cloud . . . You couldn't plan anything – people couldn't plan holidays, they couldn't go out and say 'oh well, I'll go and buy a new three-piece suite', because they never knew when they would need that money. (W7)

Second, such uncertainty was compounded by the constant difficulty miners faced in choosing the ground on which to fight. The threat of pit closures was a particularly difficult one against which to construct a coherent and sustained response. The confrontation of 1981 showed how a timely concession by the Government could undercut resistance in the coalfields. As such, NUM leaders reflected that the battleground between employer and workforce was hardly an even one. Indeed, the Derbyshire Area General Secretary argued that it was more appropriate to talk of 'industrial *re*action' on the part of workers.[70] At the local level, an NUM Lodge Chairman commented:

. . . the *problem* with working class people [is] we all . . . do things because our heart tells us to do it. And the [Coal] Board have always planned months and months and months ahead what they were going to do with the industry and the Union don't plan . . . we're always on the backfoot because the Board never tell us what they're going to do until they do it. And they know the tactics they're going to use and, unfortunately, we don't know what they're going to do . . .
We have that on the local level – the manager comes out with something, and . . . the boys . . . say to us, naturally enough, 'Well, what are you going to do about that?' And I say, 'Well, I didn't know he was going to do that until he done it. You know, he's not going to tell me he's going to hit me on the back of the head until he actually does it, is he?'
And . . . I think that's always been the case. With unions and all workers, then, we're always on the backfoot because the employer knows what he's going to do before you know. Because he's planned it, hasn't he? (W5)

Such constraints underscore the validity of a South Wales miner's observation that 'it's always a bad time to go on strike, there never is a good
time'(W22). They also remind us that assessments of workers' actions
couched in terms of 'rationality' are particularly hazardous. Thus the
confrontation of 1981, when the Government was momentarily caught
off guard, appears as a situation in which the miners should have
continued their action and pressed home a decisive advantage in the
ongoing battle over industrial contraction. In comparison, March 1984
– when, after an unusually mild winter, record coalstocks lay at the
pitheads and power stations – appears a singularly unpromising and
irrational time at which to strike. Certainly, some miners were prepared
– *in retrospect* – to view the launching of strike action in March 1984
according to such criteria. The NUM Branch President at Goldthorpe
colliery remarked that 'with hindsight, it probably was not the best thing
to do . . . the Union would have been better off seeking better terms . . .
rather than going on strike'(Y9). A miner at Whitwell colliery in Derbyshire commented that 'the overtime ban was a *good* idea, and it was
working . . . it's a pity it couldn't have kept going another year'(D41).
Even the Lodge Chairman at the solidly pro-strike Penallta colliery
declared:

> . . . you've got to *know* when to go on strike . . . not just at the drop of a hat
> . . . and I think in '84, we allowed ourselves to get suckered in to going on
> strike, before we would have. Which is our fault, not anybody else's . . . If
> we'd thought about it, we could have seen, maybe, that it was a ploy that
> they shut Cortonwood deliberately, and that they shut it in the Spring or
> latter end of the Winter – if we'd thought about it, we could have realized
> that they were conning us into it. (W5)

Throughout the coalfields, in fact, the overwhelming majority of miners
argued that in 1984 the NCB, backed by the Government, had picked the
fight with the miners at a time most opportune for itself. In South Wales,
a miner at Tower colliery remarked: 'Oh yes, there's no doubt about it
. . . they nailed those collieries at the time for closure knowing very well
the action that the men would take. And . . . I honestly believe that
[Thatcher] was set up for it, and waited for us'(W17). A Penallta miner
agreed: 'When the strike *did* come, it was motivated by the Government
as far as I'm concerned. Because they *knew*, they had *everything* they
wanted in their favour: stocks of coal, plenty of oil, plenty of gas, and
. . . they said, then, "right, we're ready for the miners, we'll take the
miners on"'(W8).

Similar sentiments were expressed elsewhere. A miner at Allerton
Bywater colliery in Yorkshire felt that 'looking back, it was a Govern-

ment ploy to get us out on strike'(Y43), while at Warsop Main colliery in Derbyshire, a miner believed 'that plans were laid down by the NCB in advance to take on the NUM when the time was right'(D20). Even some Nottinghamshire non-strikers, while remaining severely critical of the conduct of the NUM, conceded grudgingly that the Government had provoked a confrontation. At Creswell, the UDM Branch Delegate commented:

> Some of it was orchestrated . . . that was obvious, because it was the wrong time of year to go on strike . . . in a *fuel* industry, to wait [until] the start of Summer to go on strike was ludicrous. And, yes, the argument that it might have been orchestrated from the Government level to get us out of the way, to pave the way to privatization or . . . the trimming down of the industry, then I think that's got something to do with it. (N46)

None the less, as a miner at Penrhiwceiber colliery, South Wales, noted, 'everybody can be wise after the event'(W14). Thus while most miners were sure that the Government and/or the NCB had provoked a confrontation at the worst possible time for the NUM, they were equally convinced that they had had little option but to respond in the way they did. A powerful feeling therefore existed that with the Cortonwood closure, their room for manoeuvre was extremely restricted, and their control over when and how to fight very limited. At Thurcroft colliery in Yorkshire, a miner reflected that strike action in these circumstances 'was the only weapon we had really. If not, they'd have run riot. We had no option'(Y23). At Barrow colliery, a faceworker concurred: 'No one wants to strike, but it was the only thing left to do'(Y15). In Derbyshire, a miner at Whitwell colliery argued that '[Thatcher] forced us into a situation where we'd *got* to . . . respond to that closure'(D41), while a colleague at the Area's Central Workshops commented: 'I don't think we had a great deal of alternative – we all *knew* it was the wrong time' (D26). In South Wales, the Lodge Secretary at Oakdale colliery felt that 'in 1984, I don't think we had any choice. Although we didn't choose the time to come out on strike, I think we were up against a position where . . . we would have had a massive rundown of the industry'(W11). Perhaps the most sobering note, however, on the situation in March 1984 was sounded by the Lodge Secretary at Penallta colliery: 'It was the only weapon we had. We'd tried everything else . . . History shows that . . . the . . . decision to strike was taken reluctantly. Nobody wanted it. But it was the only way we had, to oppose them'(W7).

For most miners, therefore, the 1984–5 strike was undertaken against the odds – at a time not of their own choosing and over an issue on which the NUM had long struggled to forge a united front. Moreover, March 1984 was a time of considerable uncertainty. Few miners, in fact, believed they stood at the start of a year-long strike. A miner at Taff Merthyr colliery, South Wales, recalled: 'I honestly think six weeks would have been the maximum . . . no, never in my wildest dreams did I think it would last twelve months'(W3). A colleague agreed: 'You know . . . none of us ever thought we'd be on strike for twelve month . . . I mean, we were out on strike the first day . . . we was all hoping we'd be back in work the following Monday'(W2). A miner at Penallta colliery thought the strike would last 'a month, at the most, in my mind. I thought . . . it would be like '74. Not for the *world* did I ever think that . . . that would go on for a year'(W4). However, a colleague at the pit also described how March 1984, for all its uncertainties and fears, represented something akin to embarking on a voyage of possibilities and discovery:

It's a funny thing – when you get into the strike, there's something inside you . . . that: 'right, you've resigned yourself, you're into . . . the dispute now . . . the reservations that I may have had, now you had to put to one side' . . . We didn't know then . . . how far the strike – I don't think anybody, *ever*, thought the strike was going to go on for twelve months. So it's a lot easier to look back on it and analyse it, than it was then at the time, to see exactly where we were going, what we were going to achieve. We were out now, we'd resigned ourselves to being out on strike. All these other loyalties came in, as a trade unionist . . . all these other things came into play . . . so you put yourself then in with the rest. You were fighting now. (W12)

Notes

1. *G*, 11/2/81.
2. *G*, 11/2/81.
3. *MS*, 14/2/81.
4. *MS*, 18/2/81.
5. *T*, 17/2/81; *MS*, 18/2/81. The South Wales, Durham and Midlands area leaders also called for strike action (*MS*, 14/2/81; *WM*, 16/2/81).
6. The increases would have given a miner aged 30 with ten years' service in the industry £8,500 against his present £1,730; £10,300 instead of £4,880 at age 40; and £20,000 instead of £17,000 at age 60 (*DT*, 11/2/81).

7. *T*, 17/2/81.
8. *MS*, 16/2/81.
9. *WM*, 16/2/81.
10. *O*, 15/2/81.
11. *WM*, 16/2/81.
12. *O*, 15/2/81.
13. *FT*, 16/2/81.
14. *T*, 20/2/81.
15. *MS*, 20/2/81.
16. *G*, 21/2/81.
17. *MS*, 19/2/81.
18. *G*, 20/2/81.
19. This was particularly true regarding the improvements made in the NCB's redundancy scheme two months after the Government's retreat. Lump sum payments to miners between 50 and 55 (of whom there were some 62,000 of a total workforce of 225,000 in March 1981) were doubled – a miner aged 55 with thirty-five years' service, for example, became entitled to a sum of £35,481, an increase of £11,373. Thus many miners benefited from the NUM's clash with the Government. None the less such improvements in redundancy packages also underlined the Government's 'determination to "buy out" the miners' (*New Statesman*, 23/3/84).
20. The Director-General of the Institute of Directors labelled the settlement a 'scandalous surrender' (*MS*, 20/2/81).
21. See, for example, *MS*, 19/2/81; *DS*, 18/2/81; *G*, 18/2/81; *DT*, 18/2/81.
22. *T*, 17/2/81.
23. *O*, 15/2/81.
24. *MS*, 17/2/81.
25. *T*, 17/2/81.
26. *G*, 20/2/81.
27. *G*, 15/6/83.
28. *G*, 6/7/83; *T*, 1/7/83.
29. *G*, 6/7/83.
30. *WM*, 24/5/83; *SWEP*, 25/5/83. See also *SWEP*, 16/6/83; *WM*, 21/7/83.
31. *DT*, 6/7/83.
32. *DT*, 11/7/83.
33. *G*, 13/7/83.
34. *G*, 3/7/83.
35. *BS*, 5/3/84.
36. *Coal News*, Special Issue, March 1984, p. 3.
37. *BS*, 3/3/84.

38. *BS*, 5/3/84.
39. For details of this variation within Yorkshire, see Winterton and Winterton (1989:69) who conclude that 'the status of the colliery appears to have had no influence upon membership reaction, again suggesting the primacy of sociological "community" explanations over economic ones'.
40. *International Coal Report*, 16/3/84, p. 2.
41. Contrary to the fears of NUM leaders in South Wales, Welsh pickets were markedly more successful than their Yorkshire colleagues in their efforts to win over the Nottinghamshire miners. Several non-strikers in Nottinghamshire drew a sharp distinction between the actions, behaviour and achievements of the Welsh pickets and those from Yorkshire.
42. South Wales leaders also highlighted the irony of the fact that in 1983, when Welsh miners had lobbied the Yorkshire coalfield for support over the Ty Mawr/Lewis Merthyr pit, they had not been welcomed at Cortonwood. The Lodge Chairman at Oakdale commented, 'It was a hell of a situation, you see . . . because our boys went up about Lewis Merthyr [and] Cortonwood told our fellahs to get from there, they didn't want to know. And this was another one you had to get over to our boys . . . "well, why should we support them that wouldn't support us?"'(W16).
43. *WM*, 29/3/84.
44. *AL*, 27/3/84.
45. Interview, Cwmaman, 21/11/89.
46. Interview, 20/10/89.
47. Interview, Chesterfield, 31/5/90.
48. Interview, 27/6/90.
49. Interview, 27/6/90.
50. For example, redundancy payments for a miner aged 49, with thirty-three years' service, rose from £8,677 to £33,000; those for a miner aged 36, with twenty years' service, from £3,904 to £20,000 (*Coal News*, Special Issue, March 1984, p. 4).
51. *BS*, 8/3/84.
52. *BS*, 15/3/84.
53. Nor should the transformative potential of simply being caught up in the tide of events be underestimated. A South Wales miner stated, 'Well, I'm against a strike. I just can't afford it but once we're into it, well, it's a different matter then' (*FT*, 16/3/84).
54. *Socialist Organiser*, nos. 219–20, March 1985, p. 62.
55. *Socialist Organiser,* nos. 219–20, March 1985, p. 7.
56. *FT*, 14/8/84.
57. *DT*, 14/11/84.

58. *T*, 20/11/84.
59. *Source*: Industrial Relations Section, NUM National Office, Sheffield, 19/11/84.
60. *Socialist Organiser*, Nos. 219–20, March 1985, p. 62.
61. *Source*: Industrial Relations Section, NUM National Office, Sheffield, 14/2/85 [Doc. NO33/KB/CMC/IR/85].
62. *Source*: Industrial Relations Section, NUM National Office, Sheffield, 1/3/85.
63. *FT*, 4/7/84.
64. *The Miner* (Special Issue), 31/8/84.
65. *Source*: Industrial Relations Section, NUM National Office, Sheffield, 1/3/85.
66. *FT*, 21/8/84.
67. *ST*, 18/12/84.
68. *FT*, 21/8/84.
69. *Source*: Industrial Relations Section, NUM National Office, Sheffield, 14/2/85 [Doc. NO33/KB/CMC/IR/85].
Moreover, not until the *last* week of the strike did significant numbers return to work in these Areas, when 4,248 returned in Yorkshire, 2,089 in the North East, 1,029 in South Wales and 679 in Scotland (*Source*: Industrial Relations Section, NUM National Office, Sheffield, 1/3/84).
70. Interview, 31/5/90.

5

Class Consciousness and the Striking Miner I: The Context of Struggle

Introduction

> In the Falklands, we had to fight the enemy without. Here the enemy is within, and it is more difficult to fight, and more dangerous to liberty.
>
> Speech by Margaret Thatcher to the Conservative Party's 1922 Committee, 20/7/84, quoted in T. Parker, *Red Hill. A Mining Community*

> We were on strike – we were the 'enemy within' – yet we were just ordinary people fighting for what we believed in. (W28)

Few miners anticipated the ferocity with which state power was deployed against them and their Union during the 1984–5 strike, nor the costs the Government was willing to incur in the process. GDP declined by between 1.0 per cent and 1.25 per cent for 1984, while the Public Sector Borrowing Requirement (PSBR) increased by between £2.5 billion and £3.0 billion. With increased use of imported oil, the current account on the country's balance of payments deteriorated by between £2.75 billion and £3.0 billion for the 1984–5 financial year.[1] The NCB lost £1.1billion[2] with 70 million tonnes of lost production and 71 coalfaces lost or made irrecoverable.[3] The electricity industry and British Steel lost £1.2 billion and £200 million respectively, while policing costs, and lost income tax, totalled £200 million each. By the end of February 1985, the total cash costs of the strike were estimated at £3.025 billion.[4]

During the first seven months of 1984, the number of working days lost through industrial disputes was almost five times greater than that for the corresponding period in 1983. Eighty-one per cent of the 11.594 million days lost were accounted for by the miners' strike.[5] During the strike, 11,312 people were arrested for offences ranging from obstruction and breach of the peace to arson, conspiracy and murder (Percy-Smith & Hillyard 1985: 345; *Socialist Organiser* 1985: 63). Up to the end of the strike, 5,653 people – most of them miners – had been tried in the courts for alleged offences committed during the strike: 'Never before in this century has the coercive power of the state been used on such a massive scale against a clearly identified group of individuals, except in Northern Ireland against the nationalist community' (Percy-Smith & Hillyard 1985: 345). Jenkins argues that 'the strike exposed the State for what it was – or had become under Mrs Thatcher – the police force of the capitalist class' (1988: 233).

The Aims of the Struggle

The vast majority of strikers were clear about what was at stake in the 1984–5 struggle: 'to be able to keep working, and not come to the pit and [be told] "that's it, your job's finished" – the right to work'(Y51). Nor did miners limit their concerns to their *own* jobs. Many saw themselves as custodians of their jobs for future generations. A striker at Ollerton colliery, Nottinghamshire, explained: 'My family – [there would be] no future for them. I'd experienced one pit closure when I'd come from [the Northumberland coalfield]. I was fighting for the future, for the kids'(N5). A miner at Penallta colliery, South Wales, argued: 'I knew that if the pits went, there was nothing to replace them. My sons, who were young then, wouldn't have anything to do. They wouldn't have a job'(W5). A faceworker at Barrow colliery, Yorkshire, agreed: 'The immediate aim was the protection of my job. But I was also fighting for a job for my son'(Y15).

Furthermore, miners recognized the devastating impact of pit closures on community life. A striker at Bilsthorpe colliery in Nottinghamshire felt that 'the National Union was perfectly right, it *does* destroy communities, it does destroy real life, when you close a pit'(N4). A faceworker at Markham colliery in Derbyshire concurred: 'you didn't just shut a pit, you shut a community'(D22). Such views were particularly pronounced in the peripheral coalfields where the industry, though in long-term decline, still remained the dominant source of most livelihoods. An NUM Lodge official at Penallta colliery, South Wales, commented:

> . . . it was the survival, really, of . . . my pit in particular . . . When a pit falls, it's not just that pit, it's quite a number of other things – subsidiaries . . . that depends on your pit, and *their* jobs go . . . It *does* destroy a community . . . you've only got to go up and down this valley and see what have happened here . . .
>
> It was your job, it's the only job you knew . . . I've been in the pit all my life . . . and most of the miners have been in the pit all their lives, it was the only job *they* knew. And . . . we could see the pit going and . . . the present trend is 3 million unemployed, and where in hell were they going to go? Where were they going to get their living from? How were they going to go

out . . . of the area? Which they didn't want to do, because they've bought their homes, they'd set here, and their families had set here, and that was it. (W4)

Yet even if miners recognized what was at stake, what, in the circumstances, were they prepared to settle for? Throughout the dispute, the NUM leadership's position was unambiguous and unyielding: a complete halt to pit closures (unless on grounds of geological exhaustion) and, ultimately, an expansion of the industry to the levels envisaged in the 1974 Plan for Coal. Undoubtedly, many miners *explicitly* supported the Union's stance. Miners at Goldthorpe, Barrow and Silverwood collieries in Yorkshire all spoke of the need for a 'halt' to pit closures. At Penrhiwceiber colliery in South Wales, a miner characterized a successful outcome as 'no closures. It's as simple as that. You know, I had a vested interest, knowing full well that Penrhiwceiber . . . which is termed a "militant" colliery in the South Wales area, was virtually number one on the [closure] list of the NCB'(W14). The Lodge Secretary at the pit agreed: 'A successful outcome would have been, and *should* have been, the stopping of the Government, or the Coal Board . . . to close what *they* called – what's the word? – "uneconomic" collieries. That would have been a success'(W15).

However, the goals of most strikers fell somewhat short of the stated objectives of the NUM leadership. Notably, many loyal strikers retained misgivings over articulating a set of demands that appeared to completely defy the market. A miner at Tower colliery, South Wales, said 'I don't think we could have said that collieries would not close until exhaustion – that was going a bit too far'(W18). None the less, failure to support a position of total opposition to pit closures did not amount to wholesale acceptance of Thatcherism's model of the free market. Instead, most miners, while remarkably moderate in their concrete demands, clung tenaciously to an alternative vision of the market – one which encompassed different economic, social and moral dimensions. On economic grounds alone, miners scorned the Thatcher Government's rationale for reducing the capacity of the industry. An electrician at Stillingfleet colliery in Yorkshire complained that 'their economic arguments are upside-down – shutting more pits and importing more coal'(Y39). A miner at Taff Merthyr pit, South Wales, asked 'Why should we bring coal in from Australia, Poland and China to Wales, when we got the best coal in the world on our doorsteps? . . . I thought that by keeping the pits open, we had sufficient pits in . . . the valleys to . . . send to the power stations to generate all the electricity that we could produce'(W1). A miner at High Moor colliery in Derbyshire commented:

I cannot understand the way the Government has gone about closures. Take Whitwell – a lot of coal still left there, but they still closed it. And there's pits with bigger losses than Whitwell, but they've kept them going. We were losing about 7 to 8 million pounds; they closed us. The complex I'm at now – High Moor/Kiveton – we're losing a lot more than that . . . I don't know how they get round to 'it's your turn to go'. I know they have to go into losses, etc., but it didn't seem *fair*, the way they were going about it. (D41)

In criticizing the Government's economic rationale, miners did not ignore the demands of the market, but instead lamented the absence of any commitment on the part of the Government to the coal industry – '[it] has no *policy* on closures'(D41). The NUM Branch Delegate at Sharlston colliery in Yorkshire therefore viewed a victory in terms of a 'slowing down of closures, because natural wastage as far as collieries running out of coal would lead to closures, but then we'd have had another Plan for Coal – the opening up of new collieries to replace old ones. Instead of importing foreign coal'(Y40). The NUM Lodge Secretary at Penallta colliery in South Wales spoke similarly: '. . . the only thing that *really* would have solved the problem was the Government to commit itself . . . to using British coal . . . It's no good us producing . . . stacking it on the ground . . . we . . . didn't want to go down there digging the coal to put it on top of the ground, and build big mountains of coal nobody wanted. We wanted a commitment . . . to *use* that coal, that would keep us employed'(W9).

In the absence, however, of any such commitment on the government's part, most miners regarded the policy of continuing industrial contraction as arbitrary and unjustified. The rate at which pits were closing, it seemed, was out of control. Thus a striker at Ollerton colliery in Nottinghamshire wanted 'more co-operation. They were just saying, "we're closing that pit, we're closing that pit"'(N5). A striker at Bilsthorpe colliery commented:

When you get a pit exhausted, it's got to close – we all accepted that . . . we didn't like the way it was being done, while there were pits with 5 to 10 years' still left in them, which they closed down. Okay, with pits with bad geological conditions which they'd . . . struggled for two to three year . . . the board had pumped money in, and they couldn't make it pay – there again . . . I would say that's . . . in the same class as exhaustion . . . but there *was* definitely a lot of pits that didn't need to have been closed. (N4)

For a miner at Denby Grange colliery in Yorkshire, a successful outcome would have been 'if they'd said no pit closures on the scale as what they did. We accept that pits do come to the end of their life, but when they're shutting pits that's got plenty of coal reserves, to me, it's silly. Because once closed, it's very rare that they can be reopened'(Y51). A miner at Stillingfleet colliery remarked that 'pits were shutting, because they were getting worked out . . . and slowly, a lot of them would have gone anyway. But they just jumped in and said "Right, from today, we're shutting"'(Y39). In South Wales, the NUM Lodge Chairman at Oakdale colliery concurred: 'What *we* were against was *unnecessary* closures – closures for closures' sake – what we were fighting for was for pits that could be saved'(W16).

Reinforcing strikers' feelings that such closures were unnecessary was a growing sense that they were becoming powerless to stop them. Strikers felt that the established procedures of review and arbitration were being violated by the NCB and the Government. Thus a miner at Warsop colliery in Derbyshire wanted 'an agreement with the Union that pit closures would only take place subject to the agreement of all parties, including an *independent* body'(D20). A striker at Bevercotes colliery in Nottinghamshire wanted a return to the 'review procedure which was in operation prior to the strike'(N3). At Allerton Bywater pit in Yorkshire, a miner favoured 'a negotiated means of closure . . . agreements on the *grounds* for closure – geological or whatever – plus a good transfer and/or redundancy scheme'(Y43). In South Wales, the NUM Lodge Chairman at Oakdale colliery wanted 'a proper discussion before [closures] took place, not just put, say, seventy pits in front of you and [say] these have got to close – that's not the way to do it'(W16). At Tower colliery, a striker wanted the establishment of 'a body to look into pits, individually, and give a fair assessment . . . and not the NCB having the last word on it . . . [I wanted] representatives from the NCB, the NUM or any other union, to go into a room to negotiate about the pit, to talk about that pit, see what *can* be done'(W19). At Penallta colliery, a miner remarked:

> What would have represented a victory for the miners? I think, some sort of arbitration where . . . the Union and the Board . . . could call in independent people to assess whether a pit was . . . worth keeping open or not. I mean nobody in his right mind expects a pit to stay open if there's no coal in it . . . The idea of voluntary redundancy was not a bad thing, for the old people – at least they were getting out with something. If . . . they *had* to close a pit, and it was found that it wasn't viable, by the independent people, to keep it open, then, for the movement of labour, the older men could have got out, with a couple of pound in their pocket. And they could still have closed *some* pits . . . *sensibly*. But they didn't want to close them sensibly. (W6)

As ever, therefore, the miners sought to retain *some* control over their daily working lives, and a degree of protection and independence from the seemingly arbitrary decisions of government and employer. This yearning, which lent the strikers' actions a unity of purpose, was articulated by a miner at Whitwell colliery, Derbyshire:

> . . . there's some pits which were going to *have* to shut, obviously, because . . . we all live in a real world and we can't keep losing money like we *were* losing money. But, at the end of the day, success for me would have been a sensible coal policy – a proper fuel policy for the country. So that you'd *know*, if they'd say 'right, this pit is going to shut in 10 years' time' – you knew it, and people could work to that end. But when you have a threat of this month, next month, you don't know what to expect. But if there's an outlined policy, saying this pit shuts then, that pit shuts then – and give their reasons, I mean you've plenty of time to argue against it or do whatever you need to be done. But at least have some sort of policy what people can understand and follow. (D30)

In sum, the goals of the strike were remarkably moderate in scope[6] – essentially, miners sought the restoration of a system of negotiation and consultation to which they were accustomed and which they felt was being undermined in the early 1980s. Coupled with this was a clear awareness that the future of their communities was at stake. The motivations underpinning strike action were therefore largely defensive. A woman in Maerdy, South Wales said: 'We just want to keep what we've got' (Samuel 1986: 22–3), while an NUM Lodge official in the Durham coalfield spoke of the NCB's desire 'to take away our independence and our cultural heritage, our village life and our club life' (Beynon 1984: 105). Indeed, the NUM National President spoke for most strikers when he declared to the 1984 TUC: 'We are fighting for the survival of our communities, of our culture and of a way of life'.[7] But what values were embedded in such a 'way of life'? The miners' aims were shaped by a powerful sense of being wronged, a stubborn refusal to be 'pushed around', and a dogged adherence to a vision of the market wholly at odds with that of the government. As such, the strike represented a 'blind clash of moralities' (Jenkins 1988: 232).

The miners' position was therefore both defensive and defiant: 'even in those early days, people talked of being out "for as long as it takes"' (Beynon 1984: 107). The Lodge Secretary at Penallta colliery, South Wales, reflected: 'As far as I was concerned, I was prepared to sink or swim. And . . . if it meant *sinking*, then that was the way it was going to be'(W7). Such determination ensured that the miners' stance assumed a decidedly offensive quality in the eyes of the Government. A Yorkshire miner looked back: '. . . in '84, it was do-or-die on both sides. We were all out for no pit closures and they were saying "We're going to flatten you"'(Y39).

The Miners and the State

It was revenge for 1974. They'd have stuck us out if we'd . . . been out for three years. (Y1)

They done their homework . . . they dug their heels in and we *knew* we had a fight on our hands. (W13)

Most strikers knew that the battle they were entering into was part of a larger war being waged by the Government against organized labour as a whole. A faceworker at Thurcroft colliery in Yorkshire commented: 'the Thatcher Government was hell-bent, from 1979, on smashing the unions'(Y23). The NUM was not the first public-sector union to clash with the Government. In 1980, the Iron and Steel Trades Confederation (ISTC) had waged an ultimately unsuccessful three-month strike to extract a pay award from BS. Following its defeat, the workforce in the steel industry was halved (Hartley *et al.* 1983). Miners, though, were keenly aware that *they* were the key target for the Government – 'Thatcher', said a South Wales miner, 'had never made any secret of the fact that . . . the miners were a thorn in her side'(W12). Thus despite the recent difficulties of resisting pit closures, miners continued to see their Union as the focus of resistance for the whole labour movement. A Derbyshire striker felt that 'the Thatcher Government was determined to *smash* . . . the NUM, because the NUM was the last bastion of unity of the workers . . . the *defeat* of the NUM left the door open for them to attack other unions'(D20). The Lodge Secretary at Penallta colliery reflected: 'They had taken on the steel industry to a certain degree . . . but . . . the Government knew . . . that the fight against the miners, because of the traditional militancy . . . in the mines, over the years . . . would be a lot harder and the *hardest* . . . battle that they were likely to come up against'(W7).

Two important factors underscore the validity of these perceptions and explain why the Thatcher Government proved to be such a for-midable opponent. First, in challenging the assumed prerogatives of management over employment levels in the coal industry, the miners struck at the very heart of Thatcherism's strategy for the restructuring of the British economy. Its central thrust, as Gamble notes, was to break with the institutions of corporatism and interventionism, to dismantle the public sector and 'to reestablish the conditions for free markets. The state had to be strong if the market was to be free' (1985: 15). Further-more, given its monetarist goals of eliminating state subsidy of the public sector, and of breaking the power of public-sector trade unions, a 'public defeat of Scargillism would demonstrate that unions could not interfere with the restructuring of the economy' (1985: 17).

Second, the Thatcher Government took the NUM seriously as an opponent capable of wrecking this strategy. The NUM, after all, had *defeated* the Heath Government in the 1972 and 1974 strikes. Indeed, many miners felt that the Thatcher Government in 1984–5 wanted revenge for the setbacks of the early 1970s. A striker at Taff Merthyr colliery, South Wales, reflected on how 'they never forgave the miners, so they was hell-bent on beating us'(W1). At Tower colliery, a striker remarked: 'I think . . . once she came to power, she must have thought, "you beat Heath, and you're not going to beat me" – that was the attitude . . . the bitterness was there, you could see it . . . she didn't want to give us a thing'(W18a). And a Derbyshire miner commented: 'The roots of the Tory party could never forgive the miners for what they did to the Heath Government'(D20).

It is unlikely that the Thatcher Government was motivated solely by a need for revenge. However, the Conservative Party was shaken by the 1972 and 1974 strikes and subsequently formulated plans to prevent the recurrence of such a debacle. In 1972, the Government established the National Security Commission with a task of devising plans to defeat a lengthy strike and to combat 'flying pickets'. This review led to the removal from the Home Office of responsibility for dealing with civil emergencies (for example, strikes) and its transfer to the Civil Contingencies Unit in the Cabinet Office, and to the creation of a National Reporting Centre to co-ordinate Britain's regional police forces at a national level (Bunyan 1985: 294). In 1978, a report from a group of senior Conservatives argued that the presence of strong unions in the fuel and power industries made it highly unlikely that the Government – short of using the army – could win a strike in this sector (Gamble 1985: 15). An annex to the report, however, described measures to counter any 'political threat' from those they regarded as 'enemies of the next Tory government'. The group, believing that the most likely battleground would be the coal industry, urged a future Conservative Government to generate maximum coal stocks, especially at the power stations, make contingency plans for importing coal, encourage the recruitment of non-union lorry drivers to help move coal where necessary, and introduce dual coal/oil firing in all power stations as quickly as possible.[8] After winning power in 1979, the Thatcher Government acted on these proposals, especially after its concessions to the NUM in early 1981. Coal stocks rose between 1981 and 1984 from 37 to 57 million tonnes (Gamble 1985: 16). In addition, the government's trade union legislation, which placed increasingly severe legal restrictions on picketing (and sympathy action by other unions), exposed unions to crippling fines and the threat of sequestration of their funds by the State.

The circumstances in which the miners embarked on strike action in

March 1984 were therefore considerably darker than those which had prevailed in 1972 and 1974. On reflection, miners involved in all three strikes viewed the Thatcher Government as a far more determined opponent than the Heath Government. Many strikers ruefully acknowledged how well-prepared the Thatcher Government had been. The Lodge Chairman at Penrhiwceiber colliery remarked: 'I think they had organised for this strike far better than what we did . . . the Government had done their homework . . . long before actually making it a confrontation' (W15). A striker at Penallta colliery complained that 'the whole attitude of the Government had *changed* . . . Heath *did* give in to pressure . . . [but] she was motivating *everything* against . . . unions . . . you could see that with the laws she brought in . . . the picketing laws . . . they built everything up to it'(W8).

The Lodge Vice-Chairman at the pit noted the impact of sequestration: 'Everything that she legislated was to close ranks on us, so to speak, and . . . the most important thing, I thought, was a word that nobody had ever heard before: "sequestration". Now what the hell was sequestration? . . . [It] tied our funds up. You couldn't move, you couldn't go anywhere, you couldn't get anything . . . that was the nail in the coffin . . . she prepared for it. And . . . money was no object'(W4). A striker at Bilsthorpe colliery in Nottinghamshire concurred: 'She planned it very, very clever – you've got to admire her . . . it all fit in, in that ten year from '74 to '84 . . . she was determined that, at *any* cost . . . she wasn't going to be humiliated and defeated the same way Ted Heath was . . . it was all geared up for her to *smash* the *National Union of Mineworkers* – and by God, it worked. It's hard to say it, but it worked'(N4).

The miners therefore faced an opponent in 1984 that had a critical vested interest in breaking them, and a formidable array of weapons with which to do so. Yet if this was indeed the case, how was 'the State' viewed and experienced by those against whom its power was deployed? For most strikers and their families, the State was, for all intents and purposes, the massive police presence encountered on the picket lines and within their pit villages. The scale and nature of policing in the 1984–5 strike became a source of considerable public disquiet and the focus of a burgeoning body of literature.[9] Moreover, strikers (particularly those involved in picketing) highlighted not only the unevenness of the contest as compared with 1972 and 1974, but the class character of state power at a time of acute crisis.

During the 1984–5 strike, 'mass picketing proved, at certain times, to be a central issue for the [NUM], the police and other state institutions' (East *et al.* 1985: 305). Strikers described how their experience of picketing in 1984 was a world away from that of 1972 and 1974. The NUM Branch President at Maltby colliery in Yorkshire described how in 1972 'we went picketing at Rotherham, at the wharf. Workers wouldn't cross the picket lines, we'd play football. In fact, once this was known, everyone at Maltby wanted to picket at Rotherham because they'd get a game of football. They were happier times, I suppose, with none of the nastiness that has entered society in the 1980s'(Y22).

A Derbyshire miner recalled how, in 1972 and 1974, he had 'picketed locally, at Ireland colliery. It was peaceful. We made a fire at the end of the pit road, and just talked with our mates. There was no aggravation'(D14). A miner at Oakdale colliery in South Wales remembered how 'in '72 and '74, I played football with policemen . . . there was a good understanding'(W50). A striker at Bevercotes colliery in Nottinghamshire even labelled the 1974 dispute 'a happy strike – it should have been an annual event'(N7). Moreover, as the Lodge Secretary at Penallta colliery emphasized, picketing in the early 1970s had been effective: 'The . . . situation was entirely different . . . you had the flying pickets, for the first time, which had never been done before – it was a new idea which bowled them over . . . we was taking the initiative'(W9). Mass picketing scored its greatest success in 1972 when some 25,000 pickets (including approximately 10,000 members of the Amalgamated Union of Engineering Workers (AUEW)) prevented half as many police from keeping open the Saltley coke depot in Birmingham behind which lay the last large supply of coking fuel in Britain. Arthur Scargill, addressing the jubilant gathering, proclaimed 'Saltley will go down in Labour history as a great victory' (Bunyan 1985: 293–4).

The contrast in 1984 was sharp. In Yorkshire, miners highlighted the scale and impact of policing. A miner at Allerton Bywater colliery commented: 'It was unbelievable, where all the police came from'(Y43). A Derbyshire miner agreed: 'It was a lot different. In '84, it was unbelievable, the strength of the police. They were strong in '72 and '74, but even *they* seemed to be more sympathetic towards the miners, whereas in '84, they were under instructions to knock them down, and that was it. The numbers, and the money it cost, it was absolutely unbelievable' (D22). Other miners spoke in even more vitriolic terms. A Nottinghamshire striker said 'The police were like animals to us'(N7), while a miner at Warsop colliery stated 'The policing was *disgusting* – a contravention of civil liberties. It was paramilitary'(D20). As such, pickets described how their efforts had, ultimately, proved futile; a miner at Maltby colliery felt that 'the police destroyed the strike'(Y29). A picket from Taff Merthyr colliery recalled 'When it come to 1984, there was no way you could do it, because they monitored the pickets, stopped them travelling . . . you'd go halfway up the motorway, and the police patrol would stop you – "Turn back, you're not going no further" . . . From our own pit we'd have a minibus . . . police cars would stop us . . . we'd have to get out . . . and we'd walk up over the mountain . . . we didn't have no power at all'(W2).

The Lodge Chairman at Penrhiwceiber colliery, South Wales, described a visit to the North Wales coalfield:

> The determination of the Government . . . we saw it for ourselves . . . I was in Point of Ayr colliery . . . requesting . . . that they come out on strike . . . if there was, say, fifteen or twenty of us . . . that went up there, I would say that there must have been 100 police, just outside the gates of the colliery. And they came marching down the hill . . . as if there'd been thousands of miners . . . There was at least 100 . . . 150 . . . [policemen] marching down . . . I thought there was a . . . factory at the top of the hill . . . *making* them up there . . . The need for all these policemen – it truly amazed me – it just illustrated the determination of the Government to win at all costs, whatever the expense. (W15)

The NUM Branch President at Maltby colliery in Yorkshire described the limitations of picketing in Nottinghamshire:

> We went to most pits in Nottinghamshire. It was murder at Blidworth. In the early stages, the men went on strike when we spoke to them in the colliery canteen. But eventually [the police] closed off the area, there was a blue cordon around Nottinghamshire. We could get near enough the scabs to see them going into work and to shout at them, but not to talk to them and state our case. Being from an area close to the Nottinghamshire border . . . we knew all the backroads into Nottinghamshire, and we would drive across farmers' fields . . . But eventually the police had all these points covered. We couldn't get off the motorways into Nottinghamshire either. (Y22)[10]

It was, however, the failure of miners in May and June 1984 to prevent BS from moving coking coal from the Orgreave coking plant in Yorkshire to its Scunthorpe steelworks that underscored the determination of the state to defeat mass picketing. The NUM national leadership hoped for a repeat of the Saltley episode in 1972; instead, Orgreave was 'the pickets' Waterloo' (Jenkins 1988: 233). As thousands of miners from all over the country converged on Orgreave, they were met by 8,000 policemen equipped with riot helmets, shields and truncheons, and with dogs and horses at their flanks (East *et al.* 1985: 309). As Callinicos and Simons describe, the 'result was the greatest violence seen in a British industrial dispute since before the First World War' (1985: 101). For the miners involved, the experience of encountering mounted police charges was unprecedented and traumatic. A miner from Renishaw Park colliery in Derbyshire recalled: 'The police were two fields wide, twenty or thirty feet deep. They had horses at their flanks. It was an awesome sight. You knew you were going into the lion's mouth . . . I saw lampposts snap like matchsticks – levelled horizontally – under the weight of so many pickets'(D47). Miners from South Wales concurred. A miner from Maerdy colliery recalled: 'What I saw there was like nothing we'd ever had on a picket line before' (East *et al.* 1985: 309– 10), while a miner from Penallta offered a vivid account of his own experience at Orgreave:

> . . . it was a *token* gesture more than anything. We're only talking about 150 miners . . . running towards these thousands of police . . . we ended up right at the front and . . . I was stuck against this shield . . . the policemen trying to hit you with these big sticks over the top of these shields . . . and you can't push, because . . . you're like meat in a sandwich, because you've got all your miners behind you pushing, and the police the other side of you, just flat against these shields.
>   . . . it was *that* violent. They done everything bar turn guns on us . . . I think that was the only time I've ever been really frightened . . . [My brother] . . . picked up a fellow off the floor, a miner – he hadn't been touched . . . but he was *that* scared he was physically sick. And when you think of somebody working down that hole . . . he shouldn't really frighten that easily. But the man was physically sick'. (W6)[11]

The miners' experience of state power was not confined to the picket lines. Instead, most miners witnessed a growing police presence during the year within their own localities. This was particularly true of the divided pit villages of Nottinghamshire. As the strike continued, however, pit villages in strikebound areas of the coalfield also began to experience massive police presences as strikebreakers tried to return to work. The Branch President at Maltby colliery in Yorkshire, for example, described how 'when men started to go back at Maltby [around September 1984] we couldn't even get near them because of the police. We could get into the pit yard but the danger then was of being locked in and caught trespassing. Many men were sacked for this'(Y22). Moreover, the policing of the strike tended to be in the hands of non-local police forces. Indeed, many strikers distinguished between local and non-local police forces. The existence of familial ties between local police forces and local mining communities may have led to the former being viewed in a less hostile way by the latter. For the most part, non-local forces were viewed with suspicion, with particular venom reserved for the Metropolitan Police. A Derbyshire striker reflected: 'The Mets were awful. They'd split your skull as soon as talk to you. They were up front, the ones least sympathetic to you. Your village [policeman] would be the one they'd hand you to after they were done with you'(D47). At neighbouring Shirebrook colliery, a striker commented: 'The Welsh [police] were okay . . . the Devon and Cornwall police were gentlemen.

But the Met was different'(D39). A miner at Ireland colliery described how 'the Mets were awful. They taunted us and tried to provoke us' (D42), while a colleague at the pit said that 'the South Wales police were fine, but the Mets were terrible'(D45). At Bevercotes colliery in Nottinghamshire, a striker felt that 'the Met and Essex police were particularly bad, the Wiltshire and Greater Manchester police not so bad'(N32). And at Tower colliery in South Wales, a striker said that 'the Metropolitan Police were horrible – they hated us. The local police were okay'(W24).[12]

The fact that the police forces involved were *not* local merely reinforced the feeling of strikers that their villages were being occupied by something akin to a foreign army. For example, villagers in Easington in the Durham coalfield were outraged when, amidst scenes of uproar, police successfully escorted the first strikebreaker in the area back to the work at the local colliery. One woman, observing the behaviour of riot police, commented: 'It's not their village you see. They don't care.' Following the strikebreaker's return to work, 'for three days police marched through the village – Gwent Police; police from Northampton. Strangers'. Another woman proclaimed: 'I never thought I'd see what I've seen on the streets of Easington. We're occupied. We've been occupied by the police. They've brought violence to the village . . . For one man. We'll never forget this – never' (Beynon 1984: 114–15).

Strikers elsewhere recounted how their own communities had also been besieged. In South Wales, a Penallta miner commented 'As far as the miners were concerned, for that twelve months, this was a police state . . . And I'm not just talking about on the picket line. Because the police got to know the vehicles that different miners were using – myself included – to go picketing, and they'd stop you even going shopping with [your] wife . . . they'd recognize the vehicle and stop it'(W6). The Lodge Chairman at nearby Oakdale colliery concurred: 'In '72 and '74, I could get in my car and go where I wanted, no one stopped me. But in '84–'85 – I live only five miles from where Oakdale colliery was, and by the time I'd gone from where I'm living . . . to "The Crown" in Pontllanfraith, which would be about two miles, the police would be stopping me, they wouldn't let us have access anywhere . . . you couldn't move outside your own area'(W16).

In Derbyshire, a miner at Markham colliery described events in his home village: 'You couldn't get out of Killamarsh, pensioners were stopped from going to Worksop to go shopping. They'd let you picket your own pit, but it was a right job getting out of the village'(D34). In this context, the worst predicament was that faced by the minority of striking miners in the Nottinghamshire coalfield. In Ollerton, a striker, originally from the North-East, reflected:

It was the *way* this county was blockaded off – you were in this county and that was it . . . this village in *particular* . . . if I got out of the village, I couldn't get back in . . . *because* of my accent. The police would stop you, ask you, 'What you're doing here? You're going picketing?' – 'No, I'm going home' – 'With an accent like that, you're going home?' – They didn't believe you, you see . . . it took us three hours to get back in the village . . . and I've lived here nearly 28 years! (N4)

In sum, the 1984–5 strike was sustained in an environment dramatically different from that of 1972 and 1974. Indeed, the effectiveness with which state power was deployed in 1984–5 contributed critically to the tactical failure of the miners to effect cuts in the power supply. Yet it is also important to consider the impact of such state power on the consciousness of miners. Green, using a 'rigorous definition of class consciousness' (1990: 181) in her study of the impact of policing on the Nottinghamshire pit village of Ollerton argues that 'while the policing of the strike considerably heightened the political consciousness of the striking community, it did not call into question the fundamental *raison d'être* of the policing agencies nor of their more generalized role in containing industrial conflict in capitalist society' (1990: 199). This may be so, but the impact of many miners' first-hand experience of state power should not be underestimated. Violent confrontations between miners and police, or troops, were not, of course, new to the coalfields. Yet mining communities had, for the most part, been stable, peaceful and law-abiding (Beynon 1985). As such, what most strikers experienced in 1984–5 was *unprecedented* in their lifetimes. Shocked at their treatment by the police, and bewildered at being labelled criminals, many, by the end of the strike, had changed their views of the police (though often with notable reluctance). A miner at Goldthorpe colliery in Yorkshire commented: 'The aggravation was terrible . . . the police are a law unto themselves'(Y8). A miner at Cwmgwili colliery in South Wales told how 'I used to respect, have faith in, the police, but not any more'(W39). At Penallta colliery, a miner reflected: 'Out of all this . . . I don't think the police came out of it well at all. They lost a lot of respect in the community and the kids have got no respect for them. I mean . . . when I was young, if you seen a policeman coming, if you hadn't done *nothing* wrong, you'd be wanting to get out of the way; now [the kids] all . . . hate them. What can [the police] do? I think . . . they've earned it'(W6).

Furthermore, any illusions that the police had been neutral arbitrators in an industrial dispute had been shattered. The Branch Delegate at Sharlston colliery in Yorkshire spoke for many: 'They were bitter experiences in the '84 strike. The police had no mercy whatsoever . . . They'd do anything in their power to overthrow us. I believe it was a battle that the police wanted to see Thatcher win'(Y40). A miner at Allerton Bywater colliery, arrested for picketing at Babbington colliery in Nottinghamshire, reflected: 'We were taken into custody overnight . . . we were treated like scum. It's a democratic country, so they say, but at that particular time, it was a police state. When me and my son were arrested . . . police called us "Yorkshire Communist bastards" – that really got to me'(Y43). And a miner at Tower colliery in South Wales complained that the police

> were brought in . . . to break the strike . . . it's supposed to be . . . everything is right in this country, you can move around as your free will . . . free speech and everything else – but *we* wasn't allowed to travel . . . it was really rough and nasty . . . With some people, it's very bitter *now* towards the police. I know it's wrong, perhaps . . . but people have good memories . . . and they remember how they were treated . . . and they just didn't like it. The police are not there to fight other people . . . they are there to carry out the law . . . and there's no *way* in many cases that we were breaking the law . . . but they said we was, and that was an end to it . . . we had no say in the matter. And I didn't like that part of it. (W17)

That miners came to view the agencies of law enforcement in a different light is significant in and of itself. More importantly, though, the exercise of state power in 1984–5 not only reinforced the miners' conviction that the Thatcher Government was, as a Yorkshire miner described, 'rotten through to the core'(Y7), but also reawakened their well-entrenched perceptions of themselves as an historically isolated and victimized section of the working population. In forcing miners to return to their traditions of initiative and endurance in the face of adversity, the exercise of state power therefore ironically laid the basis for a wider politicization amongst the miners and their supporters. This is critical to understanding the efforts the miners made to sustain the strike, and the raising of consciousness that resulted from such efforts.

The Miners and the Labour Movement

In many ways, the miners' strike was conducted in a very traditional manner. The NUM attempted to consolidate the strike by picketing a range of industrial targets. Loyalty to the Union and respect for the picket line were major rallying cries. In addition, the miners sought support from the TUC, individual trades unions and the Labour Party. While such support was, in difficult circumstances, considerable, it is important, none the less, to note its shortcomings – for these, alongside the aggressive role played by the state, form the context in which the miners' own activities are assessed in Chapter 6.

The Miners and the Trades Unions

> In '74 . . . within the space of a week, we were down to a 3-day week – and
> that was every worker, every workplace, every factory . . . But in '84 . . . we
> *didn't* have the support of other trade unionists . . . we had a lot of people
> who were crossing picket lines . . . with the result . . . that . . . during the 12
> months of the strike, we never seen one light go out . . . we didn't see a
> flicker of any electricity cut-offs at all. (W14)

Most miners recognized that the victories of 1972 and 1974 had been
achieved with the help of other unions. Reflecting on the triumph at
Saltley in 1972, a South Wales miner described how 'there were *thousands* of workers in Birmingham come out and dropped . . . tools at that
time, and just marched to Saltley'(W12). Early on in the 1984–5 strike,
therefore, the NUM sought the support of other unions, particularly
those in the critical arena of transportation such as the Transport and
General Workers Union (TGWU), the National Union of Railwaymen
(NUR) and the National Union of Seamen (NUS). Clear statements of
support given to the NUM by the leaderships of these unions were
reaffirmed, and reinforced by others, at the September 1984 Trades
Union Congress (TUC) when delegates overwhelmingly (though not
unanimously) endorsed the TUC General Council's statement on the
strike.[13] For example, the TGWU leader proclaimed: 'From the start of
this dispute, the [TGWU] has endeavoured to give total support – moral,
physical and financial – to the NUM in its struggle to save pits, jobs and
mining communities . . . Today my union reaffirms that commitment'.[14]
Union leaders in 1984, however, struggled to deliver on their promises.
The TUC itself was divided in the face of Thatcherism's offensive
against trade unionism. While some unions embraced 'new realism' as
a means of weathering the storm, others (including the NUM) argued
for complete defiance of anti-union legislation. Furthermore, the steep
recession in manufacturing had taken its toll – union membership, which
had peaked in 1980 at over 12 million, had declined to under 10 million
by 1985 (Jenkins 1988: 234). For these reasons, 'the men who sat upon
the General Council of the TUC were generals without troops' (Jenkins
1988: 229).

   How, though, did the miners themselves assess the performance of
the wider union movement in the 1984–5 strike? As on previous occasions, relations between the miners and the TUC were strained. The
TUC had long been viewed by the miners with suspicion and contempt
– not least, as a South Wales miner noted, for its betrayal of the MFGB
in 1926: 'The TUC . . . well, we just didn't see them . . . they weren't
involved at any level . . . you can subscribe [*sic*] that, mind you, to a
reluctance by us, initially, to . . . go to the TUC . . . it's historical . . . in

'26, when we did go to the TUC [during] the General Strike . . . after nine days, they . . . recommended [a return] to work, and of course, the mineworkers struggled for another six months. So there's an *historic* . . . suspicion of the TUC'(W14).

Notably, the NUM leadership, for the first six months of the strike, did not seek the formal assistance of the TUC. Even after the TUC became involved in the strike in September 1984, relations with the NUM remained uneasy. The NUM's complaints in November 1984 that the TUC had provided little of the concrete assistance it had promised to the miners exacerbated divisions within the union movement.[15] When, at a miners' rally in South Wales later that month, the TUC General Secretary condemned violence on the picket lines 'from whatever quarter', furious strikers lowered a hangman's noose from the ceiling above him.[16] A spokesman for the South Wales Area NUM likened the speech to the 'great betrayal' of 1926. Soon after, miners' suspicions that the TUC was seeking to take the initiative in the strike away from the NUM were reinforced when the power station engineers' leader – 'a key moderate on the TUC general council' – declared that 'the TUC general council, with its wider responsibilities to the trade union movement as a whole, must establish clearly whether it has a view of its own in this protracted, bitter and ever more damaging dispute'.[17] The TUC further distanced itself from the miners following a decision by the NUM in December 1984 to adopt a position of total defiance in its ongoing confrontations with the courts and to call on the TUC to 'mobilise industrial action to stop this most vicious threat in our history to the freedom and independence of British trade unionism'. The TUC, faced with a choice of either stepping beyond the law, or 'backing away from a legal challenge which could put under threat its funds and possibly those of its affiliated unions', chose the latter course, much to the miners' dismay.[18] As such, the TUC, for most strikers, had merely confirmed its reputation as an ineffective and unreliable source of support. At Maltby colliery, Yorkshire, a miner complained that the 'TUC has sat on the fence through all of this – a waste of time and money'(Y29). At Whitwell colliery in Derbyshire, a striker agreed: 'The TUC was absolute rubbish, a waste of time. It give us nothing . . . whatsoever. In fact the TUC haven't helped *nobody*, and they never helped us. I think they just wanted to be *seen* to be helping us, but . . . they were standing on the sidelines all the time . . . We could have had a lot more help'(D41).

Condemnation of the TUC was accompanied, however, by a more mixed appraisal of the support received from individual unions. In general, miners emphasized the importance of the physical industrial support they had received in the 1972 and 1974 strikes. A Derbyshire

miner remarked that the miners 'had backing from more unions . . . in
'72 and '74. Because we stopped everything moving by road and rail
because we had the backing of the transport unions'(D22). A Yorkshire
striker felt that 'really, there was no comparison [in 1984–5] with the
backing from other trade unions in '72 and '74'(Y43).[19] In contrast,
miners noted the reluctance of unions in 1984–5 to assist the NUM by
staging industrial action of their own. Support, instead, had been
financial rather than physical. A striker at Bevercotes colliery in
Nottinghamshire felt that 'most of the support in '84 was financial –
food, soup kitchens – from the likes of the GMB and TGWU'(N32). The
NUM Lodge Chairman at Oakdale colliery in South Wales commented:
'what we had in '84–'85, we had *financial* support, but we didn't have
the physical support, and really it was the physical support we *wanted* –
people refusing to move coal, people refusing to *use* it. This is what we
wanted, but we didn't get it'(W16). A miner at Penrhiwceiber colliery
added: 'The trade union movement as a whole, you had people like [the
AEU] who . . . can give all the moral, and . . . can give all the financial
support, but . . . [are] not going to give any *practical* support. And the
practical support meant coming out on the picket line . . . and stopping
work'(W14). And a miner at Thurcroft colliery in Yorkshire complained
that 'financially, there was support, as much as in the 1970s. I don't
think *any* unions gave us industrial *muscle* . . . we had an alliance with
the NUR and the ISTC. We'd given support to the ISTC in their 1980
strike – Thurcroft came out when the ISTC sent pickets. But the ISTC
did not help us in 1984–5' (Y24).

Overall, therefore, as a South Wales miner reflected, the physical
support rendered to the miners did not live up to the pledges of help
made by trade union leaders:

> We saw different things in the '84 strike which we didn't see in '72 and '74
> . . . I remember the Trade Union Conference in . . .'84, where the leaders of
> the trade unions were getting up and pledging great support . . . from the
> rostrum, which was fine, and it was great rhetoric . . . but at the end of the
> day, when it came to deliver the goods, the very people that they were
> actually representing – they weren't there. I mean we saw the T and G Union
> members driving lorries and ferrying stuff up and down these valleys. There
> was a support as far as . . . 'yes, we agree with you' – there's a sympathy
> vote . . . and 'we'll help you all we can financially', and all the other things.
> But when it came to actual *action*, which was there in '74, . . . that wasn't
> there in '84. (W12)

None the less, miners emphasized that certain unions had been better
than others – some, after all, *did* provide industrial support for the NUM
during the strike. From its earliest stages, the NUR instructed its 150,000

members to black the movement of all coal and coking coal.[20] Between March and June 1984, BR, BS and the Central Electricity Generating Board (CEGB) (80 per cent of whose supplies were moved by rail) all acknowledged that production was being affected by the action of train drivers.[21] As such, many miners praised the NUR for its role in the strike. A miner at Allerton Bywater colliery in Yorkshire felt that the railwaymen 'put up a terrific fight for us. A lot of [train] drivers got threatened with the sack for not transporting coal'(Y43), while in South Wales, the Lodge Secretary at Penallta colliery commented: 'It was definitely the railway workers . . . There was very little coal being moved by rail . . . unless the NUM okay'd it. So I think the railway workers . . . were definitely very supportive'(W7).

To a lesser extent, the miners paid tribute to the efforts of the dockers (who staged brief, sporadic, strikes during the year) and the seamen in blocking imports of coal. A miner at Taff Merthyr pit in South Wales felt that 'the dockers . . . especially in our area . . . was helping us 100 per cent'(W2), though a colleague at the pit commented: 'We had quite good support from the dockers, when the boys used to go down . . . to Southampton . . . but . . . I found that the dockers . . . *locally* weren't so co-operative as the ones . . . from further afield . . . in England'(W3).

In addition, several other unions, while in less critical sectors of the economy, were none the less praised for their efforts. The Lodge Chairman at Penallta colliery paid tribute to the nurses who, 'when we were on strike, they give what *little* support they could give – they're not a strong union and they're not a rich union'(W5). At Tower colliery, a striker felt that the 'nurses were marvellous'(W17). A miner at Markham colliery in Debyshire mentioned the efforts of the local government workers' union, the National and Local Government Officers' Association (NALGO): 'there were unions that did back us, but they couldn't have any effect on the strike – such as NALGO – a lot of their people joined the picket lines to give financial help . . . but there was not much else they could do'(D22). One of the main printworkers' unions, the Society of Graphical and Allied Trades (SOGAT '82), was also praised. A striker at Taff Merthyr colliery reflected: 'We had the printing unions, SOGAT '82, and all the people like that . . . and without them people, we wouldn't have survived as long as we did'(W1). At Tower colliery, a striker also thanked SOGAT '82 for sending one hundred turkeys for Christmas to his home town of Treherbert (W29).

However, despite their willingness to acknowledge the support that *had* been given them, miners' perceptions of the performance of the wider trade union movement in 1984–5 were heavily coloured by the failure of several key unions to deliver effective industrial support. From the start of the strike, the two most important unions in the critical arena of electricity supply – the Electrical Electronic Telecommunications and Plumbing Union (EETPU) and the Electrical Power Engineers' Association (EPEA) – gave short shrift to the NUM's proclamation that all power stations in Britain were now 'deemed to be picketed'. Eric Hammond, the General Secretary-elect of the EETPU, stated: 'We in this union are not prepared to use our strength to bring down elected governments'.[22] In September 1984, the EETPU and the EPEA opposed the TUC's blanket endorsement of the NUM's appeal for widespread industrial action. The EETPU's General Secretary commented: 'Our members will be told to carry out their normal duties, and that means crossing picket lines',[23] while the EPEA leader declared: 'The electricity supply industry is not, and never has been, available to solve industrial disputes external to it, not even for the miners'.[24] Not surprisingly, the power unions were castigated by the miners. At Markham colliery in Derbyshire, a miner felt that 'the power workers let us down terribly. If they'd come out . . . we'd have won or at least got a settlement'(D34). The position adopted by Eric Hammond provoked particular outrage. For a miner at neighbouring High Moor colliery, leaders such as he were 'not trade unionists'(D2). At Allerton Bywater colliery in Yorkshire, a striker complained: 'Hammond was a turncoat, not a trade unionist. I never heard a trade union leader come out with speeches like he did. It was really degrading for trade unionism'(Y43).[25]

It was, however, the performance of the TGWU – Britain's largest union – that provoked the fiercest criticism from strikers. While the steadfast support offered by the TGWU's national leadership during the strike was acknowledged, it was none the less blamed for its lack of control over its large and diversified membership. A Markham miner commented: 'The T and G *said* they were supporting us, but the rank and file wasn't'(D34). The Lodge Secretary at Penallta colliery complained: 'The TGWU – they're like a dead whale on a beach, they're no good to no one. They're not even good to themselves. They're so diversified, that whenever one section . . . comes out . . . they haven't even got another section of their members [with them]. They've even got barmaids in Liverpool on their books'(W5).

Certainly, it was the TGWU's inability to prevent its lorry drivers from crossing picket lines that became one of the miners' principal sources of concern, especially as it undermined the sterling efforts of the NUR to stop the movement of coal by rail. As the strike continued, more and more coal was transported in massive convoys of lorries – many of them privately owned. As such, as a Derbyshire surfaceworker reflected, the miners' failure to turn back many lorry drivers at picket lines became a major strategic weakness of the strike: 'The TGWU – most of their members went through the [picket] lines . . . if the TGWU . . . had stopped the transportation of coal, that would have been better than money coming in'(D26). The encounters with lorry drivers on the picket lines therefore became one of the most disheartening experiences of the strike for many miners. A striker at Cwmgwili colliery in South Wales asked: 'These lorry drivers . . . the convoys of trucks . . . how could a man behave like that towards his fellow worker?'(W39), while the Lodge Secretary at Penallta colliery lamented: 'We never stopped them *once* . . . they took over the motorway, you couldn't get near them, anyway . . . so that had a bad effect on morale, watching them, travelling down the motorway, lorries that shouldn't . . . be on the road, being escorted by police'(W7). And at Taff Merthyr colliery, a striker agreed: 'While we were picketing locally . . . it was sort of soul-destroying to think that we'd been out all them months and you had transport drivers just ignoring us and taking coal . . . into power stations . . . if you'd stop them, and you pleaded our case, they'd just . . . ignore you . . . you've got to single the Transport and General workers out because . . . they did sweet bugger-all to . . . help us . . . They worked against us, they did' (W1).[26]

Such frustrations were symptomatic of the miners' wider strategic failure to effect an industrial shutdown, as in 1972 and 1974 (McIlroy 1984: 12). As such, the NUM leadership (especially the National President) cited the lack of industrial support given to the NUM when branding the union movement in general as 'class traitors'. How, though, did the miners themselves view the actions of other workers in the strike? Some felt that the strike had highlighted a change in attitudes amongst workers. A miner at Markham colliery argued that 'In '84, the days of not crossing a picket line had gone . . . [Thatcher] had broken . . . the heart of the trade union movement'(D34). A miner at Goldthorpe colliery in Yorkshire reflected: 'There was a lack of industrial muscle – after four years of Thatcher, she'd got everyone looking after their own backs – "I'm alright, Jack" – that's the result of Thatcherism'(Y9). Other miners pointed to the perennial problem of sheer selfishness: 'I think this selfish attitude comes into it. The lorry drivers were making thousands of pounds on the back of that strike. And . . . they would have been glad to see that strike going for another year'(W5).

None the less, overall, miners were *restrained* in their assessments of why they had not received more physical support from other workers. This, in turn, suggests that their bonds of solidarity with other workers remained resilient despite the strains of the strike. Indeed, the miners themselves were more accommodating than their own Union leadership in two important respects. First, miners were sensitive to the plight of other workers during a period of high unemployment in which employers and the Government were attacking unions in general. A miner at

Penallta colliery commented: 'I think why we didn't get a lot of support
was . . . people were frightened . . . very frightened, because the Government had proved that they intended to win and never mind what it
cost'(W6). A colleague at the pit agreed: 'Why we didn't get that
support . . . is because . . . the propaganda that Thatcher was putting
about, a lot of people unemployed, who were *fighting* for jobs, and there
was people then that were employed who knew that if they didn't play
ball with the employers they would be pushed out'(W9). The Branch
Delegate at Sharlston colliery in Yorkshire spoke similarly: 'The whole
trade union movement has gone through a low ebb . . . they'd seen other
people, before the miners, being attacked . . . the establishment of
industrial laws. I believe people were looking after their own jobs – they
were threatened with "if you do support the miners with industrial
action, you could close your own factory down"'(Y40).

The pressure exerted by the employer was highlighted by the
experiences of a South Wales miner who had picketed the railwaymen:
'We was on the picket lines up in Derby. You'd get one train going
through, but then you'd get some of the drivers *not* going through . . .
they were explaining to us: "we'll stop, and not go through, but they'll
get people then – because we've refused – to get on [the train] and take
it through"'(W18a). A miner at Penrhiwceiber colliery commented on
the predicament of most workers thus: 'there's a lot of the trade unions
had gone through the early '80s when a lot of engineering jobs . . . were
decimated . . . and everybody was losing members and I think there was
a *fear* of Thatcher – there's no doubt about that – the steelworkers had
been out for 13 weeks over the wages issue, and they'd lost, and there
was *definitely* a fear of Thatcher'(W14).

Relations between the miners and the steelworkers during the strike
do, in fact, capture the contrast between the miners' more accommodating attitude towards the plight of other workers and the decidedly
more abrasive attitude of the NUM's national leadership. From the start
of the strike, the NUM leadership aimed to halt steel production as part
of its larger strategy of reducing the country's industrial output.
However, by attempting to impose a blockade of BS's five integrated
plants, the NUM clashed with the priorities of the ISTC which was
determined to maintain what remained of its own industry and membership. In May 1984, Arthur Scargill wrote to Bill Sirs, the ISTC's General
Secretary: 'Throughout this dispute the attitude you have displayed has
been diabolical and in violation of every principle understood and
accepted by the trade union and Labour movement' (McIlroy 1984: 12).
In response, Sirs retorted that the NUM's threat to cut off supplies of
iron ore and coal would be 'catastrophic' for the steel industry.[27] By
September 1984, the ISTC leadership was ignoring requests to accept

only that amount of coking coal and iron ore to the five main steel plants which maintained the safety of the furnaces but produced no steel.[28]

In contrast to the insults being exchanged at the national level, however, miners and steelworkers locally reached a working agreement on the amount of coal to be delivered to the steel plants. In South Wales, where the coal and steel industries remained central to the regional economy, miners allowed coal to be delivered to the Llanwern steel plant in return for which the steelworkers limited production to 75 per cent of normal output. Consequently, steelworkers had lost their production bonus payments (accounting for 40 per cent of their total earnings) but had still raised over £4,000 for miners in collections at the plant gates.[29] In June 1984, however, the NUM's national leadership ordered a halt to supplies to steel plants. Following its decision, local agreements between the NUM and the ISTC collapsed. At Llanwern, the ISTC, angered by the threat of a total blockade, decided to restore full production levels as soon as possible. As a result, therefore, of national-level interference, miners locally lost all control of the situation. Notably, though, both miners and steelworkers were united in directing their anger towards the NUM's national leadership, and not towards each other – the steelmen's leaders 'still had the highest regard for the *Welsh* NUM . . . the understanding between them and the Welsh NUM had been marvellous'. This situation, however, had been transformed by 'outside interference from the national scene'.[30] For the miners, the Lodge Secretary at Penallta colliery could only reflect ruefully on how a painstaking compromise had been undermined:

> Prior to the strike . . . a delegation of workers came to meet us from Llanwern steelworks . . . and essentially, what they were asking was: 'Don't close us down' . . . So when the strike actually took place . . . agreement was reached between . . . Llanwern steelworks . . . and the South Wales NUM, that we would allow . . . a limited amount of coal to go in there, to keep the furnaces hot, but the amount of steel that would be produced would be very minimal . . . And that agreement was used . . . but then it came from 'on high', that that was not to be the case, that they were not to have any fuel at all – that was a national decision, which overruled our *Area* decision. Consequently, you saw then the convoys [of lorries] . . . that had a *very* bad effect on morale. (W7)

The second way in which striking miners demonstrated restraint in their views of other workers' actions was by acknowledging the damaging consequences of their own internal divisions. With most Nottinghamshire miners working, many strikers accepted that other workers could question, with some justification, the strength of the NUM's own case. In Yorkshire, a miner asked: 'Who's going to back the miners with

Nottinghamshire working? If they'd have all come out, *then* we'd have got the backing of other trade unions'(Y43). In Derbyshire, a miner at Markham colliery commented: 'You asked lorry drivers to back you, and they said "get your own men out first", which you couldn't argue with, because our own men weren't backing us'(D22). And in Nottinghamshire itself, a striker lamented the fact that the issue of non-striking miners had been raised 'all the time . . . especially from the lorry drivers . . . and it was understandable . . . we were trying to stop them going into the pit . . . to transport coal . . . and they came out with a bit of an argument. They turned around . . . and said "How do you expect to picket us out when you can't even get your own men out, get your own house in order, *before* trying to get other trade unionists out", which . . . is perfectly true'(N4).[31]

The Miners and the Labour Party

Reflecting on the Labour Party's role in the 1984–5 strike, the Party's Chairman wrote: 'The Labour Party, as a whole, did a good job during that year. According to Arthur Scargill, it raised more money than any other section of the movement. The NEC has given its unqualified support and has been right behind the miners from the very beginning. That is something of which I am proud' (Heffer 1985: xiv). In April 1984, the party's NEC voted unanimously to provide more than £100,000 per week for the miners' strike fund.[32] At its Annual Conference in October 1984, delegates overwhelmingly endorsed a motion expressing full support for the miners and their families 'in their struggle to defend the coal mining industry'.[33] Yet the strike also exposed deep divisions within the party, especially at the national level. The Parliamentary leadership, reeling from the General Election disaster of June 1983, and still under a cloud from the 1979 'Winter of Discontent' which had destroyed the last Labour Government, enjoyed a distinctly uneasy relationship with the NUM throughout the strike. The newly-elected leader, Neil Kinnock, occupied a particularly uncomfortable position. Viewing Labour's close association with the unions as an electoral liability, he was, at the same time unable – and unwilling – to distance himself completely from the miners. He had little influence over the Union's NEC. Consequently, 'throughout the strike Kinnock was powerless; he was unable to end it, unable to control it, unable to condemn it' (Jenkins 1988: 237). His discomfort was exacerbated by the NUM leadership's persistence in blaming the police alone for violence in the strike. He did not share a platform with the miners' leader until June 1984, and did not visit a miners' picket line until January 1985. As Leader of the Opposition, he did not force an Emergency Debate in Parliament until the dying weeks of the strike (Jenkins 1988: 237). In addition, his scathing description of Arthur Scargill as 'the Labour Movement's nearest equivalent to a First World War general' (Jenkins 1988: 237) enraged the Union's NEC.[34]

In contrast, the Labour Party Left supported the miners unambiguously and complained continually of the half-hearted approach of the party's Parliamentary leadership. In August 1984, *Labour Herald* attacked Kinnock for criticising picket line violence: 'Neil Kinnock seems unable to make mention of the strike without a compulsory condemnation of picket line violence . . . The Tories and the press have deliberately set out to portray the strikers as mindless thugs who are keeping the majority of decent miners out by sheer intimidation. Kinnock's statements only help to give credence to this thoroughly false picture'.[35] At the party's 1984 Annual Conference, pandemonium ensued when the EETPU leader criticized a motion condemning 'police-violence against the miners'.[36] And in December 1984, much to the annoyance of the Labour leadership, Tony Benn MP, the longest serving member of the Party's NEC, called for a General Strike of twenty-four hours or longer 'to protect free trade unionism, political freedom and civil liberties in Britain'.[37]

Given these internal divisions, how did the miners – traditionally the most loyal of Labour voters – view the party's performance? Regarding the party nationally, strikers were divided. Surprisingly, many sympathized with the party leadership's predicament, and emphasized the limitations of being in opposition: 'The . . . party, I believe, tried to do their *best*, but . . . the Government at that time was too strong . . . we know they spoke out in many cases . . . what was going on in the strike and the way it was being handled . . . but it was falling on deaf ears, wasn't it? So . . . I think Labour tried to play their part, but they was in opposition and they had no . . . say in it really . . . their hands were tied' (W17). A miner at Markham colliery in Derbyshire concurred: 'They backed us . . . in words, but if they're not in power, what could they have done? If they had been in power, the strike wouldn't have lasted long, but they weren't, and they could only keep shouting, they could criticize the government over the strike, but what [they could] do was very limited'(D22).

Additionally, some strikers defended the Party Leader in 1984–5. A miner at Penrhiwceiber colliery in South Wales declared: 'I won't criticize [Kinnock] too much – he *did* stand on picket lines – I think people ought to be made aware of it – he was outside Oakdale colliery – which is his own constituency – he was outside South Celynen [colliery], which is his own constituency, so . . . he *was* there'(W14). The Lodge Secretary at Oakdale colliery applauded the Party Leader's even-handed condemnation of picket line violence:

If you're leader of the party . . . you've got to work within the confines of
the laws of the country . . . I mean Neil Kinnock was accused, you know, of
not supporting us. But . . . I've got a copy of most of his speeches, that he
made throughout the strike, and he was backing us all the way . . . this is
what I say was the difference between him and Arthur Scargill – Neil
Kinnock would condemn violence . . . on all sides, not on one, but Arthur
would condemn it only on one, and not accept the other side. (W16)

Finally, some strikers were acutely aware of the constraints imposed by
the party's weak electoral position and the dangers of being seen to ally
itself too closely with the NUM. An electrician at Stillingfleet colliery
in Yorkshire felt that 'the party was in a funny situation. They have to
be cautious to get into power . . . The party needed the votes of people
hostile to us'(Y39). At Penallta colliery in South Wales, a miner agreed:

I've heard Neil Kinnock strongly criticized as a leader of the party. Then
again, I had to think well, let's put ourselves in his position, let's put
ourselves in the Labour Party's position. Now we were having a media . . .
that was homing in mostly on the violence that was taking [place] during
the strike . . . and the Tory Party really capitalized on it, didn't they? . . . The
Labour Party leadership . . . they supported the miners and the party and
Neil Kinnock made that quite plain, I thought. But . . . I can understand they
had to be very careful how close they associated themselves because . . . the
violence, it would have [been] construed . . . that 'the Labour Party . . .
accepts violence on the picket lines, the Labour Party don't care about those
innocent people' . . . Now, the Labour Party . . . had to be very careful that
they weren't associated with . . . 'the reds', the 'militants' . . . you know,
the 'stonethrowers' as Neil Kinnock said. And he condemned the
stonethrowers, he also condemned the shield-batterers [riot police] too, if
you remember his speech in the . . . Party Conference at the time . . . and I
think that speech that [he] gave . . . clarified the position they were in. (W12)

In contrast, however, many other strikers had little patience with the
difficulties facing the Labour Party; reactions to its performance at the
national level ranged from despair to disgust. At Sharlston colliery in
Yorkshire, the NUM Branch Delegate commented: 'The philosophy of
certain [leaders] of the Labour Party . . . was not to rock the boat,
to keep on the path of right-wing Labour policies . . . they . . . never
worked for us at all, nationally'(Y40). A striker at Bilsthorpe colliery in
Nottinghamshire added: 'I'd criticize Kinnock . . . I mean [he] couldn't
help his own people, could he? He sat on the fence in *Wales*!'(N4). Some
of the strongest criticism of the Party Leader did, in fact, come from
miners in South Wales, especially those from his own constituency: 'I
think in the main they were rubbish – especially the leader'(W9). The
Lodge Secretary at Penallta colliery remained outraged:

Nationally, they weren't helpful at all. When Neil Kinnock was asked – and he's my local MP – when he was asked to stand on the platform . . . with us, he turned around and said his diary was full, I thought that was a *pathetic* thing to say . . . absolutely *pathetic* – we was in the middle of the . . . biggest strike this country has ever seen . . . every day, people were being lambasted by the television with the sort of scenes that we saw on picket lines . . . with police . . . and confrontations taking place . . . The strike was being watched . . . all through Europe and . . . he couldn't speak on behalf [of us] because his *diary* was full – which was a *ridiculous* statement. Ridiculous. (W7; see also Saville 1986)

However, regardless of their views of the party's performance nationally, the vast majority of strikers praised the activities of the party locally.[38] Thus the Lodge Secretary at Penallta colliery, quoted immediately above, felt that 'on a . . . local basis, I found that they were, on the whole, *helpful* . . . nobody ever thought that this strike was going to last as long as it did. So therefore perhaps they were a bit slow in mobilizing themselves . . . but once asked for [support], it was there. Because I went all over the country, and I found the Labour Party – *local* Labour parties – very helpful'(W7). A miner at the pit agreed: '*Locally*, they were very good. And I think, if the truth were known, locally – right throughout the country . . . right throughout the mining communities, the Labour Party was supportive . . . on a *local* basis, the support was excellent'(W6). A miner at Taff Merthyr colliery spoke in similar terms: 'They was excellent, locally, you couldn't fault it'(W1).

Elsewhere, the Branch Delegate at Derbyshire's Central Workshops recalled how his local party had organized soup kitchens, delivered food parcels and provided information on welfare benefits (D26). In Yorkshire, a miner at Allerton Bywater colliery felt that 'the *local* Labour parties up here were great. They did everything for us – couldn't do enough for us – fundraising, everything'(Y43). At Barrow colliery, a striker described how his local Labour council had helped him during the strike: 'I was a council [house] tenant, and the council froze the rents – I didn't have to pay them'(Y16).

A report in *The Guardian* in December 1984 highlighted how Labour-controlled local authorities throughout the country, but particularly those in the mining areas, were helping the striking miners. In Yorkshire, Barnsley Council spent £1.4 million in extra rates and rent rebates, free school meals for strikers' children and weekly food vouchers to strikers' families. Doncaster Borough Council allocated £85,000 to provide children with food vouchers for Christmas. Leeds City Council spent £68,200 financing free school meals during the holidays, and food for under-fives. Derbyshire County Council spent £233,000 on food parcels for strikers' families. Nottinghamshire County

Council gave £21,000 to miners' wives' support groups and to organizations providing food parcels. West Glamorgan County Council spent £9,500 providing food for local miners. Meanwhile, to the fury of the Conservative opposition, Sheffield City Council raised local taxes by £42,000 to pay for Christmas food hampers for strikers. Across Britain, local authorities made donations to hardship funds, including £200,000 from Tyne and Wear County Council, £100,000 from South Yorkshire Council, £50,000 from Strathclyde Regional Council and £10,000 from Dyfed County Council.[39]

The role of local Labour parties in *non*-mining areas was also critical. A striker at Stillingfleet colliery in Yorkshire acknowledged the efforts of adjacent Castleford Council in setting up kitchens for local miners: 'I lived under Selby Council. Selby is a Tory village – about six NUM families in a village of 300 – so you can understand what pressure we were under – in general, we were struggling for support'(Y39). A striker from the Cynon Valley, South Wales, praised the efforts of Bristol West CLP: 'I done a lot of speaking at the time in Bristol West . . . and spoke in different wards, and . . . the difference between Bristol West and the Cynon Valley . . . there's a vast difference, a *vast* difference. And yet, the support we had from Bristol West was *unbelievable* to this particular village, *unbelievable* – every weekend . . . there were convoys of food coming in here . . . financial help'(W14). Similarly, the hard-pressed minority of strikers in Ollerton, Nottinghamshire, described how Norwich CLP had sustained them through the strike. One miner recalled:

> The most effective [support] we had in the village at the time was Norwich Support Group . . . it was mainly the Labour Party . . . they was coming up every other weekend . . . a convoy, two big transit vans . . . *full* of vegetables, food . . . tins . . . clothes . . . I would *definitely* say Norwich Labour Party was our biggest asset here . . . on one occasion, [it] even financed *our* Labour Party . . . because they needed £200 to get them out of the mess they were in. (N4)[40]

Assessment

Overall, the performance of the labour movement as a whole during the 1984–5 strike, though viewed by strikers as uneven, should not be underestimated. With respect to the Labour Party, its shortcomings at the national level[41] were overcome in the eyes of most strikers by its sterling efforts at the local level.[42] As such, miners remained loyal to the party after the strike – *no* striker interviewed had switched his voting allegiance after 1985.[43]

Similarly, the performance of the trade unions should not be underestimated. Miners paid tribute to those unions that *had* delivered critical industrial support, and were well aware that the demands they made of other workers were difficult ones. Taking into account the other forms of support that unions delivered, it would be wrong, consequently, to argue that the unions 'failed' the miners, for the support they gave was indeed considerable. Indeed, 'faced with the deepest divisions within the NUM , with a marked reluctance of ordinary trade unionists to jeopardise their own jobs by industrial solidarity, and with a massive onslaught by the state, the movement's response has been creditable' (Field 1985: 14). However, in terms of the striking miners' objectives, such a 'creditable' performance was, ultimately, inadequate. As miners testified, the level of *industrial* support was much lower than it had been in 1972 and 1974. Most support given by the unions, and all the support given by the Labour Party, 'helped sustain the strike, but could not win it' (Field 1985: 14). This general absence of industrial solidarity ensured that the strike would not be sustained (let alone won) in an *exclusively* traditional manner. Instead, the shortcomings of the labour movement's help not only reinforced the miners' own traditions of resilience, but pushed them and their communities into new fields of struggle.

Notes

1. *FT*, 4/3/85.
2. *FT*, 4/3/85.
3. *Colliery Guardian*, September 1985, p. 418. This journal placed the NCB's losses at £1.75 billion. Young, though, refers to the NCB's 'record loss' of £2.2 billion in the summer of 1985. (1990: 376).
4. *FT*, 4/3/85. The *MS* (4/3/85) placed the cost at £7.0 billion.
5. *DT*, 30/8/84.
6. A South Wales miner wanting the 'downfall of the government' represented a tiny minority of strikers (W50).
7. *Report of 116th Annual Trades Union Congress* (3–7/9/84, Brighton), London: Trades Union Congress, p. 401.
    Samuel writes, 'The animating spirit of the 1984–5 strike – its "common sense" or implicit ideology – was that of *radical conservatism*. As very often in popular movements of the past, it was a defence of the known against the unknown . . . The miners were fighting against *losing* something . . .' (1986: 22).

146   *Miners on Strike*

8. *The Economist*, 27/5/78, pp. 21–2.
9. See especially Fine and Millar (eds) 1985, and Coulter *et al.* 1984. See also Beynon 1985; Beynon and McMylor 1985; Bunyan 1985; East *et al.* 1985; Geary 1985; Green 1990; Home Office 1985; Jackson and Wardle 1986; Leonard 1985; Lustgarten 1985; McIlroy 1985; Labour Research 1984; Reiner 1984; Scraton 1985; Spencer 1985; Walker and Miller n.d.; Winterton 1984; Wright 1985.
10. East *et al.* cite official police figures stating that during the first twenty-seven weeks of the strike, 164,508 'presumed pickets' were prevented from entering Nottinghamshire (1985: 308).
11. In June 1991, the South Yorkshire police agreed to settle all claims for the violence on the picket lines at Orgreave. Thirty-nine miners wrongly arrested were paid damages totalling £425,000: Following the settlement, the NUM National President and several individual miners demanded a public inquiry into the affair (*I*, 20/6/91; *G*, 21/6/91).
12. Though see Percy-Smith and Hillyard who, calculating the percentage of arrests resulting in injury to the person being arrested, found that the West Yorkshire police were the most heavy handed (24.5 per cent), followed by South Yorkshire (20.2 per cent), Greater Manchester (16.2 per cent) and the Metropolitan Police (14.8 per cent) (1985: 348).
13. See *Report of 116th Annual Trades Union Congress* (3–7/9/84, Brighton), pp. 398–410; 653.
14. Ibid., p. 405.
15. *FT*, 9/11/84.
16. *T*, 14/11/84.
17. *T*, 15/11/84.
18. *FT*, 3/12/84; *G*, 5/12/84.
19. Only a minority of strikers felt that given the length of the 1984–5 strike, the support from other unions had been remarkable. For example, a miner at Barrow colliery in Yorkshire observed, 'In 1984, we got fantastic support from other unions . . . I think it was better than in the '72 and '74 strikes which were not so long'(Y15).
20. *FT*, 3/4/84.
21. *DT*, 26/3/84; *DT*, 8/6/84; *G*, 26/6/84; *G*, 5/7/84.
22. *DT*, 14/5/84.
23. *T*, 2/9/84.
24. *Report of 116th Annual Trades Union Congress*, p. 405.
25. Support for the miners from workers in Britain's power stations was by no means absent in 1984–5. A miner at Tower colliery pointed to isolated pockets of support within the EETPU: 'The big union – the Electrical union – I didn't like their attitudes – and yet having

said that, some of the people in their union was sympathetic towards us anyway. But . . . Hammond . . . wasn't very helpful . . . as a *leader* . . . you could pick individuals out of their union who were probably *very* helpful, in many ways'(W17).

Furthermore, other power station unions were more supportive. In October 1984, TGWU members at seven power stations voted to refuse fresh supplies of coal (*G*, 10/10/84). And the GMB, the union with the largest membership in the electricity industry, distributed £1,000 per day in food vouchers to the miners and their families for the duration of the dispute (*Report of 116th Annual Trades Union Congress*, p. 404).

26. However, as a colleague at the pit recalled, many lorry drivers were non-union labour anyway: 'The T and G – terrible . . . we had lorry drivers driving straight through picket lines . . . it was no help to us at all. Although half of them wasn't even members of the T and G anyhow'(W2). In June 1984, with non-union lorry drivers allegedly being paid £180 per day for two trips to and from the Orgreave coking plant in Yorkshire, a TGWU organiser commented: 'They are highly-paid strike breakers – scab labour. We cannot think of anything so low' (*DT*, 8/6/84).

27. *DE*, 5/7/84.

28. *FT*, 28/9/84.

29. *STe*, 2/7/84.

30. *STe*, 2/7/84.

31. Indeed, the only weak spot in the NUR's otherwise robust support for the miners was in North Nottinghamshire where the majority of local miners were working and where, in June 1984, the national leaders of the NUR and the Associated Society of Locomotive Engineers and Firemen (ASLEF) failed to persuade local railwaymen to respect striking miners' picket lines (*DT*, 8/6/84).

32. *DT*, 26/4/84.

33. *DT*, 2/10/84.

34. *DT*, 14/9/84.

35. *FT*, 20/8/84.

36. Jenkins 1988: 238; *DT*, 2/10/84.

37. *T*, 7/12/84.

38. A *minority* of strikers were equally critical of the party's performance at the national and local levels. For example, a miner at Goldthorpe colliery in Yorkshire felt that 'the Labour Party, in '84–5, were a waste of time . . . They were no better at the local level' (Y8).

39. *G*, 13/12/84.

40. Of course, local Labour parties in Nottinghamshire were in a

particularly difficult situation. The miner quoted above added: 'Our *own* Labour Party here – they didn't know which way to go . . . 'cause they were in the middle . . . it's alright for people to say that they sat on the fence, *but* . . . how could they represent people that were working and people that was . . . on strike . . . I didn't think they *could* take sides . . . although they could have done a lot more than they actually done'(N4).

41. Field, though, pointing to the support provided to local branches by the Party press, regional organizations and Labour authorities, argues that the role of the Party nationally should not be under-estimated (1985a: 14).

42. A small minority of strikers emphasized the role of other parties at the local level. The efforts of the Communist Party of Great Britain (CPGB), though wracked by divisions between its pro-Moscow and Eurocommunist wings, were acknowledged by the Branch Delegate (a Party member) at Sharlston colliery in Yorkshire: 'A mass of the "old brigade" people gave their hearts and soul, but the "Euros", they did very little'(Y40). A miner at Penallta colliery in South Wales also praised the CPGB: 'Even the Communist Party around here – militants and all that – they couldn't do enough for us, and I'm not a militant, I've never agreed with the Militant Tendency and all that, but we were getting help from everywhere'(W5). Meanwhile, a miner at nearby Oakdale colliery paid tribute to Plaid Cymru (the Welsh Nationalist Party): 'The Labour Party, locally, was fairly good, but Plaid Cymru beat them hands down . . . I'm not a supporter, but Plaid Cymru was very supportive during the strike' (W50).

43. For example, a Taff Merthyr miner commented: '[The party] doesn't show up all that well . . . in my opinion . . . [I] never had a lot to thank them for, actually . . . but that don't mean to say I wouldn't vote Labour again'(W3).

6

Class Consciousness and the Striking Miner II: The Experience of Struggle

Introduction

> The wild men are coming down from the mountains of history and out of the dark past.
>
> D. Douglass, *Come and Wet This Truncheon: The Role of the Police in the Coal Strike of 1984/1985*

In the 1984–5 strike, the localized world of the miner was a source of great strength. Many of the activities in which the mining communities engaged assumed – out of necessity – a very traditional character. For example, the establishment of soup kitchens to feed the local population, and the picking of coal from slag heaps to fuel local fires, reawakened memories of the 1926 strike. However, the length of the struggle ensured that strike action in 1984–5 assumed many new dimensions. The role played by the women of the coalfields astounded not only the urban Left watching from afar but, more importantly, the miners themselves. In attempting to sustain themselves and their families, and to rally support for their cause, the women and men of the coalfields entered new worlds and established links with individuals and groups with whom they had hitherto enjoyed little contact.[1] As such, the localized world of the miner was, in 1984–5, both reinvigorated and, to a large degree, transcended. Indeed, the strike embodied a shift, however tentative, from an old to a new form of struggle – 'an industrial dispute was transformed into a communal act'. Consequently, the mining communities did indeed emerge from their 'dark past'.

The Substance of Struggle

Community Action in the 1984–5 Strike

> This village has had its share, if that is the word, of fatalities; men have paid for the coal lying on the coal tips with their blood, and morally the coal is

ours. And we will win, through principle, determination, guts. We will obtain an honest and just victory.[2]

The sentiments of a Yorkshire striker underscore the determination with which mining communities sustained themselves during the 1984–5 strike. Such endurance, however, was not rooted in determination alone, but in the ability to meet the concrete costs of forgoing wages for an entire year – as a miner at Cynheidre colliery, South Wales, noted, 'It's all very well to talk of the *miners* on strike – really, the whole family was on strike'(W43). Lacking any strike pay and adequate welfare benefits, the mining communities established an 'alternative welfare distribution system' (Massey & Wainwright 1985: 8) on a massive scale: 'the network of women and mixed support groups has given rise to an alternative, community-based system of food, clothing, financial *and* morale distribution which has sustained about half a million people for nearly a year' (Francis 1985d: 14).

Faced with the need to feed striking miners and their families, soup kitchens were established across the coalfields for the first time since 1926. The many women's action groups and support groups which emerged in pit villages early in the strike played a central role in the provision of meals and distribution of food parcels to strikers' families. The scene in June 1984 at the strike centre at Newbridge Miners' Institute, South Wales, where a group of women had just cooked and served ninety-seven free meals, was typical.[3] At Keresley in Warwickshire, the sports pavilion – commandeered by strikers' wives – served 200 men, women and children with free daily meals, while another 250 people went to two other soup kitchens in the village.[4] At a food depot (loaned by the local council) in Abertillery, South Wales, a miner and his family prepared weekly food rations valued at roughly £5 each – 'Five thousand of these go to the neediest in a community of 8,000 miners across this valley'.[5]

The funding of such a support system, and the preservation of morale, depended largely on the initiative of the mining communities themselves. A miner's wife in Newbridge, South Wales, commented: 'We run raffles, coffee mornings, collections at churches, beg, you know, anything to get money for food'.[6] In West Wales, an array of activities took place in the Neath, Dulais and Swansea valleys to sustain the strike. In May 1984, at a rally organized by a local women's support group, a thousand people marched behind Dulais Valley Silver Band to Seven Sisters to raise funds and to hear speeches from local NUM leaders, Labour Party members and leaders of women's support groups.[7] Throughout the year, events were organized both to boost morale and fund the increasing demand for food parcels. In June 1984, coffee evenings, dances and barbecues were held at local Miners' Welfare Institutes, as well as various public meetings and a national lobby of Parliament.[8] Jumble sales, auctions and children's discos were held regularly during the strike. At Christmas, every striker received a fowl, and every striker's child sweets, a gift, a Christmas party and a visit to a pantomime.[9]

Not surprisingly, strikers overwhelmingly praised their local communities during the strike. Often, as the Branch Delegate at Sharlston colliery in Yorkshire observed, miners were supported by their family and relatives: 'Naturally, if you came from a mining background, you'd got aunties and uncles, mothers, fathers, sisters . . . [who] . . . supported you . . . in lots of ways – food, financially'(Y40). Furthermore, some strikers were able to rely on their wife's wages: '. . . the men around here had food parcels, but because . . . I had (my) wife working . . . with a full wage . . . I wouldn't take a food parcel'(W17). Mostly, however, miners praised the local community as a whole. A Derbyshire striker recalled that his home village of Glapwell 'responded very well. People all threw in together – it's a small village'(D20). Similar sentiments were expressed in the tight-knit communities of the South Wales coalfield. A striker from Cwmdare said that 'the community here was tremendous . . . they had every sympathy'(W18).

In addition, miners pinpointed the various sources of, and dimensions to, the support from their communities. Undoubtedly, donations to food collections were especially prized. A miner at Tower colliery, South Wales, recalled: 'The community was *excellent* . . . because I . . . went around . . . the houses . . . for donations toward food parcels . . . and people put in – every door you knocked – they were only too willing to give . . . something'(W17). A miner from Cefn Forest, near Penallta colliery, recalled: 'You know, it's not very nice when you've got to go around knocking on people's doors, asking them whether they'd like to support the miners, with food and such things – but we *did* it. And the support you had was *tremendous*. The boys were taking home a bag of food *every* week, after the first few weeks . . . the *communities* themselves – it was the best backing we ever had'(W8).

Older members of the community were especially praised. A striker's wife at High Moor colliery, Derbyshire, described how 'it was the old people, from the old mining industry – pensioners who'd been miners themselves who would chuck the odd fiver into your pocket during the strike. The younger ones couldn't manage that, but they did what they could'(D7). A miner at Cwmfelinfach commented that 'during the '84 strike, you had sympathy off the older person . . . people who could ill afford [it] . . . the older person would give you food . . . because they could remember what happened in the past'(W13).

Naturally, such support was a boost to morale. A Yorkshire striker described the support given to him: 'Here at Garforth, it was originally a mining village, but it's grown into a town . . . My own neighbours –

I'd just moved, I didn't know them – brought vegetables, bread, the odd
five pounds – you found out who your true friends were in that strike'
(Y43). A South Wales miner concurred: 'Everybody was helpful . . . in
many ways . . . whether giving you a bit of food, or if . . . they seen you
out, always come on to you and have a few words with you, *about* the
strike – "How's it going?" "Are you doing well?" . . . that kind of support'(W17).

Additionally, local businesses donated to the miners' cause – accepting perhaps 'with varying enthusiasm . . . that the fate of their business
is inextricable from the goodwill of the miners' families'.[10] Thus a
striker at Taff Merthyr colliery noted that 'we had tremendous support
from the community as a whole . . . even local shopkeepers, business
people . . . small factories'(W1). A wool shop in the West Wales village
of Duffryn Cellwen offered cut-price clothing for miners' children.[11]
NUM Branch Officials at Brodsworth colliery, Yorkshire, cited the support of Heinzel's Frozen Cakes, a local company employing many
miners' wives.[12] Local banks and building societies were also praised for
their generally understanding attitude. A Penallta miner commented: 'I
mean even people we owed money to, didn't press: the mortgage people
. . . during that twelve months . . . didn't put pressure on us to pay, at
all'(W6).[13] Public houses enhanced their status as the mainstay of social
life in the mining areas by raising money through raffles, as was the case
at 'The Red Lion' in Crynant, South Wales,[14] or offering cut-price beer,
as in the case of 'The Poachers' in Rossington, Yorkshire.[15] Several
strikers recalled the goodwill of both proprietors and patrons of their
local pub. A miner at Penallta colliery described how he 'had a lot of
support from the pub . . . in the end it was getting embarrassing to go in
there, because I'd start off with the landlady saying there was a pint
behind the bar for me, and in the end, there'd be about eight pints there.
And then you'd go home sometimes with more money than I was going
out with'(W5). A Derbyshire striker commented: 'I went to "The White
Hart" in Eckington – it had a smashing landlord. I had a job getting
home. They wouldn't let you spend your own money!'(D34).

However, it is crucial to underscore strikers' emphatic acknowledge-
ment of the role played by women in the strike. Some viewed the
women's role simply in terms of having stood by their husbands. A
Penallta miner commented: 'I think in a *non*-active way . . . that women
played a dramatic role in it, by *allowing* the men to do what they felt was
right, at the time. Because they didn't . . . put any pressure . . . on the
men to get back to work'(W7). A colleague at the pit agreed, seeing the
most effective source of support as 'the women. Without a doubt. Full
stop. If you didn't have that support, the strike would have crumbled in
the earlier part of the year. And I don't only mean . . . the women who

were active in gathering food . . . money, and things like that. I mean the
. . . women who stood behind their husbands during the strike, which is
more important. Which they *did*'(W4).

Many more miners, though, were keen to emphasize the *active* role
of women. A miner at Markham colliery in Derbyshire felt that 'some
of the women did marvellous jobs . . . fantastic – they helped with
breakfasts, put meals on, issuing food parcels, they really put some
work in'(D22). A miner at Thurcroft colliery in Yorkshire described the
women's support groups as 'fantastic. If these hadn't been formed, by
our wives and girlfriends . . . things would have been tight'(Y23), while
at Stillingfleet colliery, a striker commented: 'We got food parcels from
the Women's Support Group . . . without them, a lot more would have
gone under a lot quicker . . . the Women's Support Group based in Selby,
incorporating all the Selby pits – this was the only support we got . . .
it's a Conservative area'(Y39).

Furthermore, as the NUM's National Vice-President noted, the
women had been 'out in *front* of the miners on many occasions'[16] – not
least, as a South Wales miner observed, on the picket lines: 'I [think] the
women were a lot more effective than us . . . because the police couldn't
go in so hard with them . . . and the women seemed to do a lot better.
They seemed to go out on the roads, they seemed to stop things better
than men, because the men were just getting pushed back or [were]
fighting . . . but [the police] couldn't do it to the women'(W19).

Thus the activity and support *within* the mining communities themselves in 1984–5 outlined here is key to understanding how the strike
was sustained for so long. Yet it is not the whole story, for the miners'
endurance was reinforced, and their experiences enriched, by the help
they sought and received from other places.

Localism Transcended

We got fantastic support from all over the country. (D22)

Undoubtedly, the traditional isolation of the mining communities was
shattered in 1984–5. The miners sought and received support from
individuals, groups, organizations and communities in non-mining, and
non-industrial, parts of Britain and beyond. Formidable links were established, for example, between the pit villages of South Wales and many
rural and urban centres across England. A miner at Oakdale colliery
praised the efforts of supporters in Bristol and the London borough of
Hackney (W50). At Betws colliery, a miner cited the London borough
of Lambeth as a significant source of support (W38). The Lodge Chairman at Penrhiwceiber colliery described how 'we had affiliations with

people in . . . Chertsey, Walton-on-Thames . . . Hastings . . . we sent children away on holiday and [these people] provided buses for the children' (W15). By January 1985, the people of Oxford were contributing nearly £2,000 per week to Maerdy in the Rhondda valley.[17] In Nottinghamshire, the small band of strikers at Bevercotes and Bilsthorpe collieries paid tribute to the efforts of supporters in Norwich, Basingstoke, Manchester, Liverpool, Stoke and Scotland (N3, N4, N7, N32).

In addition, and for the first time since 1926, substantial support for the miners came from abroad (Saunders 1989). Strikers at Betws and Penallta collieries in South Wales, Bilsthorpe colliery in Nottinghamshire and Maltby colliery in Yorkshire praised the efforts of supporters – especially the mining unions – in France and Belgium (W38, W6, N4, Y29). A miner at Sharlston colliery in Yorkshire recalled the provision of food and clothing by miners from the Donbass coalfield in Ukraine (Y40). With the forging of such links, money, food and clothing poured into pit villages from all over the world. The Gwent and Rhymney Food Fund, in South Wales, received cheques from Norway, Ireland and Australia.[18] Clothes at a strike centre in Abertillery were sent from France, Belgium and Sweden,[19] while at Mardy, clothes donated by Dutch trade unionists arrived in time for Christmas.[20] A miner at Markham colliery in Derbyshire recalled how his backyard had been used as a food storage depot by the local Women's Action Group: 'My garage was full of Spanish jam, Russian flour and tins with no labels on!'(D48). Overall, the scale of non-local support for the mining communities in 1984–5 is demonstrated by analysing the funds collected by and through the NUM Lodge at Oakdale colliery in South Wales, and passed on to the Gwent Food Fund. Of the £57,272.95 collected during the year, £47,030.20 – or 82.1 per cent of the total – came from non-local sources.[21]

The construction and maintenance of such alliances between the pit villages and other communities was a two-way process. Much depended, for example, on the initiative of those in the non-mining areas – as a South Wales miner noted, 'The help we had from people who had nothing to do with mining – who'd never seen a mine – was tremendous'(W38). The Mayor of Hackney 'adopted' the children of South Wales as a charity for Christmas of 1984 (W50). The town of Swindon forged links with the western area of the South Wales coalfield by sending van loads of food, and raising over £30,000 in the course of the year.[22] Mining communities, moreover, hosted various groups and organizations throughout the strike. For example, the London-based Lesbians and Gays Support the Miners twinned itself with the South Wales pit village of Dulais, raising £11,000 in the process, and attending dances in the miners' Welfare Hall (Flynn *et al.* 1985: 40–1; 44). At Crynant,

the Women's Support Group met in November 1984 with represent-
atives of the *News of the World* and *The Sun* newspapers at the local
Welfare Hall, while at Seven Sisters, miners hosted a visit from Brent
Teachers' Miners' Support Group.[23]

The localized world of the pit community was also transcended, however, by the way in which miners themselves *travelled* – as they had
never done before – to rally support for the strike throughout the country
and beyond. A Nottinghamshire striker from Ollerton village visited
Stoke, Manchester, Liverpool and London during the year (N7). A
striker from Penywaun, South Wales, described how the strike 'was a
hard time, but we had some fun. I went to Tolpuddle, Yeovil . . . all over
the country. I made a lot of friends – and enemies'(W24). Miners from
Blaenant colliery in South Wales travelled to London in June 1984
soliciting support from the Union of Construction, Allied Trades and
Technicians (UCATT) in Haringey, a hospital in Bethnal Green and the
City Polytechnic.[24] In September 1984, the South Wales Striking Miners
Choir performed at the Albany Empire in London, before moving on to
the Labour Party's Annual Conference.[25]

Many went further afield. The Branch Delegate at Sharlston colliery
in Yorkshire joined a delegation of 250 British miners touring the
Ukrainian coalfields to receive food and clothing (Y40). A miner from
Whitwell colliery in Derbyshire led a delegation of thirty miners on a
five-week tour of the USSR, including visits to Moscow, Tula and Sib-
eria, and spent two weeks in the Basque region of Spain meeting with
local labour unions (D51). In South Wales, the Treforgan NUM Lodge
sent representatives not only to North Wales, Swindon, the Midlands,
Southampton and Leicester, but also to Paris to meet with the *Confederation General du Travail* (CGT).[26] Two women from Hirwaun,
meanwhile, travelled in late 1984 to Ferrara, Northern Italy, and subsequently addressed twenty-seven meetings.[27]

The testimony of strikers who had travelled during the year highlights
the broad base of support obtained. Some pinpointed certain groups in
particular. A Derbyshire miner described the 'very sympathetic' response from students at Essex University (D36). A South Wales miner
who had travelled to Derby and Oxford also said that 'the students were
marvellous . . . collecting for us . . . they'd go to the cafe, fetch us fish
and chips . . . they wouldn't take no money off us . . . and we'd meet
these students in the evening and fair play, they'd put . . . a social
evening on for us . . . to keep us going'(W18a). A Nottinghamshire
striker, visiting London described the robust support given to the miners
by 'gays and lesbians' and 'blacks who were not impressed by my
experience of being beaten up by the police, as this was the norm for
them'(N7). A striker from Whitwell colliery in Derbyshire spoke of the

support in London from 'Asians and coloured people' and the 'abuse from some white people'(D30). Some strikers had been surprised by certain sources of support. A Nottinghamshire striker told of getting 'abuse at the London School of Economics from the Young Conservatives, but then arguing with one of them and getting a donation'. Back in Nottingham, meanwhile, 'we got abuse from "yobboes", but twenty-pound notes from pinstriped gentlemen'(N7).

Mostly, though, miners emphasized that support had come from *all* quarters. In Yorkshire, a miner at Silverwood colliery commented that 'it was the ordinary person in the street, in my experience' (Y7), while at Penrhiwceiber colliery, South Wales, a miner praised 'ordinary rank-and-file people up and down the country'(W14). For a striker at Betws colliery, it was 'all kinds of people. All races, black and white'(W38). At Oakdale colliery, a striker reflected: 'The ordinary, non-politicized person was very very supportive'(W50).

Many of the support networks that emerged within and between the mining and non-mining communities were solidified during the strike. For example, the women's support groups and action groups that sprang up in the pit villages and localities in the early stages of the strike joined together to stage a 12,000-strong national rally in Barnsley, Yorkshire in May 1984. Latterly, Women Against Pit Closures was established as a national organization: 'By the end of the strike, the women's groups were linked together in a national federation, were demanding associate membership status within the NUM, and had firmly established themselves as a distinctive voice within the coalfields and beyond' (Field 1985a: 17; 1985b: 17–18, 21). The establishment of the Wales Congress in Support of Mining Communities in October 1984 reinforced the existing support for the miners and 'very quickly received the backing from over 300 prominent people in Welsh politics (Plaid [Cymru], Labour and Communist Party), local government, trade unions, the churches, the arts, farmers, the women's movement and the peace movement' (Francis 1985d: 14–15). By the end of 1984, local Congresses were established in North Wales, the Rhondda valley, London and Ireland (Francis 1985d: 15). In addition, the multiple strands of international support were strengthened by the establishment of various miners' support groups in dozens of countries. Barnsley Women Against Pit Closures, for example, had, by the end of the strike, established offices in Belgium, France, West Germany, Holland, Ireland and Italy. The Save Easington Colliery Campaign had established a presence in Canada, Denmark, France, Italy and the USA (LRD 1985: 38–9).

Thus to a remarkable degree, the mining communities in 1984–5 demonstrated 'how people begin to take control of their own lives' (Francis 1985d: 15). Facing a vindictive government, and lacking complete industrial support from the wider labour movement, these communities created a resilient support system for themselves. Certainly, 'the Government could never have anticipated . . . the strength of the resolve in the coalfields to resist for so long against such massive odds' (Francis 1985c: 32). Nothing demonstrates this better than the success of the mining communities' Christmas celebrations. Diggins *et al.* describe how the national Christmas Appeal for striking miners and their families, which raised nearly £400,000 'brought support from every area of the country and from social groups far beyond organised labour' – from retired miners and unemployed workers to doctors and company directors; from civil servants at the Ministry of Defence to a branch of the Indian Workers' Association (1985: 22–3). Many of the accompanying letters saluted the dignity of the miners. A retired social worker wrote: 'I worked in the coalfields for 17 years. I know how quickly miners responded to the appeals for help from those who were less fortunate than themselves. They most certainly do not deserve the abuse that flows from those who know so little about them' (1985: 22).

Consequently, many strikers described 1984 as 'the best Christmas we've ever had as a community'(Y9). At Bevercotes colliery in Nottinghamshire, a striker described Christmas 1984 as 'the best ever. The people of Norwich said they would deal with Christmas, and send food, money and toys for the children – it didn't cost me a penny'(N7). And a striker at Betws colliery in South Wales recalled how 'the people of Lambeth [came] down in coaches to Ammanford Miners' Welfare Hall. The coaches were loaded with food and Christmas presents for the children . . . It took my wife, who was active in the local Women's Support Group, and other women, several weeks to sort it out and wrap it up. They had a list of all the children, it was very well organized' (W38).

Overall, the activities described here demonstrate how an essentially defensive struggle had become 'a resistance movement of the coalfield communities' (Carter 1985: 29). Out of this emerged 'a support network at home and abroad the like of which Britain has never witnessed. This went far beyond traditional union and political structures' (Francis 1985c: 32). What, though, was the impact of having been involved in such a struggle?

Victory or Defeat? Consciousness and the Experience of Struggle

Given the scale of the strike, it is hardly surprising that the judgements formulated in its aftermath were couched in grand terms. Interpretations, however, with respect to the implications of the strike for issues of class and consciousness in advanced industrial societies, diverged sharply. Some saw the strike as a massive reawakening of class conflict in Britain

(Meiksins Wood 1986: 180–200) and a major vehicle for the creation of a popular socialist consciousness – the NUM President argued that 'the most important victory of all [was] the struggle itself' (Goodman 1985: 200). Tony Benn asserted that 'the miners' strike was the greatest piece of political radicalisation I've seen; there have never been so many socialists in the country in my lifetime . . . We're only half-way between Dunkirk and D-Day' (Adeney & Lloyd 1988: 300). *New Socialist* editorialized that the Government's 'long march against the miners' represented, ultimately, 'Thatcher's Moscow'.[28]

Others, however, viewed the outcome as a significant setback for organized labour: 'For all the brave initial denials, the outcome was a crushing defeat, mitigated only partially by the positive and perhaps enduring achievements of those twelve months in transforming social relations in the striking communities and the broad movements of support' (Hyman 1986: 330). Field argues that 'the miners' strike has turned out to be the labour movement's Dunkirk' (1985a: 11), while Hall, though acknowledging that the strike was 'in fact instinctually with the politics of the new', none the less argues that it was 'fought and lost as an old rather than as a new form of politics . . . imprisoned in the categories and strategies of the past" (1988: 205). And Jenkins writes 'The striking miners were the past challenging the present . . . the . . . strike was an ending, not a beginning. It was the last hurrah of the old Labour Movement, the closing of a chapter which had opened in the nineteenth century, the explosion of a proud myth founded in the struggles of the General Strike of 1926, and another landmark of the Thatcher Revolution' (1988: 228–9).

What unites these diverging views is the way in which the strike is viewed as a landmark – either as the 'rebirth' or 'death' of class politics, broadly defined. Yet any assessment of how the strike changed the consciousness of striking miners must be undertaken, in the first instance, in terms of their own class experience – an experience defined by a close relationship between the miners, their Union and their communities. Any adequate judgement of the effects of the strike must be informed by the concrete experience of the miners both during and after 1984–5 and the way in which this altered their relationship with their Union and their communities.

The two contending perspectives outlined above are inadequate. On the one hand, those arguing for a flowering of radical consciousness should ignore neither the material costs borne by those involved in the struggle, nor the damaging legacy of industrial defeat, organizational division and divided communities. On the other hand, those viewing the strike and its aftermath as the demise of class politics *per se* should neither underestimate the resilience of the Union and the mining communities, nor the resolve with which the miners forged new alliances to defend themselves. The strike, in fact, was neither a 'rebirth' nor a 'death'; instead, it laid the basis for a *changing* consciousness amongst those clinging tenaciously to a declining sector of industrial society.

The Miners and the Union

On 5 March 1985, the NUM ended the strike following its failure to extract an agreement from the NCB on the pit closures issue. The following day, miners marched behind their Branch and Lodge banners back to work with a mixture of dignity and defiance. A miner at Denby Grange colliery in Yorkshire recalled: 'I did not like the idea of a return to work without an agreement. But what could we do? We'd done twelve months, and got nowhere, more or less. But I didn't like the idea. It was not a total defeat because I know, at this pit, when we came down the pit lane, we were proud'(Y51). At Mardy, the last pit in the Rhondda valley, the NUM Lodge Chairman proclaimed: 'We are not coming back on our knees. We are not crawling back'.[29]

Undoubtedly, many strikers felt that having made a stand against the Government and the NCB for a year was a victory in and of itself. In South Wales, the Lodge Secretary at Penallta colliery said that 'a lot of us feel more proud that we *did* take action, and didn't do nothing'(W9). In Nottinghamshire, a Bevercotes striker felt that 'it showed the government we were willing to take them on over pit closures . . . we weren't a spent force'(N3). In Derbyshire, a miner at Warsop colliery argued that 'to some extent, it showed this country the unity that can be achieved through a national industry against the provocatism [*sic*] from an ultra Right-wing Tory Government'(D20). In Yorkshire, a faceworker at Thurcroft colliery concurred: 'We came out with a bit of credibility. The Tory Government was hell-bent on smashing the Union . . . we weren't completely devastated . . . it cost the Government [billions of pounds] to . . . lick us'(Y23).

Such defiance had, in turn, reinvigorated an intense loyalty to the NUM – sticking with the Union to the bitter end was regarded as an accomplishment and a source of pride (Samuel 1986: 25). A miner at Tower colliery, South Wales, said that 'I would never have gone back as a scab'(W27). In Yorkshire, a miner at Thurcroft colliery commented 'It were recommended from the Union to return to work with our heads held high, and we had not lost faith . . . as long as I live, I'll be able to hold my head up high, and from the bottom of my heart I know that I remained loyal to the Union'(Y23). A miner at Allerton Bywater colliery testified:

> We made our point, and we did twelve month of it, and we couldn't do no more. I felt as though we'd won in one way – all them men who stuck it out for that twelve month – I thought we'd won it *that* way . . . I cried when the

dispute were over . . . I really felt it . . . but a return to work on an organized basis was better than just trickling in. And we all marched to work, and even then, I felt really proud to be a member of the NUM. (Y43)

None the less, many strikers emphasized that such loyalty had involved horrendous costs. Some miners had seen their houses repossessed or marriages destroyed; many had exhausted their savings and incurred huge debts; *all*, at the very least, had lost thousands of pounds in earnings. As such, many strikers emphasized the darker aspects of struggle. In South Wales, a Penallta striker commented that 'there was a hell of a lot of families that had to get back on their feet . . . people had . . . lost their homes . . . people . . . had to pay back money that they had borrowed to keep their mortgages going . . . it took them years to get themselves back on their feet. So it was a costly, costly strike, to the individual anyway'(W4). In Yorkshire, the NUM Branch Secretary at Maltby colliery told how 'it's not an experience I would like to go through again'(Y22). A miner at Markham colliery reflected that 'I was more fortunate than others . . . having their houses taken off them – that's when it does come bad, and they're still sticking out. No, personally, I would say '84 was the worst year of my working life'(D22). The Branch Secretary at neighbouring High Moor argued therefore that loyalty had to be placed in perspective: 'The only thing the strike really did show was to display the enormous loyalty of the men to the Union. It proved that men would go through hell to support the Union that had supported them. But when you see men who've been proud to be miners, and to be in the NUM, picking clothes out of rag heaps – this didn't do too much for me'.[30]

As such, the fact that the strike reinforced many strikers' loyalty to the NUM should be tempered by the view of many – equally loyal – strikers that the NUM's refusal to end the strike earlier than it did had turned many 'good Union men' into 'scabs' and, as a consequence, had damaged the authority and respect it commanded in the coalfields. A Derbyshire striker complained: 'What I will say about the NUM – it made scabs out of good Union men – because the strike went on too long. You can't call a man a scab what's been out of work ten months' (D34). In Yorkshire, a striker at Stillingfleet colliery thought

it was left a month too late to go back, I think the Union lost a lot of integrity by letting it drag on as long as it did, from a lot of its own members. Around here, the biggest majority of men came back in the last *fortnight* – I think the Union got away from the grass-roots level as to what was actually happening, what men was actually thinking. I think they left it just a little too late to turn around and say 'Right, let's go back, we're not going to win'. (Y39)

The Branch Delegate at the pit agreed:

> I think Arthur Scargill was developing a bunker mentality towards the end of the strike. He was playing for a 'hard-line' position where he could later claim that *he* didn't urge the men back to work – this was less than honest – it's the *miners* that mattered, not so much the leaders. In [March] 1985, you were not talking about hunger or destitution, but you *were* talking about *total* demoralization – the men had given everything for a year, and now they were saying, 'For God's sake, lead us out of this mess'. (Y38)

In general, Union officials expressed unease regarding the prolonged nature of the strike. For example, at High Moor colliery, Derbyshire, the Branch Secretary commented that 'we moved further and further away from the hardship of our people by not recognizing unpalatable things. There were casualties as in any war, but it's easy for leaders to talk . . . I can't see how a Derbyshire Area [Union] Official could relate to some people who'd lost *everything* . . . we took a bloody-minded position of 'no compromise' . . . and pushed loyalty beyond the limit'.[31] Even in South Wales, which recorded the lowest number of strikebreakers any-where in the coalfield, the Area President thought that local miners' legendary loyalty to the Union had been pushed to the limit.[32]

Regardless, however, of whether their loyalty to, and respect for, the Union had been strengthened or impaired by the strike, miners were almost unanimous in their assessment of the outcome of the strike. Few could ignore the phenomenal contraction of the coal industry after 1985. For most miners, therefore, some of the more spectacular scenarios of 'longer-term victories' belonged to the intellectual stratosphere. In particular, the NUM President's persistent refusal to see the 1984–5 struggle as a defeat was given short shrift – a Derbyshire surfaceworker noted that 'it might not be a defeat for Scargill, but Scargill ain't on the sharp end of it'(D26). In South Wales, a Penrhiwceiber miner com-mented: 'Arthur would say "Well, we *didn't* have the closures we *would* have had if we hadn't come out on strike" . . . but I don't think anybody could subscribe to a position where we had 200,000 mineworkers before the strike, and now four years later, we're down to . . . under 80,000' (W14). The Lodge Chairman at Oakdale colliery was even more direct: 'The *damnable* part is . . . that Arthur still says we won the strike. Well if we won it, God help us if we'd bloody lost it – what the hell would have happened?'(W16).

Mostly, miners everywhere highlighted the strike's outcome for what it was – an industrial defeat of shattering proportions. In South Wales, a striker at Oakdale colliery reflected: 'I can understand when Scargill says it was a victory, because it caused the Government's plans to be set back . . . and it did prevent them from privatizing the industry during their last term. But other than that, it was a massive defeat, we were forced back to work . . . and though we can hold our heads up and say we gave it our best shot, in the end we were defeated'(W50). The Lodge Secretary at the pit agreed:

> It was a *total* defeat . . . I think that's proved by the fact that they're just doing what they want with the coal industry now . . . and anyone with a *grain* of intelligence is *bound* to see . . . that there is no way of stopping them . . . shutting any pits they want to, introducing all . . . methods of work . . . contract work . . . all these kinds of things now they're doing completely at will. So, it was certainly a massive defeat for the miners. (W11)

Similarly grim appraisals were presented elsewhere. In Yorkshire, the Branch President at Goldthorpe colliery argued that it was a 'total defeat. No one realistic can say otherwise. We put all our eggs in one basket, and dropped them'(Y9). In Derbyshire, meanwhile, a miner at Markham colliery commented that 'we'd lost, and it's the worst feeling I've ever had in my life'(D34).

It is clear that during and after the 1984–5 strike, the NUM had remained, for many miners, the focus of great loyalty. Given the harsh circumstances of the mid-1980s, this was no mean achievement. None the less, it is equally clear that such loyalty had been pushed to the absolute limit; miners emphasized that the exceptional length of the strike had involved heavy costs – not least in turning 'good men' into strikebreakers. Moreover, few underestimated the scale of the defeat they had suffered.

The Miners and their Communities

The aim of the strike was to defend communities and the mines on which they depended. Some strikers felt that regardless of its outcome, the strike had at least advertised to a wider audience how the fate of their communities was tied to that of the coal industry. The Lodge Secretary at Penallta colliery, South Wales, argued that

> Perhaps if we'd sat back quietly and let them pick the pits off one at a time, then the pits would have just gone and nobody would perhaps have taken any notice of them going . . . I think the strike highlighted the problems that do arise when a pit goes. You're talking about a *large* number of men *from* the community being out of work – it isn't as if it's, say, Ford . . . where people commute from all the different valleys and the coastal towns . . . *to* the factory. I mean everyone that works in this pit, or *did* work in this pit at the time of the strike, was all local people . . . when a pit actually goes, it's a lot of jobs go from one spot in one fell swoop . . . so all this . . . publicity about communities and . . . suffering, *is true* . . . and I think . . . if the strike

hadn't gone on, then that message wouldn't have gone across . . . so I think *that* came out of it. (W7)

However, the almost umbilical link between mine and community characteristic of the 'traditional' pit village had been under strain for a long time prior to the 1984–5 strike: 'Today there are pit villages without pits and pits without pit villages' (Gibbon 1988: 151). As such, one important effect of the strike was the way in which it reawakened a strong sense of community in the coalfields (Samuel 1986: 6). In July 1984, a Derbyshire miner's wife noted: 'The morale is something to be seen. There has been a sort of re-birth of the community spirit that was traditional in mining communities and which had been lost. A lot of us thought it was dead and gone, but that's not so. It's been fantastic' (Marxism Today 1984: 28). A miner at Penrhiwceiber colliery, South Wales, felt that the strike 'brought a lot of closeness to the community, a lot of camaraderie – not only in Penrhiwceiber, but in virtually every pit village'(W14). The Branch Secretary at Rossington colliery, Yorkshire, described how 'the community has drifted apart in recent times, but up against it as we [are] now, the old spirit comes back, and people support each other'.[33]

However, though communities were indeed reinvigorated by the strike, they were also wracked by internal divisions – especially as growing numbers of miners returned to work. This was especially true of pit villages in and near Nottinghamshire. For example, the Derbyshire pit village of Whitwell was badly divided during the dispute between local miners on strike at Whitwell colliery and those working at Creswell colliery just two miles away in Nottinghamshire. A Whitwell striker described how his own street had been divided between three strikers from Whitwell and three miners working at Creswell – 'there's still a lot of bad feeling'(D30). A colleague recalled: 'There was hassle . . . At the Welfare, quite a few times there were confrontations when having a drink, between working and striking miners . . . There were scuffles on Saturday nights, often, with working miners being given a good hiding by strikers. Which was to be expected'(D41). In Creswell itself, matters were even worse. At the height of the strike, the pubs and clubs of the village were divided into those serving working and striking miners. Throughout the strike, claims and counter-claims were exchanged between strikers and working miners regarding threats, injuries and damage to property.[34] The same applied to Shirebrook, Derbyshire,[35] and Keresley, Warwickshire.[36]

As ever, strikebreakers were ostracized by their former workmates. A strikebreaker at Coventry colliery in Warwickshire, no longer able to attend his local club, described how his best friend, a striker, 'doesn't bother with me now'.[37] In this way, the strike not only regenerated traditions of resilience and initiative, but also the darker side of mining community life. A striker at Ireland colliery, Derbyshire, remained on strike, but still underscored the fear of being labelled a 'scab': 'All my friends were already back at work – including my father-in-law – It was just a waste of time [by March 1985] . . . I wanted to go back, but just couldn't stand the thought of the divisions, and the possible abuse I'd get if I went back. I had friends at work, friends not at work, and me stuck in the middle. So I thought I'd stop out [the whole time] so I could talk to everybody'(D14).

How enduring, though, was such bitterness? After all, a badge worn by many strikers had proclaimed 'We'll not always be poor, but they will always be scabs'.[38] Immediately after the strike, a miner at Bevercotes colliery in Nottinghamshire recalled: 'Relations between strikers and scabs were initially very bad. A lot of scores were settled underground' (N7). A Derbyshire striker concurred: 'There was a lot of fighting at Ireland colliery after the strike, from Day One in fact. I mean it was OK if you were on a face-team where everyone had stayed out, but that was a rarity . . . there was fighting in the baths, underground. Insults were exchanged'(D54).

Undoubtedly, many strikers continued to hold in contempt those who had returned to work. A South Wales miner declared: 'They're scabs. I'm as bitter now as I was in '84. They let down their fellow workers' (W22). A miner at Cwmgwili colliery described how 'the boys who went back to work – you'd have to see them to believe them . . . they just didn't give a damn. They were not people who were nice to know before the strike'(W43). At Taff Merthyr colliery, a striker recalled how he 'was on the picket line and [saw] a father on strike and his son passing him [on the picket line] – my father was in the strike, I could never have gone back to work with my father on strike . . . never in a lifetime'(W2). In Yorkshire, a miner at Allerton Bywater colliery said 'You call them miners. But they're scabs, and always will be'(Y43), while at Grimethorpe colliery, a striker stated: 'I have no respect for them whatsoever, they're traitors to us, and traitors to . . . themselves'(Y1).

Such hostility ensured that the wounds suffered by certain mining communities were slow to heal. A striker from Ollerton in Nottinghamshire described how

> there's still animosity in the village . . . I don't think there's a day gone by in the Welfare . . . where the strike isn't raised . . . it's always there. And I think it's going to take a hell of a long time to die . . . how can I term a bloke a 'friend' now, when he turned his back on you for a year and watched you struggle? . . . There is people like myself . . . I know it's a horrible thing to say – we will not let it die, we'll let them *remember* what they done. (N4)

A miner from Cwmfelinfach, South Wales, agreed: 'You've got a few people *here* [who returned to work] . . . I feel that I'm their conscience. You know, if I see him, I think "he scabbed", but he's also thinking when he sees me "you wasn't a scab" – he's *aware* of it, so I feel I'm their conscience for ever and a day . . . they done it for their Judas money . . . they were the spineless ones'(W13).

In general, such animosity resulted in the ostracism of, rather than violence towards, strikebreakers. A South Wales miner described the continuous shunning in Penrhiwceiber of members of the pit deputies' Union, the National Association of Colliery Overmen, Deputies and Shotfirers (NACODS), who had worked through the strike: 'That evidence is still about now. And unfortunately that carries over four years on, in that I can go in the Working Men's Club, and the NACODS lads are there, and we totally . . . wouldn't bother with each other . . . they're in a corner on their own . . . they're ostracized by the community'(W14). A striker at High Moor colliery, Derbyshire, described how 'the kids who went back . . . you don't talk to them . . . it's a terrible atmosphere. I can go anywhere – I didn't go back, but these lads can't go very far . . . they're known as scabs in local pubs'(D2). In Nottinghamshire, a striker from Bevercotes colliery felt that 'locally, there's still a lot of ill-feeling amongst people. I mean, I was very good friends, obviously, prior to the strike with a lot of lads I worked with, but from then on, I've never spoken to them since'(N3). A colleague agreed: 'When we went back, we had to speak to them and work with them. But . . . I didn't socialize with them – I haven't got a lot in common with them, I'm not bothered with them. I've got my own mates'(N32). And in Yorkshire, a miner at Thurcroft colliery felt that 'there is now a barrier at the pit between those who struck and those who scabbed'(Y23). For a miner at Maltby colliery, 'strikebreakers don't exist, as far as I'm concerned. They've destroyed the mining industry'(Y29).

None the less, other strikers – many from the same communities as those quoted above – were more forgiving of those who had returned to work. As such, the divisive aftermath of the strike should not be exaggerated.[39] In Yorkshire, a miner at Stillingfleet colliery commented that 'five years is a long time, a lot have mellowed. Some people ostracize [members of] their own families, but not me'(Y39). A surfaceworker at Barnsley Main colliery added: 'I don't hold it against men who went back near the end of the strike'(Y16). In Derbyshire, the Branch Delegate at the Central Workshops told how 'I decided that people who went back in November [1984] onwards, I would tolerate'(D26). Even in Nottinghamshire, a striker at Bevercotes felt that 'things have got better – at least the taunting and provocation of strikers by scabs has died away'(N7). Even in South Wales, where the wrath incurred by strikebreakers was legend, an Oakdale miner commented: 'There's bitterness, yes, but I feel sorry for the people who returned to work – they've paid their penance'(W50). The local Lodge Chairman agreed:

> Let's be fair – a man remains out eleven months, and everyone's not built the same, you can't call a man a scab if he goes back after eleven months, it's . . . too much, in my opinion . . . people have got different breaking points – for someone, it wouldn't matter if the bloody house fell on their ears, they'd just go on . . . reading the papers, it wouldn't matter to them, but if someone [else] had a little leak in the tap, they'd be worried to bloody death. (W16)

This recognition amongst strikers that many strikebreakers, too, had made sacrifices during the year was best articulated by a miner at Tower colliery, South Wales: 'You've got to forget the past, or you're not going to go forward . . . you've got to forget about the strike, forget about the men that worked, and get back to work – together'(W19).

Finally, it is worth emphasizing that miners who had remained on strike for the entire year were *unanimous* in wanting the re-establishment of a single Union in the coal industry.[40] In Yorkshire, a miner at Allerton Bywater colliery felt that 'it's far better to have one Union . . . a miner's a miner, whether he's a Nottingham miner . . . or . . . an African miner. I'd like to see one amalgamated Union'(Y43). A miner at Maltby colliery agreed: 'You must stick together . . . you've got to have one Union'(Y29). In Derbyshire, a miner from Ireland colliery argued that the return of a single Union was the 'only way they're going to achieve anything'(D14). In South Wales, a Penallta miner noted that 'while you've got two Unions, then the government have got the whip-hand . . . the Coal Board couldn't have it better'(W6). And a Nottinghamshire striker commented: 'Definitely, I'd like to see one Union again . . . back in the NUM'(N3).

In expressing this desire, it is noteworthy that many strikers were unhappy with the NUM national leadership's continuing refusal to recognize the UDM. Indeed, some singled out the NUM President for criticism in this context. An Allerton Bywater miner felt that 'the NUM and the UDM will have to sit down together – get leadership to one side, personalities should have nothing to do with it. It's time to get together. Let's fight together – that's what it's all about'(Y43). A Derbyshire miner commented that 'I don't want [Arthur Scargill] to go, but he's an obstacle [to reunification]'(D34). And a miner at Taff Merthyr colliery, South Wales, said 'I would be willing to sit around this table tomorrow, as long as we come back to one Union . . . to the NUM. And this is what Arthur Scargill has got to do'(W2).

The strike strained the traditional unity of the mining communities. Yet despite its legacy of defeat and organizational division, crucial components of the miners' identity remained intact – the Union continued to maintain a presence, unanimous support existed for the re-establishment of one Union in the coalfields, and relations between strikers and strike-breakers showed signs of improvement. Yet for striking miners, if the struggle itself had proved the resilience (and indeed the rediscovery) of their traditional 'community' of pit, Union and village, had it not also involved the discovery of *new* communities?

Strike Action and the Politicization of Miners

The notion that miners jettisoned a 'trade union' consciousness and acquired a 'revolutionary' one is an inadequate means of measuring how they were transformed in the course of struggle – the aims of the strike remained defensive, and the activities of the miners and their communities amounted very much to a *resistance* movement. Yet undoubtedly the strike had done *something* to those involved – after all, for most strikers, it remained the major event in their lives. A miner at Thurcroft colliery in Yorkshire labelled it 'the best year I've ever had in my life'(Y23). In South Wales, a Penallta miner reflected that 'some of it was good, some of it was bad. As an experience, it was excellent'(W6). And a miner at Markham colliery in Derbyshire remarked: 'You'll remember it all your life. I've never, ever regretted it . . . never'(D34). Thus even if the strike did not transform the miners – even those most active in the struggle – into models of revolutionary ardour, it *changed* them none the less. It may well be the case that after the strike, 'members of mining families have relapsed into a traditional, and somewhat parochial, form of class consciousness: an unpractised and largely untheorized brand of socialism based on a pragmatic distinction between us and them' (Waddington *et al.* 1991: 148). My evidence, however, suggests the need to use a more modest benchmark – that is, any change in consciousness should be measured within the parameters of the miners' own class experience. Whether 'untheorized' or not, the strike produced its own spectrum of raised consciousness from those who discovered it was possible to fend for themselves for twelve months to those who were liberated from the old order that they struggled to defend.

Undoubtedly, some miners retained a circumspect view of their experiences. The Lodge Secretary at Oakdale colliery, South Wales, for example, commented: 'I think the only point that did come out of it really was that it did prove that you can stick twelve months on strike!' (W16). Many others, however, felt that the strike had had a wider effect. A miner at Bevercotes colliery, Nottinghamshire, spoke of discovering one's abilities during the strike – whether it was the fundraising that he himself had undertaken or a colleague's debut as a public speaker – in front of 2,000 people in Liverpool, following on from veteran Labour MPs Eric Heffer and Tony Benn (N7). A South Wales striker, arrested four times during the strike, described how 'personally, I became completely anti-authority . . . I just couldn't . . . contemplate it at all . . . and the longer the strike went on . . . I think the harder my attitude got'(W7). Others described how the strike had increased their political awareness. A South Wales miner argued that 'what [Thatcher] managed to do and perhaps what she . . . wouldn't have *wanted* to do: she made a lot more people – women and men – not just the men – she made them more politically aware'. He continued:

> What '84 done to me was made me a lot more politically aware . . . because I never took no notice before. Just wasn't particularly interested. *Now* . . . I haven't joined the Labour Party . . . but I am a lot more interested in the political side of things . . . Before '84, the simplest way of putting it is that I never watched the news – I wasn't even interested . . . Not no more. I'm interested now in what's happening, practically all over the world . . . one particular thing . . . that sticks in my mind . . . where [our] Prime Minister, going over to Poland, congratulated Lech Walesa and his trade unions . . . for fighting for their freedoms and fighting for their union rights, and at the same time, she was trying to . . . hit the unions in this country . . . I mean the woman . . . comes over to me as a hypocrite. Before I wouldn't have even realized, or recognized that fact, it would have just been something that was said. *Now*, you tend to take things in. (W6)

For many miners, increased political awareness meant a significantly sharpened view of the Conservative Party as a traditional foe. A South Wales miner reflected: 'a lot of miners were politicized – [the strike] reminded them what our forefathers went through . . . and what a Tory Government is all about'(W50). A miner at Whitwell colliery in Derbyshire described how 'I became more bitter . . . towards the Government. The strike reminded me how rotten the Tories are'(D30). The Branch Delegate at the Central Workshops told of how 'a lot of people were politicized. A lot of young miners . . . who'd got no interest in trade union activity . . . saw the police and Government tactics – and it politicised these people'(D26). And a striker at Bilsthorpe colliery in Nottinghamshire argued that 'it's surprising, there's a lot of people that got a good education through that strike – and I mean that – it opened their lives to . . . how the system worked, how *vicious* this Government *can* be – through its policing and its methods'(N4).

To a lesser extent, growing political awareness led to increased involvement with the Union. A miner at Penallta colliery, South Wales,

described how 'when the strike first started . . . I didn't even know it was
going to *start* until the day before, because I wasn't interested – I was
one of the . . . soldiers . . . who was just told what to do'. During the
strike, however, he took 'more interest in the Union then I ever did
before' and afterwards became Chairman of the NUM Lodge at the pit
(W5). Undoubtedly, many others followed a similar path – Clapham
notes how after the strike, 'the branch officials tend to be younger men.
Most of them came through and were politicized by the 1984/85 strike'
(1989: 17). Thus the Branch President at Barnsley Main colliery, Yorkshire, recalled how 'I never used to be involved in the Union . . . I would
never go to Branch meetings except at times of strikes. But I would
always follow the Union . . . I reckon they knew what was going [on] –
well, it was the only way of finding out. I got involved in the Union a bit
before the 1984–5 strike . . . [but] . . . if it hadn't been for the strike, I
probably wouldn't be "on the Union" now'(Y14).

Perhaps the most spectacular growth of activism and politicization
was that seen amongst the women of the coalfields. Just as they had
acknowledged the *role* of many women in sustaining the strike, many
miners were convinced that the lives of such women had been dramatically changed by the experience – as a striker at Silverwood colliery,
Yorkshire, declared: 'The strike fetched a lot of women out, the women
could stand up and talk; previously they'd done the cooking and the
washing up'(Y7). The Branch Delegate at Sharlston colliery felt that the
strike 'made quite a lot of people more politically aware . . . including a
hell of a lot of women'(Y40). In Derbyshire, a miner at Markham colliery commented: 'I think it must have changed some women's lives
completely. And in fact, some of the women'll have benefited by it,
through getting together and showing strength as they did'(D22). In
South Wales, the Lodge Secretary at Oakdale colliery said 'I can't
see that experience that they had, of speaking on platforms, collecting
money or going on the picket lines, is going to ever leave them, it's
going to be with them. So they're that much more independent, self-
assertive than they would have been before the strike'(W11).[41]

It is important, however, not to exaggerate the effects of politicization. Undoubtedly, continuing industrial contraction damaged morale.
In South Wales, for example, the Lodge Chairman at Penallta colliery
commented: 'I think it's just broken the heart of many people around
here – many people have just had a guts-full. I wouldn't be surprised if
the pit went, they wouldn't care, half of them. Which is a sad state of
affairs to be in'(W5). In fact, at Oakdale, where the local pit *had* closed,
the Lodge Secretary argued:

I think it's a very small minority of people who were politicized because . . . the majority of *miners* involved in the strike are asking . . . 'what was the point of us being out on strike?' Now if they're asking *that* question, that must be, to my mind anyway, a clear indication that they learnt little or nothing from the strike – only that they lost a *lot* of money, that they were *totally* defeated, and what was the point of being out on strike? Which seems to point to the fact that they couldn't possibly have been politicized at all. (W11)[42]

None the less, miners around the country, while agreeing that 'the heightened sense of community generated during the course of the strike had since dissipated' (Waddington *et al.* 1991: 49) still felt that an undercurrent of politicization endured in their communities. The Lodge Vice-Chairman at Penallta colliery, South Wales, felt that the strike

. . . revitalized this community spirit . . . they say time heals all wounds . . . I think time deadens people's enthusiasm a little bit, too. I think people became more politically aware . . . more aware of the dangers of that Government, during that strike, and more interested in what was going on than they ever did. Well, there's probably some of that still left . . . In general, I would say that people will gradually start . . . quietly to go back to the same apathetic ways, probably. But at least it did revitalize it . . . I think there is definitely some groups who . . . still . . . thrive on it. (W12)

A Derbyshire Branch Delegate felt, too, that 'there is still something lying dormant' (D26), while at Rossington in Yorkshire, the NUM Branch Treasurer remarked:

The strike did bring the community together, but this tended to die away. There's always an undercurrent, which will come out in a crisis, but take that crisis away and it goes away . . . the women – if ever there was a crisis situation again, in the mining industry, or a local crisis, it would come out again. They came out of the woodwork during the strike and went back in after the strike was over. But you know it would come out again in another crisis, you know it's there, you can't put your finger on it . . . But it helps you sleep at night. (Y27)

Ultimately, though, the most powerful case for a raised consciousness as a result of the 1984–5 strike is rooted in the testimony of miners for whom the experience of struggle remained of *enduring* quality. At the 1990 Durham Miners' Gala, Labour MP Dennis Skinner described how the 'strike is etched in my memory. I can't forget it, it'll live with me for ever'.[43] Reflecting on what the strike had done for miners in general, Skinner described how they 'found out when they were collecting, that some of the coloured people – the blacks, the Asians, the ethnic groups . . . were paying a lot of money into the strike fund – I mean they were really marvellous. And [the miners] – working-class people who'd been born in these narrow . . . communities . . . they were coming back and having a different perception about coloured people . . . and they'd also got a different view about homosexuals . . .'.[44]

Without question, the experience of moving *beyond* their communities had stayed with many miners. The Lodge Secretary at Oakdale colliery in South Wales reflected: 'What has come out of the strike . . . are *positive links* between communities – I mean like the Oakdale community and the Hackney community which we were very much linked up with – people still meet, from one community to the other, and there was a lot of barriers broken down – racial barriers, people with different . . . lifestyles and cultures'(W11). At Penallta colliery, a striker recalled '. . . the friends you made – and I'm not talking about miners now – I know I slept in people's houses that I never knew . . . I'd never even seen before. People were coming up to you, wanting to buy you a drink in the pub, or buy you food in the cafe – you would never have thought it possible'(W6).

In Yorkshire, a Stillingfleet miner described how 'I met people and made friends that I'd never have met, due to the help from everywhere'(Y39). In Nottinghamshire, a Bilsthorpe miner felt 'there's a lot come out of that strike, in respect that we've got a very longstanding relationship . . . with the rest of the country . . . which we wouldn't have ever had . . . the people of Norwich *still* come up, they come up *at least* three or four times a year. We've made friends that we never had, and we've seen another way of life . . . it *did* do a lot of good'(N4). An Ollerton striker thought the strike 'proved that people could unite. I met people in the strike that I'd never have met . . . people from London bringing food parcels, miners from Wales and Scotland . . . it united people'(N5). A Bevercotes striker told how he 'made a lot of good friends in Norwich, Basingstoke, and places like that – people I'd probably never have met'(N3), while a colleague reflected: 'We made many new friends, and we learnt a lot. It widened our experience . . . compared to the rather closed world of the mining community'(N7).

In defending their 'old order', therefore, the miners moved beyond their own communities and into new worlds. The strike enabled them to see others in a new light, and to re-evaluate the problems of those with whom they had enjoyed little previous contact. More important, though, was the way in which such experiences allowed the miners to re-evaluate *themselves*, and their own attachment to a brutal industry. When a Derbyshire striker remarked that the strike gave him 'a year of sunshine for the first time in eighteen years'(D14), he was by no means being flippant. Instead, as a striker at Bilsthorpe colliery in Nottinghamshire noted, 'There was a *lot* of things learned during that year. There was people [who] . . . realized they didn't have to go down the pit to make a living, which they'd done all their lives, there was other jobs to go to' (N4). Nothing, however, better demonstrates how the defence of 'the old' had led to the discovery of 'the new', than the testimony of a veteran South Wales miner: 'I suppose . . . having been in the industry for thirty-two years – leaving school at fifteen and going straight into mining – we enjoyed it because we knew nothing else. But during that year away from it . . . we went everywhere, we saw how others lived, what they had to do to earn their money . . . well, having seen all this, we didn't enjoy going back down the mine'(W34).

Notes

1. It is impossible to capture fully the range of community activity in 1984–5. For a general account, see Samuel *et al.* 1986. For accounts of individual communities, see especially Beynon 1984; Douglass 1986b; People of Thurcroft 1986; Levy 1985; Parker 1986.
2. H. Hancock, *London Review of Books*, 15 November–6 December 1984, p. 5.
3. *G*, 28/6/84.
4. *T*, 8/10/84.
5. *G*, 4/12/84.
6. *G*, 4/12/84.
7. *The Valleys' Star*, No. 2, 22/5/84.
8. *The Anthracite Star*, No. 4, 7/6/84.
9. *The Valleys' Star*, No. 18, 21/11/84.
10. *T*, 18/6/84.
11. *The Valleys' Star*, No. 7, August 1984.
12. Notes from conversation with NUM Branch President, and Branch Treasurer, Brodsworth colliery, 26/4/90.
13. It appears, though, that miners whose mortgage-lenders were not locally based were less fortunate. A striker at Frickley colliery in Yorkshire, whose lender was based in London, had his house quickly repossessed and he and his family evicted on to the street (Y28).
14. *The Valleys' Star*, No. 2, 22/5/84.
15. *T*, 18/6/84.
16. Interview, 15/12/89.
17. *G*, 2/1/85.
18. *G*, 28/6/84.

19. *G*, 4/12/84.
20. *G*, 2/1/85.
21. I am grateful to Alan Baker, former NUM Lodge Secretary at Oakdale colliery, for these details.
22. *The Valleys' Star*, No. 7 (August 1984) and No. 25 (23/1/85).
23. *The Valleys' Star*, No. 18, 21/11/84.
24. *The Anthracite Star*, No. 4, 7/6/84.
25. *The Valleys' Star*, No. 10, 26/9/84.
26. *The Anthracite Star*, No. 4, 7/6/84.
27. *The Valleys' Star*, No. 23, 8/1/85.
28. *New Socialist*, No. 26, April 1985, p. 2.
29. *MS*, 6/3/85.
30. Interview, 23/5/90.
31. Interview, 23/5/90.
32. Interview, 20/10/89. A small minority of strikers felt, however, that the strike should have been prolonged by the NUM. A miner at Grimethorpe colliery in Yorkshire commented that 'I was upset, I would have carried on. At that point, the membership should have been asked, instead of being told it was over'(Y1).
33. *T*, 18/6/84.
34. *DT*, 12/4/85.
35. *DT*, 28/6/84.
36. *T*, 8/10/84.
37. *T*, 8/10/84. In Nottinghamshire, it was the minority of strikers who were ostracized by working miners. At Harworth, where in June 1984, only 30 per cent of miners remained on strike, the leader of the local Striking Miners' Wives' Group remarked, 'When you're spat at walking to the shops and people refuse to serve you, you don't forget. It will take years for that bitterness to die' (*T*, 18/6/84).
38. *T*, 8/10/84.
39. As ever, the dangers of the working environment meant that even the most vitriolic critics of strikebreakers still recognized a basic common identity. An NUM member at Ollerton colliery in Nottinghamshire commented: 'If I was down the pit, and a UDM man was in an accident ... I'd still carry him out – he's a miner'(N5). A miner at Allerton Bywater colliery in Yorkshire stated 'Any grievances – keep them out of the pit'(Y43).
40. *Every* striker interviewed expressed this preference (as, indeed, did every *non*-striker). Waddington *et al.*'s survey showed that more than 80 per cent of 'mining families' wanted the reunification of the NUM and UDM (1991: 69).
41. For accounts of the activity of women in the strike from the perspective of women themselves, see, amongst others: Dolby 1987;

Evans *et al.* 1985; Miller, J. 1986; Miller, S. 1985; Salt and Layzell 1985; Seddon (ed.) 1986; Stead 1987; Witham 1986. See also Louisa Sanders, 'Striking a blow for unity', *G*, 7/3/90; Beatrix Campbell, 'Pitting their wits', *G*, 25/8/86; Hilary Rose, 'Securing Social Citizenship', *New Socialist*, 25 (March 1985): 16–18; 'Coalfield Women at the Face: A Roundtable Discussion', *Marxism Today*, 28, 7 (July 1984): 28–30.

42. Furthermore, for all the miners' glowing assessments of what the strike had done for women, the fact remains that traditional attitudes die hard. Thus at the NUM's 1985 Annual Conference, delegates voted narrowly against giving Women Against Pit Closures associate membership of the Union. Incredibly, the South Wales and Yorkshire Areas opposed the reform. One Yorkshire Area delegate grumbled, 'The women are trying to take over' (Field 1985b: 18). Michael McGahey, National Vice-President of the NUM during the strike, reflected, 'The strike was a tremendous development for the feminine [*sic*] movement. The women came out of the kitchen. There should have been a constitutional attachment of the women to the Union' (Interview, 15/12/89).

43. Speech at 106th Annual Durham Miners' Gala, 14/7/90.

44. Interview, 9/11/89.

7

Class Consciousness and the Non-Striker: The Roots of Disunity in the 1984–5 Strike

Introduction

> Solidarity, isn't it? Everybody was together in 1972 and 1974. In 1984, we wasn't. We split in two different groups. And in 1972, 1974, it was 100 per cent solid. And when you're like that . . . you've got power, haven't you? But when you're split . . . there was no way we were going to win it then. (W2)

During the 1984–5 strike, most Nottinghamshire miners refused to support the NUM and, as a result, were vilified by most strikers as scabs and traitors. In October 1985, they broke with the NUM (of which their forefathers had been founder members in 1947) and voted, by a majority of 72 per cent, to form their own union, the Union of Democratic Mineworkers (UDM).

What, though, is the meaning of the divisions within the miners' ranks which undermined the 1984–5 strike and which were then institutionalized by the formation of the UDM? By the mid-1980s, were the Nottinghamshire miners a breed apart – unthreatened, and therefore unwilling to act with and for fellow-workers who *were* under threat? Does the record support the argument that the bonds of solidarity are waning amongst workers in industrial societies? In this chapter, I reject these notions. Instead, the roots and significance of divisions during and after the 1984–5 strike underscore the *complexity*, rather than the death, of class solidarity and politics broadly defined.

The Extent of Disunity: Nottinghamshire and the 1984–5 Strike

> We never envisaged the rebellion of the Nottinghamshire men against the general movement. Our thoughts of unity, as in 1972 and 1974, didn't happen.

> Interview with Peter Heathfield, NUM National General Secretary, 23/8/90

On 8 March 1984 the Union's NEC endorsed, under Rule 41, the strikes underway in Scotland and Yorkshire, and extended approval to any other Area of the coalfield joining the strike. Nottinghamshire soon emerged as the most important site of opposition to strike action. On 8 March, the Area NUM President declared that he would not call his membership out on unofficial strike without a secret ballot,[1] while a day later the Area Executive demanded a national ballot. This initial recalcitrance made Nottinghamshire the immediate target of pickets from other Areas. Notably, hundreds of Yorkshire pickets streamed southwards to halt production in the area. Such efforts undoubtedly enjoyed several successes. On 12 March, 150 pickets turned back the afternoon shift at Harworth, the Nottinghamshire pit closest to the Yorkshire border (Callinicos & Simons 1985: 47). On 13 March, all three shifts at Harworth, Bevercotes and Thoresby collieries were picketed out (Winterton & Winterton 1989: 295), while over the next two days, pickets stopped various shifts at Cotgrave, Hucknall and Creswell collieries (Callinicos & Simons 1985: 50). On 14 March, at Blidworth colliery, 'pickets succeeded in turning away most of the late afternoon shift . . . as the evening wore on more and more men were persuaded not to work as hundreds of Yorkshire miners poured into the area'.[2] Meanwhile, pickets turned back '2 coachloads of workers' at Bilsthorpe colliery, and at Ollerton stopped 'nearly all the night shift going in'.[3] At this point, the NCB admitted that the afternoon shift at nine Nottinghamshire pits had been stopped while at several others it was 'undermanned' (Callinicos & Simons 1985: 53).

Nevertheless, these sporadic successes proved to be short-lived as pickets were soon outnumbered by a growing police presence in the Nottinghamshire coalfield. By 14 March, 8,000 policemen had been drafted into the area from over twenty regional forces around Britain (Winterton & Winterton 1989: 295). On 15 March, a Yorkshire miner died amid scenes of mayhem at Ollerton colliery as hundreds of Yorkshire pickets clashed with police and local miners. The following day, in an Area Ballot, the Nottinghamshire miners voted by 20,188 to 7,285 (73.5 per cent to 26.5 per cent) to continue working until a national ballot had been held.[4] When a Special Delegate Conference of the NUM decided on 19 April 1984 not to hold a national ballot, Nottinghamshire's position as the centre of opposition to the strike was sealed. During 1984–5, a serious rupture emerged between the majority of Nottinghamshire miners and the NUM at Branch, Area and National levels.

The Collapse of the NUM in Nottinghamshire

The problems faced by the NUM in winning the support of the Nottinghamshire miners were epitomized by the excruciating position in which the Union's Area leadership found itself at the start of the dispute. Henry Richardson, the Area General Secretary, remarked later: 'In my job I wear two hats. I am general secretary in a dual union. I have my loyalty to the National Executive and my loyalty to the Notts area of the NUM'.[5] Such dilemmas led eventually to divisions within the Area's leadership which, in turn, destroyed the NUM's authority in the coalfield.

However, early in the dispute, the Area leadership was united both in its calls for a national ballot and in its concern for the potentially alienating effects of picketing. On 13 March 1984, the Area's General Secretary and President declared:

> We abhor the situation that is now arising in the Area. The Yorkshire pickets are in the Area unofficially, as the Yorkshire leaders have undertaken to keep them out of the Area until the Notts Ballot has taken place . . . We have instructed our members not to cross picket lines, but the type of action taking place is not picketing, but purely mass blockading . . . what is taking place now . . . will be counter-productive. No Union can sustain a strike under these circumstances.[6]

However, after the Nottinghamshire miners' decision to continue working until a national ballot was held, a rift emerged within the Area leadership. The increasingly hopeless predicament of those Area leaders sympathetic to the strike in trying to integrate pressure for conformity from the National Union with defiance from local miners was underscored by the Area General Secretary on 21 March: 'We respect the fundamental right of Members not to cross picket lines, but . . . we must respect the mandate of the Notts Area Ballot decision which gives the fundamental right of a Member to go to work, if he wishes'.

On 5 April, a recommendation from the Area Executive Committee for local Branches to set up their own picket lines was rejected by Branch Officials and Committee members.[7] At this point, the rift within the Union's Area leadership solidified, with the two most senior Officials – the General Secretary and the President – supporting the National Union, and most of the remaining leadership adhering to the Area decision to continue working. The General Secretary subsequently called on local miners to 'get off their knees' and join the strike[8]. When the NUM decided not to hold a national ballot and instead declared the strike 'official', he repeated his call: 'We have to accept the majority decision at the special conference which instructs Notts men and all who are still working to come out on strike. We are isolated'.[9] Such calls, however, failed to resolve the NUM's problems in Nottinghamshire: on 1 May 1984, at the Area's headquarters, about 7,000 working miners demanding the resignation of their Area President and General Secretary clashed with 3,500 strikers. The Area President's call to working miners to join the strike was met with a barrage of jeers and anti-strike placards (Griffin 1985: 50–1).

The Area leadership's waverings provoked growing discontent amongst working miners which eventually led to a rupture between the bulk of the rank-and-file membership and the NUM at Branch level. In early April, five miners at Ollerton colliery staged a two-day 'sit-in' at the coalface to protest the Area General Secretary's instruction to members to set up official picket lines at their pits. At Mansfield colliery, 1,300 miners voted unanimously to call for the resignation of the Area's General Secretary and President.[10] Meanwhile, working miners began to lose patience with those Branch Officials supporting the strike. In May, the pro-strike Branch Delegate at Calverton colliery was ousted by a vote of 695 to 90.[11] When annual Branch elections were held in Nottinghamshire in July 1984, working miners won substantial gains at the expense of striking officials. At Ollerton and Blidworth collieries, both the entire Branches were replaced by working miners. At Thoresby, the Branch President, Delegate and Secretary (all strikers) were defeated. At Rufford, all Branch officials except for the Delegate (a striker) were re-elected. At Mansfield, the working President and Secretary were re-elected, while the striking Delegate was defeated. At Bilsthorpe, the whole Branch – made up entirely of working miners – was re-elected.[12]

For the NUM nationally, the success of working miners in these elections confirmed an alarming trend – the growing isolation of the Nottinghamshire coalfield, and the Union's complete inability to win it over to the national strike. At the Special Delegate Conference of 19 April 1984, the NUM implored non-strikers to stop work: 'It is . . . agreed that the National Union call on all Areas to join the 80 per cent who are already on strike and thereby ensure the maximum unity in the Union'.[13] This exhortation subsequently had little impact as was implicitly recognized by the NUM National President on 30 April 1984 when he declared that the strike could be won without the Nottinghamshire miners (Winterton & Winterton 1989: 73). Even a rally of 15,000 striking miners held on 14 May 1984 in Mansfield, in the heart of the Nottinghamshire coalfield, failed to increase local support for the strike.

With the defiance of the majority of Nottinghamshire miners well entrenched, other events contributed to the 'irrevocable polarization of Nottinghamshire and the National Union' (Winterton & Winterton 1989: 73). In particular, the NUM's decision to introduce disciplinary rule changes against working miners provoked outrage in Nottinghamshire. The new Rule 51 would establish a National Disciplinary Committee – quickly dubbed the 'Star Chamber' by working miners – to consider complaints against members for 'any act (including any omission) which may be detrimental to the interests of the Union'. This rule change was agreed at a Special Delegate Conference of the Union on 10 August 1984 which was boycotted by delegates from Nottinghamshire, Leicestershire and South Derbyshire. The rule change was clearly designed to make the Nottinghamshire Area more accountable to the NEC; in response, Nottinghamshire miners in December 1984 voted heavily in favour of a new constitution giving the Area greater autonomy from the National Union (Winterton & Winterton 1989: 74, 301). In January 1985, the pro-strike Nottinghamshire General Secretary was suspended, and in March, dismissed, by the Area Executive Committee.

After the national strike ended in March 1985, the Nottinghamshire coalfield became a highly charged battleground between those area leaders arguing for greater autonomy and, if needs be, independence from a now distrusted National Union, and those within and beyond Nottinghamshire pleading for the maintenance of one national Union in the industry. At the NUM's 1985 Annual Conference, however, delegates voted for a new disciplinary rule against dissident Areas whereupon the Nottinghamshire delegation abandoned the proceedings and shortly afterwards voted to leave the NUM. Despite subsequent pleas from the TUC and Labour Party to remain in the NUM, Nottinghamshire miners voted in October 1985 to form a new union. The rift between Nottinghamshire and the rest of the coalfield was now complete.

The Roots of Disunity: Nottinghamshire – A Coalfield Apart?

> The Nottinghamshire miners . . . their problems is the same as ours, no different. The only thing different was the accents. (W16)

> The Nottinghamshire miners have always felt themselves sort of apart from the National Union. (W50)

The Working Miner

Why did the majority of Nottinghamshire miners refuse to strike in 1984? Overwhelmingly, working miners (whether they favoured or opposed strike action) pointed to the absence of a national ballot as their principal reason. The response of a faceworker at Mansfield colliery was typical: 'There was no vote, that was my main reason . . . If there'd been a vote, I'd probably have voted "no", but if the vote had gone for a strike . . . I'd have gone with the majority, same as would everybody in Nottinghamshire'(N57). Furthermore, in the absence of a *national* ballot, the authority of the Area Ballot against strike action became, for most Nottinghamshire miners, unimpeachable:

> . . . we had a set of rules and one of the rules was for national action to have
> a national ballot . . . That never took place and they tried to steam-roller it –
> a domino effect – well, none of that's in the rulebook. So our representatives
> went to the (NEC) and said 'Look, we want an area Ballot', they said yes
> . . . we had the ballot . . . it was overwhelmingly in favour of not to strike.
> So even though I voted 'for', I've got to go along with the majority decision
> – and up to that point, that was the only majority decision that had affected
> me. Everybody . . . fully expected a national ballot to come along, and *fully*
> expected the decision . . . to be strike action – everybody thought they'd be
> on strike in a matter of weeks. (N11)

For working miners, therefore, the absence of a ballot legitimized the
breaching of that most potent symbol of collective solidarity – the picket
line. The UDM Branch Delegate at Sherwood colliery commented: '. . .
the picket line was sacrosanct. And a picket line had not been breached
in Nottingham while ever I'd been in the pits. The problem was that the
lack of a national ballot gave the men – they felt – the right to cross
picket lines. So the lack of a national ballot did untold damage to the
Union at the time . . . picket lines had been breached, and obviously, the
sanctity of the picket line had been destroyed'(N55).

In addition, many working miners underscored the alienating effects
of heavy picketing from the Yorkshire coalfield. Such tactics represented
a blatant attempt by the NUM to force them out on strike without a say
in the matter. A faceworker at Calverton colliery reflected: 'They went
about it all wrong – forcing, not asking. We had all these bully boys here,
pickets from Yorkshire'(N53). A surfaceworker at Rufford likened the
picketing to the 'bullying tactics . . . of a "rent-a-mob"'(N31). And a
chargeman at Harworth colliery argued that 'it wasn't as though we were
against a strike, it was against the way it was put about – being told,
trying to take our vote away from us'(N25). Moreover, the violence of
some of the picketing reinforced the determination of some miners to go
into work. A faceworker at Creswell complained: 'I don't want Yorkshire men coming down here and smashing my house, and smashing my
car – which happened . . . I weren't having that, not off a fellow-miner'
(N45), while at Mansfield colliery, a faceworker described a damaging
sequence of events:

> . . . when they came to our colliery, at the very beginning of it . . . they
> approached us like they normally do – with pickets. Nobody knew what
> were going [on] . . . so we decided, we'll work tonight and see what the
> Union Secretary says in the morning when we come off shift. I think *then*
> they attacked us, and . . . if that hadn't . . . happened, they'd have had a lot
> more men supporting them. Because police were there – they got us through
> the [picket] lines, but a minority of [the pickets] broke through and attacked
> some of the lads, and that were it, that were end of support – for *me*. And a
> lot more felt like it. (N56)

Overall, objections to the NUM's strategy of mobilizing strike action through picketing rather than through the mechanism of a national ballot produced a tenacious determination on the part of Nottinghamshire miners to continue working. A miner at Bolsover colliery – scene of some of the heaviest picketing in the coalfield – summarized the situation thus: 'No matter how many pickets came, or where they came from, it wouldn't have stopped me from coming to work. Whether the police were there or not, it wouldn't have stopped me. I was abiding by an area ballot decision . . . as far as we were concerned, we were in the right'(N39).

The Striking Miner

Were such arguments, however, merely the excuses of a section of the workforce unwilling to support strike action? Many strikers thought so. At Penrhiwceiber colliery in South Wales, the NUM Lodge Chairman remarked, 'I think that the Notts Area *used* the fact that we didn't have a ballot simply as an excuse to work'(W15). Nor were such attitudes confined to the threatened 'peripheral' areas of the British coalfield. At High Moor colliery in Derbyshire, a miner felt that the 'Notts men went into work because they were in a rich coalfield. [A national ballot] would have made no difference. The Notts men would not have abided by it'(D2). And a miner at Barrow colliery in Yorkshire commented 'They weren't going to back us . . . they've got plenty, so they think, f**k them. A national ballot in 1984 would have made no difference. It would not have brought the Notts miners out . . . they're in clover, so they think: we're not going to back other areas in a strike'(Y15).

The existence of two sharply contrasting accounts of the defiance of the Nottinghamshire coalfield has critical implications, of course, for the larger issue of whether the disunity displayed in 1984–5 was a manifestation of declining collective consciousness amongst miners. On the one hand, a materialist explanation for the actions of Nottinghamshire miners implies that they could not have been won over: they shared no common interest with their fellow workers and on that basis were not going to support strike action. On the other hand, the non-strikers' protestations that the national ballot and picketing issues were legitimate grievances implies that the Nottinghamshire men could have been won over, regardless of whether they were better off or not.

I believe that first, the grievances of the Nottinghamshire miners *were* legitimate, and that therefore, given different tactics adopted at the national level, they could have been won over to supporting the strike. Second, the articulation of these grievances, far from heralding the emergence of a new or declining consciousness on the part of the

Nottinghamshire miners, was in keeping with a well-entrenched political and industrial tradition which Nottinghamshire miners saw as being under attack by the NUM nationally.

Undoubtedly, Nottinghamshire miners were, in the early 1980s, relatively secure. The introduction of the AIS in the late 1970s put them at or near the top of the wages league. In terms of job security, the contrast with other Areas is a little less stark. After all, for many Nottinghamshire miners, the experience of job losses was not unknown – pit closures in the 1960s in areas such as South Wales, Scotland and Durham had forced thousands of miners to uproot themselves and move to core coalfields like Nottinghamshire. Moreover, as the Area NUM emphasized in 1983, Nottinghamshire *had*, like other areas, suffered pit closures in the recent past, and was vulnerable in the future to government plans for the expansion of nuclear power and greater reliance on cheap foreign coal (NUM Notts Area 1983).

As such, several Nottinghamshire miners, while agreeing that their jobs were more secure, none the less shared *some* of the insecurities felt by miners in the peripheral coalfield areas. A Bolsover miner remarked wryly that 'old miners have told me they've been going to close Bolsover colliery since 1950 – every three to four years, they've been going to shut it'(N47). And a mechanic with twenty-eight years' service at Creswell colliery reflected:

> We've had closures here . . . when I first started working for the NCB, they gave me three pits to choose from. I chose Creswell No.1, Whitwell No.2 and Langwith No.3. And I got advice at the time that Creswell was due to close – we live under that sort of atmosphere. As time has told, Langwith and Whitwell have gone before Creswell. So we're all aware that pits can come and go . . . But . . . I didn't honestly think that I personally was in any greater danger [in the early 1980s] than what I'd been through all my working life with regards my position at the pit. (N46)

However, with pit closures and job losses in the early 1980s hitting the peripheral coalfields significantly harder than Nottinghamshire, a feeling existed amongst most local miners that their jobs were secure. Of twenty-three non-strikers expressing a direct opinion, nineteen (83 per cent) felt their own jobs were not under any threat.[14] Thus at Bilsthorpe colliery, a surfaceworker commented: 'Whitburn closed in the late 60s, and that's why I came from the Durham coalfield to Notts . . . I transferred here . . . Notts was . . . the big money maker, the star area . . . I've been at pits in Notts that weren't doing well, but you never had that feeling that you were under any immediate threat . . . I felt I'd got a secure future until I retired'(N13).[15]

Undoubtedly, the general feeling of well-being amongst Nottingham-shire miners generated precious little support for strike action in the three national ballots held in 1982 and 1983. Thus an electrician at Bilsthorpe colliery stated: 'Job prospects seemed to be so good, and we was earning *good* money, and we didn't see any reason *to* strike. I think it was possibly a feeling of "we're alright" – it's probably the wrong attitude, but I think that's what it was, in all honesty. We never wanted to strike, in case it jeopardized our pit, and that's what it boiled down to'(N19).

The assumption that miners in secure positions would not support strike action seemed to have been borne out by these results. As such, it had a profound impact on the attitudes of both miners elsewhere and their national leadership towards the Nottinghamshire coalfield (and the other smaller central coalfields). Beynon reports, for example, on the demoralization caused in the peripheral areas by the decisive rejection of strike action in the ballot of March 1983:

> Again just [39 per cent] had voted for the strike and again the main source of opposition to the strike was certain groups, like COSA (Colliery Officials and Staffs Association), the white-collar section, and areas like Nottingham and Leicester. The scale of this defeat forced miners in South Wales and some of the other threatened areas to ask deep questions about strategy . . . Notts and the Midlands, so many people argued, would *never* support threatened miners in South Wales, Scotland and the North-East. (1985: 11; original emphasis)

One of the main conclusions drawn – as several South Wales miners testified – was that a national ballot was an inherently unfair method of mobilizing strike action given the uneven impact of pit closures. A miner at Penallta colliery argued that 'it's alright to have a ballot over pay, and them sort of things, but when you're asking a man in a safe job to vote on a man in a not-so-safe job, on his livelihood, it's totally wrong. I would never have gone along with a ballot on that'(W6). While this perspective was by no means universally shared by striking miners, it undoubtedly gained currency with the NUM's national leadership. Defending the decision to reject a national ballot, Peter Heathfield, the NUM's National General Secretary argued:

> There was a lot of nonsense talked about the demand for a ballot . . . with 80 per cent of the men *out*, why did they then want a ballot? I'm an advocate of ballots on major issues, with one qualification – the issue on the ballot equally affects everyone participating in the ballot – for example, wages, or hours of work. But on the question of colliery closures, the issues were affecting a minority. So people working at long-life pits – especially Notts – don't see themselves as affected, leading to a tendency to vote against [a

strike]. If a national ballot had been held, there would have been an overwhelming majority, but Notts would still have gone against.[16]

By 1984, therefore, many within the NUM viewed the demands for a
ballot with deep suspicion: 'The feeling had grown . . . that Nottingham
would *never* vote for strike action, and that on an issue which didn't
directly affect them, like colliery closures, they could not be relied on to
adhere to a national decision' (Beynon 1985: 13). Or, as Winterton and
Winterton argue: 'The Notts miners called for a ballot as a way of
stopping the strike; the ballot issue was a *result* of their disaffection for
the strike rather than a *cause* of it' (1989: 75; original emphasis).

    In addition, however, it is crucial to note that for the NUM's national
leadership, and for many strikers, the Nottinghamshire miners' defiance
was not just rooted in their immediate conditions of well-being in the
1980s, but in the fact that in terms of earnings, working conditions and
job security, the Nottinghamshire coalfield had *always* been better off.
This, it was argued, had shaped a long tradition of parochialism, political
moderation and general abhorrence of acting on anyone's behalf but
their own. The determination of Nottinghamshire miners in 1984 to go
to work was typical of such a tradition – as the Yorkshire Area NUM
President noted, he 'didn't really trust' the Nottingham Area (Beynon
1985: 13).

    Was this fair? I argue not, because the above, while containing grains
of truth, essentially mischaracterizes the traditions of the Nottinghamshire miners. The attitudes and practices of the Nottinghamshire miners
represented a tradition *within*, rather than *in opposition to*, the NUM at
large. As such, it was the violation of this tradition, rather than the
tradition itself, which explains the Nottinghamshire miners' decision to
work. What, therefore, was the substance of this tradition, and in what
ways was it compatible with loyalty to the national Union? Furthermore,
did the events of 1984–5 represent a rupture or continuation of this
tradition?

The Nottinghamshire Tradition within the NUM

The Notts miners have always been a thorn in our flesh.

Conversation with Mr Tom Brunkner, Sr, Treorchy, 7/12/89

The judgement of a 97-year-old ex-South Wales miner and veteran of
the 1926 General Strike demonstrates how well entrenched the feeling
was amongst miners that Nottinghamshire had traditionally been a coalfield apart. For many miners, its reputation had been tarnished forever
by its role in undermining the 1926 national coal strike. From this

point on, it seems, Nottinghamshire had earned for itself a tradition of selfishness and a decided lack of industrial and political militancy. This view was particularly pronounced among miners from the central South Wales coalfield, for whom the secure working conditions, union traditions and attitudes of the Nottinghamshire miners belonged to a different world – 'they're selfish buggers . . . they're all "self"'(W5). For a miner at Penrhiwceiber colliery, their recalcitrance in 1984 was unsurprising: 'In regards to the Notts area, it was most disappointing that they didn't come out . . . it's historic, there . . . after the 1926 strike they broke away, and they formed the non-political union . . . and . . . it's something that's spread in a lot of people in Notts, this non-political issue – "if they keep their heads down, then everything will pass over"' (W14). Two critical questions are generated by these perspectives on the alleged 'apartness' of the Nottinghamshire coalfield – what was the substance of this tradition, and was it incompatible with a wider loyalty?

The reflections of a miner at Creswell colliery underscore Nottinghamshire's position as a bastion of peaceful industrial relations within an otherwise turbulent industry: 'I've always thought Notts . . . one of the most stable areas in the coalfield . . . we've always felt that in Notts they protect all pits, and it's such a good producing area, they can afford to do that'(N43). Moreover, 'easy coal meant less rank-and-file pressure for militant leadership' (Winterton & Winterton 1989: 75), unlike South Wales and Kent, for example, where perpetual geological problems led to constant delays, disputes and strikes. Consequently, many Nottinghamshire miners felt themselves to be part of a moderate political and industrial tradition. At Bolsover colliery, a miner described how 'Notts has a really funny history – it's peculiar. They're always last to come out on strike, and they've always been first to go back. I think that kind of history's gone against them' (N47). Often, the area's moderation was contrasted with the traditions of Yorkshire, its militant neighbour to the north. A miner at Silverhill colliery commented 'If there's a right-wing and a left-wing, I would have said we're more right of centre than what Yorkshire were'(N17), while a miner at Welbeck was more blunt: 'There's never been any love lost between Notts men and Yorkshiremen, because we've always been moderates'(N16).

How, though, did such a tradition of moderation manifest itself? Easier working conditions created the opportunities for high earnings; this, in turn, undoubtedly underpinned an instrumental attachment to work: 'We come to work for one thing – to get paid on a Friday, that's it – a good wage'(N20). Thus the Nottinghamshire miners resented the imposition of national wage parity, seeing it as an obstacle to making the most, financially, of locally favourable working conditions. Consequently, they voted in 1974 and 1977 for the reintroduction of incentives to the industry's wages structure. A Bilsthorpe miner noted that 'we hadn't got to produce a deal more coal to earn a lot more money . . . there's nothing wrong with a man getting paid for working hard – because down the pit, you've got men who *will* work hard, and men who won't . . . men who work *bloody* hard should be rewarded'(N13). A Mansfield miner favourably compared incentive payments to national wage parity: 'When they set us on the NPLA, you couldn't earn no more . . . no matter what they did, they still got the money. Yet when you went on [incentives], . . . everybody was different again – busy beavers, earning money – men *worked*, and I was in favour of it'(N57).

Traditionally higher earnings, rooted in less arduous working conditions, also generated support for a general industrial relations strategy of consultation rather than confrontation. For example, a Gedling miner reflected, 'I . . . believe that . . . it's absolutely the *very last* thing that you start talking industrial action before you do anything . . . It's necessary to make a compromise between the union and management, for the good of everybody'(N28). Not surprisingly, Nottinghamshire miners overwhelmingly favoured the consensually minded NUM leadership of Gormley in the 1970s over that of the more confrontational style adopted by Scargill in the 1980s. Of forty-two interviewees who did not strike in 1984–5, thirty-two (76.2 per cent) viewed Gormley as the better defender of miners' interests, compared to four (9.5 per cent) for Scargill, and six (14.5 per cent) undecided. A Rufford miner complained that Scargill 'seemed to have . . . a one-track mind – confrontation, that was his middle name, "confrontation"'(N20), while a miner at Welbeck colliery compared the two leaders thus: 'Gormley negotiated on behalf of the membership. Arthur Scargill has never negotiated anything in his life . . . from Day One, he has wanted to confront the leadership of our industry . . . his philosophy is "we'll have everything we demand, or we're not talking". But there's got to be give and take'(N16).

This pragmatic attitude towards industrial relations was reflected in traditionally low levels of strike action in Nottinghamshire and a general dislike of the strike as an industrial weapon.[17] An electrician at Bolsover commented: 'A strike never wins anything – you never get *back* what you've lost during a strike, no matter how long you go'(N40). Furthermore – unlike Yorkshire and South Wales where miners argued that the defence of their communities was at stake in the fight against pit closures – there was a tendency in Nottinghamshire to accept the language of the market regarding allegedly uneconomic capacity in the industry: 'Most people in Notts . . . look at it like this: if a concern's not paying and . . . it's taking taxpayers' money, you couldn't keep that pit going – if it's not paying its way, there's no place for it'(N57). Even those with working experience in declining coalfields viewed the issue likewise: 'I mean, alright, we in the Notts area, we were doing very well . . . I used to travel about and saw these mines in other areas, and I said to myself, I don't know why the [NCB] keeps these places open . . . because . . . they were losing money hand over fist – well . . . you're in business to either break even or make a profit, not to keep losing money as they were'(N31). A Bilsthorpe miner concurred, 'It's inevitable – you can't go on indefinitely pouring money into a pit that's not making its way . . . there comes a time when you've got to say "enough's enough", and the pit's got to go – rough as it is on your communities'(N13).

Acceptance of the language of the market underpinned a mood of resignation on what could be done to prevent pit closures: 'No matter what happened, they was going to shut them . . . it's all about economics really, that's the top and bottom of it'(N56). A Gedling miner stated baldly, 'If a pit's going to shut, it'll shut, and that's it'(N28). As such, Nottinghamshire miners were divided as to the efficacy of strike action as a means of fighting pit closures in the 1980s. Only 41 per cent of respondents saw striking as the best means of doing so, with 55 per cent favouring other measures such as an overtime ban. Indeed, many viewed strike action as futile and even counter-productive: 'I just couldn't see what could be gained through going on strike. Actually, when you're on strike, and the pit's stuck, there's more chance of something happening, because when a pit's working, it keeps open, on strike, it shuts itself. So . . . you'll end up shutting your own pit'(N24). A miner at Calverton added, 'I wouldn't go on strike to keep a pit open, keep my job open for me – if it's going to go, it's going to go, there's nothing you can do about it'(N53).

Such attitudes support the notion of the 'apartness' of the Nottinghamshire coalfield – one whose economic interests, and industrial and political outlook, often differed from those of neighbouring coalfields. Yet the Nottinghamshire Area did remain a loyal component of the NUM for nearly four decades. That it did so is largely a function of the nature of the NUM's structure and constitution – borne of the painstaking process in the 1940s of bringing together a diverse group of coalfields. The Nottinghamshire coalfield, like others, entered into a federal structure allowing individual areas large degrees of autonomy. A robust belief developed amongst Nottinghamshire miners that membership of a national organization – with whose interests they often clashed – was acceptable only as long as the Union's rules, constitution and procedures were strictly observed – 'No man', stated a Harworth miner with thirty-seven years in the industry, 'is going to stop me saying my piece'(N25). A Bolsover miner described how 'the National Rule Book is there to be adhered to, not to be broken'(N39). A Creswell miner stated, 'I've not had a lot to do with Unions, but a Union's a good thing, except in one way – if it uses its rules to win, good; but if breaks those rules to win, it's wrong'(N44). And a Mansfield miner argued that 'if you've got a constitution set up, you've got to stick to it, no matter what, or you might as well not have one'(N56).

Certainly, such views reflected a desire to maintain and protect local interests. By the same token, however, where the national Union was seen to be acting legitimately and according to procedure, Nottingham-shire miners *were* capable of forgoing local concerns in the interests of national solidarity. This was undoubtedly so with the NPLA, where a prolonged and painstaking campaign in the Nottinghamshire coalfield by the NUM's national leadership succeeded in winning over the Nottinghamshire miners to the principle of national wage parity. As noted earlier, the NPLA was disliked in Nottinghamshire since the move towards wage parity hit the higher-paid coalfields harder than the older peripheral coalfields. Indeed, the NUM's General Secretary Lawrence Daly testified to the Wilberforce Inquiry in 1972 thus: 'Many thousands of men in coalfields like Nottingham, who knew they were going to experience actual, and in many cases very substantial, net reductions in their cash wages, were opposed to [the NPLA] and it was not without great difficulty that this became the official policy [of the NUM]' (Hughes & Moore 1972: 22). Yet remarkably, the Nottinghamshire miners did subsequently adhere to a system which saw their pay decline in real terms between 1966 and 1972 by 15 per cent, compared to only 1.8 per cent in South Wales (Hughes & Moore 1972: 29).

Again, in the 1972 national strike, the Nottinghamshire miners demonstrated their traditional moderation by returning a 'Yes' vote in their area ballot of 54 per cent, just below the constitutional requirement for a 55 per cent majority to sanction strike action. Yet because the national ballot returned an overall 'Yes' vote of 58.8 per cent,[18] they struck with the rest of the coalfield. Several Nottinghamshire miners reflected approvingly on how the 1972 strike had been conducted by the NUM's national leadership. A Mansfield miner said: 'It were done right. Every man was allowed a vote . . . it was organized from Day One right through . . . the constitution of the Union'(N56). A Creswell miner thought the strike had been 'handled very well by the NUM – all organized, a ballot, everything done properly – asking our opinion, not *telling* us'(N51). And a Harworth miner reflected:

> We'd all been put in the picture . . . no . . . trying to wangle things. Gormley went to the NCB, then to the Government, it was all brought back and dis-cussed at Branch level. Everybody knew what was happening . . . and it was voted for a strike. That's what I like, democracy, that's all I want. I mean I've voted at Branch, Area, Nationally, ever since I've been down the pits, and there's a lot of things I've voted for that haven't come about. But I'll abide by the majority, and I'll eat grass before I go against it. (N25)

The same adherence to Union procedure was demonstrated again by Nottinghamshire miners when they observed the overtime ban imposed by the NUM in November 1983 in response to the NCB's pay offer. Cutting deep into bonus earnings, the overtime ban was, like the NPLA two decades earlier, deeply unpopular in Nottinghamshire. The Branch Secretary at Bilsthorpe colliery recalled, 'It was passed at Area Council by sixteen votes to fifteen . . . a very unpopular decision in Notts . . . and I had to go round the pit defending this decision to people who were losing a lot of money. *But*, we stuck by it'(N11). A Welbeck miner commented that 'this Area stuck to that agreement . . . because it was a national policy on an overtime ban. And this area adopted it'(N16). Moreover, the Nottinghamshire miners *continued* to observe the overtime ban into the tenth month of the 1984–5 strike. As such, an Annesley miner emphasized that 'we kept to [the overtime ban] right through to March 1985 at this colliery. So we did take part – if anybody says Notts men didn't take part in industrial action, they're wrong'(N38).

This appraisal of the Nottinghamshire coalfield suggests a need to reconsider what the defiance of 1984–5 actually tells us about the bonds of solidarity between miners nationally. Undoubtedly the economic security and traditional moderation of the Nottinghamshire coalfield posed a strategic problem for a national Union leadership campaigning over an inherently divisive issue. The Nottinghamshire miners in the early 1980s felt themselves to be under little immediate threat, and demonstrated this in the 1982 and 1983 national ballots by recording characteristically low levels of support for strike action. However, such attitudes and perceptions were not new – nor were they incompatible with the expression of solidarity with the coalfield as a whole. The defiance of the Nottinghamshire miners did not amount, therefore, to a set of *ad hoc* excuses invented by a disinterested section of the national mining workforce. Nor did it signify the development of a tradition in opposition to the NUM at large. Instead, it very much represented the continuity of an authentic tradition *within* the NUM which the Nottinghamshire miners saw as being violated by the tactics and strategy of the NUM. It is in *this* context that the criticisms levelled by the Nottinghamshire miners against the NUM's national leadership, and parts of their own Area leadership, must be placed.

Thus the refusal to strike was rooted in a genuine belief that the rule book of the Union was being violated by the NUM. Moreover, Nottinghamshire miners, far from seeing themselves as intractable opponents of the NUM, saw themselves very much as a 'loyal opposition'. A Harworth miner remarked

It was things inside the Union's structure that was being attacked . . . we
were fighting on two fronts . . . certain elements in our union, as well as the
Government . . . and that's where we weakened ourselves . . . when you start
attacking the principles of your rule book and the constitution of the Union,
then that's when people have gone away from the true facts they were there
for. Arthur Scargill did good, but . . . he attacked something that didn't suit
[him] . . . he tried to destroy that framework – that framework was good
enough for miners, not forgetting that our forefathers . . . had *fought* and
died for them rules and rights, and we weren't prepared to see them . . .
thrown out'. (N26)

Similarly, an Annesley miner argued that 'you've got to have a strategy,
and the strategy was the rules of the NUM – not rules written by any
Tory or landowner – they were written by our forefathers for us, for our
generation. And certain NUM leaders chose to ignore them'(N38).
Indeed, many Nottinghamshire miners viewed the application of such
rules as the only means of overcoming the different traditions within the
coalfield. Thus an Annesley miner argued that the 'main stumbling block
was the unity – the only way to unite mineworkers is with a national
ballot, because you've got little pockets of mineworkers everywhere,
each have got their own folklore, each Area with its own structure – so,
to unite a mineworker in South Wales that knows his area, a miner in
Durham, and a lad in Notts, it's the only thing you've got'(N38). As
events unfolded, therefore, the issues underpinning the strike became
rapidly submerged by concerns over the way it was being conducted:

We all operated under a Rule Book – the South Wales miners, the Yorkshire
miners, Notts miners, Scottish miners – we *all* operated under one national
Rule Book, and if you read that Rule Book as it was then, it stated before
any national strike there must be a national ballot of the membership. Now
whether your head rules your heart, or your heart rules your head, if you've
got a Rule Book, you're supposed to operate under it. Now if it had been
my pit that were going to close, I may well have felt like saying 'Well, they
should have supported us' – but the fact remains that you have to operate
under [rules], and the Area . . . and National Officials are there to implement
[them]. (N16)

As such, the grounds on which to criticize the absence of a national
ballot in 1984, the mass picketing from Yorkshire, and the 'defection'
of their two senior Area leaders to the National Union, were legitimate
and crystal clear. On the ballot issue, a Gedling miner commented:

If those that said we should have gone out and supported them, if they are
Union-minded, there's a rule book . . . and that says there should be a national ballot for strike action. And we need to abide by the rules. And that's
what we did – that's all, there's nothing more about that – my paramount

thoughts all the while were: national ballot – if we have one I am *certain* we will be out on strike. But we didn't have [one], so there was no way we were going to. (N28)

Picketing was also seen as a violation of Union procedure: 'We had a democratic vote in this Area to work . . . and he sent his bully boys down to get us out . . . I don't see why we should have gone through all that hassle what we did, when we voted to work'(N23). At Bilsthorpe, a miner reflected: 'If they'd come about it the proper way, they'd have had us out, but they didn't . . . we weren't having them ruling the roost down here'(N12).

In similar fashion, the Nottinghamshire Area General Secretary and President were castigated not so much for supporting a strategy of strike action against pit closures, but for ignoring the Area Ballot decision to continue working until a national ballot had been held. A strong feeling existed across the coalfield that the Area Officials were delegates to, and not servants of, the Union's NEC. For an Annesley miner, therefore, the Area leaders were 'turn-coats'(N37) while the UDM Branch President at Silverhill colliery argued that 'their members told them what they wanted, and they didn't do as the workforce wanted. They should have told the [National leadership] that "my men have voted 74 per cent to go to work" and that's it . . . but they didn't want to abide by their own rules'(N17). Overall, little sympathy existed for the pressure that Area leaders came under from the Union's National leadership to toe the national line. At Creswell, the home pit of Henry Richardson, the Area General Secretary, a miner reflected:

> . . . he came to Creswell and told the men his thoughts – you ought to be supporting the other Areas. *But,* if you have a ballot and it goes against strike action, I will support you . . . The Area ballot went against strike action, and a week later, they organized a meeting in the village – there were about 2,000 pickets there. I went through the pickets into the meeting. Henry . . . called us all scabs, it was time to get off our knees, and he wasn't going to [National Headquarters] anymore to be kicked and spat at in order to support us. From then on, he distanced himself from us – that's when I turned against him . . . the men in Notts voted the [Area leaders] in, not the men in Yorkshire and Wales. We voted them in, they should have been there to carry out our mandates. They didn't. (N43)

Moreover, surprising levels of support for the Nottinghamshire miners' position existed in other coalfields – overall, *strikers* were generally divided, for example, on the question of the national ballot. Even in Yorkshire, where the majority of strikers demonstrated their historic dislike for Nottinghamshire miners by arguing that a national ballot

would have changed nothing, several loyal strikers, including an electrician at Thurcroft colliery, were emphatic that 'there *should* have been
a national ballot, it *would* have been won, the Notts men *would* . . . have
abided by the result . . . and we should have left them alone, and not
gone picketing'(Y24). Indeed, a majority of South Wales miners felt that
errors had been committed by the NUM. Some argued that a national
ballot would at least have removed the excuses emanating from the
Nottinghamshire coalfield. Miners at Penallta colliery argued that a
ballot 'would have proved a *point*'(W4), and ensured that 'their excuse
would have gone'(W10). One miner at the colliery, like the Annesley
miner quoted earlier, saw a ballot as the only practical means of uniting
a traditionally fragmented coalfield:

> . . . loyalties aside . . . I looked at it purely on *tactics* . . . it's alright for
> Arthur Scargill to say that this is the way working men and miners should
> react to the call. But all working men don't react to the call. But . . . when
> you have a ballot, they *will follow* it . . . once they see that this is . . .
> national . . . there will be virtually no need to picket any colliery in the
> British Isles. I'm all for calling strike action without the ballot, but what
> we're . . . depending on then is men's . . . convictions and principles and . . .
> everybody's not as highly principled, are they? . . . and my tactical argument
> was . . . let's not give anyone the excuse to say I will cross the picket line
> because I didn't have the ballot. (W12)

Some South Wales strikers went even further than this by arguing that
the defiance of the Nottinghamshire men, though regrettable, was not
without justification. The NUM Lodge Secretary at Penallta reflected:

> Notts, as an Area, had the right to vote, or *decide*, whether they went on
> strike. And when they decided they weren't going on strike, they weren't
> breaking any rule by not coming out on strike. Because they decided as
> an Area . . . There was quite a few mistakes, and I've been at loggerheads
> with rules most of my life – yet you've *got* to have rules, and you've got to
> *change* them – it's no good ignoring them . . . you've got to keep the *unity*
> amongst men, even if you've got to alter what you think, sometimes, as
> leaders . . . to get the maximum of unity. And I think this was thrown to the
> wind. And we paid for it. (W9)

The NUM Lodge Chairman at neighbouring Oakdale colliery agreed:

> . . . what people don't realize is that Notts didn't do anything wrong – under
> rule. They went to their men, but they didn't want to strike, which they was
> quite entitled to do. So they didn't do anything wrong . . . I think the biggest
> thing against the Notts miners coming out was the way they went in
> picketing . . . I've always found if you ask someone to do something, it's a
> lot better than trying to *tell* them they've got to do it . . . I think it was

handled wrongly. And I think we ought to be big enough, you know, to *admit* that. (W16)

Undoubtedly, not all strikers were as forgiving as this towards the Nottinghamshire miners; it is also probable that some Nottinghamshire miners did indeed use the ballot, and associated issues, as excuses not to strike. However, my conclusions are three-fold. First, given different tactics adopted at the national level, the Nottinghamshire miners could have been won over to the national struggle. Second, their actions were in keeping with a well-entrenched tradition. Third, their actions and attitudes amounted to an internal critique of the NUM which was shared by other miners in other parts of the coalfield. In terms of the allegedly changing bonds of solidarity between industrial workers, therefore, Nottinghamshire was not such a 'coalfield apart' as events in 1984–5 would, at first glance, indicate. That this is so is underscored by considering the position of the Nottinghamshire miners within the post-strike landscape of industrial defeat and organizational division.

The Meaning of Disunity: Continuity and Change in the Consciousness of the Non-Striker

I think the Notts miners were misled in breaking away from the NUM. But at the same time I think we've got to find a means of working with them . . . I don't treat 20,000 Nottingham miners, their wives, their families and their communities as outcasts, untouchables – they're *miners*. They've got basic problems, the same as other miners . . . and *that's* the avenue upon which we must build the basis of unity . . . they have not breached from the labour movement, they have breached from the national leadership of the miners.

Interview with Mick McGahey, NUM National Vice-President, 18/12/89

The establishment of the UDM represented the continuity of a tradition and did not amount to a rejection of the labour movement in particular, or a class outlook in general. Furthermore, a strong basis existed for the reunification of the miners.

The Establishment of the UDM

The decision of Nottinghamshire miners to form the UDM represented, obviously, an emphatic desire to break with the NUM. But did they jump or were they pushed? The distinction is critical if we are to understand the meaning of the NUM–UDM split in the period after the 1984–5 strike. Without doubt, the NUM's tactics at the national level during and after the strike alienated large swathes of the Nottinghamshire coalfield.

Indeed, the failure to hold a national ballot, the consequent attempt to
spread the strike through picketing, and the subsequent efforts to make
dissident Areas more accountable to the National Union and to punish
working miners for their actions, all ensured that with near-unanimity,
Nottinghamshire miners felt they had been forced into breaking from the
NUM – 'It was a reaction to what had gone on over twelve months'
(N48). A Silverhill miner argued, 'People say we're the guilty party
because we split. I think we were forced into it by people *in* the NUM'
(N17). A Creswell miner agreed, 'It wasn't really a breakaway, we were
thrown out . . . we were forced into it'(N44). In particular, UDM Branch
Officials pointed to the implications of actions by the national leadership
for local Area autonomy. The UDM Branch Delegate at Welbeck colliery commented:

> It was inevitable . . . the way we were forced to go. They . . . didn't give us
> any option. They were going to victimize all Branch officials in the Notts
> Area . . . for the fact that they had been at work. But . . . the workforce at
> the pit have elected those people to represent them, not miners nationally –
> I've been elected here by the men who work at Welbeck. Now if I was to be
> expelled by someone at [National Headquarters] for supporting men that
> worked all along here, where would that leave these men? So . . . a split was
> inevitable. (N16)

The UDM Branch Treasurer at Gedling colliery concurred: 'It was
inevitable . . . the NUM leadership – Scargill and co. *pushed* us, they
didn't give us an olive branch, they turned round and said they'd introduce this new Star Chamber . . . get rid of working miners, all Branch
Officials that worked . . . and "We're going to hammer you". And the
lads themselves, at the pits, said "You're not going to" – that's why the
UDM was formed'(N33).

However, this near-universal feeling of being forced into breaking
from the NUM did not mean there was unmitigated enthusiasm for a new
Union. Certainly, some relished the prospect: 'I thought it was great . . .
just to get away from that rabble'(N57). A Rufford miner described how
he was 'elated at the time. Because it meant we was on us own, on our
own footing, we'd got us . . . destiny in our own hands, by being on our
own as a Union'(N22). And an Annesley miner said:

> I felt great about it, because I thought Arthur had done that much damage to
> our Union, I thought it was time that someone told him he couldn't do just
> as he liked. And I was all in favour of a new Union – we were treated very
> bad throughout that strike . . . they tried to bully us out . . . and none of it
> worked. And in the end . . . I said it's time we did break away . . . because
> they were doing nothing for us, we'd have been lepers for the rest of time.
> (N37)

The majority of Nottinghamshire miners, though, viewed the emergence of the new Union with misgivings and regret. Naturally, this was strongest among the minority of Nottinghamshire miners voting 'no' to the new Union: 'I voted for the Union *not* to split up, and I still don't think it's right that we split up, we should be *one* Union, because they're going to get nowhere with two'(N49). A Calverton miner commented, 'I thought it were wrong, it was splitting a group of men what had been together since 1926 [*sic*]. We'd always been together'(N54). Even those in favour of the UDM still expressed similar sentiments: 'It had to be done. I'm a UDM member now . . . but it was a crying shame when we split the NUM up. I just wish it could be forgot about, and everybody got back together'(N45). A Gedling miner said, 'I was reluctantly in favour . . . very disappointed that it had got to happen . . . but there was no other means [for] the Notts miners'(N33). And a Creswell miner reflected, 'It sticks in my mind quite keenly. I thought at the time that both sides of the argument had pushed each other into a corner, and that the only way out of it was a fragmentation of the NUM resulting in the UDM being formed. It were mixed feelings – probably the saddest day of the NUM, but it was the best way out for people like myself . . . but at the time I had . . . enormous sadness about the NUM'(N46).

Such testimony hardly amounts to a ringing endorsement for the formation of a new Union. Nor does it signify the emergence of a new consciousness amongst Nottinghamshire miners. Instead, miners were acting within a tradition increasingly at odds with the tactics of a belligerent national leadership. Indeed, many miners, especially those with many years' service, insisted that it was the NUM national leadership that had changed, not them. Their hostility to the NUM leadership in 1984–5 was matched only by the stress they placed on their mining roots and their many years of loyalty to the NUM. A Harworth miner reflected:

> When I left school, I walked straight from the school gates to the pit gates and signed on. My father did it, my grandfather did it – it was something that went through the family . . . it was *in* you – you'd got coal dust in you when you were still at school, because you knew you were going to go down the pit . . . But no way am I going to work down a pit for thirty-seven years, gobbling dust, grime and filth, and sweat, like thousands of other miners – I didn't just *want* my vote, I *demanded* it. (N25)

A Gedling miner with thirty-nine years' service underground spoke in similar terms: 'How can I say it? . . . I felt really *terrible* at having to leave the NUM – I'd supported it since I was 16, and my father and grandfather before . . . but I couldn't accept the point that the NUM

wanted to change the rulebook . . . so . . . I just had to go into the UDM'
(N42). The UDM Branch President at Harworth also stressed the element of continuity:

> I was not very happy. Because . . . my father was NUM, my grandfathers
> were . . . NUM. I was taken to my first NUM meeting when I'd just started
> at the pit. And the split was the greatest catastrophe that ever happened to a
> trade union in this country . . . it will go down in my memory as the greatest
> catastrophe I've ever known, and one of the most *sorrowful* I've ever known
> . . . it was the worst day of my life when that happened. (N26)

Despite stressing the pain of leaving the NUM, he once again emphasized that the Nottinghamshire coalfield had not changed – even
pointing to Harworth's role in the suppression of 'scab' unionism in the
1930s:

> I would like to think that we're the same people that fight under, and had
> same beliefs, as when we were in the NUM . . . The UDM – structure-wise,
> everything, a *lot* of the people are just the same people which . . . were in
> the NUM . . . I can only speak of Harworth colliery, that we've had a proud
> tradition, here in the days of Spencerism, when the streets here ran red with
> blood, and a reporter said 'Harworth was the *making* of the [NUM]' – we're
> the sons of those people who fought hard and got locked up by the police.
> So I don't think we're any different – we're no gaffers' men. (N26)

Given this testimony, I conclude that the formation of the UDM, far
from heralding the development of a new consciousness, became the
reluctantly-adopted means of preserving a well-entrenched tradition.
Moreover, this tradition remained compatible with loyalty to the miners
nationally, and the wider labour movement.

Strike Aftermath: Class Politics and the Non-Striker

After the 1984–5 strike, Nottinghamshire itself was engulfed by the
wave of contraction sweeping the British coalfield generally. By March
1989, nine of the twenty-five pits in existence in Nottinghamshire before
the strike had closed, with manpower cut from 29,200 to 15,200. By
1995, UDM membership numbered only *4,000*.[19] Thus while it remained
intact as an organization and continued to command the loyalty of most
Nottinghamshire miners, it suffered, like its arch-rival, a declining membership base. Yet despite this disastrous trend, the bonds of solidarity
between striker and non-striker, though undoubtedly strained, proved
resilient. The *basis* for a reunification of the miners survived, while the
commitment of Nottinghamshire miners to the wider labour movement
remained strong.

First, all UDM members interviewed – like those in the NUM – supported the principle of re-establishing one Union for all miners. As a Harworth miner noted, 'That's how it should be'(N34). The damage done by the presence of two rival Unions to the overall bargaining power of miners was lost on few men. A Bilsthorpe miner commented that 'while there's a split, the Government knows if ever there is another dispute, it can always play one against the other – they've got the two sides'(N19). A Harworth miner emphasized the weakened power of miners with respect to wage bargaining: 'The split is divisive. The Coal Board is implementing the NUM's pay rises, even without a ballot . . . the Coal Board just pays the NUM what they pay the Notts miners – they can do it while ever there are two unions'(N34). And a Gedling miner described how the split hindered a collective response to continuing industrial contraction: 'In the long term, it must be damaging. Because once they've picked the NUM off, and got them down to the size they want them, it's our turn next. And over the last couple of years, that's been seen with what's happened with Notts, where pits have shut' (N33).

However, the overwhelming desire of Nottinghamshire miners to rejoin a single national Union was heavily qualified. They remained both wary and resentful of the NUM's national leadership – particularly in the person of Arthur Scargill – for its role in the 1984–5 strike. Indeed, it was seen by a majority of Nottinghamshire miners as a major obstacle to the reunification of the two Unions. A small minority couched their criticisms of the NUM leadership in ideological terms: a Mansfield miner declared, 'To me, they want hanging – they're militants, Communists, that's all they are'(N57). A Bilsthorpe miner also referred to the militancy of the NUM President: 'I've got to mention Arthur Scargill – while he's head of the NUM, no way will they ever get back together again! I suppose if someone takes over from him who's a lot more moderate in their outlook, [it might happen]'(N19). For the majority, however, any personal or ideological dislike for Scargill was outweighed by his continuing adherence to the rule changes which, during and after the 1984–5 strike, had threatened the area's autonomy. Few countenanced rejoining the NUM, therefore, with its current constitution: 'I wouldn't mind [getting back] into a single union, under the *old* rule book. But not under this new one that Arthur Scargill wanted to bring out'(N42). A Bilsthorpe miner commented, 'The rule book that the [NUM] changed – it would have to go back to what it was. Through my eyes, I see that book stood there all that time and then all of a sudden a man turns round and says he's going to change it so he can call you out on strike anytime, that's wrong, without a ballot . . . If they had their old rule book back, they'd get back together again'(N12).

In addition, the Nottinghamshire miners, recognizing the bitterness felt by strikers towards the UDM, appeared willing to sacrifice their own leadership (in particular, Roy Lynk, the UDM General Secretary) as well as that of the NUM in order to facilitate the process of reunification: 'Some obstacles could be quickly moved, which could pave the way – sacrifice . . . Scargill, and we'd probably have to get rid of Roy Lynk' (N13). An Annesley miner stated bluntly, 'Get rid of the two leaders, re-establish the pre-1984 rule book, and then you might get it'(N37). And the UDM Branch President at Harworth commented, 'I don't think it'll ever come with the leaders we've got on both the NUM and UDM sides . . . I don't agree with everything *our* leaders do, but you abide by the majority decision . . . it's inevitable that no way will we get back together again with the current leaders . . . ordinary working people, there's no problem. I think we could get back together tomorrow'(N26).

This testimony demonstrates that despite the institutionalized divisions of the post-strike period, the foundations for a possible reunification of the mining workforce remained strong. Nottinghamshire miners were clear about what was needed to effect such an outcome. Moreover, the positions adopted – removal of the current NUM leadership and a restoration of the old rule book – again represented an internal critique of the NUM. They did not amount to the embracing of a new anti-union stance. In an appraisal of the post-strike situation in Nottinghamshire, Schwarz writes, 'To suppose that the working miners have all been gripped by the truth of Thatcherism is rubbish' (1985: 62). The role of Nottinghamshire as the 'weakest link in the strike', and the government's success in winning the strike and dividing the miners did 'not necessarily mean a complete abandonment of working-class instincts for solidarity and collectivism, a collapse into the possessive individualism of Thatcherism' (1985: 63). Research undertaken in the Nottinghamshire coalfield five years after the strike underlines the validity of this perspective. Far from embracing the tenets of Thatcherism, the Nottinghamshire miners continued to identify strongly with the mainstream labour movement.

First, they continued to support free and independent trade unionism. They were divided, for example, on whether legal action taken against the NUM during the 1984–5 strike by the courts, and by some working miners, had been legitimate. The NUM's ability to conduct the strike had been severely hindered when, as a consequence of legal action, its funds were sequestrated by the courts. Fifty per cent of interviewees thought that the NUM itself was to blame for this, and condemned the Union's leadership for defying court injunctions prohibiting the picketing of working areas: 'Arthur thought he was *above* the law, and nobody's above the law – you must abide by it . . . the same thing applies with

Union funds etc. – Arthur thought he could do as he wanted . . . and it was *inevitable* that people would use the law courts to defeat him if necessary'(N16).

Surprisingly, though, the other 50 per cent disapproved of such action taken against the NUM. While criticizing the NUM for adopting tactics inviting legal retribution, many viewed such retribution as part of a wider strategy on the government's part, and condemned it accordingly: 'The NUM had itself to blame, but I believe that a lot of the court orders that came in were orchestrated by the Conservative Government through back door means'(N39). A Gedling miner felt that 'in some cases it had itself to blame, but I think it did go too far – that is, in the case of the Government's [use of] sequestration, I think it was to belittle the NUM even more. I think that was a Government policy, I'm sure Maggie Thatcher just wanted to hammer them down as far as she could get them down'(N41). The former Branch Secretary at Silverhill colliery remarked, 'The action went too far . . . I'd got a lot of sympathy with the NUM . . . it was the Tory Government's tactics which were wrong. I didn't agree with that, even though I were working and not supporting the strike – the [Government] should not have took the funds . . . off those lads'(N30). The UDM Branch President at Annesley colliery agreed, 'I thought that action were going too far, personally. There were people used by people what were anti-union. They used them as puppets . . . to do that, and personally, being a trade union official now, and having always been interested in the union movement, I thought it were going too far, and I didn't agree with it'(N38).

Second, many Nottinghamshire miners continued to situate themselves and their new Union within the traditions of the labour movement. Notably, towards the end of the strike, when a breakaway from the NUM was becoming increasingly likely, Roy Lynk (later the UDM leader) argued that 'the Nottingham Area is totally opposed to the anti-working class policies of this Tory Government. We campaigned against them during the last General Election. And nothing has happened since then to change our views'.[20] Once formed, the UDM subsequently demonstrated its commitment to the labour movement by applying for affiliation to the TUC and the Labour Party (both of which rebuffed the applications).

Third, the style of industrial relations espoused by the UDM remained very much in keeping with the traditions of the Nottinghamshire Area. Several Branch Officials stressed the emphasis placed by the UDM on consensus, partnership and a moderate attitude towards gains for its members – compared with the continuing hardline approach of the NUM's leadership. The Branch Secretary at Gedling colliery said, 'All we are as a Union is a negotiating team between men and management . . . you don't need to be super-strong as long as you come out with an acceptable pay deal, and we've done this over the last four years'(N28). The Branch Treasurer at Rufford commented that 'since being in the UDM, we've had at least three pay rises – not brilliant ones, but at least we've had them'(N23). At Bilsthorpe, the Branch Delegate argued that 'I don't think we've done too badly, in terms of conditions – not just wages, but early retirement, pensions, holiday bonuses. We're working away at it, we don't get big results overnight, but we're chipping away at things'(N13). And the Branch Secretary at Bilsthorpe stated:

> We're a lot more forward-thinking union, and we have a lot of benefits now available to the membership which move away from the older ideas of trade unions – apart from just representation and pay and conditions. We have a whole range of benefits that a man can come and get, so I think we've set the blueprint for the future – you must have these types of benefits – a social service, if you like – as *well* as fighting for better pay and conditions. (N11)

Moreover, such a philosophy, while at odds with the intensely ideo- logical stance adopted by the NUM national leadership in the 1980s, was none the less hardly exclusive to Nottinghamshire.

Fourth, support for the Labour Party itself amongst Nottinghamshire miners who refused to strike in 1984–5 remained relatively strong des- pite misgivings over the Party's role during the strike and its subsequent attitude towards the UDM. Certainly, a minority of non-strikers had stopped supporting Labour. An Annesley miner complained that the Party had been '. . . pathetic. Kinnock . . .as leader, should have said the strike was wrong – the whole handling . . . we've got a local MP here who to this day has failed to recognize the UDM . . . these militants damage the labour movement'(N38). A Rufford miner said, 'I've voted Labour all my life . . . but never no more, because [it's] slagging the UDM off something rotten . . . Kinnock has declined invitations to UDM conferences'(N23). A Creswell miner was equally bitter: 'I've been brought up in a Labour family, they've always been for the working man . . . but when Mr Kinnock says there's only room for one Union in the mining industry, then . . . he's dismissing people out of bounds' (N46). Such disgruntlement with Labour certainly accounted for a fall in support for the Party amongst miners not on strike in 1984–5. Of the forty-four non-strikers interviewed, while thirty-eight (86 per cent) had voted Labour in 1983, only thirty (68 per cent) did so in 1987. However, only two of the eight defectors had switched their support to the Conservatives, with five moving to the Liberal Democrats. Moreover, if we factor in *striking* Nottinghamshire miners (thirteen) – all of whom voted Labour – 75 per cent of all local miners continued to vote Labour in 1987.

Thus a substantial majority of non-strikers in Nottinghamshire continued to identify with the Labour Party – 'I'm not a "Leftie", but I'm a Labour man through and through'(N45). A Gedling miner stated, 'I could never vote other than Labour. It's either Tory or Labour – I don't agree with everything Labour does, but you've got to look at what they do for the working class as a whole, and Tories do *nothing* for the working class'(N33). An Annesley miner remarked, 'I think Labour's the working man's party, and I've always been a working man. I shall go on voting Labour . . . because they're the right party'(N37). A Silverhill miner added, 'I will vote Labour again . . . I detest this Tory government'(N17). Indeed, the fact that such views were likely to flourish, rather than wither, in the face of continuing Government attacks on the coal industry was demonstrated in the General Election of April 1992 when the Labour Party scored decisive victories in Sherwood and Mansfield, the two main mining constituencies in Nottinghamshire.[21]

The Non-Striker and the Death of Class Politics?

Class politics with respect to Britain's miners always encompassed a multiplicity of economic, industrial and cultural traditions. The Nottinghamshire tradition was but one of them. It was the violation of this tradition by the NUM leadership, not the development of a new consciousness, that explained the decision of most Nottinghamshire miners to work through the 1984–5 strike. These divisions – grim and damaging though they were – were in keeping with the class politics of the miners, and were not without historical precedent. The refusal of most Nottinghamshire miners to strike does not therefore 'prove' that they lacked 'class consciousness'.

None of this is to deny the severity of the defeat suffered by the miners in 1985. The strikers' loss in 1985 became a loss for the Nottinghamshire miners in the 1990s as they too began to suffer the effects of pit closures. *However*, despite the strike's legacy, the basic bonds of solidarity between miners remained robust. In the final analysis, therefore, the venom directed by Nottinghamshire miners towards the NUM's national leadership should not obscure the fact that the feeling, on the part of non-strikers, of having something *in common* with miners who were on strike, survived intact. This is no mean consideration, for it constitutes – to repeat McGahey's words – 'the avenue upon which we must build the basis of unity'.

This feeling of retaining something in common with other miners manifested itself in different ways. For many non-strikers, the decision to work through the strike was not taken lightly and still remained the source of considerable reflection. A Rufford miner said, 'I admire the

men who stood on picket lines for a year. They stood up for what they
believed in'(N23). An Annesley miner commented ruefully, 'I regret the
split of the Union. And I should like to have thought I'd have been on
strike . . . if the Area had voted to have been, then I would have been,
and supported it fully. I feel in my heart that I should have been on
strike, I feel as though I've let people down, to be honest'(N36). And a
Creswell miner reflected, 'I did a lot of soul-searching . . . our UDM
Delegate has an NUM father – this led to serious arguments. Would that
have occurred between me and my father, or would he have understood
why I did what I did? *Should* I have done it? What of my wife – from a
very left-wing family? She never said she didn't support me, though she
questioned me about going through picket lines'(N43).

However, for most Nottinghamshire miners – like those elsewhere –
the basis for a renewed unity lay, as ever, in the dangers and demands of
everyday working life – 'I think if you work in a pit you've got something in common with miners anywhere irrespective of political views,
or whether you were on strike or not on strike – it's still a dirty, dark
bloody hole where you've got to go down and earn a crust'(N55). An
Annesley miner agreed:

> . . . we're all miners. It were always a common bond to be a miner . . . and
> personally I still feel that it is. I still feel for them people, and I'll tell you
> something else, I admired them for stopping out like they did, for sticking
> to their principles as they did, just as much as we stuck to our principles . . .
> and I can still say that I look upon them as a brother – because they're
> miners. I know what mining's about, *they* know what [it's] about. (N37)

Even those miners alluding to any enduring bitterness between strikers
and non-strikers in the social life of Nottinghamshire's pit villages
stressed that the working environment remained a powerful force for
unity: 'They can still work together. And they've still got that comradeship when they're at work. *Although*, when you come out from
work, you're against one another, sort of thing'(N31). A Welbeck miner
reflected, '[The strike has] split a lot of families, split this village up . . .
but fair enough, if you got trapped underground, the NUM men would
still come and dig you out'(N15). And a Rufford miner argued, 'If you
work underground, and you find someone that's in trouble . . . you don't
go up to him and ask him what union's he in . . . you just help him. And
that's throughout mining – an unwritten law, an unwritten *element*, if you
like – it's a natural element – if somebody's injured . . . you're there'
(N20).

Such testimony demonstrates that the recriminations between striking and non-striking miners took place, for the most part, within the

parameters of a common language. That non-strikers, vilified by many strikers as scabs and traitors, persisted, in various ways, in claiming a common interest with those that vilified them, underscores the resilience of the miners' collective identity. Despite the consequences of defeat and division, the basis of solidarity remained intact.

Notes

1. *Chad*, 8/3/84.
2. *Chad*, 15/3/84.
3. *Chad*, 15/3/84.
4. Source: *NUM, Nottingham Area, Minutes, 1984*, p. 114. Not one of the Area's thirty-one Branches voted to strike, though support varied greatly – from 46.4 per cent at Blidworth to 4.1 per cent at Bestwood.
5. *MO*, 31/1/85.
6. Source: Letter from Nottinghamshire Area General Secretary to Nottinghamshire Branch Officials, 13/3/84.
7. Letter from Nottinghamshire Area General Secretary to Nottinghamshire Branch Officials, 5/4/84.
8. *Chad*, 19/4/84.
9. *Chad*, 26/4/84.
10. *Chad*, 12/4/84.
11. *Chad*, 31/5/84.
12. *Chad*, 5/7/84.
13. Source: *NUM, Nottingham Area, Minutes, 1984*, pp. 148–50.
14. Interviewees were asked, 'In the early 1980s, before the year-long strike, did you yourself feel that your own job was under threat from the pit closure programme?'
15. Not surprisingly, as the national strike gathered momentum, the NCB sought to reassure Nottinghamshire miners about the future of their coalfield: 'There will be no closures and no compulsory redundancies in 1984/5 . . . [a]lthough there is a small planned cut-back in output from the older South Notts pits, the impact is being softened by a helping hand from neighbouring North Notts'(*Coal News*, Special Issue, March 1984, p. 2).
16. Interview, 23/8/90.
17. Between 1970–1 and 1983–4, of the four areas in which research was conducted, Nottinghamshire recorded the lowest levels of

204 Miners on Strike

industrial action in ten (and the equal lowest in two) of the fourteen years. Source: NCB, *Report and Accounts*, for *1971–72* (p. 89); *1973–74* (p. 5); *1975–76* (p. 5); *1976–77* (p. 5); *1978–79* (p. 5); *1980–81* (pp. 34–5); *1982–83* (pp. 22–3); *1984–85* (pp. 38–9).

18. *NUM, Annual Report and Proceedings, 1971*, p. 599.
19. *NCB, Report and Accounts, 1984/5*, pp. 28–9; *BC, Report and Accounts, 1988/9*, pp. 30–1. *New Statesman and Society: 1996 Guide to Trade Unions and the Labour Movement*, p. 36.
20. *The Nottinghamshire Miner*, No. 1, February 1985.
21. *G*, 1/4/92; *FT*, 11–12/4/92.

8

Defiance in Defeat: Britain's Miners since 1985

Introduction

The decade following the 1984–5 strike saw the near-disappearance of the British coal industry. What befell the miners after 1985 represents a social and economic catastrophe. Their collective identity, however, remained resilient. Despite the massive contraction of the industry, many of the values and attitudes which had underpinned community-level struggle in the past remained intact. Loyalty to the Union, concern for the preservation of jobs, and for dignity and influence in the workplace survived the trauma of industrial collapse.

Labour Relations in the Coal Industry after 1985

The Context of Changing Industrial Relations

It would be difficult to exaggerate the scale of the problems which engulfed the NUM after the 1984–5 strike. It faced a triumphant Conservative Government now able to supplement its long-standing commitment to the privatization of the electricity industry (the principal consumer of British coal) with a pledge to privatize the coal industry itself. Both these commitments threatened gravely the longer-term viability of what many miners continued to view as 'their' industry. Few of them, however, could possibly have foreseen the scale of restructuring which was to affect the industry following the strike, though it was they themselves who were destined, as ever, to bear the brunt of such changes.

Certainly, the privatization of the electricity industry had devastating consequences for the coal industry. Relieved of their state-owned predecessor's obligation to rely primarily on domestic coal, the newly privatized electricity generators increased their use of cheaper imported coal and alternative fuel sources such as natural gas. Following the strike, therefore, NUM officials (and latterly, even BC management) complained bitterly of the threats posed to the industry. In November 1988, BC announced the imminent closure of ten pits and the loss of some 20,000 jobs.[1] In February 1989, the Coalfield Communities Campaign (CCC) predicted that large areas of the British coalfield would be wiped out if privatization of the electricity industry started a 'free-for-all by British coal importers'. Indeed, BC itself announced that 11,000 mining jobs would be threatened by the proposed construction of two new coal-handling terminals in Northwest England. This was in addition, moreover, to the 15,000–20,000 job cuts already planned for the following financial year.[2] In March 1989, the Labour Party castigated the electricity industry for importing US coal for trial use at a South Wales power station[3], while later in the year, both miners and management claimed that increasing use of imported coal would force a cut in British output of 25 million tonnes per year, the closure of twenty pits and the loss of 30,000 jobs.[4] In August 1989, such fears were confirmed when National Power – destined to generate two-thirds of Britain's electricity needs – announced tentative plans for the development of two new ports capable of handling 10 million tonnes of imported coal annually.[5]

Not surprisingly, the NUM, by 1990, was warning of the 'virtual demise' of the British deep-mined coal industry by the end of the century. The switch to cheap foreign coal and to gas-fired power stations by the privatized electricity generators and the scaling down (under government pressure) of BC's commitment to the desulphurization of domestic coal, all threatened the eventual displacement of 75 per cent of the industry's current output and the loss of 60,000 jobs.[6] By 1992, BC itself argued that *firm* plans by the electricity generators to switch from coal to gas would displace 25 million tonnes of output and 20,000 jobs in the industry, while *tentative* plans for the construction of more gas-fired power stations – if confirmed – would leave the industry as a 'tiny rump' employing only a few thousand miners.[7]

For the miners, the threats posed by the privatization of electricity were exacerbated by the proposed privatization of the coal industry itself. Under pressure from the government to prepare the industry for privatization, BC management sought to cut operating costs drastically, close 'uneconomic capacity', boost productivity levels and restrict any influence the NUM might have on the future course of the industry to an absolute minimum. It is in this context that NCB Chairman Ian MacGregor declared in the wake of the strike: 'People are now discovering the price of insubordination and insurrection. And, boy are we going to make it stick'.[8]

Thus in 1985–6, BC noted that twenty-seven collieries had closed during the year, representing an annual capacity reduction of approximately 9 million tonnes. Meanwhile, compared to the 1983–4 level, productivity in the industry had risen by 21.5 per cent.[9] In the year from November 1985, output per manshift (o.m.s.) had increased by a further 23 per cent (Glyn 1988: 161, 173). By the end of 1988, in comparison with the 1982–3 financial year, daily output per coalface had increased by 94 per cent and o.m.s. by more than 85 per cent; saleable output had been cut by 59 per cent, manning levels by 58 per cent and the number of pits by 51 per cent.[10] The eight years following the strike saw 135,000 miners leave the industry, an exodus representing a 79 per cent cut in manpower.[11] In November 1992, BC reported that its forty remaining pits had achieved record productivity levels of 6.72 tonnes o.m.s. (compared to 2.7 tonnes o.m.s. before the strike).[12] By July 1993, o.m.s. had risen to 8.5 tonnes – a 23 per cent increase over the previous year[13] – while BC's stated intention of driving productivity levels up to 9.37 tonnes o.m.s. by 1997–8[14] appeared to have been exceeded in March 1994 when *The Times* reported a productivity level of *12.0* tonnes o.m.s. in the industry.[15]

Changing Industrial Relations and the Problems of Resistance

None of these changes could have occurred without altering profoundly the state of labour relations in the industry (Glyn 1988: 173). Indeed, any lingering notion of the coal industry as the 'paradigm case' of the post-war consensus did not survive the 1984–5 strike. Instead, miners everywhere pointed to a sharp deterioration in industrial relations in which management had gained the upper hand at the expense of the NUM, and to the consequent disappearance of any sense of job security. For example, a miner at Whitwell colliery in Derbyshire commented, 'I felt sick. If we didn't win, we'd go back a hundred years. There was nothing to look forward to in going back'(D30). A colleague at the pit – which closed one year after the strike – reflected, 'It was terrible . . . they won, and believe you me, they made us know they'd won. They really put their foot down' (D41). At Markham colliery, a striker agreed, 'We lost, and they put the boot in. And they're still putting it in. Management now are just tolerating us. They *tolerate* the NUM. And that's all they do . . . it's a horrible . . . terrible atmosphere'(D34). A Shirebrook miner told of how 'managers [used to be] a lot more sympathetic to us. Now, they're cost-conscious – it's all market forces now, there's no concern for the social side of things . . . if the pit loses money, it shuts'(D36). Relations were no better elsewhere. A striker at Bevercotes colliery in Nottinghamshire returned to work to be told by the pit manager 'I am the Union now' (N7), while a colleague spoke of being 'kicked from pillar to post' in the aftermath of the dispute (N14). In sum, as a miner at Cwmgwili colliery in South Wales commented, 'The situation has changed . . . the employer tells us now "You can join *four* Unions if you like . . . but I call the tune"'(W39). What, though, did 'calling the tune' amount to? Two broad developments are noteworthy.

Back to the Future?

First, the continued viability of all mines was seen to depend on the willingness of miners to accept sweeping changes in long-established working practices. By 1993, managers aimed to cut deep-mine operating costs by 28 per cent over the next five years.[16] Consequently, BC sought to remove the 80-year-old maximum restriction on working hours to allow longer shifts underground,[17] to introduce 10-hour shifts and weekend working (that is, a repeal of the 5-day week agreement), and to repeal Section 46 of the Coal Industry Nationalization Act which laid down joint consultation and conciliation procedures.[18] In addition, the use of outside, non-unionized, private contractors in the mining work-force was to be increased.

For its part, the NUM continued to oppose such changes. As late as June 1993, delegates to its Annual Conference voted overwhelmingly to oppose longer working hours. A delegate from Selby argued that the Government's attempts to repeal legislation limiting working hours aimed to make the industry more attractive to private investors, while the NUM President predicted that a 10-hour day and a 7-day working week would leave no more than twelve mines in Britain.[19] Meanwhile, miners themselves emphasized how, after the strike, the post-war system of consultation and negotiation had given way to one in which many established working arrangements were now either modified unilaterally, or retracted completely, by management. A miner from Betws colliery, South Wales, reflected:

> I never enjoyed the work after the '84–5 strike – in fact, it was a nightmare up until the time I finished (in 1989). We were squeezed . . . and squeezed by the managers. It was a totally different atmosphere. We had to give up concessions which we'd fought for, and maintained, for many, many years. For example, it *had* been the case that if you were working in water,[20] you would get an hour off (your shift) but still get paid for it . . . After the strike, that was finished – you could be up to your neck in water but still have to work the full (shift) . . . Mind you, when it was put to the vote – strike action or accept the change – the majority of men voted not to strike. The pit was in trouble and the men were afraid of losing the pit. (W34)

Similarly, a miner at Denby Grange colliery in Yorkshire described how 'management now just turns around and says "I want this, you'll do that, you'll do this". Whereas before, our Union at pit level could go into the office and talk to the manager and come to agreements. Now he just puts a paper on the table and says "that's what you're getting, take it or leave it". And that's all happened since the strike. Our Union now can't negotiate like it could before the strike'(Y51).

At the NUM's Central Workshops Branch in Derbyshire, the Union Delegate commented, 'The attitude of management, when you tried to negotiate locally, wasn't there. You have to rely on the manager being reasonable . . . [but] . . . the defeat made our job on the shop floor ten times, a thousand times, worse – because management were really cock-a-hoop, weren't they? . . . Consultative meetings are not consulting at all – they inform you of what they're going to do'(D26). The Branch Secretary at nearby High Moor colliery complained that 'we've not won one thing since the end of the strike. Everything has been imposed, locally-agreed arrangements have been squashed. We were told to work under national agreements – "if you don't like it, f**k off". It's a *big* contrast with before the strike when everything was negotiable and the Union was seen as having some power, particularly with respect to local agreements'.[21]

Overall, however, the relaxing of *safety standards* in the industry was of greatest concern to most miners. In 1987, the NACODS General Secretary argued that BC's official figures revealed that the company's safety record had 'worsened significantly' in recent years. For example, the number of 'dangerous occurrences'[22] per pit per year had more than doubled from 1.0 in 1979 to 2.2 in 1986–7. The total number of dangerous occurrences had risen from 272 in 1985–6 to 362 in 1986–7. In addition, there had been a 25 per cent increase in the major injury accident rate since 1981–2; 843 had occurred in 1986–7 alone.[23] As such, miners expressed concern over constant management pressure to meet production and productivity targets. For example, at Hem Heath colliery in Staffordshire, where three men died in separate incidents during the 1988–9 year, a miner commented, 'We all try to do it by the rules but if you're taking your time they lay into you for not getting the stuff in quick enough'. A colleague added, 'You get fatigued, and people die'.[24] Such worries were not isolated, either. In 1990, after two fatal accidents at local collieries, the North East Area NUM warned that the Mines Inspector's report for 1988–9 'revealed staggering increases in accidents' in which fatal accidents had risen by 100 per cent, all accidents by 14.6 per cent, dangerous occurrences by 27.5 per cent, underground fires by 58.9 per cent and incidents involving locomotives by 40 per cent.[25]

None the less, the assault on safety standards continued unabated in the 1990s, as the NUM struggled to preserve the Mines and Quarries Act, one of the country's most rigorous pieces of health and safety legislation.[26] Claiming that detailed provisions in the Act had made British mines three times as safe as those in the US,[27] delegates at the Union's 1993 Annual Conference warned of the dangers of attempting to boost productivity levels.[28] Such fears proved well-founded when, during the summer of 1993, in the worst single mining accident in Britain for twenty years, three miners died when a roof-bolted area collapsed at Bilsthorpe colliery in Nottinghamshire. The use of roof-bolts – reckoned by BC to double productivity – had long been condemned by the NUM as unsafe.[29]

The Return of Mass Unemployment

If, however, a harsher working environment had not already reawakened dark memories in the coalfields of the interwar period, then the second major manifestation of increased management power could not have failed to do so. Following the 1984–5 strike, management proceeded to implement a programme of massive job losses which led, in turn, to high levels of chronic unemployment in most coalfield areas.

It is true that many miners, demoralized after the defeat of 1985, actively sought to leave the industry. Many changed their attitudes towards a working environment in which they had previously thrived. In addition, the dogged persistence of striking miners in equating acceptance of redundancy with 'selling' one's job was undermined as thousands of disheartened miners left the industry. A miner at Ireland colliery in Derbyshire reflected, 'I used to like working at the pit, but after the strike, I couldn't get away fast enough. As soon as they mentioned redundancy, I was straight into that office'(D14). A miner at Markham colliery concurred, 'The atmosphere changed . . . a lot of people wanted to get out, they'd had enough . . . I've had some real happy times – I know it don't seem right having happy times in a pit – but I have. I've had some good mates, and it used to be a laugh – you used to have fun as well as work. But that part seemed to go . . . I wasn't sorry to leave . . . only sorry to leave my . . . good mates'(D22). Meanwhile, the President of the Yorkshire Area NUM, in a sombre valedictory speech in 1990, noted how miners were now 'so low that it will be too low to lift them . . . Men used to talk about "our" industry. Now they no longer feel part of it in the same way. The gap between us and them has widened. The miners are no longer convinced they have a future in the industry'.[30]

However, it would be wrong to assume that after 1985 the majority of miners acquiesced willingly in the wave of pit closures that now engulfed them. They did not. Instead, they were forced to make the traditionally difficult choice of accepting redundancy, transferring to another pit, or actually fighting a closure, in extraordinarily harsh circumstances. First, no matter how generous redundancy payments appeared,[31] the consequences of accepting the loss of one's job were dire for most miners. Traditionally high rates of unemployment in the coalfield areas afforded miners few opportunities for alternative work. For example, the 700 miners made redundant when Marine colliery in South Wales closed in March 1989 entered a local job market in which the unemployment rate was already approaching 20 per cent.[32] When neighbouring Oakdale colliery closed later in 1989, the local council spoke of the 'social and economic devastation' that would be caused by an overnight jump in the local unemployment rate from 15 per cent to 25 per cent (Francis 1989: 10). Redundant miners elsewhere faced similarly bleak prospects. In North Derbyshire, the closure of Renishaw Park colliery in 1987, with the loss of 400 jobs, exacerbated the problems of local and regional decline. Around Renishaw itself, 12,000 jobs had been lost since 1980, including more than 2,000 in 1986 alone. The local rate of unemployment approached 18 per cent. Across the North Derbyshire coalfield as a whole, 23 per cent of unemployed men had been out of work for more than three years, while youth unemployment accounted for almost 40 per cent of total unemployment. Thus there was little alternative work available for both old and young miners alike.[33]

Similarly, in Nottinghamshire, when BC decided in 1989 to close Blidworth colliery, with the loss of 850 jobs, the most pessimistic estimates of the impact of the closure suggested a *doubling* of the existing 20 per cent unemployment rate in the village.[34] Meanwhile, the proposed closure of nearby Bilsthorpe colliery in October 1992 threatened to throw 965 miners out of work – of whom one-half lived in the local village, with no other source of mass employment available.[35] The proposed simultaneous closure of neighbouring Clipstone colliery, meanwhile, threatened to push the unemployment rate in nearby Mansfield to over 20 per cent.[36] In South Yorkshire, when Grimethorpe colliery closed in October 1992, with the loss of 800 jobs, many miners (mostly in their 30s and 40s) at the pit, pointing to a local unemployment rate of 17 per cent, were pessimistic about finding other work.[37] Ninety-five per cent of those in work in the village had had a job at the mine.[38] In the North East coalfield, the closure in October 1992 of Vane Tempest and Easington collieries, with the loss of almost 2,300 jobs, pushed local unemployment rates to 17 per cent.[39] The first wave of 940 redundant miners encountered a local market listing just thirteen job vacancies.[40]

Meanwhile, the possibility of transferring to other pits, as a means of avoiding redundancy outright, became increasingly improbable as more and more pits around the country closed. In many cases, therefore, miners were cynical and sceptical about offers of transfers to other pits.

For example, at Renishaw Park in Derbyshire, there was no opportunity to transfer to neighbouring collieries – Ireland colliery had closed recently after a run-down costing 450 jobs; Arkwright colliery was earmarked for closure in 1988 with the loss of 300 jobs; Markham colliery was cutting its workforce from 2,100 to 1,600, and at Shire-brook, 400 of the 2,000-strong workforce were losing their jobs.[41] Similarly, at Marine colliery in South Wales, a local NUM official commented, 'There are lot of young miners who transferred here and some will be losing their jobs for the second or even third time'.[42] At Blidworth colliery in Nottinghamshire, some younger miners had worked at three pits in two years.[43] Thus one local miner noted, 'We've got lads at Blidworth from Linby Colliery. Now Linby closed outright after the [1984–5] strike, and the lads that were transferred to us were promised thirty years' working here at Blidworth. That was ten months ago' (Gray 1989: 31). And when Parkside colliery in Lancashire closed in October 1992 with the loss of 720 jobs, the NUM's Area Secretary reported that some miners at the pit had worked at four pits in fifteen months as mines had closed around them.[44] In sum, the *Independent* editorialized, 'The market is no fairer than the weather . . . Yet it seems outrageously unfair when . . . several thousand men are thrown out of work by the closure of a pit in an area where no other jobs are to be found, and where little prospect of creating work exists. However good the redundancy money, however earnest the efforts to attract new employers, this community may well have suffered a mortal blow'.[45]

Despite the uncertainties surrounding future employment prospects, however, the ability of miners to protect their jobs was severely undermined by the ruthless manner in which the redundancy scheme was operated by BC. In most cases after the 1984–5 strike, enhanced redundancy terms (as opposed to basic state payments) were offered to local miners on a short-term basis only. As such, many miners complained of being blackmailed into accepting the swift closure of their pits, or risk losing redundancy payments altogether. The use of this tactic was particularly pronounced in the South Wales coalfield where, after the strike, BC moved quickly to shut loss-making pits. For example, when in August 1989 BC announced the closure of Merthyr Vale, Trelewis Drift and Oakdale collieries (with a combined loss of 1,600 jobs), miners spoke of the pressures exerted by short-term offers of redundancy money. At Merthyr Vale, where BC intended to withdraw redundancy payments within forty-eight hours if the workforce did not agree to the closure, the local miners' leader talked of 'shotgun industrial relations' and of 'men being treated like cattle' (Francis 1989: 10). A colleague complained that 'they have put a gun to the men's heads. Men have been offered up to 35,000 [pounds], but if the vote had been to fight the closure those poor buggers would have been turned out with 5,000 [pounds] instead. It's disgusting. We've given our all to this industry and now they have shit on us.' A younger colleague under-scored the divisiveness of BC's tactics: 'My uncle, who is thirty-eight and has been down the pit since he was sixteen, was going to lose 20,000 [pounds] if we voted to fight on . . . That was in the back of my mind. And he would have had it in his mind that by voting for closure he would have cost me my job. I've got nearly 3,000 [pounds] for eight years' work. That's rubbish'.[46]

Moreover, miners were further constrained by the inadequacies of the independent colliery review procedure to which, ostensibly, they were entitled to refer BC's closure decisions. As many miners complained, the findings of such review bodies – though supposedly impartial and exhaustive – were not in fact binding on BC. In theory, the right of the NUM (or any other union) to challenge closure proposals had survived (though in a somewhat revised form) the strike defeat of 1984–5 – yet as of 1989, BC had refused to be bound by any recommendations of the independent review body.[47] Consequently, the risks of referring a closure decision to an independent review procedure that was liable to take several months to reach its verdict were very great. A miner at Blidworth colliery in Nottinghamshire remarked, 'The miner's greatest fear is that at the end of six months, at the end of the review, the decision will be the same. Then he'll face possibly compulsory redundancy, the loss of severance pay . . . and the fact that jobs that might have come up in other pits in the meantime will have already gone' (Gray 1989: 31). For these reasons, the NUM Branch President at Creswell colliery in Nottingham-shire, noting in 1990 that few pits had actually survived the review procedure, commented, 'The future is black. For the last five years (BC) has systematically raped the industry and the review procedure is nothing but a sop to public opinion'.[48]

Defiance in Defeat? Industrial Action in the Coal Industry since 1985

The Union in the Aftermath of the Strike

In such circumstances, how had the NUM fared as the traditional focus of miners' loyalties? Nationally, it struggled constantly during the late 1980s and early 1990s to retain its authority in the coalfields. A miner at Taff Merthyr colliery in South Wales saw the strike's outcome as 'the ruination of the NUM'(W1) while a miner at Barnsley Main colliery in Yorkshire lamented the fact that 'Thatcher broke the finest . . . union in the country'(Y15). In Derbyshire, a miner at Markham Main colliery complained that 'we've not spoke to the bloody NCB since we went back to work . . . we're not *talking* to British Coal . . . we're just going through the motions. We're not a Union, we're not united at all, we're infighting'(D34). A miner at Ireland colliery spoke in similar terms, 'It was a defeat for the NUM, and the Union is still suffering. The Union has met with British Coal for forty-five minutes this year – if this isn't a defeat, I don't know what is'(D14).

At least *some* of the blame for the NUM's post-strike problems was directed at the Union's national leadership, particularly in the person of Arthur Scargill.[49] Many worried that the Union leadership's hostile attitude towards the UDM was hindering the restoration of a single union in the industry. Meanwhile, the President's seemingly ritual calls for industrial action to prevent further pit closures were seen by some as damaging to the Union's credibility nationally. In May 1990, after BC announced the imminent loss of 7,500 jobs, a miner reflected, 'No one listens to Arthur anymore'.[50] In fact, by 1992, Scargill had called for industrial action every year since being in office, yet had won favourable majorities only twice. Furthermore, he had failed to negotiate a pay rise since 1985.[51] Such intransigence at the national level was scorned in some parts of the coalfield, particularly those suffering the worst of the post-strike rundown of the industry. Notably, by the early 1990s, a rift had developed between the Union President and his erstwhile allies in the traditionally militant Scottish coalfield. When in April 1993 the NUM leadership won a majority vote for a national one-day strike to protest pit closures, the Scottish NUM Vice-President's pledge of support, though loyal, was qualified: 'The men are obviously upset about the closures . . . However, they didn't feel industrial action was the right step to take . . . but we accept the democratic decision of members nationally and will support the day of action . . . This is [Scargill's] tenth ballot and the first one he's won. The days of bringing down governments are gone, but Arthur's about 20 years behind the times'.[52]

If, however, after the strike, the Union's federal structure creaked louder than ever, the picture at the local level was somewhat different. Certainly, miners emphasized the continuing difficulties of the NUM at the pit level in dealing with management. Moreover, as the Branch Secretary at Warsop Main colliery in Derbyshire acknowledged, the Union now had to proceed with considerable caution with respect to striking: 'The days are gone when we as union officials could blow the whistle and clear the pit. I think everybody realises that we have to think three or four times instead of twice on how to respond as particular conflicts arise'.[53] Nevertheless, the Union 'at local level . . . proved its durability' (Clapham 1989: 17). Many miners stressed that the Union retained a *presence* at pit level despite the grim post-strike environment. A miner at Stillingfleet colliery in Yorkshire felt that the strike 'hasn't been a defeat as far as [Thatcher] tried to flatten the Union and its membership as a whole. She failed, so in that respect, it was not a defeat'(Y39). And in Nottinghamshire, the minority of striking miners continued to show fierce loyalty to the Union despite the fact that locally it was no longer recognized by BC. A Bilsthorpe miner commented, 'The *National Union* of *Mineworkers* is still functioning, still working. Thatcher didn't actually achieve the ultimate goal of smashing it altogether'(N4). In this context, it is crucial to note that the coalfields were by no means free of industrial conflict after the 1984–5 strike. Regardless of any wider demoralization, therefore, miners continued to struggle for an element of control over their working lives, and to show a continuing resentment at being 'pushed around' – a resentment with which the Union was able to generate a certain degree of industrial militancy. This was particularly evident in the immediate aftermath of the strike. For example, at High Moor colliery, the Branch Secretary recalled, 'We came in on the 5 March 1985 behind the [Union] banner, went into the canteen, held a meeting and promptly called a 24-hour strike as an act of defiance against British Coal. So as to let them know they couldn't take liberties. There were six 24-hour strikes in rapid succession within two months of the end of the strike'.[54]

Such a mood of defiance prevailed well beyond the strike, particularly in the Yorkshire coalfield. The Branch Secretary at Thurcroft colliery commented, 'Obviously it'll take us time at national level to rebuild. Locally – it certainly wasn't a defeat – we've had disputes at Thurcroft almost continuously since 1984. The workforce here is still solidly together, and we would come out on strike together'(Y24). The Branch Treasurer at Rossington colliery described how 'it's not as bad as it was five years ago – the lads are getting a bit of fight back, we've had a couple of local strikes. They're not kowtowing anymore, and in this respect, things are getting better'(Y27). And at Barnsley Main colliery, a surfaceworker commented that 'it's not a *total* defeat, because the Union still has a bit of strength at this Branch – there've been ten strikes here since 1985, so it can't be a total defeat'(Y16). The Branch President at the pit added, 'It's still pretty good at this pit . . . there's still a lot of togetherness. If one team comes out on strike, then everyone comes out with them . . . They've been trying to break us, fragment us, but it hasn't worked. We get about 500 men at a Branch meeting. It can be rowdy . . . shouting . . . but they're good meetings'(Y14).

Thus despite the quickening pace of pit closures after 1985, miners continued to combat, as best they could, the effects of increased management power. Such attempts ensured, in fact, that in 1986 only fifteen of BC's 125 mines were free of industrial action,[55] while widespread strikes

in 1987–8 'illustrated the disruptive power of strikes at the point of
production when the power of management was seriously challenged'
(Clapham 1989: 18). In June 1987, BC complained that it had lost approximately £2 million worth of production during the previous two months
as a result of nine unofficial strikes at eight pits. In South Wales, 2,800
miners at four pits had staged a 24-hour strike against BC's proposals to
reduce the allowance of anthracite coal for local miners.[56]

In July 1987, miners at Frickley colliery in South Yorkshire walked
out in support of six workmates facing disciplinary action by BC. Reflecting growing resentment at what were seen as draconian revisions to
disciplinary procedures, 6,000 miners had, within forty-eight hours,
honoured picket lines at six other collieries. A day later, 14,000 miners
at sixteen South Yorkshire pits were on strike, with promises of support
coming from several NUM branches in North Yorkshire.[57] Though South
Yorkshire's miners, fearful of the consequences of a prolonged strike,
returned to work within a matter of days,[58] the NUM leadership, in receipt
of a growing chorus of complaints regarding the new disciplinary code
from miners' leaders in Durham, Nottinghamshire and South Wales,[59]
subsequently won support for a national overtime ban which held fast
from September 1987 to March 1988. This ban, together with 331 separate disputes throughout the coalfields, ensured that during the 1987–8
year, BC lost over 400,000 shifts (a four-fold increase on the previous
year) and 4.505 million tonnes of coal (equivalent to 5.47 per cent of
total national output for the year).[60] Indeed, as Table 7 demonstrates,
national levels of industrial action in 1987–8 were the highest of the
decade (excluding the 1984–5 strike itself), and exceeded easily those
for the early 1980s.[61] Clearly, the willingness of miners to take industrial
action had not been destroyed completely by the experience of defeat in
1985. In this sense, as the NUM Branch Secretary at Shirebrook colliery
in Derbyshire noted, the Union had been able to retain a credible role:
'Alright . . . British Coal can shove to one side, the National Union of
Mineworkers – nationally, but what they can't do, they can't shove it to
one side *locally*. Because the power of the Union is locally-based.'[62]

Such resilience casts doubt on the assertion that after the strike,
'many employees appeared to be undergoing a transformation in their
orientation to work, from that of the "traditional proletarian" to one
more characteristic of the "privatized worker"' (Waddington *et al.* 1991:
72). Instead, the miners' long-standing culture of resistance and protest
remained intact, despite the difficulties of the post-strike environment.
Yet even allowing for this, few could have foreseen the ability of the
miners to stage, in late 1992, a final attempt to halt the near-total demise
of their industry now planned by a Conservative Government recently
elected to a fourth term of office.

Table 7. Levels of Industrial Action in the British Coal Industry, 1980–89

Year	A Saleable Output lost to Disputes (millions of tonnes)	B Total Saleable Output for the year (millions of tonnes)	A as % of B
1980/1	1.467	110.287	1.33
1981/2	1.133	108.871	1.04
1982/3	3.640	104.938	3.47
1983/4	13.055	90.062	14.50
1984/5	67.244	27.644	243.00
1985/6	1.022	88.418	1.16
1986/7	1.044	87.953	1.19
1987/8	4.505	82.399	5.47
1988/9	0.630	85.035	0.74

Source: Calculated from BC, *Report and Accounts* for *1988/9* (pp. 30–1); *1986/7* (pp. 18–19); NCB, *Report and Accounts* for *1984/5* (pp. 28–9); *1982/3* (pp. 22–3); *1980/1* (pp. 34–5).

The Miners' Last Stand

Even by the standards of the 1980s and 1990s, BC's announcement on 13 October 1992 of a massive round of pit closures was a stunning development. Blaming 'harsh conditions' in the electricity market,[63] BC declared the imminent shutdown of thirty-one of the industry's fifty remaining mines, with the loss of 30,000 jobs.[64] The decision – quickly endorsed by the Government – meant reducing the mining workforce from 53,000 to 23,000, cutting output by 25 million tonnes per year, ending mining completely in Lancashire, North Staffordshire, North Wales and North Derbyshire, and leaving just one mine each in South Wales, Scotland, Warwickshire, South Staffordshire and the North East.[65] Even more staggering than the scale of the cutback was the proposed manner of its implementation. Labelling the colliery review procedure 'inappropriate to the circumstances',[66] BC announced that six mines (affecting 6,000 miners) were to close that week, a further thirteen by December 1992, and a total of twenty-seven by March 1993. In addition, four would be retained on a 'care and maintenance' basis only.

Reaction to the decision, which represented one of the largest set of redundancies ever announced at once,[67] was swift. In the coalfields themselves, the announcement was greeted with a mixture of bewilderment, despair and fury. Describing the decision as 'an act of industrial vandalism',[68] the NUM President attacked the 'total lack of compassion by both a management and a Government devoid of anything except malice and the determination to repay what they see as a defeat inflicted upon them by the miners' union in 1974'.[69] The Union's Vice-President agreed, labelling the proposals 'criminal stupidity on a massive scale . . . The social consequences of the planned closures . . . will be catastrophic'.[70] Many within the NUM (especially in Yorkshire) immediately called for a strike.[71] However, at a national conference held on 15 October to debate the closures, many NUM delegates – aware of both the Union's industrial weakness and the difficult financial circumstances of its members – warned of the dangers of a strike and argued instead for a broader strategy of protest. A Derbyshire delegate felt that local miners would not strike because of the fear of either losing their jobs or redundancy payments.[72] As such, an NEC member declared, 'We have to broaden the campaign. What we are saying is, give us some help. Let's all get on the streets or let's all give up'.[73] The Union leadership therefore deferred a ballot on strike action and instead launched a public appeal to save the industry. Arthur Scargill declared that a strike ballot would be conducted 'only after we have exhausted all options of trying to persuade this Government, who appear impervious to logic, either of the economic or political variety'.[74]

The NUM's decision won it swift support from the wider labour movement. The Parliamentary Labour Party (PLP), arguing that the closures could put 100,000 out of work, demanded a Government statement and Emergency Debate in Parliament for 21 October. The TUC called for a national day of action in support of the miners for 25 October.[75] Its General Secretary declared that the manufacturing core of the country was 'starting to melt', and appealed to the Prime Minister to halt the closures.[76] Individual unions, aghast at both the demise of the coal industry itself, and its implications for other sections of the British economy, also quickly pledged their support. The railway unions, fearing the loss of 13,500 jobs in their own industry as a result of the pit closures,[77] condemned the Government and agreed to lobby Parliament.[78] The leader of the Associated Society of Locomotive Engineers and Firemen (ASLEF) declared, 'We are not in the area of fighting the last battle of the Alamo, but we are seriously concerned that something has to be done. It's much, much wider than the NUM'.[79] In addition, and less predictably, the mines received support from unions in other parts of the energy sector. Six unions representing 10,000 blue-collar employees of British Nuclear Fuels and the Atomic Energy Authority called for a common front of all energy workers. The Amalgamated Engineering Union (AEU) declared that any differences between the miners' leaders and power workers now belonged 'in the past' because of the urgent need to win the battle on behalf of the energy industry.[80]

In addition to the labour movement, the NUM was aided by a storm of public protest against the Government's proposals. Indeed, it was with considerable confidence that the NUM President called for a national referendum on the issue.[81] The TUC General Secretary commented, 'Over the past few days we have been inundated with calls from the public including many who admit to not being the natural allies of the trade union movement. All have asked how they can help in the campaign to reverse the pit closures and express in a practical way their anger and frustration at what is happening to our country'.[82]

Indeed, following BC's announcement, public protests erupted throughout the country. On 16 October in South Wales, protestors marched behind a brass band to Tower colliery (destined to be the last surviving mine in Wales were the closures to proceed[83]), while in the North East, the Energy Minister was bombarded with eggs by 350 protestors as he arrived at the doors of BC Enterprises in Gateshead.[84] At a rally of several thousand people in Chesterfield on 17 October, Dennis Skinner MP declared, 'We got rid of the poll tax and we are going to get rid of this closure programme. Thatcher has gone but Scargill and the NUM are still here. The nation is stirring'.[85] The following day, 5,000 people marched in Mansfield, Nottinghamshire,[86] whilst in Cheltenham, a crowd of 3,000 protestors – in which Socialist Workers, Liberal Democrats, Conservatives and church leaders marched together – brought the town to a standstill.[87] On 21 October, a crowd of some 50,000 miners and their supporters marched through central London on its way to lobby Parliament during the latter's emergency debate on the coal crisis.[88] Five days later, more than 250,000 people rallied in London despite atrocious weather conditions.[89]

Finally, the NUM's campaign was reinforced by three less expected developments. First, the crisis created – for the first time since 1985 – the *basis* for some common ground between the NUM and the UDM. The latter, with 10,000 of its 14,000 members in Nottinghamshire,[90] was stunned to learn of BC's intention to close seven of Nottinghamshire's remaining thirteen mines.[91] Indeed, the UDM leader labelled the decision a 'deliberate attempt to smash the miners'[92] and promptly locked himself down Silverhill colliery in protest.[93] However, the role played by the UDM in opposing the closures was limited. First, although the UDM was officially opposed to the privatization of coal, it was significantly less aggressive than the NUM, being compromised by its involvement in a variety of private consortia bidding for parts of the industry.[94] Second, the UDM, in the midst of a leadership election campaign, was divided on the means of combating the closures. While the incumbent leader opposed the use of industrial action,[95] his challenger called for a general strike.[96] Consequently, no coherent strategy of opposition to the Government emerged in the ensuing months from the UDM leadership.[97] Third, the institutional rupture between the NUM and the UDM remained in place despite the severity of the crisis facing both unions.

Thus while the NUM continued, as ever, to appeal to UDM members to return to the fold, no initiative was undertaken to bridge the institutional divide. For example, at its 1993 Annual Conference, in the face of exhortations from the Scottish Area to negotiate alongside the UDM on the issue of pay, the NUM President pronounced himself 'absolutely staggered' that any NUM member could suggest sitting down with the UDM.[98] A Yorkshire delegate was even more uncompromising: 'The UDM has managed to get everything wrong. They threw their lot in with this government. They have made a terrible mistake. They have been stabbed in the back. We said they would be, and they will pay the price'.[99]

A second unexpected source of assistance for the NUM came on 16 October 1992 when the Union scored a rare victory in the High Court. Reviewing a case brought by the NUM and NACODS, the court declared the closure decisions by BC and the Government unlawful, and ordered the first four pit closures planned for the end of the week halted.[100]

Finally, and ironically, support for the miners (or, at least, opposition to the Government) emerged from within the ranks of the Conservative Party itself. Aware of the public outcry, many Tory backbenchers voiced misgivings over, or outright opposition to, the closures, and warned the Government of a possible Parliamentary defeat. By 18 October, a poll of one hundred backbenchers reported forty-four opposed to the closures, with only forty in favour.[101]

In the face of such pressure, the Government (though initially unmoved) staged a retreat on 18 October. The next day, the Prime Minister conceded that the Government had been 'too hasty'[102] while in Parliament, amidst scenes of near pandemonium, a beleaguered Trade and Industry Secretary announced an amended closure programme. Of the thirty-one pits earmarked for closure, the ten pits destined to be closed within days of the original announcement would now be placed in the normal ninety-day consultation process (and in the meantime would be retained on a 'care and maintenance' basis). The other twenty-one pits would be 'reprieved' pending the completion of a Government review of their long-term viability. In addition, a 'job regeneration' programme would be established to help redundant miners find new work,[103] £165 million would be granted to mining communities affected by closures, while some areas would gain Enterprise Zone and Assisted Area status. On 20 October, the Government decided that the House of Commons Select Committee on Trade and Industry should execute a full review of the coal and electricity issue. For its part, the Government committed itself to conducting a review of energy policy over the next three months and publishing its conclusions in a White Paper. In the ensuing division, the Government's amended closure programme was carried by 320 votes to 307.[104] Thus 'in the course of 8 days, the government moved from supporting a savage cut in the coal industry to carrying out a full review of the nation's energy policy, while putting mine closures on hold'.[105] The miners, it seemed, had achieved a late and unexpected victory in their struggle to save the remnants of the industry.

1992 and its Aftermath

In a sense, the events of October 1992 demonstrated how 'coal retained a special symbolic significance in the mind of the nation, which [the Government] had underestimated: a black seam runs through our national psyche'.[106] Yet what kind of a victory had the miners achieved? In fact, the Government's concessions were condemned by the miners and their allies. The NUM President, who called for the whole closure programme to be withdrawn,[107] was supported by other Union members. For example, the Yorkshire Area leader commented, 'We are not prepared to accept the statement . . . and we will still campaign to get a decision . . . opposing the immediate closure of the 10 pits and the possible closure of a further 21. Heseltine has not said that those 21 pits will remain open'. The UDM leader was equally vociferous: '[Heseltine] is just trying to buy a bit of time. He has treated the British public, the Houses of Parliament, and the miners with contempt'.[108] In addition, the TUC General Secretary observed that the Government statement amounted to a 'massive climbdown on tactics but clearly no climbdown on policy'.[109]

Such doubts were well-founded, as 'keeping up the pressure' proved to be an intensely difficult task. In fact, in a pattern of events depressingly reminiscent of that which followed the Thatcher Government's 'retreat' on pit closures in 1981, the miners quickly found themselves under renewed siege, as the Government and BC resorted to a strategy of 'closure by stealth'. As such, the victory of October 1992 was short-lived, and its aftermath deeply sobering. Indeed, by February 1994, BC was left with sixteen deep mines – three *fewer* than were expected to survive when it had provoked the initial furore in October 1992.[110] A brief review of the continuing contraction of the coal industry between late 1992 and 1994 serves to underscore the long-standing difficulties faced by a war-weary set of workers now facing overwhelming odds in their bid to resist the final demise of their industry.

Soon after the October 1992 debacle, BC revealed that it had no intention whatsoever of easing the pressure on its workforce. The weapons deployed to restructure the industry since 1985 were taken up again with renewed vigour. First, the potential blackmail power of the redundancy scheme remained. This was the case even at those ten pits ostensibly reprieved by the Government. For example, at Trentham colliery in Staffordshire, the local (Conservative) MP complained that miners were being threatened with loss of severance pay unless they accepted redundancy immediately.[111] Meanwhile, at Markham Main colliery the NUM reported that local management was intensifying pressure on miners to take 'voluntary–compulsory' redundancy, and regrading miners refusing to accept lower pay.[112] Miners *still* faced, therefore, an excruciating dilemma – should they take redundancy now, thereby increasing their chances of obtaining a new job before their pit eventually closed, or, hope to strengthen the NUM's campaign against closures by staying put?[113] Well aware of such dilemmas, the NUM struggled in the ensuing months to advertise the corrosive effects of redundancy blackmail. In January 1993, both the NUM and NACODS argued before the High Court that BC was trying to intimidate miners into giving up their jobs by threatening the withdrawal of special redundancy terms at the end of the ninety-day consultation period.[114] Such efforts, though, were increasingly in vain. In June 1993, for example, BC proceeded to impose its first formal compulsory redundancies since nationalization of the industry in 1947, after all other measures had failed to oust miners from their jobs at Trentham colliery in Staffordshire, Parkside colliery in Lancashire and Vane Tempest colliery in the North East.[115]

Of further threat to the NUM was the manner in which BC held to the terms of the revised review procedure forced on it both by the High Court and the Government's decision to reprieve ten of the thirty-one pits originally earmarked for closure. These actions had supposedly nullified BC's initial declaration that normal pit closure procedures were to be set aside. Yet once again, the concessions wrought by the miners ultimately proved illusory. For one thing, review procedure findings were *still* not binding on BC. For example, in March 1993, a Government-appointed independent consultant rejected BC's argument that Grimethorpe colliery in Yorkshire was financially unviable, and determined also that the shutting down of Taff Merthyr colliery in South Wales had not met BC's own closure criteria. In neither case, however, were such findings able to prevent the subsequent closure of the mine in question.[116] Furthermore, there is strong evidence to suggest that in the case of the ten pits reprieved in late October 1992, BC disobeyed a High Court order to maintain the fabric of the mines for the duration of the ninety-day consultation period.[117]

In these circumstances, many miners – weary of such pressures, and uncertain of the Government's true intentions for the industry – gave up the fight to retain their jobs. Within three weeks of the Government's initial statement on 13 October 1992, some 2,976 miners had taken 'voluntary redundancy',[118] with the majority of these reportedly from the ten reprieved pits placed in the ninety-day review process.[119] By mid-March 1993, 8,094 miners had left the industry since the October 1992 announcement,[120] rising to just over 17,000 by early June 1993,[121] and to approximately 21,000 later the same month.[122] Naturally, such an exodus weakened the NUM's campaign to halt the closures and undermined those miners still willing to stay in the industry and fight for their jobs. Even so, despite the unfavourable odds, resistance in the coalfields by no means disappeared altogether. At some pits, miners who had been resigned to redundancy changed their minds during the national outcry against the Government's original plans. In late October 1992, for example, an NUM Branch meeting at Parkside colliery in Lancashire voted to reverse its previous position, resist redundancy and use 'any means possible' to fight a shutdown of the pit.[123] For its part, the NUM's national leadership strove, as best it could, to maintain pressure on both the Government and BC. Increasingly aware that Government concessions, review procedures and High Court injunctions were not enough to prevent the continuing contraction of the industry, the Union leadership, by late 1992, was reconsidering the use of the more militant tactics from which it had shied away during the initial furore. In late November, the NUM called for a national 'stay-away' day of action to be held in mid-January 1993. However, the TUC rejected the call – the first public difference to emerge between the NUM and the TUC since the current crisis had developed.[124]

Despite such differences, however, the NUM persevered. In January 1993, the Union's growing fears for the fate of the industry were confirmed when the House of Commons Select Committee on Trade and Industry recommended that only half (and possibly fewer) of the thirty-one threatened collieries be saved. Calling the Committee's findings 'totally unacceptable',[125] the Union's NEC called for a national ballot on a series of one-day strikes to protest the closures; this decision was subsequently endorsed by NUM delegates on 4 February 1993.[126] One month later, to the astonishment and fury of both the Government and BC, miners decided, by 12,913 votes to 8,465, to support the NUM's call for a 24-hour strike, to be followed by a 'rolling programme of industrial action'. Ten of the Union's thirteen Areas voted to strike.[127] The ballot success was reinforced when the Government finally published its White Paper on the coal industry on 25 March 1993. Of the thirty-one pits on the original closure list, only twelve would be reprieved, twelve others would be closed, six would be 'mothballed', and one would undergo development work only.[128] The privatization of BC was to be accelerated, while the 'dash for gas' would continue with no restrictions on gas-fired power stations.[129] In short, the White Paper made no attempt to restructure the market, and offered a short-term subsidized future to only twelve of the original pits.[130]

As such, the mining unions were unanimous in their condemnation of the Government's latest proposals. The NUM President declared that the Union would continue its campaign to keep all thirty-one pits on the original hit list open. The arguments, he added, had 'not moved one inch since October [1992]'.[131] The UDM, enraged by the plans to close five pits in Nottinghamshire, proceeded to organize a strike ballot. Its President added, 'This is the first time we have ever gone down the path of industrial action . . . The white paper is an absolute disgrace'.[132] Meanwhile, the TUC, though still wary of the NUM's plans for strike action, nevertheless called for a protest rally and lobby of Parliament for 29 March 1993, and issued a strong statement of support for the miners: 'This is a deliberate deception. What is in offer is nothing more than a confidence trick . . . to cover up the truth that in 2 years the British coal industry will be dead and buried'.[133]

Once the Government's proposals won parliamentary approval,[134] the NUM proceeded with its programme of industrial action. On 2 April 1993, the first of two 24-hour strikes was held, for which support appears to have been exceptionally strong – 'most' of the NUM's 30,000 members obeyed the strike call,[135] while BC assessed the level of support for the strike as follows: in Yorkshire, of twenty pits, only Manton produced coal (in the morning only); in the Midlands and Wales, eleven of twelve pits ceased production; Scotland's sole remaining pit closed down; in the North East, coal was produced (during the nightshift only) at just one of five pits. In Nottinghamshire, where UDM members worked normally, nine of twelve pits produced coal, though at Thoresby and Ollerton, where key faceworkers remained in the NUM, production was affected. Incensed by the robust support for the strike, BC retaliated by 'immediately' ending the 46-year-old 'check-off' system of collecting union subscriptions directly from NUM members.[136] Support for the NUM's second 24-hour strike, held on 16 April 1993, though labelled 'magnificent' by the Union President, was weaker. BC claimed that coal had been produced at twenty of the forty pits still in production, with UDM miners again working normally, and a 'sizeable minority' of NUM members reporting for work.[137]

Regardless of the exact degree of solidarity achieved, the ability of the NUM in 1993 to generate significant levels of support for two national protest strikes was no minor feat. Amongst miners, it demonstrated, at the very least, a continuing loyalty to the Union, and a determination to retain their jobs in the industry. Nevertheless, the ultimate *impact* of these strikes was minimal. In the absence of effective support from the wider labour movement, the strikes in and of them-selves could not halt the continuing demise of the industry. Indeed, by June 1993, only fifteen coal mines (employing fewer than 15,000 miners) appeared to have a secure future.[138] In addition, by mid-1993, the Union was beset by internal divisions regarding the best course of action in the circumstances. At its 1993 Annual Conference, the President's call for further industrial action to pursue a pay claim, and to oppose continuing pit closures and the privatization of the industry, was criticized severely by the Union's Scottish delegates.[139] By late 1993, the viability of the NUM as a functioning national organization was called into question when a ballot of NUM members on a campaign of selective industrial action had to be aborted subsequently because of 'logistical difficulties'.[140] And in June 1994, the Union, once a key player in the internal affairs of the Labour Party, suffered the ignominy of being unable to participate in the Party's leadership election. In a letter to the Party's NEC, the Union President pointed to the prohibitive costs of holding either a postal or workplace ballot of its membership.[141]

Given this, the two strikes of April 1993 represented, in all prob-ability, the last-ever national-level industrial action taken by the NUM. Such an outcome, wrote Seumas Milne in June 1993, represented a 'far cry' from the 'spontaneous outburst of popular revulsion against the Government' seen in October 1992. In lamenting the subsequent inability of the miners and their Union to prevent the continuing demise of the industry, Milne not only blames the '20-year Tory vendetta' against the miners, but also delay and inaction at the national level of the wider labour movement which allowed the public mood to be dis-sipated.[142] Certainly, moves by the TUC General Council and the Labour Party leadership to distance themselves from calls for industrial action severely constrained the NUM's ever diminishing room for manoeuvre.

However, in keeping with the central theme of this study, it would be wrong to equate the physical destruction of the coal industry, and the undermining of the NUM at the national level, with the disappearance of the spirit, attitudes and culture which had informed and animated grass-roots struggle in the industry for so long. Indeed, the sporadic and often surprising episodes of resistance seen in the post-1985 period were, in large measure, rooted in the resilience of such a spirit at the community level, despite the increasingly formidable obstacles to the waging of such resistance. That this is the case was demonstrated vividly by the spirited attempt in 1994 by miners and their supporters to resist the closure of Tower colliery, the last deep mine in South Wales.[143]

Despite making a profit of £28 million between 1991 and 1994, BC, in October 1993, began to reduce progressively the pit's production targets. Calling for 200 redundancies, BC warned that a loss of bonus and overtime pay would halve miners' wages if volunteers were not forthcoming. In response, nearly 2,000 people – including Tower miners, colleagues from closed local pits and from the North East and Yorkshire coalfields, and members of other unions – marched through Aberdare in a rally of support. Despite such protests, BC had succeeded in halving the pit's workforce by the end of 1993. However, when, in early April 1994, it announced its plans for the final closure of the colliery, it encountered unexpected opposition. Despite being offered an extra £9,000 in addition to the usual redundancy terms in return for leaving immediately, a meeting of the pit's 250 miners decided that the pit be put through the independent colliery review procedure. Their decision generated wide popular support throughout Wales. Stunned by developments, BC, in 'the most far-reaching reversal in its closure programme since . . . October 1992',[144] decided that the colliery would remain open. A delighted local borough council leader declared that 'the victory has put new heart into the community' (Heath 1994: 13). Yet once again, this victory was short-lived. Worries emerged very quickly over the terms and conditions on which miners would continue to be employed after BC hinted at impending pay cut of up to £95 per week. Moreover, as ever, the risk of losing redundancy payments (due to finish at the end of April 1994) if miners held out for the duration of the review process began to damage the miners' morale. At a gloomy Union meeting held within four days of BC's retreat, the Tower miners voted reluctantly to accept the closure of the pit. One miner commented, 'We were hit in all directions. Suppose the pit had stayed open for six or nine months and then closed without us getting proper redundancy?' A colleague added, 'The pressure was too intense . . . Don't forget it's British Coal that's closed the pit, not the men' (Heath 1994: 13).

The spirited attempts by the people of the Cynon Valley to defend the last mine in South Wales demonstrated that a willingness to persevere in the face of adversity did not belong to the past. By April 1994, however, 'the Tower men did their best, but the odds against them were just too great' (Heath 1994: 13). With the closure of Tower, it is reasonable to assume that the long rearguard action fought by the miners and their Union to defend jobs, mines and communities – their 'way of life', no less – is over.

Postscript: The Miners' Experience in Perspective

A central focus of this study has been the richness and resilience of the miners' collective identity, as defined by the robust relationship, at the local level, between the mine, the Union and the surrounding community. This relationship, forged in the tumultuous years of the early twentieth century, survived the steady contraction of the coal industry in the 1960s, was reinvigorated (and indeed, rediscovered) during the 1984–5 strike, and remained durable even in the face of defeat, division and the industry's precipitous decline after 1985. However, the long and ultimately unsuccessful struggle of the miners to defend their industry and communities is in keeping with broad international trends affecting organized labour. Indeed, nothing epitomizes the contemporary predicament of traditional blue-collar workers more strongly, or more poignantly, than the miners' fate in the 1980s and 1990s. Most miners, after the defeat of 1985, were painfully aware that a familiar – and cherished – world was disappearing. A miner at Taff Merthyr colliery, South Wales, reflected in 1989: 'I was up in Swansea library three years ago, and they got a map up there showing you, years ago in the twenties and thirties . . . and the pits that was in South Wales then . . . and there was dots all over the map . . . you've got a map up to date now and . . . you're lucky . . . [to see] six dots on there now . . . they've just demolished the industry . . . as far as South Wales is concerned'(W2). A miner at Markham colliery, Derbyshire, noted that 'thousands and thousands of men have left the industry since the strike. One word sums it all up – decline'(D54), while a miner at Celynen North colliery felt that 'it's the end of an era'(W53). Certainly, the near-collapse in 1994 of the 110th Durham Miners' Gala[145] – as one of Britain's proudest and most colourful labour rallies – illustrated the demise of a distinctive brand of working-class politics in Britain, while the NUM's inability to participate in the Labour Party's 1994 leadership election demonstrated, brutally, how the miners had been forced to relinquish their position at the core of the labour movement.

What, therefore, in theoretical and empirical terms, *is* the wider significance of the miners' experience? After all, because of the swift demise of the coal industry, there has been a tendency, even amongst the most sympathetic of commentators, to consign the relevance of the miners' struggles to the past.[146] As such, there is a danger that the miners of the late twentieth century may well come to be seen in much the same way as the '"obsolete" hand-loom weaver[s]' of the late eighteenth century (Thompson 1966: 12) or as 'inevitable victims' inasmuch as they ran 'dead against the current of history' (Hobsbawm 1971: 11–12; cited in Scott 1976: 3). For example, Waddington *et al.* conclude that the outcome of the 1984–5 strike 'was a significant step in the victory of exogenous forces for change over endogenous defences of *tradition*' (1991: 179; emphasis added). Jenkins, meanwhile, cites the coal industry in the early 1980s as 'a vivid example of the triumph of the past over the present at the expense of the future' (1988: 224).

Yet it is essential that any study of the miners should seek to rescue them from 'the enormous condescension of posterity' (Thompson 1966: 12). It is with this in mind that the following conclusions on the miners' experience are presented. First, the miners' experience underscores the importance of the concept of solidarity in explaining how and why workers act collectively. For miners, the brutal nature of their work, and the traditional isolation of the pit village, forged just such a sense of solidarity. Miners recognized that a grim life could be made more bearable only by acting together. Below the ground, the dangers of the working environment taught the miner that his own fate was tied inextricably to that of his fellow workers. Above the ground, a similiar sense of solidarity underpinned the array of community-level institutions of welfare and recreation. In particular, robust support for one such institution – the Union – grew out of a recognition that the lot of the individual could only be improved through collective effort. At times of acute crisis, such a recognition was capable of generating astounding loyalty to the Union, even in the most dire circumstances. Indeed, it is only as an act of class-based solidarity that the 1984–5 strike, and the various hardships and material sacrifices that it involved, may be understood fully: 'The strike went beyond any conceivable utilitarianian calculations of self-interest: the sacrifices were out of all proportion to any conceivable financial gain, even if money had been an issue in the strike, which it was not' (Samuel 1986: 6).

However, the 1984–5 strike, as an example of *national* level industrial action amongst miners, was a rarity. A second conclusion of this study therefore concerns the *nature* of solidarity amongst workers. Such solidarity is, in fact, very much a *local-level* phenomenon. Thus the powerful structural factors noted above tended to promote a powerful sense of solidarity at, but not necessarily beyond, the pit level. As such, local-level solidarity had a decidedly double-edged quality. On the one hand, it tended to perpetuate local and regional identities within the coalfields, thereby affecting profoundly the structure and capacities of the Union as a national institution. The federal structure of the Union, rooted in the desire of miners to guard jealously their local autonomy, limited its ability to institutionalize a sense of collective identity among all miners. It also made the coordination of industrial action at the national level (especially over as inherently a divisive issue as pit closures) a particularly hazardous enterprise. On the other hand, through several tumultuous decades of industrial expansion and contraction, the *importance* of local-level solidarity in the coalfields cannot be underestimated. Indeed, the historical and contemporary struggles described here demonstrate that local-level solidarity *did* provide a firm foundation for wider unity. The resilience of national-level strike action in 1926, 1972, 1974 and 1984–5 was rooted in the robust quality of solidarity at the community level.[147]

Given the ambiguous nature of local-level solidarity, the national unity of miners, far from being a structurally determined given, was very much a contingent, constructed phenomenon – clearly, the common fate of all miners down a 'wet, mucky hole' (Gittins 1986: 29) was never a *guarantee* of national unity. The miners, contrary to their popular image as the 'shock troops' of the British labour movement, never *did* enjoy a golden age of solidarity. In terms of the intricate problems of class-formation, therefore, the miners' experience underscores how unity needs always to be seen as the product of a painstaking process of construction from the bottom up – it could *never* simply be proclaimed by leaders and activists and, as events in Nottinghamshire in 1984–5 demonstrated, it most certainly could not be imposed.

A third conclusion concerns this very process of construction – namely, the critical role played by ordinary men and women at the local level in constructing a wider unity.[148] Such local-level activity was of a predominantly defensive nature – whether resisting pay cuts in the 1920s or pit closures in the 1980s. That this is so is not, in and of itself, surprising. The nature of the miners' demands, and the severe obstacles to pursuing such demands, were rooted in their position of class subordination. This was seen vividly in the difficulties encountered by the miners in the early 1980s in constructing a united front against the threat of industrial contraction. The Government and BC were in a position to exacerbate long-standing material differences between and within the coalfield areas and, for the most part, were able to choose the ground on which to fight the NUM. Consequently, miners testified to the circumstances of fear and uncertainty in which they found themselves – all of which tended to push self-interest to the fore. As such, attempts to resist pit closures in the early 1980s were generally uncoordinated and fraught with internal division and recrimination.

Yet such defensiveness *did*, ultimately, assume an offensive quality. The miners' goal of preserving pits and communities clashed increasingly with the government's attempts to restore management's 'right to manage'.[149] In a situation of growing crisis in the coal industry, the closure of Cortonwood colliery in March 1984 – the proverbial 'last straw' – precipitated a spontaneous revolt at the local level in which, to a remarkable degree, the individual miner cast aside any initial misgivings in the interests of wider solidarity.[150] It is worth reiterating, moreover, the role of grass-roots action and initiative in mobilizing strike action at a national level. The NUM national and area leaderships, far from 'starting' the strike, responded to actions already underway – notably, a series of local conflicts in various parts of the coalfields (not all of which were related directly to the issue of pit closures) and, of course, the activities of picketing miners.[151] Furthermore, despite such chaotic beginnings,[152] the 1984–5 strike generated a tenacious will to resist the Government, proving that, for the men and women of the coalfields, persevering in the face of adversity, and fighting to retain an element of control over, and dignity in, their working lives were not traditions confined to the past. Such resistance was rooted, as ever, in the ability of the miners to show initiative and fend for themselves:

> With no prompting from *Marxism Today*, the *New Left Review* or *Labour Weekly*, the people of the coalfields created the basis for a new politics which grew out of experience and necessity. [Politicians] . . . found themselves straggling badly behind, lost in a mist of worries about parliamentary whips and TUC guidelines. Others became near-sighted, so hard did they search the small print of their constitutions and manifestos for guidance on how to relate Trotsky and Tawney to food-parcel distribution . . . (Howells 1985: 146)

A fourth conclusion to be drawn from the miners' experience concerns the critical role of action, in and of itself, in the generation of collective consciousness.[153] In this regard, the length and, for many, the brutality, of the 1984–5 strike reinvigorated key elements of the miners' identity. The array of activities and initiatives undertaken by the miners and their supporters to sustain the strike reawakened a strong sense of community in pit villages (thereby reversing the debilitating effects of long-term industrial contraction), and intensified loyalty to the Union. Encounters with the police, meanwhile, reinforced perceptions of the Conservative Party as the traditional class enemy, and 'the state' as an instrument of class interest. For many miners and their supporters, therefore, the strike increased their political awareness. Significantly, the NUM, in the wake of the strike, gained an influx of newly politicized and committed leaders at the local level.

In addition, however, and even more importantly, it is quite clear that local-level struggle to defend their communities took miners beyond the confines of the traditional labour movement. In so doing, their own consciousness was raised. Entering the world of new-found allies, miners not only re-evaluated their own attachment to a brutal industry, but discovered that their struggle for control and dignity in the workplace resonated far beyond the coalfields themselves. The uproar of October 1992, moreover, confirmed that it continued to do so despite the crushing nature of the miners' own defeat in 1985. Herein lie some of the most significant aspects of the events described in this study. From a certain standpoint, much of what the miners sought to preserve was indeed 'traditional'; the issues at stake, however, were and are of extreme contemporary significance. In this context,

> The miners' strike is being represented as the last kick of an old order. Properly understood, it is one of the first steps towards a new order. This is especially the case in the emphasis they have put on protecting their *communities* . . . what the miners, like most of us, mean by their commun-

ities is the places where they have lived and want to go on living, where generations not only of economic but of social effort and human care have been invested, and which new generations will inherit. Without that kind of strong whole attachment, there can be no meaningful community. (Williams R. 1985: 8; original emphasis)

It is this trenchant view of the miners' precarious socioeconomic position which, in an age of increasingly globalized capitalist operations, lends their particular experience a much wider relevance: 'In a period of very powerful multinational capital, moving its millions under various flags of convenience, and in a period also of rapid and often arbitrary takeover and merger by financial groups of all kinds, virtually everyone is exposed or will be exposed to what the miners have suffered' (Williams R. 1985: 7).

What the miners' struggles of the 1980s pointed to is the way in which *new* communities of interest could be forged through the fierce defence of an old one. In so doing, miners at the grass-roots level appeared to adapt to important ongoing changes in the class structure of late industrial societies far better than many elements of the traditional labour movement: 'What emerges is a network of unexpected alliances which go far beyond the traditional labour movement. It is a broad democratic alliance of a new kind . . . in which the organised working class has a central role but a role henceforth it will have to *earn* and not *assume*' (Francis 1985d: 14; original emphasis).

None of this is meant to romanticize either the 'old order' itself or those that fought so hard to defend it. None the less, while the demise of a brutal industry in and of itself may be a legitimate measure of progress, there seems little reason to celebrate the demise of the traditions of solidarity and community which such an industry engendered. In the final analysis, it is worth emphasizing how miners lamented the decline of their pit villages as *communities*. A Yorkshire miner spoke of how his village had 'changed a lot . . . with pit closures . . . and everything. The old miners are dying off, and [as] younger miners have got transfers to other pits, they've left. So as a mining community itself, it's starting to totally die off'(Y51). A Derbyshire miner spoke in similar terms of how his village had '*grown* and *modernized*. There are a lot of fresh faces in the village not connected with mining. When I was first here, there was just a corner shop and the co-op. There was no [housing] estate as there is now . . . It's a cheap place for commuters to Sheffield – that's why the village has grown. It's not to do with the mining community'(D34). Furthermore, whether glad or not to have left the industry in the harsh circumstances following the strike, miners hankered after the comradeship of working life in happier times – this after all, had been the basis of such cherished community traditions. A miner at Celynen North colliery in South Wales commented, 'If you went on a shift with those men, you'd remember it for the rest of your life. Brilliant men. A law unto themselves underground. The comradeship was great. Other work – it's just not the same'(W53). A retired miner(W8) from neighbouring Penallta colliery reflected:

> I do miss the mining industry . . . because it's a very *close* community . . . when you're down there, you're one. There's six, seven hundred men there but you're all as one . . . you work for one another. You would *never* find another community like miners – if you work in a factory, a shop anywhere – you can be friends, but you would *never* find a close . . . knitness . . . as you've got underground . . . It's a *tremendous* feeling . . . it's the nature of the work, yes. It knitted you into one.

And it was a good thing.

Notes

1. *FT*, 15/11/88.
2. *FT*, 1/2/89.
3. *FT*, 4/3/89.
4. *G*, 24/8/89.
5. *I*, 8/8/89; *I*, 24/8/89.
6. *O*, 20/5/90.
7. *I*, 3/3/92; *I*, 10/3/92.
8. *STe*, 10/3/85.
9. Significant regional variations, however, saw productivity rise in the Doncaster section of the Yorkshire coalfield between 1983 and 1985 by 58.2 per cent, but only 2.9 per cent in North Derbyshire (Glyn 1988: 161).
10. *FT*, 14/2/89.
11. *FT*, 16/3/93.
12. *GH*, 26/11/92.
13. *FT*, 1/7/93.
14. *FT*, 16/3/93.
15. *T*, 1/3/94.
16. *FT*, 16/3/93.
17. *FT*, 26/3/93.
18. *FT*, 16/3/93.

19. *PAN*, 30/6/93. Opposition to such changes in working practices was not unanimous. The UDM was nowhere near as vigorous as the NUM in opposing BC. Indeed, in January 1993, UDM leaders were willing 'to discuss sweeping changes in working practices if it would help save threatened pits' in the Nottinghamshire coalfield (*GH*, 29/1/93).

    Nor was the NUM itself united, with some local branches – for example, Longannet in Scotland – considerably more accommodating than others (*GH*, 2/4/93). Moreover, in April 1993, 10-hour shifts and Saturday working were reportedly the norm 'at pit level in most NUM mines' (*FT*, 5/4/93).

20. See Edwards 1992, Metcalf 1989, Park 1962.

21. Interview, 23/5/90. Moreover, conditions were even worse for the nearly 2,000 miners working in the 140 private mines in existence in Britain by 1994. For an account of the situation in South Wales, see *G*, 10/2/94.

22. Such occurrences were defined as those 'which could potentially cause serious accidents and loss of life' (*FT*, 1/8/87).

23. *FT*, 1/8/87.

24. *G*, 26/8/89. Two observations in this report are noteworthy. First, higher productivity areas of the coalfield were undoubtedly experiencing higher accident rates. Second, the proposal to abolish the role of the pit deputy, if implemented, would obviously remove the pit deputy's statutory duty – and *power* – to stop any job considered unsafe – a contrast with practice in US mines, for example, where the job of pit deputy did not exist.

25. *The North East Miner*, No. 6, April 1990, p. 5.

26. *FT*, 2/4/93. The Government, meanwhile, pledged that safety standards in the industry would remain of 'paramount' concern. (*DT*, 3/12/93).

27. *FT*, 5/4/93.

28. *PAN*, 30/6/93.

29. *G*, 10/2/94. Roof bolts – six-foot-long steel screws used to bind rock together into a beam – are increasingly used in British mines as roof supports in preference to the costlier, but stronger, system of steel arches.

    Again, conditions in the private sector were even worse. In July 1992, a Labour MP demanded a Government inquiry into safety standards at privately-owned mines after a fatal accident in South Wales. The victim, crushed by a ten-foot boulder, was the third miner to die in privately-owned mines in South Wales in a year (*DT*, 23/7/92). By 1993, the fatal accident rate in privately-owned mines was *23* times that for mines operated by BC (*G*, 10/2/94).

30. *IS*, 3/6/90.
31. The steeply falling average age of the mining workforce meant that by October 1992, typical redundancy payments amounted to less than £10,000 – well below the sum of '£37,000' to which BC, the Government and the media referred continually in the post-strike period (*FT*, 3/11/92; *FT (Power Europe)*, 23/10/92).
32. *FT*, 4/3/89.
33. *G*, 3/12/87.
34. Gray 1989: 30; *G*, 3/3/89.
35. *T*, 14/10/92.
36. *FT*, 14/10/92.
37. *NYT*, 25/10/92.
38. *The Reuter European Business Report*, 15/10/92.
39. *T*, 14/10/92.
40. *T*, 15/10/92.
41. *G*, 3/12/87.
42. *FT*, 4/3/89; *G*, 6/12/88.
43. *G*, 3/3/89.
44. *T*, 14/10/92. Moreover, the private reopening of a mine previously closed by BC did little to alleviate local unemployment. For example, when Clipstone colliery in Nottinghamshire was reopened by RJB Mining in January 1994, it employed only 100 miners compared to the *565* men working at the mine when it had ceased production in April 1993 (*T*, 25/2/94).
45. *I*, 25/8/89. For an account of the damage inflicted by pit closures on the general economic health of South Wales, and on the mental and social well-being of its population, see *WM*, 14/10/92. For an account of the impact of the closure in 1987 of Polmaise colliery on the Scottish community of Fallin, see *GH*, 15/10/92. For a shattering description of the 'loss of community' in Mardy, South Wales, see *T*, 15/10/92.
46. *G*, 25/8/89. Similar tactics were used by BC to close Betteshanger in Kent in 1989 (*G*, 26/8/89; *I*, 25/8/89), Barnburgh in Yorkshire in 1990 (*I*, 7/2/90) and Blaenant in South Wales in 1990 (*MS*, 12/5/90).
47. *FT* 4/2/89.
48. *DT*, 6/8/90.
49. Though Scargill was re-elected NUM President in 1988, albeit with a substantially reduced majority and by a greatly diminished electorate.
50. *IS*, 3/6/90.
51. *I*, 18/10/92.
52. *GH*, 2/4/93.

53. *FT*, 3/3/86.
54. Interview, 23/5/90.
55. *FT*, 11/6/87.
56. *FT*, 11/6/87; *FT*, 9/6/87.
57. *FT*, 16/7/87; *FT*, 17/7/87.
58. *FT*, 22/7/87.
59. *FT*, 17/7/87.
60. Clapham 1989: 18; BC, *Report and Accounts 1988/9*, p. 31.
61. The national trend concealed significant regional variations. Using the same method of calculation for Table 7 (output lost to disputes as a percentage of total output for the year), levels of industrial action by areas of the coalfield (as organized by BC) varied, for example, as follows: South Yorkshire (9.64 per cent); North West (5.24 per cent); North East (0.95 per cent) (*Source*: BC, *Report and Accounts, 1988/9*, pp. 30–1).
62. Interview, 27/6/90.
63. *DM*, 14/10/92; see also *FT*, 14/10/92.
64. *FT*, 14/10/92.
65. *T*, 14/10/92.
66. *FT (Power Europe)*, 23/10/92.
67. *FT*, 13/10/92.
68. *FT*, 14/10/92.
69. *PAN*, 13/10/92.
70. *GH*, 9/10/92.
71. *PAN*, 12/10/92; *O*, 11/10/92.
72. *FT*, 16/10/92.
73. *T*, 15/10/92.
74. *G*, 16/10/92.
75. *PAN*, 20/10/92.
76. *T*, 15/10/92.
77. *DT*, 15/10/92.
78. *T*, 15/10/92.
79. *DM*, 15/10/92.
80. *GH*, 20/10/92.
81. *T*, 15/10/92.
82. *PAN*, 17/10/92.
83. *PAN*, 17/10/92.
84. *GH*, 17/10/92.
85. *GH*, 19/10/92.
86. *PAN*, 20/10/92.
87. *GH*, 19/10/92.
88. *FT (Power Europe)*, 23/10/92.

89. *GH*, 18/1/93. These demonstrations marked the high point of overt public opposition to the closures. However, in January 1993, the TUC delivered a 500,000-name petition to Parliament (the largest ever submitted by the trade union movement) demanding a halt to the closures (*GH*, 21/1/93). (The following month, Women Against Pit Closures delivered a similar 35,000-name petition to 10 Downing Street (*GH*, 5/2/93).) On 29 March 1993, between 2,000 and 5,000 miners and their supporters rallied in London to protest the Government's White Paper on the coal industry (*FT*, 30 and 27–8/3/93; *PAN*, 29/3/93). Meanwhile, throughout the winter of 1992–3, opinion polls showed more than 90 per cent of the electorate opposed to pit closures (*G*, 7/6/93).

90. *I*, 13/10/92.

91. *FT*, 14/10/92.

92. *The Age* (Melbourne), 15/10/92.

93. *PAN*, 20/10/92.

94. *T*, 1/3/94; *I*, 13/10/92; *T*, 9/10/92.

95. *I*, 9/10/92.

96. *GH*, 17/10/92.

97. In January 1993, for example, the UDM criticised the NUM's decision to hold a strike ballot (*GH*, 21/1/93). In late March 1993, however, the UDM leadership itself voted to organize a strike of its own to protest the Government's White Paper on the industry (*GH*, 27/3/93), only to be rebuffed subsequently by its membership in the strike ballot itself (*GH*, 6/4/93).

98. *GH*, 30/6/93.

99. *DM*, 14/10/92. UDM miners were, at best, divided on the implications of the crisis for relations with the NUM. On one hand, the NACODS secretary at Silverhill colliery in Nottinghamshire commented, 'Three quarters of the men would go over to the NUM straightaway if it ran a recruitment campaign down here' (*G*, 9/11/92). On the other hand, miners at neighbouring Bilsthorpe colliery clearly remained hostile to the NUM and steadfast in their opinions on the 1984–5 strike (*T*, 14/10/92). However, another report on the situation at Bilsthorpe contrasts sharply with that of *The Times*. The *Financial Times* correspondent, visiting Bilsthorpe Miners' Welfare, found pickets drinking 'side by side with those they picketed eight years ago'. An NUM miner commented, 'A lot of people here sold their souls, but by God they wish they hadn't now', while a UDM miner conceded to another NUM member: 'You were right and I was wrong' (15/10/92).

100. *GH*, 18/1/93; *FT (Power Europe)*, 23/10/92; *PAN*, 20/10/92.

101. *O*, 18/10/92; *DM*, 15/10/92; *PAN*, 20/10/92.

102. *FT (Power Europe)*, 23/10/92.
103. *GH*, 20/10/92.
104. *FT (Power Europe)*, 23/10/92.
105. *FT (Power Europe)*, 23/10/92.
106. *ST*, 27/12/92.
107. *PAN*, 20/10/92.
108. *GH*, 20/10/92.
109. *GH*, 20/10/92.
110. *T*, 4/2/94.
111. *G*, 26/10/92.
112. *G*, 3/11/92.
113. *FT*, 3/11/92; *FT (Power Europe)*, 23/10/92.
114. *G*, 21/1/93.
115. *G*, 7/6/93.
116. *FT*, 16/3/93.
117. A survey undertaken by *The Guardian* in November 1992 (3 and 9/11/92), which eluded a BC news blackout, corroborated the NUM President's earlier allegation that BC was deliberately allowing conditions to deteriorate at the mines in question (*G*, 26/10/92).
118. *FT*, 7–8/11/92.
119. *G*, 3/11/92.
120. *FT*, 18/3/93.
121. *G*, 7/6/93.
122. *GH*, 26/6/93.
123. *G*, 26/10/92.
124. *G*, 24/12/92; *GH*, 26/11/92. In April 1993 also, the Welsh TUC overwhelmingly defeated calls for a 24-hour general strike in Wales over pit closures (*PAN*, 29/4/93).
125. *GH*, 5/2/93; *GH*, 30/1/93.
126. *GH*, 5/2/93.
127. In a 75 per cent poll, 60 per cent voted to strike. For Area returns, see *FT*, 2/4/93; *FT*, 8/3/93; *DT*, 8/3/93.
128. *FT*, 26/3/93.
129. *FT*, 26/3/93.
130. *G*, 7/6/93.
131. *PAN*, 29/3/93.
132. *FT*, 27–28/3/93; *GH*, 27/3/93; *FT*, 26/3/93.
133. The TUC General Secretary quoted in the *FT*, 26/3/93; *FT*, 27–28/3/93.
134. *FT*, 30/3/93.
135. *I*, 3/4/93.
136. *FT*, 3–4/4/93; *PAN*, 2/4/93.

137. *DT*, 17/4/93. BC refused, however, to identify all the pits where
     miners were working (*DT*, 17/4/93; *PAN*, 17/4/93).
138. *GH*, 26/3/93.
139. *GH*, 30/6/93; *PAN*, 29/6/93; *GH*, 28/6/93.
140. Reasons for the Union's decision are not clear. BC's decision to
     end the check-off system, and the continuing severe and rapid loss
     of membership, may have been contributing factors (*DT*, 12/11/93;
     GH, 12/11/93; *PAN*, 11/11/93).
141. The Party, moreover, rejected the Union's request that it be
     allowed to hold cheaper branch ballots instead (*FT*, 30/6/94).
        The Union's immediate future did, however, appear to have been
     secured when, in March 1994, 88 per cent of Yorkshire miners
     voted to transfer their Area's £5.8 million of assets to the impo-
     verished National Union (*FT*, 26/3/94; *FT*, 10/3/94).
142. *G*, 7/6/93. See also Negrine 1995: 53–6.
143. For an account of Tower's colourful role in South Wales labour
     history, see Heath 1994.
144. *T*, 16/4/94.
145. See *FT*, 15/3/94; 16/2/94; 2/2/94.
146. Well before the 1980s, Thompson noted the habit of urging the
     miners to 'get back into history where we can honour you!' (1980:
     67).
147. I therefore concur with Sabia who argues that the presence or
     absence of strong local–level bases is an important factor in
     accounting for the successes and failures of many large-number
     collective efforts by workers (1988: 67). Shorter and Tilly, in their
     survey of strike activity in France between 1830 and 1968, argue
     that solidarity at the community level was crucial in the generation
     of class action. For example, French artisans, well-organized at the
     local level, played a critical role in unionizing industrial workers
     and generating mass strike action prior to World War One (1974,
     cited in Sabia 1988: 67). Moore also provides a similar account of
     German workers between 1848 and 1920. In the Ruhr prior to
     1914, for example, he notes that unlike their counterparts in the
     iron and steel industries, coal miners were able to carry out 'major
     strikes and other forms of collective action' because they were
     well-organized locally (1978, cited in Sabia 1988: 67).
        What matters, as Sabia notes, is not so much the size of the local
     community but its features – namely its density exclusivity, and the
     overlapping nature of its interactions (1988: 69). Thus Lipset, in
     his study of working-class movements in the nineteenth and twen-
     tieth centuries, argues that the more the workers felt themselves
     to be a part of a distinctive community, the more they developed

strong feelings of collective identity and the more they supported enduring large-scale organizations and movements (1983, cited in Sabia 1988: 70). Similarly, Piven and Cloward have argued that feelings of solidarity, based on a sense of sharing a common fate, and often rooted in small local associations and informal groups, accounts for the large-scale movements during the Great Depression in the US that campaigned for union recognition several years prior to the Wagner Act (1977: 96–131, cited in Sabia 1988: 70).

148. This is not to deny the role of leadership but to emphasize that a focus on the grass-roots level is key to understanding the resilience of the concrete struggles in which the miners were involved. This is true even in the case of the NUM President's charismatic and indefatigable leadership of the 1984–5 strike. As Dave Hill remarks, 'To demonise Arthur Scargill – or to deify him as a prophet – is to obscure the great mass of grassroots activism which weaved together the daily fabric of the strike' (*G*, 4/3/94).

149. The miners' goals validate Calhoun's observation that '"conservative" attachments to tradition and community may be crucial bases for quite rational participation in the most radical of mobilizations' (1988: 132). In this context, there are parallels between the motivations that lay behind the miners' strike and the actions of pre-industrial artisans in early nineteenth-century England 'who called for changes which were at once founded on traditional aspirations and almost diametrically opposed to the dominant economic and social trends of their day' (Calhoun 1988: 139). One cannot push the parallel too far, however. The subjects of Calhoun's study were quintessential 'machine–breakers' – something the miners were not, and never had been. Indeed, the NUM, in the course of its history, erred by being far too willing to embrace the introduction of new technology into the mines without calculating its possible effects on employment levels in the industry (Winterton & Winterton 1989: 9–52).

150. Thereby confirming the validity of Rosa Luxemburg's memorable observation: 'At the moment that a real, earnest period of mass strikes begins, all these "calculations" of "cost" become merely projects for exhausting the ocean with a tumbler' (1925: 51, cited in Holmstrom 1983: 315).

151. I am not seeking to romanticize actions at the local level, merely to underscore their importance. For example, the largely spontaneous actions of Yorkshire pickets in streaming into the Nottinghamshire coalfield undoubtedly forced the hand of their own area's Union leadership and, as such, had a powerful impact on the way in which wider strike action was generated. However, the *results* of such

picketing were anything but positive (as, indeed, several Yorkshire miners acknowledged).

152. The process whereby individual workers in a situation of general upheaval do not, ultimately, stay on the sidelines is captured by Roemer thus: 'The participants act, in a sense, despite their better judgement. They do not calculate rationally whether or not to strike, walk out, or fight the police. People are pushed, they retreat, they seek individual solutions; they are pushed farther, conditions become intolerable, some incident occurs, and there is an eruption' (1979: 763).

153. In this context, Sartre's observations remain trenchant: 'The working class can never express itself completely as an active political subject . . . There is a strong tendency today to generalise the concept of *class consciousness* and of *class struggle* as pre-existing elements antecedent to the struggle. The only *a priori* is the objective situation of class exploitation. Consciousness is only born in struggle: the class struggle only exists insofar as there exist places where an actual struggle is going on' (1970: 237).

Appendix

Interviews

Mineworkers

One hundred-and-seventy-three members of the NUM (including fifty-four in South Wales, fifty-two in Yorkshire, fifty-four in Derbyshire and thirteen in Nottinghamshire) and forty-four members of the UDM (all in Nottinghamshire) were interviewed by means of a tape-recorded, semi-structured questionnaire. The principal qualification for an interviewee was that he had worked in the coal industry during the period covering the 1972, 1974 and 1984–5 strikes.

Given the absence of a definitive and comprehensive list of employees, no random sample of the mining workforce was possible. As such, contact with interviewees was made, in the first instance, through as many as possible of the NUM and UDM branches in existence in 1989–90 in the South Wales, Nottinghamshire, Derbyshire and Yorkshire coalfields. As such, interviewees were drawn *mainly* from those pits which had survived the contraction of the industry between 1985 and 1989. *However*, the process of contraction itself (whereby miners had transferred *to* pits in existence in 1989–90), and the use of a 'snowballing' technique of making contacts, ensured that interviews were also conducted with miners from pits which had closed since 1985.

The list below denotes the date of the interview, and the mine at which the interviewee was working at the time of the 1984–5 strike. I choose not to reveal the name of the interviewee.

South Wales, November 1989–January 1990

W1 Taff Merthyr, 17/11/89.
W2 Taff Merthyr, 17/11/89.
W3 Taff Merthyr, 17/11/89.
W4 Penallta, 28/11/89.
W5 Penallta, 29/11/89.
W6 Penallta, 29/11/89.
W7 Penallta, 30/11/89.

W8   Penallta, 30/11/89.
W9   Penallta, 30/11/89.
W10   Penallta, 30/11/89.
W11   Oakdale, 30/11/89.
W12   Penallta, 1/12/89.
W13   Taff Merthyr, 1/12/89.
W14   Penrhiwceiber, 4/12/89.
W15   Penrhiwceiber, 4/12/89.
W16   Oakdale, 4/12/89.
W17   Tower, 4/12/89.
W18   Tower, 4/12/89.
W18a Tower, 5/12/89.
W19   Tower, 5/12/89.
W20   Tower, 5/12/89.
W21   Tower, 5/12/89.
W22   Tower, 5/12/89.
W23   Tower, 5/12/89.
W24   Tower, 6/12/89.
W25   Tower, 6/12/89.
W26   Tower, 6/12/89.
W27   Penrhiwceiber, 6/12/89.
W28   Penallta, 6/12/89.
W29   Tower, 7/12/89.
W30   Tower, 7/12/89.
W31   Tower, 7/12/89.
W32   Tower, 7/12/89.
W33   Blaenant, 7/12/89.
W34   Betws, 12/12/89.
W35   Betws, 12/12/89.
W36   Betws, 12/12/89.
W37   Betws, 13/12/89.
W38   Betws, 13/12/89.
W39   Cwmgwili, 19/12/89.
W40   Cwmgwili, 20/12/89.
W41   Cynheidre, 21/12/89.
W42   Tower, 21/12/89.
W43   Cynheidre, 22/12/89.
W44   Abernant, 9/1/90.
W45   Blaenant, 9/1/90.
W46   Blaenant, 9/1/90.
W47   Abernant, 10/1/90.
W48   Blaenant, 10/1/90.
W49   Penrhiwceiber, 10/1/90.

W50   Oakdale, 16/1/90.
W51   Oakdale, 16/1/90.
W52   Oakdale, 16/1/90.
W53   Celynen North, 16/1/90.
W54   Cwmgwili, 17/1/90.

Nottinghamshire, February–March 1990

NUM:
N1   Bevercotes, 4 + 7/2/90.
N2   Bevercotes, 5/2/90.
N3   Bevercotes, 5/2/90.
N4   Bilsthorpe, 5/2/90.
N5   Ollerton, 5/2/90.
N6   Ollerton, 6/2/90.
N7   Ollerton, 6/2/90.
N8   Thoresby, 6/2/90.
N9   Bevercotes, 7/2/90.
N10   Blidworth, 18/2/90.
N14   Bevercotes, 19/2/90.
N27   Bevercotes, 26/2/90.
N32   Bevercotes, 1/3/90.

UDM:
N11   Bilsthorpe, 19/2/90.
N12   Bilsthorpe, 19/2/90.
N13   Bilsthorpe, 19/2/90.
N15   Welbeck, 21/2/90.
N16   Welbeck, 21/2/90.
N17   Silverhill, 21/2 + 21/3/90.
N18   Silverhill, 21/2/90.
N19   Bilsthorpe, 21/2 + 5/3/90.
N20   Rufford, 22 + 28/2/90.
N21   Rufford, 22/2/90.
N22   Rufford, 22/2 + 15/3/90.
N23   Rufford, 22 + 28/2/90.
N24   Harworth, 26/2/90.
N25   Harworth, 26/2/90.
N26   Harworth, 26/2/90.
N28   Gedling, 27/2/90.
N29   Silverhill, 27/2/90.
N30   Silverhill, 27/2/90.
N31   Rufford, 28/2/90.

N34   Harworth, 5/3/90.
N35   Annesley, 6/3/90.
N36   Annesley, 6/3/90.
N37   Annesley, 6/3/90.
N38   Annesley, 6/3/90.
N39   Bolsover, 7/3/90.
N40   Bolsover, 7/3/90.
N41   Gedling, 9/3/90.
N42   Gedling, 9/3/90.
N43   Creswell, 12/3/90.
N44   Creswell, 12/3/90.
N45   Creswell, 12/3/90.
N46   Creswell, 12/3/90.
N47   Bolsover, 12/3/90.
N48   Bolsover, 14/3/90.
N49   Bolsover, 14/3/90.
N50   Creswell, 15/3/90.
N51   Creswell, 15/3/90.
N52   Calverton, 16/3790.
N53   Calverton, 16/3/90.
N54   Calverton, 16/3/90.
N55   Mansfield, 20/3/90.
N56   Mansfield, 20/3/90.
N57   Mansfield, 20/3/90.

Yorkshire, April–May 1990

Y1   Grimethorpe, 3/4/90.
Y2   Grimethorpe, 3/4/90.
Y3   Grimethorpe, 3/4/90.
Y4   Grimethorpe, 3/4/90.
Y5   Allerton Bywater, 5/4/90.
Y6   Silverwood, 6/4/90.
Y7   Silverwood, 6/4/90.
Y8   Goldthorpe, 9/4/90.
Y9   Goldthorpe, 9/4/90.
Y10   Goldthorpe, 9/4/90.
Y11   Goldthorpe, 9/4/90.
Y12   Goldthorpe, 9/4/90.
Y13   Rossington, 10/3/90.
Y14   Barnsley Main, 11/4/90.
Y15   Barrow, 19/4/90.
Y16   Barrow, 19/4/90.

Y17   Barrow, 19/4/90.
Y18   Brodsworth, 20/4790.
Y19   Brodsworth, 20/4/90.
Y20   Brodsworth, 23/4/90.
Y21   Brodsworth, 23/4790.
Y22   Maltby, 24/4/90.
Y23   Thurcroft, 25/4/90.
Y24   Thurcroft, 25/4/90.
Y25   Barrow, 26/4/90.
Y26   Brodsworth, 26/4/90.
Y26a   Bentley, 27/4/90.
Y27   Rossington, 30/4/90.
Y28   Frickley, 30/4/90.
Y29   Maltby, 1/5/90.
Y30   Maltby, 1/5/90.
Y31   Dinnington, 3/5/90.
Y31a   Dinnington, 3/5/90.
Y32   Dinnington, 3/5/90.
Y33   Manton, 4/5/90.
Y34   Manton, 4/5/90.
Y35   Manton, 8/5/90.
Y36   Manton, 8/5/90.
Y37   Gascoigne Wood, 9/5/90.
Y38   Stillingfleet, 9/5/90.
Y39   Stillingfleet, 9/5/90.
Y40   Sharlston, 10/5/90.
Y41   Kiveton, 11/5/90.
Y42   Kiveton, 11/5/90.
Y43   Allerton Bywater, 12/5/90.
Y44   Wiston, 12/5/90.
Y45   Savile, 15/5/90.
Y46   Allerton Bywater, 15/5/90.
Y47   Allerton Bywater, 15/5/90.
Y48   Allerton Bywater, 15/5/90.
Y49   Sharlston, 16/5/90.
Y50   Sharlston, 16/5/90.
Y51   Denby Grange, 18/5/90.
Y52   Brookhouse, 27/5/90.

Derbyshire, May–July 1990

D1   High Moor, 22/5/90.
D2   High Moor, 22/5/90.

D3	High Moor, 22/5/90.
D4	High Moor, 22/5/90.
D5	Westthorpe, 22/5/90.
D6	High Moor, 23/5/90.
D7	High Moor, 25/5/90.
D8	High Moor, 25/5/90.
D9	Renishaw Park, 27/5/90.
D10	Renishaw Park, 29/5/90.
D11	Renishaw Park, 29/5/90.
D12	Westthorpe, 29/5/90.
D13	Renishaw Park, 29/5/90.
D14	Ireland, 31/5/90.
D15	Markham, 4/6/90.
D16	Workshops, 5/6/90.
D17	Workshops, 5/6/90.
D18	Workshops, 5/6/90.
D19	Warsop, 5/6/90.
D20	Warsop, 5/6/90.
D21	Markham, 7/6/90.
D22	Markham, 7/6/90.
D23	Markham, 7/6/90.
D24	Workshops, 11/6/90.
D25	Workshops, 11/6/90.
D26	Workshops, 11/6/90.
D27	Workshops, 11/6/90.
D28	Markham, 12/6/90.
D29	Markham, 13/6/90.
D30	Whitwell, 19/6/90.
D31	Shirebrook, 20/6/90.
D32	Shirebrook, 20/6/90.
D33	Warsop, 20/6/90.
D34	Markham, 20/6/90.
D35	Workshops, 21/6/90.
D36	Shirebrook, 22/6/90.
D37	Shirebrook, 25/6/90.
D38	Whitwell, 25/6/90.
D39	Shirebrook, 27/6/90.
D40	Westthorpe, 27/6/90.
D41	Whitwell, 28/6/90.
D42	Ireland, 29/6/90.
D43	Whitwell, 29/6/90.
D44	Shirebrook, 2/7/90.
D45	Ireland, 2/7/90.

D46   Ireland, 2/7/90.
D47   Renishaw Park, 3/7/90.
D48   Markham, 3/7/90.
D49   Workshops, 3/7/90.
D50   Workshops, 3/7/90.
D51   Whitwell, 5/7/90.
D52   High Moor, 6/7/90.
D53   Westthorpe, 7/7/90.
D54   Ireland, 13/7/90.

Union Officials

The position of the interviewee is that pertaining at the date of the interview.

NUM

Peter Heathfield, National General Secretary, NUM; Chesterfield, 23/8/90.

Mick McGahey, former National Vice-President, NUM; Edinburgh, 15/12/89.

Des Dutfield, President, South Wales Area NUM; Pontypridd, 20/10/89.

Gwyn Williams, Vice-President, South Wales Area NUM; Taff Merthyr colliery, 17/11/89.

Tyrone O'Sullivan, NUM Lodge Secretary, Tower colliery, South Wales; Cwmaman, 21/11/89.

Glyn Roberts, NUM Lodge Vice-Chairman, Tower colliery, South Wales; Tower colliery, 24/11/89.

Henry Richardson, General Secretary, Nottinghamshire Area NUM; Mansfield, 10/10/89.

Philip Thompson, Administrative Officer, Yorkshire Area NUM; Barnsley, 11/11/89.

Gordon Butler, General Secretary, Derbyshire Area NUM; Chesterfield, 31/5/90.

Austin Fairest, President, Derbyshire Area NUM; High Moor colliery, 23/5/90.

Alan Gascoigne, Vice-President, Derbyshire Area NUM; Shirebrook colliery, 27/6/90.

Peter Elliott, Chief Executive Officer and Financial Secretary, Derbyshire Area NUM; Chesterfield, 11/10/89.

John Burrows, Compensation Agent, Derbyshire Area NUM; Chesterfield, 13/6/90.

Mick Clapham, Industrial Relations Officer, NUM; Sheffield.

UDM

Roy Lynk, General Secretary, UDM; Mansfield, 10/10/89.

Other Trade Union Leaders

Norman Willis, General Secretary, TUC; London, 25/10/89.
John Edmonds, General Secretary, GMB; London, 6/11/89.

NUM-sponsored Labour MPs

Kevin Barron (Rother Valley), Parliamentary Private Secretary to Leader of H.M. Opposition; London, 24/10/89.
Eric Illsley (Barnsley Central), former Administrative Officer, Yorkshire Area NUM; London, 7/11/89.
Dennis Skinner (Bolsover), former President, Derbyshire Area NUM; London, 9/11/89.

Other Labour MPs

Tony Benn (Chesterfield), Secretary of State for Energy, 1975–79; London, 24/10/89.
Eric Heffer (Liverpool, Walton), Chairman of the Labour Party, 1984–85; London, 11/12/89.

Archive and Library Sources

Benn Archives, London
British Coal, National Headquarters Library, London
British Coal, Employee Relations Department, Edwinstowe, Nottinghamshire
British Coal, Statistics Department, Doncaster, Yorkshire
Central Library, Barnsley, Yorkshire
Chesterfield Public Library, Chesterfield, Derbyshire
Coalfield Communities Campaign, Barnsley, Yorkshire
Labour Party, National Headquarters, London
Mansfield Public Library, Mansfield, Nottinghamshire
National Union of Mineworkers (Industrial Relations Department), National Headquarters, Sheffield, Yorkshire
Northern College Library, Barnsley, Yorkshire
South Wales Miners' Library, University College, Swansea

Newspaper Sources

National Newspapers:

Daily Express *(DE)*
Daily Mail *(DM)*
Daily Mirror *(DMi)*
Daily Star *(DS)*
Daily Telegraph *(DT)*
Financial Times *(FT)*
The Guardian *(G)*
The Independent *(I)*
The Independent on Sunday *(IS)*
Morning Star *(MS)*
The New York Times *(NYT)*
The Observer *(O)*
The Times *(T)*
Sunday Telegraph *(STe)*
Sunday Times *(ST)*
Western Mail *(WM)*

Regional and Local Newspapers:

Aberdare Leader *(AL)*
Barnsley Star *(BS)*
Glasgow Herald *(GH)*
Mansfield Chronicle and Advertiser *(Chad)*
Mansfield Observer *(MO)*
South Wales Echo *(SWE)*
South Wales Evening Post *(SWEP)*

Other Press Sources:

The Anthracite Star (Newsletter)
Coal News
The Colliery Guardian
International Coal Report
The Miner
The North East Miner
The Nottinghamshire Miner
Press Association Newsfile *(PAN)*
The Reuter European Business Report
The Valleys' Star (Newsletter)

Bibliography

Adeney, M., and Lloyd, J. (1988), *The Miners' Strike 1984–5. Loss without Limit*, London: Routledge and Kegan Paul.

Allen, S. (1989), *Gender and Work in Mining Communities*, Paper presented to BSA Conference, Plymouth.

——, Littlejohn, G., and Warwick, D. (1989), *Gender and Work in Mining Communities*, unpublished paper, University of Bradford.

Allen, V. (1977), 'The Differentiation of the Working Class', in A. Hunt (ed.), *Class and Class Structure*, London: Lawrence and Wishart.

——, (1981), *The Militancy of British Miners*, Shipley, Yorkshire: The Moor Press.

——, (1982), 'The Miners on the Move', *Marxism Today*, vol. 26, no. 2, pp. 17–21.

Arnot, R.P. (1949), *The Miners. A history of the Miners' Federation of Great Britain, 1889–1910*, London: George Allen and Unwin Ltd.

——, (1953), *The Miners: Years of Struggle. A history of the Miners' Federation of Great Britain (from 1910 onwards)*, London: George Allen and Unwin Ltd.

——, (1961), *The Miners in Crisis and War (from 1930 onwards)*, London: George Allen and Unwin Ltd.

——, (1979), *The Miners – One Union, One Industry: a history of the National Union of Mineworkers, 1939–46*, London and Boston: George Allen and Unwin Ltd.

Aronowitz, S. (1983), *Working Class Hero. A New Strategy for Labor*, New York: The Pilgrim Press.

Ashworth, W. (1986), *The History of the British Coal Industry. Volume 5. 1946–1982: The Nationalized Industry*, Oxford: Clarendon Press.

Bain, G.S., and Price, R. (1972), 'Who is a White Collar Worker?', *British Journal of Industrial Relations*, vol. 10, no. 3, pp. 325–39.

——, and Price, R. (1980), *Profiles of Union Growth. A Comparative Statistical Portrait of Eight Countries*, London: Basil Blackwell.

Barrioz de Chiungara, D., and Viezzer, M. (1978), *'Let Me Speak'. Testimony of Domitilia, a Woman of the Bolivian Mines*, New York: Monthly Review Press.

Beaumont, P.B. (1987), *The Decline of Trade Union Organisation*, London; Wolfeboro, NH: Croom Helm.

——, and Harris, R.I.D. (1995), 'Union De-recognition and Declining Union Density in Britain', *Industrial and Labor Relations Review*, vol. 48, no. 3, pp. 389–402.

Benn, T. (1985), 'Who Dares Wins', *Marxism Today*, vol. 29, no. 1, pp. 12–15.

Benney, M. (1978), 'The Legacy of Mining', in M. Bulmer (ed.), *Mining and Social Change*, London: Croom Helm.

Beynon, H. (1985), 'Authority and Change in the Coalfields', *Journal of Law and Society*, vol. 12, no. 3, pp. 395–403.

——, (1984), 'The Miners' Strike in Easington', *New Left Review*, no. 148, pp. 104–15.

——, and McMylor, P. (1985), 'Decisive power: the new Tory state against the miners', in H. Beynon (ed.), *Digging Deeper. Issues in the Miners' Strike*, London: Verso.

Blackwell, T., and Seabrook, J. (1985), *A World Still to Win. The Reconstruction of the Post-War Working Class*, London: Faber and Faber.

Bone, I., Pullen, A., and Scargill, T. (eds) (1991), *Class War. A Decade of Disorder*, London; New York: Verso.

Boston, S. (1987), *Women Workers and the Trade Unions*, 2nd edn, London: Lawrence and Wishart.

Brody, D. (1994), 'The Future of the Labor Movement in Historical Perspective', *Dissent*, Winter, pp. 32–41.

Bulmer, M. (1975), 'Sociological Models of the Mining Community', *The Sociological Review*, vol. 23, no. 1 (New Series), pp. 61–92.

——, (1978a), 'Social Structure and Social Change in the Twentieth Century', in M. Bulmer (ed.), *Mining and Social Change*, London: Croom Helm.

——, (1978b), 'The Decline of Mining: A Case Study in Spennymoor', in M. Bulmer (ed.), *Mining and Social Change*, London: Croom Helm.

——, (ed.) (1978), *Mining and Social Change*, London: Croom Helm.

Bunyan, T. (1985), 'From Saltley to Orgreave via Brixton', *Journal of Law and Society*, vol. 12, no. 3, pp. 293–304.

Calhoun, C. (1988), 'The Radicalism of Tradition and the Question of Class Struggle', in M. Taylor (ed.), *Rationality and Revolution*, Cambridge: Cambridge University Press; Paris: Editions de la Maison des Sciences de l'Homme.

Callinicos, A., and Simons, M. (1985), *The Great Strike. The Miners' Strike of 1984–5 and Its Lessons*, London: Socialist Worker.

Campbell, A., and Warner, M. (1985), 'Changes in the Balance of Power in the British Mineworkers' Union: an Analysis of National Top-office Elections, 1974–84', *British Journal of Industrial Relations*, vol. 23, no. 1, pp. 1–24.

Campbell, A. (1974), 'Honourable men and degraded slaves: a comparative study of trade unionism in two Lanarkshire mining communities,
1841–1871', *Bulletin of the Society for the Study of Labour History*,
no. 28, pp. 9–11.
Campbell, B. (1986), 'Proletarian Patriarchs and the Real Radicals', in
V. Seddon (ed.), *The Cutting Edge: Women and the Pit Strike*, London: Lawrence and Wishart.
Carter, P. (1985), 'Striking the Right Note', *Marxism Today*, vol. 29, no.
3, pp. 28–31.
Chaplin, S. (1978), 'Durham Mining Villages', in M. Bulmer (ed.), *Mining and Social Change*, London: Croom Helm.
Church, R. (1986), *The History of the British Coal Industry. Volume 3.
1830–1913: Victorian Pre-eminence*, Oxford: Clarendon Press.
——, Outram, Q., and Smith, D. N. (1991), 'The "isolated mass" re-
visited: strikes in British coal mining', *The Sociological Review*, vol.
39, no. 1, pp. 55–87.
Clapham, M. (1989), *Relations at Colliery Level Since the Strike*,
Sheffield: Industrial Relations Department, National Union of Mine-
workers. (Mimeo).
Coates, D. (1989), *The Crisis of Labour: Industrial Relations and
the State in Contemporary Britain*, Oxford; Atlantic Highlands, NJ:
Philip Allan Publishers.
Cobble, D.S. (1994), 'Labor Law Reform and Postindustrial Unionism',
Dissent, Fall, pp. 474–80.
Coggins, J. *et al.* (1989), *Trade Unions of the World 1989–1990. Second
Edition*, Chicago and London: St. James Press.
Coote, A., and Campbell, B. (1987), *Sweet Freedom: the Struggle for
Women's Liberation*, 2nd edn, Oxford: Blackwell.
Coulter J., Miller, S., and Walker, M. (1984), *State of Siege*, London:
Canary Press.
Craver, C.B. (1993), *Can Unions Survive? The Rejuvenation of the
American Labor Movement*, New York: New York University Press.
Cronin, J. E. (1983), 'Politics, Class Structure and the Enduring Weak-
ness of British Social Democracy', *Journal of Social History*, vol. 16,
no. 3, pp. 123–42.
Crouch, C. (1986), 'The Future Prospects for Trade Unions in Western
Europe', *Political Quarterly*, vol. 57, no. 1, pp. 5–17.
——, (1992), 'The Fate of Articulated Industrial Relations Systems: a
Stock-taking after the Neo-Liberal Decade', in M. Regini (ed.), *The
Future of Labour Movements,* London: Sage.
——, (1995), 'Exit or Voice: Two Paradigms for European Industrial
Relations after the Keynesian Welfare State', *European Journal of
Industrial Relations*, vol. 1, no. 1, pp. 63–81.

Bibliography

253

Davis, M. (1986), *Prisoners of the American Dream. Politics and Economy in the History of the US Working Class*, London; New York: Verso.

——, and Sprinker, M. (eds) (1988), *Reshaping the US Left. Popular Struggles in the 1980s*, London; New York: Verso.

Dennis, N., Henriques, F., and Slaughter, C. (1969), *Coal is Our Life*, 2nd edn., London: Tavistock Publications.

Diggins, L., Massey, D., and Wainwright, H. (1985), 'The comfort of strangers', *New Socialist*, vol. 24, pp. 22–3.

Disney, R., Gosling, A., and Machin, S. (1995), 'British Unions in Decline: Determinants of the 1980s Fall in Union Recognition', *Industrial and Labor Relations Review*, vol. 48, no. 3, pp. 403–19.

Dolby, N. (1987), *Norma Dolby's Diary: An account of the Great Miners' Strike*, London: Verso.

Dorey, P. (1991), 'Thatcherism's impact on trade unions', *Contemporary Record*, vol. 4, no. 4, pp. 9–11.

Douglass, D. (1986a), *Come and Wet this Truncheon: The Role of the Police in the Coal Strike of 1984/1985*, David John Douglass / Doncaster, Cambridge and London groups of DAM-IWA (Direct Action Movement-International Workers Association [Anarcho-Syndicalists]) / Canary Press, London.

——, (1986b), *A Year of Our Lives: A Colliery Community in the Great Coal Strike of 1984/85*, London: Hooligan Press.

——, and Krieger, J. (1983), *A Miner's Life*, London, Boston, Melbourne and Henley: Routledge and Kegan Paul.

Duckham, H., and Duckham, B. (1973), *Great Pit Disasters. Great Britain 1700 to the Present Day*, Newton Abbot: David and Charles.

East, R., Power, H., and Thomas, P. A. (1985), 'The Death of Mass Picketing', *Journal of Law and Society*, vol. 12, no. 3, pp. 305–19.

Edwards, N. (1936), *History of the S.W.M.F. Vol. II*, Oxford: Uncorrected proof copy, unpublished, Nuffield College Library.

Edwards, P.K. (1992), 'Industrial Conflict: Themes and Issues in Recent Research', *British Journal of Industrial Relations*, vol. 30, no. 3, pp. 361–404.

Edwards, R. (1979), *Contested Terrain. The Transformation of the Workplace in the Twentieth Century*, New York: Basic Books.

Ellis, A. (1929, reprinted 1980), *The Life of an Ordinary Woman*, Lincoln: University of Nebraska Press.

Evans J., Hudson C., and Smith, P. (1985), 'Women and the Strike: it's a whole way of life', in B. Fine and R. Millar (eds), *Policing the Miners' Strike*, London: Lawrence and Wishart.

Fantasia, R. (1988), *Cultures of Solidarity. Consciousness, Action, and Contemporary American Workers,* Berkeley; Los Angeles; London:

University of California Press.

Feldman, R., and Betzold, M. (1988), *End of the Line. Autoworkers and the American Dream. An Oral History*, New York: Weidenfeld and Nicolson.

Field, J. (1985a), 'Labour's Dunkirk', *New Socialist*, no. 26, pp. 11–14.

——, (1985b), 'Police and Thieves. The British Miners' Strike of 1984–85', *Radical America*, vol. 19, no. 2–3, pp. 7–22.

Fine, B., and Millar, R. (eds) (1985), *Policing the Miners' Strike*, London: Lawrence and Wishart.

Flynn, B., Goldsmith, L., and Sutcliffe, B. (1985), 'We Danced in the Miners' Hall. An Interview with "Lesbians and Gays Support the Miners"', *Radical America*, vol. 19, no. 2–3, pp. 39–46.

Fosh, P. (1993), 'Membership Participation in Work-place Unionism: The Possibility of Union Renewal', *British Journal of Industrial Relations*, vol. 31, no. 4, pp. 577–92.

Francis, H. (1976), 'The Origins of the South Wales Miners' Library', *History Workshop*, no. 2, pp. 183–205.

——, (1980), 'The Secret World of the South Wales Miner: The Relevance of Oral History', in D. Smith (ed.), *A People and a Proletariat. Essays in the History of Wales 1780–1980*, London: Pluto Press.

——, (1985a), 'That Tearing Sound', *Marxism Today*, vol. 29, no. 12, pp. 56–7.

——, (1985b), 'Unfinished Business: The breaking of the NUM?', *Marxism Today*, vol. 29, no. 8, pp. 22–4.

——, (1985c), 'NUM United: A Team in Disarray', *Marxism Today*, vol. 29, no. 4, pp. 28–34.

——, (1985d), 'Mining the Popular Front', *Marxism Today*, vol. 29, no. 2, pp. 12–15.

——, (1985e), 'The Law, Oral Tradition and the Mining Community', *Journal of Law and Society*, vol. 12, no. 3, pp. 267–71.

——, (1989), 'Denial of Dignity', *New Statesman*, 1 September 1989, pp. 10–11.

——, and Rees, G. (1989), '"No Surrender in the Valleys": the 1984–5 Miners' Strike in South Wales', *Llafur (Journal of Welsh Labour History)*, vol. 5, no. 2, pp. 41–71.

——, and Smith, D. (1980), *The Fed. A History of the South Wales Miners in the Twentieth Century*, London: Lawrence and Wishart.

Gallie, D. (1983), *Social Inequality and Class Radicalism in France and Britain,* Cambridge: Cambridge University Press.

Gamble, A. (1985), 'The strike the Tories wanted', *New Socialist*, vol. 26, pp. 15–17.

Garside, W.R. (1971), *The Durham Miners 1919–1960*, London: George Allen and Unwin Ltd.

Gaventa, J. (1980), *Power and Powerlessness*, Urbana; Chicago; London: University of Illinois Press.

Geary, R. (1985), *Policing Industrial Disputes, 1893–1985*, Cambridge: Cambridge University Press.

Geoghagan, T. (1991), *Which Side Are You On? Trying to Be for Labor when It's Lying Flat on Its Back*, New York: Plume.

Gibbon, P. (1988), 'Analysing the British miners' strike of 1984–5', *Economy and Society*, vol. 17, no. 2, pp. 139–94.

Gifford, C. D. (1990), *Directory of U.S. Labor Organizations. 1990–91 Edition*, Washington, D.C.: The Bureau of National Affairs, Inc.

Ginzberg, E. (1991) [1942], *A World Without Work. The Story of the Welsh Miners*, New Brunswick and London: Transaction Publishers.

Gittins, J. A. (1986), *Striking Stuff*, Bradford, England: "1 in 12" (Publications) Collective.

Glyn, A. (1984), *The Economic Case Against Pit Closures*, Sheffield: National Union of Mineworkers.

——, (1988), 'Colliery Results and Closures after the 1984–85 Coal Dispute', *Oxford Bulletin of Economics and Statistics*, vol. 50, no. 2, pp. 161–73.

Goldfield, M. (1987), *The Decline of Organized Labor in the United States*, Chicago; London: University of Chicago Press.

Goldthorpe, J.H. *et al.* (1969), *The Affluent Worker in the Class Structure*, Cambridge: Cambridge University Press.

Goldthorpe, J.H. *et al.* (1968), *The Affluent Worker: Industrial Attitudes and Behaviour*, Cambridge: Cambridge University Press.

Goodman, G. (1985), *The Miners' Strike*, London and Sydney: Pluto Press.

Gormley, J. (1982), *Battered Cherub. The Autobiography of Joe Gormley*, London: Hamish Hamilton.

Gray, S. (1989), 'Dole not coal', *New Socialist*, vol. 25, pp. 30–1.

Green, F. (1992), 'Recent Trends in British Trade Union Density: How Much of a Compositional Effect?', *British Journal of Industrial Relations*, vol. 30, no. 3, pp. 445–58.

Green, H. S. (1990), *On Strike at Hormel: The Struggle for a Democratic Labor Movement*, Philadelphia: Temple University Press.

Green, P. (1990), *The Enemy Without: policing and class consciousness in the miners' strike*, Milton Keynes; Philadelphia: Open University Press.

Griffin, A. R. (1962), *The Miners of Nottinghamshire 1914–1944. A History of the Nottinghamshire Miners' Unions*, London: George Allen and Unwin Ltd.

——, (1985), *County Under Siege. Nottinghamshire in the Miners'*

Strike 1984–5, Ashbourne, Derbyshire: Moorland Publishing Company Ltd.

Hall, P. (1987), 'European Labor in the 1980s', *International Journal of Political Economy*, vol. 17, no. 3, pp. 3–25.

Hall, S. (1988), *The Hard Road to Renewal. Thatcherism and the Crisis of the Left*, London; New York: Verso.

Handy, L.J. (1981), *Wages Policy in the British Coalmining Industry. A Study of National Wage Bargaining*, Cambridge: Cambridge University Press.

Hartley J., Kelly J., and Nicholson, N. (1983), *Steel Strike*, London: Batsford.

Heath, T. (1994), 'Tower's collapse', *New Statesman and Society*, vol. 22, pp. 12–13.

Heffer, E. (1985), 'Preface', in H. Beynon (ed.), *Digging Deeper. Issues in the Miners' Strike*, London: Verso.

Hobsbawm, E. (1952), 'The Machine Breakers', *Past and Present*, no. 1, pp. 57–70.

——, (1971), 'Class Consciousness in History', in I. Meszaros (ed.), *Aspects of History and Class Consciousness*, London: Routledge and Kegan Paul.

——, (1978), 'The Forward March of Labour Halted?', *Marxism Today*, vol. 22, no. 9, pp. 279–86.

——, (1982), 'The State of the Left in Western Europe', *Marxism Today*, vol. 26, no. 10, pp. 8–15.

——, (1989), 'Farewell to the Classic Labour Movement?', *New Left Review*, no. 173, pp. 69–74.

Holmstrom, N. (1983), 'Rationality and Revolution', *Canadian Journal of Philosophy*, vol. 13, no. 3, pp. 305–25.

Home Office (1985), *Policing the miners' dispute; the National Reporting Centre*, London: Home Office.

Howell, D. (1989), *The politics of the NUM. A Lancashire view*, Manchester and New York: Manchester University Press.

Howells, K. (1985), 'Stopping Out. The Birth of a New Kind of Politics', in H. Beynon (ed.), *Digging Deeper. Issues in the Miners' Strike*, London: Verso.

Hughes, J., and Moore, R. (1972) (Edited for the NUM), *A Special Case? Social Justice and the Miners,* Harmondsworth: Penguin Books.

Humphries, J. (1981), 'Protective Legislation, the Capitalist State, and Working Class Men: The Case of the 1842 Mines Regulation Act', *Feminist Review*, no. 7, pp. 1–33.

Hyman, R. (1978), 'Occupational Structure, Collective Organisation and Industrial Militancy', in C. Crouch and A. Pizzorno (eds), *The Resurgence of Class Conflict in Western Europe Since 1968. Volume Two,*

London and Basingstoke: Macmillan.

——, (1986), 'Reflections on the miners' strike', in R. Miliband *et al.* (eds), *The Socialist Register 1985/86*, London: The Merlin Press.

——, and Price, R. (eds) (1983), *The New Working Class? White Collar Workers and their Organizations*, London: Macmillan.

Jackson, B., and Wardle, T. (1986), *The Battle for Orgreave*, London: Canary Press.

Jackson, M.P. (1974), *The Price of Coal*, London: Croom Helm.

Jacobi, O. *et al.* (eds) (1986), *Economic Crisis, Trade Unions and The State*, London; Sydney: Croom Helm.

Jenkins, P. (1988), *Mrs. Thatcher's Revolution. The Ending of the Socialist Era*, Cambridge: Harvard University Press.

Kahn, P. (1987), 'Coal Not Dole: The British Miners' Strike of 1984–85', *Socialist Review*, vol. 17, no. 3 and 4, pp. 57–88.

Katz, H.C. (1993), 'The Decentralization of Collective Bargaining: A Literature Review and Comparative Analysis', *Industrial and Labor Relations Review*, vol. 47, no. 1, pp. 3–22.

Kerr, C., and Siegel, A. (1954), 'The Interindustry Propensity to Strike – An International Comparison', in A. Kornhauser, R. Dubin, and A.M. Ross (eds), *Industrial Conflict*, New York; Toronto; London: McGraw-Hill Book Company, Inc.

Kingsolver, B. (1989), *Holding the Line: Women in the Great Arizona Mine Strike of 1983*, Ithaca, NY: ILR Press.

La Botz, D. (1990), *Rank-and-File Rebellion. Teamsters for a Democratic Union*, London; New York: Verso.

Labour Research (1984), 'Miners: policing the dispute', *Labour Research*, vol. 73, no. 9, pp. 227–9.

LRD (1985), *Solidarity With the Miners*, London: LRD Publications Ltd.

——, (1989), *The Hazards of Coal Mining*, London: LRD Publications Ltd.

Lange, P. (N.d.), *Union Democracy and Liberal Corporatism: Exit, Voice and Wage Regulation in Postwar Europe,* Cornell University: Western Societies Program, Occasional Paper No. 16, Center for International Studies.

Laslett, J. (1974), 'Why some do and some don't: some determinants of radicalism among British and American coalminers 1872–1924', *Bulletin of the Society for the Study of Labour History*, no. 28, pp. 6–9.

Lenin, V.I. (1973), *What Is To Be Done?*, Peking: Foreign Languages Press.

Leonard, T. (1985), 'Policing the miners in Derbyshire', *Policing*, vol. 1, no. 2, pp. 96–101.

Levy, C. (1985), *A Very Hard Year: the 1984–85 miners' strike in*

Mauchline, Glasgow: Workers' Educational Association.

Lewis, R. (1993), *Leaders and Teachers: Adult Education and the Challenge of Labour in South Wales, 1900–1940*, Cardiff: University of Wales Press.

Lipset, S. M. (1950), *Agrarian Socialism*, Berkeley and Los Angeles: University of California Press.

——, (1983), 'Radicalism or reformism: The sources of working-class politics', *American Political Science Review*, vol. 77, no. 1, pp. 1–18.

——, (ed.) (1986), *Unions in Transition. Entering the Second Century*, San Francisco: Institute for Contemporary Studies.

Lloyd, J. (1985), *Understanding The Miners' Strike*, (Fabian Tract 504), London: Fabian Society.

Lockwood, D. (1975), 'Sources of Variation in Working-Class Images of Society', in M. Bulmer (ed.), *Working-Class Images of Society*, London and Boston: Routledge and Kegan Paul. Originally in *The Sociological Review* (1966), vol. 14, pp. 249–67.

——, (1989), *The Blackcoated Worker. A study in Class Consciousness*, 2nd edn, Oxford: Clarendon Press.

Longstreth, F. (1988), 'From corporatism to dualism? Thatcherism and the Climacteric of British Trade Unions in the 1980s', *Political Studies*, vol. 36, no. 3, pp. 413–32.

Lustgarten, L. (1985), 'The long-distance policemen', *New Society*, 3 January, pp. 24–5.

Luxemburg, R. (1925), *The Mass Strike*, London: The Merlin Press.

MacInnes, J. (1987), *Thatcherism at Work: Industrial Relations and Economic Change*, Milton Keynes, UK; Philadelphia, USA: Open University Press.

Maksymiw, W., Eaton, J., and Gill, C. (1990), *The British Trade Union Directory*, Harlow, Essex: Longman.

Mann, M. (1973), *Consciousness and Action among the Western Working Class*, London and Basingstoke: Macmillan.

Marks, G. (1989), *Unions in Politics. Britain, Germany, and the United States in the Nineteenth and Early Twentieth Centuries*, Princeton: Princeton University Press.

Marsh, D. (1989), 'Review Article. British Trade Unions in a Cold Climate', *West European Politics*, vol. 12, no. 4, pp. 192–8.

Marshall, G. (1988), 'Some remarks on the study of working-class consciousness', in D. Rose (ed.), *Social Stratification and Social Change*, London: Hutchinson.

Marshall, P. (1984), 'Following the Fight to the Finish', *Marxism Today*, vol. 28, no. 12, pp. 38–40.

Marxism Today (1984), 'Coalfield Women at the Face. A roundtable discussion', *Marxism Today*, vol. 28, no. 7, pp. 28–30.

Massey, D., and Wainwright, H. (1985), 'Keep Moving On . . .', *New Socialist*, no. 26, pp. 8–9.

Maynard, S. (1989), 'Rough Work and Rugged Men. The Social Construction of Masculinity in Working Class History', *Labour/Le Travail*, no. 23, pp. 159–69.

McCormick, B.J. (1979), *Industrial relations in the coal industry*, Hamden, CT.: Archon Books.

McIlroy, J. (1984), 'On Second Fronts and Allied Commands', *New Statesman*, 24 August, pp. 12–13.

——, (1985), 'Police and Pickets: the Law against the Miners', in H. Beynon (ed.), *Digging Deeper. Issues in the Miners' Strike*, London: Verso.

Meiksins Wood, E. (1986), *The Retreat from Class*, London: Verso.

Mény, Y., and Wright, V. (eds) (1986), *The Politics of Steel: Western Europe and the Steel Industry in the Crisis Years*, Berlin: W. de Gruyter.

Metcalf, D. (1989), 'Water Notes Dry Up: the Impact of the Donovan Reform Proposals and Thatcherism at Work on Labour Productivity in British Manufacturing Industry', *British Journal of Industrial Relations*, vol. 27, no. 1, pp. 1–31.

Miliband, R. (1964), 'Socialism and the Myth of the Golden Past', in R. Miliband and J. Saville (eds.), *The Socialist Register 1964*, New York: Monthly Review Press.

——, (1985), 'The New Revisionism in Britain', *New Left Review*, no. 150, pp. 5–26.

——, *et al.* (eds) (1986), *The Socialist Register 1985/86*, London: The Merlin Press.

Miller, J. (1986), *You can't Kill the Spirit: Women in a Welsh Mining Village*, London: The Women's Press.

Miller, J. (1974), *Aberfan: A Disaster and Its Aftermath*, London: Constable.

Miller, S. (1985), '"The Best Thing that ever Happened to Us": Women's Role in the Coal Dispute', *Journal of Law and Society*, vol. 12, no. 3, pp. 355–64.

Milne, S. (1994), *The Enemy Within. MI5, Maxwell, and the Scargill Affair*, London: Verso.

Mineworkers, National Union of (1989), *A Century of Struggle. Britain's Miners in Pictures 1889–1989*, Sheffield: National Union of Mineworkers.

Mineworkers, National Union of, (Industrial Relations Department) (1983), *Study of the Incentive Scheme*, Sheffield: National Union of Mineworkers.

Mineworkers, National Union of, (Nottinghamshire Area) (1983), *An Appraisal of the British Coalmining Industry and an Examination of the Possible Consequences Following Pit Closures in the N.U.M. (Nottinghamshire Area)*, Mansfield, Nottinghamshire: National Union of Mineworkers (Nottinghamshire Area).

Moore, B. (1978), *Injustice: The Social Bases of Obedience and Revolt*, White Plains, NY: Sharpe.

Morris, T. (1995), 'Annual Review Article 1994', *British Journal of Industrial Relations*, vol. 33, no. 1, pp. 117–35.

Nairn, T. (1964), 'The English Working Class', *New Left Review*, no. 24, pp. 43–57.

Negrine, R. (1995), 'The "Gravest Political Crisis Since Suez": the Press, the Government and the Pit Closures Announcement of 1992', *Parliamentary Affairs*, vol. 48, no. 1, pp. 40–56.

Ollman, B. (1972), 'Toward Class Consciousness Next Time: Marx and the Working Class', *Politics and Society*, vol. 3, no. 1, pp. 1–24.

Orwell, G. (1986), *The Road to Wigan Pier*, The Complete Works of George Orwell, Volume Five, London: Secker and Warburg.

Panitch, L. (1981), 'Trade Unions and the Capitalist State', *New Left Review*, no. 125, pp. 21–43.

Park, R.C.R. (1962), *A Study of Some of the Social Factors Influencing Labour Productivity in Coal Mines*, Ph.D. dissertation, University of Edinburgh.

Parker, T. (1986), *Red Hill. A Mining Community*, London: Heinemann.

Parkin, F. (1971), *Class Inequality and Political Order*, London: MacGibbon and Kee.

Patton, K. (1978), 'The Foundation of Peterlee New Town', in M. Bulmer (ed.), *Mining and Social Change*, London: Croom Helm.

Paynter, W. (1972), *My Generation*, London: George Allen and Unwin Ltd.

People of Thurcroft (1986), *Thurcroft. A Village and the Miners' Strike. An Oral History*, Nottingham; Atlantic Highlands, NJ: Spokesman.

Percy-Smith, J, and Hillyard, P. (1985), 'Miners in the Arms of the Law: A Statistical Analysis', *Journal of Law and Society*, vol. 12, no. 3, pp. 345–54.

Pérez Díaz, V. (1987), 'Unions' Uncertainties and Workers' Ambivalence. The Various Crises of Trade Union Representation and Their Moral Dimension', *International Journal of Political Economy*, vol. 17, no. 3, pp. 108–38.

Phillips, A. (1983), *Hidden Hands*, London: Pluto Press.

Pitt, M. (1979), *The World on Our Backs*, London: Lawrence and Wishart.

Piven, F.F., and Cloward, R.A. (1977), *Poor People's Movements. Why They Succeed, How They Fail*, New York: Vintage.

Pollard, M. (1984), *The Hardest Work under Heaven. The Life and Death of the British Miner*, London: Hutchinson.

Popkin, S.L. (1979), *The rational peasant: the political economy of rural society in Vietnam*, Berkeley: University of California Press.

Przeworski, A. (1980a), 'Material Interests, Class Compromise, and the Transition to Socialism', *Politics and Society*, vol. 10, no. 2, pp. 125–53.

——, (1980b), 'Material Bases of Consent: politics and economics in a hegemonic system', *Political Power and Social Theory*, I, pp. 23–68.

——, (1980c), 'Social Democracy as a Historical Phenomenon', *New Left Review*, no. 122, pp. 27–58.

——, and Wallerstein, M. (1982), 'The Structure of Class Conflict in Democratic Capitalist Societies', *American Political Science Review*, vol. 76, no. 2, pp. 215–38.

Rees, G. (1985), 'Regional restructuring, class change, and political action: preliminary comments on the 1984–1985 miners' strike in South Wales', *Environment and Planning D: Society and Space*, no. 3, pp. 389–406.

——, (1986), '"Coalfield culture" and the 1984–1985 miners' strike: a reply to Sunley', *Environment and Planning D: Society and Space*, no. 4, pp. 469–76.

Regini, M. (ed.) (1992), *The Future of Labor Movements*, London: Sage.

Reid, D. (1981), 'The Role of Mine Safety in the Development of Working-Class Consciousness and Organization: The Case of the Aubin Coal Basin, 1867–1914', *French Historical Studies*, vol. 12, no. 1, pp. 98–119.

Reiner, R. (1984), 'Is Britain turning into a police state?', *New Society*, 2 August, pp. 51–6.

Rhodes, M., and Wright, V. (1988), 'The European Steel Unions and the Steel Crisis, 1974–84: A Study in the Demise of Traditional Unionism', *British Journal of Political Science*, vol. 18, no. 2, pp. 171–95.

Richards, A. J. (1995), *Down But Not Out: Labour Movements in Late Industrial Societies*, Madrid: Estudio/Working Paper 1995/70, Centro de Estudios Avanzados en Ciencias Sociales, Instituto Juan March de Estudios e Investigaciones.

Richards, F. (1984), *The Miners' Next Step*, London: Junius.

Rimlinger, G. V. (1959), 'International Differences in the Strike Propensity of Coal Miners: Experience in Four Countries', *Industrial and Labor Relations Review*, vol. 12, no. 3, pp. 389–405.

Roemer, J. E. (1979), 'Mass Action is *Not* Individually Rational: Reply', *Journal of Economic Issues*, vol. 13, no. 3, pp. 763–7.

Sabia, D. (1988), 'Rationality, Collective Action, and Karl Marx', *American Journal of Political Science*, vol. 32, no. 1, pp. 50–71.

Salt C., and Layzell, J. (1985), *Here We Go: Women's Memories of the 1984/85 Miners' Strike*, London: London Political Committee, Co-operative Retail Services.

Salvatore, N. (1992), 'The Decline of Labor. A Grim Picture, A Few Proposals', *Dissent*, Winter, pp. 86–92.

Sampson, A. (1962), *Anatomy of Britain*, London: Hodder and Stoughton.

Samuel, R. (1986), 'Introduction', in R. Samuel, B. Bloomfield and G. Boanas (eds), *The Enemy Within. Pit Villages and the miners' strike of 1984–5*, London and New York: Routledge and Kegan Paul.

——, Bloomfield, B., and Boanas, G. (eds) (1986), *The Enemy Within. Pit Villages and the miners' strike of 1984–5*, London and New York: Routledge and Kegan Paul.

——, Stedman Jones, G., and Weir, S. (1985), 'Thatcher's Moscow', *New Socialist*, no. 26, pp. 2–3.

Sartre, J.P. (1970), 'Masses, Spontaneity, Party', in R. Miliband and J. Saville (eds), *The Socialist Register 1970*, London: The Merlin Press.

Saunders, J. (1989), *Across Frontiers. International Support for the Miners' Strike 1984/85*, London: Canary Press.

Saville, J. (1986), 'An Open Conspiracy: Conservative Politics and the Miners' Strike 1984–5', in R. Miliband *et al.* (eds), *The Socialist Register 1985/86*, London: The Merlin Press.

Scargill, A. (1975), 'The New Unionism', *New Left Review*, no. 92, pp. 3–33.

——, (1981), *Miners in the Eighties*, Barnsley, Yorkshire: Yorkshire Area NUM.

——, (1987), *'New Realism': The Politics of Fear*, Merthyr Tydfil, Wales: Merthyr Tydfil Trades Union Council.

——, (1990), *Response to the Lightman Inquiry*, Barnsley, Yorkshire: Campaign to Defend Scargill and Heathfield.

Schwarz, B. (1985), 'Let Them Eat Coal: The Conservative Party and the Strike', in H. Beynon (ed.), *Digging Deeper. Issues in the Miners' Strike*, London: Verso.

Scott, J. C. (1976), *The Moral Economy of the Peasant*, New Haven and London: Yale University Press.

——, (1985), *Weapons of the Weak*, New Haven and London: Yale University Press.

Scott, Joan (1988), 'Women in the Making of the English Working Class', in J. Scott (ed.), *Gender and the Politics of History*, New York: Columbia University Press.

Scraton, P. (1985), *The State of the Police*, London: Pluto.

Seddon, V. (ed.) (1986), *The Cutting Edge: Women and the Pit Strike*, London: Lawrence and Wishart.

Seifert, R., and Urwin, J. (1987), *Struggle Without End: The 1984/85 Miners' strike in North Staffordshire*, Newcastle, Staffordshire: Penrhos Publications.

Shorter, E., and Tilly, C. (1974), *Strikes in France, 1830–1968*, Cambridge: Cambridge University Press.

Smith, C., Knights, D., and Willmott, H. (1991), 'Introduction', in C. Smith, D. Knights and H. Willmott (eds), *White-Collar Work. The Non-Manual Labour Process*, Basingstoke: Macmillan.

Smith, P., and Morton, G. (1994), 'Union Exclusion – next steps', *Industrial Relations Journal*, vol. 25, no. 1, pp. 3–14.

Socialist Organiser (1985), 'Magnificent Miners', *Socialist Organiser*, no. 219–20, pp. 1–64.

Spencer, S. (1985), *Police Authorities during the Miners' Strike*, London: Cobden Trust.

Stead, J. (1987), *Never the same again: women and the miners' strike*, London: The Women's Press.

Stern, G. M. (1977), *The Buffalo Creek Disaster*, New York: Vintage Books.

Strath, B. (1987), *The Politics of Deindustrialisation: The Contraction of The West European Shipbuilding Industry*, London; Wolfeboro, NH: Croom Helm.

Sunley, P. (1986), 'Regional restructuring, class change and political action: a comment', *Environment and Planning D: Society and Space*, vol. 4, pp. 465–8.

Supple, B. (1987), *The History of the British Coal Industry. Volume 4. 1913–1946: The Political Economy of Decline*, Oxford: Clarendon Press.

Taylor, A.J. (1982), 'Miners in the Eighties – An Analysis', *Political Quarterly*, vol. 53, no. 2, pp. 218–21.

——, (1984), *The Politics of the Yorkshire Miners*, London: Croom Helm.

——, and Townsend, A.R. (1976), 'The Local "Sense of Place" as evidenced in North–East England', *Urban Studies*, vol. 13, no. 1, pp. 133–46.

Thompson, E.P. (1966), *The Making of the English Working Class*, New York: Vintage Books.

——, (1980), *Writing by Candlelight*, London: The Merlin Press.

Thorpe, E. (1978), 'Politics and Housing in a Durham Mining Town', in M. Bulmer (ed.), *Mining and Social Change*, London: Croom Helm.

Tilly, C., and Tilly, L. (eds) (1981), *Class Conflict and Collective Action*, Beverly Hills, CA: Sage.

Towers, B. (1989), 'Running the gauntlet: British trade unions under Thatcher, 1979–1988', *Industrial and Labour Relations Review*, vol. 42, no. 2, pp. 163–88.

Trent, R.B., and Stout-Wiegand, N. (1987), 'Attitudes toward Women Coal Miners in an Appalachian Coal Community', *Journal of the Community Development Society*, vol. 18, no. 1, pp. 1–14.

Trumka, R.L. (1992), 'On Becoming a Movement. Rethinking Labor's Strategy', *Dissent*, Winter, pp. 57–60.

Visser, J. (1989), *European Trade Unions in Figures*, Deventer, Netherlands; Boston, USA: Kluwer Law and Taxation Publishers.

——, (1992), 'The Strength of Union Movements in Advanced Capitalist Democracies: Social and Organizational Variations', in M. Regini (ed.), *The Future of Labour Movements*, London: Sage.

Waddington, D., Wykes, M., and Critcher, C. (1991), *Split at the seams? Community, continuity and change after the 1984–5 coal dispute*, Milton Keynes; Philadelphia: Open University Press.

Walker M., and Miller, S. (N.d.), *The Iron Fist: A State of Siege Vol. 2: Policing the coalfields in the second six weeks of the miners' strike*, London: Yorkshire Area NUM and Greenwich NALGO.

Waller, R. J. (1983), *The Dukeries Transformed. The Social and Political Development of a Twentieth Century Coalfield*, Oxford: Clarendon Press.

Walsh, K. (1985), *Trade Union Membership. Methods and measurement in the European Community*, Luxembourg: Office for Official Publications of the European Community.

Warwick, D., and Littlejohn, G. (1992), *Coal, capital and culture*, London and New York: Routledge.

Westergaard, J. (1970), 'The Rediscovery of the Cash Nexus', in R. Miliband and J. Saville (eds), *The Socialist Register 1970*, London: The Merlin Press.

——, and Resler, H. (1975), *Class in a Capitalist Society*, New York: Basic Books, Inc.

Western, B. (1995), 'A Comparative Study of Working-Class Disorganization: Union Decline in Eighteen Advanced Capitalist Countries', *American Sociological Review*, vol. 60, no. 2, pp. 179–201.

Wilentz, S. (1984), 'Against Exceptionalism: Class Consciousness and the American Labor Movement, 1790–1920', *International Labor and Working Class History*, no. 26, pp. 1–24.

Williams, G. (1982), *The Welsh in Their History*, Beckenham: Croom Helm.

Williams, J.E. (1962), *The Derbyshire Miners. A Study in Industrial and Social History*, London: George Allen and Unwin Ltd.

Williams, R. (1985), 'Mining the Meaning. Key Words in the Miners' Strike', *New Socialist*, no. 5, pp. 6–9.

Williamson, B. (1982), *Class, Culture and Community. A Biographical Study of Social Change in Mining*, London, Boston and Henley:

Routledge and Kegan Paul.

Winchester, D. (1989), 'Sectoral Change and Trade-Union Organization', in D. Gallie (ed.), *Employment in Britain*, New York: Basil Blackwell.

Winterton, J. (1984), 'Police activities', *New Statesman*, 27 April, p. 8.

——, and Winterton, R. (1989), *Coal, Crisis and Conflict*, Manchester and New York: Manchester University Press.

Witham, J. (1986), *Hearts and Minds: the story of the women of Nottinghamshire in the miners' strike, 1984–1985*, London: Canary Press.

Wolfe, J. D. (1985), 'Corporatism and Union Democracy. The British Miners and Incomes Policy, 1973–74', *Comparative Politics*, vol. 17, no. 4, pp. 421–36.

Wright, E. O. (1985), *Classes*, London and New York: Verso.

Wright, P. (1985), *Policing the Coal Industry Dispute in South Yorkshire*, Sheffield: Report to South Yorkshire Police Committee for the Chief Constable, South Yorkshire Police.

Yarrow, M. (1992), 'Class and Gender in the developing consciousness of Appalachian coal-miners', in A. Sturdy, D. Knights and H. Willmott (eds), *Skill and Consent. Contemporary Studies in the Labour Process*, London and New York: Routledge.

Young, H. (1990), *The Iron Lady. A Biography of Margaret Thatcher*, New York: The Noonday Press. (Originally published as *One of Us*, London, Macmillan, (1989).)

Zeitlin, M. (1966), 'Economic Insecurity and the Political Attitudes of Cuban Workers', *American Sociological Review*, vol. 31, no. 1, pp. 35–51.

Zolberg, A. R. (1986), 'How Many Exceptionalisms?', in I. Katznelson and A.R. Zolberg (eds), *Working-Class Formation. Nineteenth-Century Patterns in Western Europe and the United States*, Princeton: Princeton University Press.

Index

Index